*Resurgent Politics
and Educational Progressivism
in the New South*

Resurgent Politics
and
Educational Progressivism
in the New South

North Carolina, 1890–1913

H. Leon Prather, Sr.

Rutherford • Madison • Teaneck
Fairleigh Dickinson University Press
London: Associated University Presses

© 1979 by Associated University Presses, Inc.

Associated University Presses, Inc.
Cranbury, New Jersey 08512

Associated University Presses
Magdalen House
136–148 Tooley Street
London SE1 2TT, England

Library of Congress Cataloging in Publication Data

Prather, H   Leon, 1921–
    Resurgent politics and educational progressivism in the new South,
North Carolina, 1890–1913.

    Bibliography: p.
    Includes index.
    1. Education—North Carolina—History.   2. Afro-Americans—Educa-
tion—North Carolina—History.   3. School integration—North Carolina—
History.   I. Title.
LA340.P72   370'.9756   77–74394
ISBN 0-8386-2071-X

To Audrey

Contents

Preface

Education is viewed by most Americans as the avenue to success, or at least as a necessary tool to escape poverty. That public school systems in some states lagged behind those in the rest of the nation is a prima facie case. In his studies on the New South, C. Vann Woodward clearly demonstrates that the post-reconstruction South had more than its share of the nation's poverty. Southern politicians were belated in accepting the proposition of universal education. Walter Hines Page charged the "stump and pulpit" as the chief backward influences. But to be sure, there were other impeding forces. North Carolina, like a lot of other Southern states, had settled in a sort of racial ooze of hyperconservatism; attitudes hardened, while political and social institutions rigidified. Public education was a perplexing social problem that had long frustrated the social reformer. It reached its nadir in North Carolina by the end of the nineties, at which time the state maintained perhaps the poorest public educational system in the South. Universal education, constitutionally and politically, meant a four-months school term, yet more than a thousand school districts in that state failed to meet even that meager requirement. In the sparse rural areas, where 82 percent of the population lived, the "common schools" (one-room ungraded schools) predominated. Here, incompetent whites (standards of the teaching corps for the Negro population were lower) conducted classes during an average seventy-day school term for less than $30 a month. Succinctly stated, public education was well anchored in the sod of public and political apathy, poverty, and racism, and made a travesty of the concept of the American public school system as exemplified by Massachusetts. Educational leaders and humanitarians had spoken out against $3.50 per child annually, but their voices

9

resounded in the wilderness; and whatever were the deficiencies in the existing system, no real interest was manifested to correct them.

Fortunately, forces in operation opened the way for educational progress. During the 1890s political-economic grievances surfaced in North Carolina to destroy the white solidarity of the Democratic party. The Populist revolt representing agrarian radicalism spawned third-party movements throughout the South. The Populists converted the Black man because he was included among the downtrodden and suffered from the same "common oppressor"—the Democratic party as controlled by the economic oligarchies. According to the Populist view, "the problem was poverty, not *color*." But could men of common interests, yet of different races, be united in a quest for economic and social justice? Populism was only a brief interlude in some states, but in North Carolina it released cataclysmic changes. In 1894 and 1896, after a reign of almost twenty years, the Democrats were toppled from power by the so-called Fusion ticket, a combination of Populists (disgruntled Democrats) and Republicans. Because the Negro constituted a large segment of the Republican party, he re-appeared as a potent political force. A clean sweep of public offices occurred in many places, and new men now filled these positions. Some of the smaller offices went to Blacks, who, nevertheless, were enough to play into the hands of the Democrats, a trump card to propagandize "Negro Rule" or "Black Domination." This could mean only one thing—the return of racism to North Carolina politics.

Fusion politics resulted in a resurgence of the Democrats' aim to regain political ascendancy in 1898, as an emotional white campaign was fought on a pledge to extirpate the Black man's political power. To accomplish this objective, the Democrats fashioned a suffrage amendment with a temporary "grandfather clause" to disfranchise the illiterate Negro voter, while accepting the illiterate white voter. It also had great educational significance, for section 4 of the amendment mandated that after 1908 only literate persons would be enfranchised. The amendment was the major issue in the 1900 gubernatorial election. An embryonic educational question surfaced and rode the political storm to become a significant issue after the amendment began to encounter staunch opposition, especially in counties where a large percentage of white illiteracy prevailed. To insure acceptance of the measure, the Democrats promised the creation of educational facilities adequate to overcome illiteracy among white children in 1909. But they failed to fulfill their campaign pledge of universal education. Their victory of 1900, nevertheless, marked the dawn of a remarkable era of educational progress. The Conference for Education in the South, along with the famous Ogden movement, supported by Northern philanthropy (General Education Board and

10

the Southern Education Board), moved into North Carolina to help fill the educational vacuum created by the Democrats. This conference prepared to inaugurate a great public school movement, aimed at redeeming what Walter Hines Page dubbed the "Forgotten Man," meaning the illiterate masses—men, women, and children bypassed by Southern civilization.

During the early decades of the twentieth century, a momentous educational movement, a "crusade against ignorance," exploded throughout the South, and it originated in and received its impetus from North Carolina, the home state of the South's foremost educational progressives. Accordingly, the major purposes of this study are to describe how a unique mixture of politics and racial attitudes coalesced to involve education, and to identify and analyze the major forces associated with and propelling the public school movement between 1902 and 1913. The movement is considered against a backdrop of sociopolitical forces that give it an added dimension. The period selected falls between the years so skillfully depicted by the eminent Southern authority C. Vann Woodward in his classic, *Origins of the New South, 1877–1913*. The year 1890 is a logical beginning date, since it is the approximate time of the rise of the populism, racism, and state politics that made public education a paramount issue at the turn of the twentieth cenury. And 1913 serves well as the terminal date, for during this year the Conference for Education in the South was dissolved; the education campaigns had run their course.

Although this study is basically confined to North Carolina, it is likely to shed some light on the educational problems of the entire South. Moreover, the study is not isolated from central themes in American historiography, for it possesses a relevancy to the Farmer's Alliance and to the Populist and Progressive movements that dominated the national political scene from 1890 to 1916. The public school movement, to be sure, was the most discernible manifestation of Southern progressivism, but this has been overlooked by far too many historians. How Southern progressivism manifested itself separately in individual states and the relation of racism and public education to it are significant.

Is there a historical "gap" within the literature related to this subject that justifies a study of this nature? The volumes written and the research performed by educational historians are not impressive. What about the resulting impact of politics and racism as these two forces indirectly or directly relate to public education? The two general educational histories of North Carolina, which are highly regarded scholarly works, are those of Edgar W. Knight and Marcus C. S. Noble. However, both of these historians fall somewhat short of expectation. Charles W. Dabney, one of the leading participants in the Southern crusade for public education, has written the most comprehensive account of the regional movement, but he employs great restraint in dealing with the problems of racism and education. One may safely conclude that these historians were. too much a part of the era of which they wrote to have the detached perspective demanded in present-day historiography. But here I do not want to deprecate, or express disapproval of, their contribution to scholarship. On the other hand, it was clear to me at the outset that education could not be studied apart from politics and racism. The political threat that the Black man poses was certainly the central theme that gave impetus to the white supremacy campaigns underlying the public school movement in North Carolina at the turn of the twentieth century. But social historians have been noticeably timorous in relating the educational movement to racism. Indeed, this makes Southern educational history a complex subject that involves many facets of social interaction.

I may confess here a personal feeling about this book and my approach to the subject, which has a unique fascination. My hope in writing this volume is that I can make a contribution to human knowledge, or at least suggest a fresh approach to an issue. New insights and interpretations can be grasped from the study of a state or region's educational history, and an adequate understanding of this history is essential, since education plays a cardinal role in molding the minds, attitudes, and character of people. Furthermore, in the South public school systems in general are not seen as obvious arms of the political order. But in the large, they play a significant role in the perpetuation of the historical lore of a society: the myths, the mores, and traditions; the patterns of action and the loyalties that are fundamental to the political order and to the Establishment—the power structure. Moreover, social historians who take a stand at any point in history can see evidences of a new educational growth emerging out of the past. Much too often such progress is recorded merely in statistical or clerical data. And whenever educational deficiencies crop up, the social reformers try to effect changes. They often lament—as does Jeremiah—while the Establishment ignores them. When there is great progress during one era, the educational journals record such advancement in quantative data, including variables and the like, but they ignore the forces that influence the conservative power structure to change. With the exception of the works of Horace Mann Bond (*Education of the Negro in the American Social Order* [1934]; *Negro Education in Alabama* [1939]) and Louis R. Harlan (*Separate and Unequal* [1958]) , Southern educational histories of the Progressive era have been basically "inbred, in-house encomiums."

Hence, this volume is offered as the study of a viable and neglected phase of Southern progressivism. Here I can plead, but might not persuade. North Carolina is the watershed in the history of and is crucial for a study of this type. I also strongly believe that such a study is needed to fill a very considerable gap in our knowledge and understanding of the Southern educational revival and of the Progressive movement. The resources of North Carolina are abundant, and other scholars have not undertaken to deal with the question of racism and public education within a broad political context. Such political focusing, in my opinion, is the only proper way for a social historian to approach the problem. It is my hope that this book will be of special interest to social historians, political scientists, sociologists, textbook writers, educators, the general public, and the new wing of historians—the cliometricians.

A few words about organization. This work is constructed so that each chapter offers an explanation of or a basis for understanding later parts of the exposition. Educational background is provided, which exposes the nadir of North Carolina's post-Reconstruction problem. Beginning with part 2, the study progresses from movement to movement, presenting important data on the ascendancy of agrarian radicalism, the Alliance-Populist interlude, Fusion politics, and the political specter of the Negro. All these forces became caught up in the political battles of the era. There follows an account of the white supremacy movements, with some attention paid to character and drama. From this point on much new information is uncovered—most notably, the futile populist educational movement of 1897; the giant political rallies (truly a study in rustic politics and pageantry); the "Red Shirts" movement; the origin of the Democrat's promise of universal education; the helping hand of Northern philanthropy; and the numerous colorful rallies in the quest for universal education. The educational changes that followed these events were of marked significance.

This study of Southern progressivism and pervasive institutional racism is examined by a Negro historian, which should give it a certain uniqueness. As much as historians try to be dispassionate, our experiences often condition the choices we make, and few historians agree to the notion of objectivity. The Black scholar should have a deep commitment to scholarship and a deep involvement in research, for he has been *greatly outdistanced by this Caucasian counterpart.* This volume, it is hoped, will make a distinctive contribution to American historiography.

Acknowledgments

Professor Carl N. Degler in the preface of his study *Neither Black or White* expressed my own sentiments when he wrote: "Like any scholar, I have learned much in the course of writing this book." One of the ways I have learned is from the writings, talks, and advice of many persons.

It is impossible for me to acknowledge adequately the many individuals who gave valuable assistance in the preparation of this book. The research was made possible by a grant from the Ford Foundation. I would like to thank Hugh T. Lefler, Kenan Professor of History Emeritus at the University of North Carolina, who performed a chore of expert reading and made corrections throughout· the manuscript, which saved me from many errors. I would also like to thank Susan Stock Means of Associated University Presses, Inc., who skillfully edited the entire manuscript, helping me over numerous rough spots. My thanks are also due Charles B. Fancher, formerly vice-president of the faculty of Tennessee State University, presently associate vice-chancellor for Academic Affairs of the Tennessee Board of Regents, for his encouragement during my early research efforts and for his arrangement of leaves of absence for me during the writing of this book. I also wish to thank two colleagues, Lois C. McDougald and Samuel H. Shannon, for reading parts of the manuscript at various stages and for offering valuable suggestions. Acknowledgment must also be made to those who rendered assistance during the formative stages of this study: Dewey W. Grantham, Jr., Vanderbilt University; George B. Tindall, University of North Carolina; and Stanlake Samkange of Northeastern University.

I would like to acknowledge the courteous aid given me by the staffs of many depositories and libraries, including: the Houghton

Library of Harvard University; the New York Public Library; the Schomburg Center for Research in Black Culture; the Manuscript Division of the Library of Congress; the Alderman. Library, University of Virginia; the Southern Historical Collection and the North Carolina History Room in the Wilson Library, University of North Carolina; the William R. Perkins Library, Duke University; the North Carolina Department of Archives and History; the University of North Carolina Library at Greensboro; the Andrew Carnegie Library, Livingstone College; the Estes Kefauver Room, University of Tennessee Library; the Joint University Libraries, Vanderbilt University; the Tennessee State University Library; and the Fisk University Library.

No author can ever sufficiently express his appreciation for the services of those who served as typists. I do all my writing in long-hand, and I am especially indebted to Mrs. Lynn Hill, who typed the original draft and countless revisions of the manuscript; also to Mrs. Louise N. Watson, who typed various key revisions and also had the responsibility of typing the manuscript in its final form; and to Mrs. Lillian C. Swingley, who helped to edit the final draft.

The dedication of this work to my wife, Audrey Minga Prather, is an inadequate gesture of gratitude for her sacrifices. Although she is employed full-time and shares the major responsibility for rearing two dynamic children afflicted with growing pains, she read the tedious longhand drafts and all revisions to me, rendering editorial assistance, criticism, and advice. In this capacity, she is my "girl Friday"—competent, patient, and always supportive of my efforts at scholarly writing.

16

Note to the Reader

Particularly disturbing to Negro scholars and others is the inadequate representation of Blacks in the professions, where scholarship is crucial, as compared with the increasingly discernible Negro image in sports. Blacks constitute approximately 65 percent of the National Basketball Association; 42 percent of the National Football League; and 19 percent of baseball's Major League. In great contrast, Blacks constitute only 2 percent of the nation's physicians, 3 percent of its lawyers, and 1 percent of its engineers. At this point a significant question is raised: How do we explain that *less than one-half of one percent of the scholarly works are produced by Blacks?* In general, the voice of the Negro is missing from historiography. And no scholar is likely to doubt that whites write from an elitist perspective, which makes obtuse their conceptualization of the "Black Experience." Professor William M. Tuttle, Jr., put it well when he wrote in *Race Riot: Chicago in the Red Summer of 1919:* "Unfortunately much that has been written about black Americans by whites has been written from the point of view of Ellison's liberal antagonist." This is true, for example, of much of the literature on racial violence. Professor Tuttle goes on to point out the propensity for distortion among white authors, who tend to interpret the Black Experience from their own middle-class perspective. The definitive pen of the Black scholar is needed to correct the distortions and/or to fill in the glaring omissions. The author of this volume possesses an acute awareness of the Black Experience and writes from the point of view of Black people themselves who lived through that experience and who were aware of the continuities and the discontinuities in the unceasing struggle for survival and development. While utilizing only relevant literature of enormous proportion, he was very careful to document his conclusions with the best sources.

17

Prologue

Public schools, Horace Mann Bond observed, are the "product of a variety of forces, set in motion by human beings equipped with a social heritage, and reacting to a particular kind of natural and physical environment."[1] These perceptions apply especially to North Carolina, where the educational process suggests a continuous effort of adaptation to an array of environmental influences. The conclusion is inevitable that the unique topography and sparse population of North Carolina at the turn of the century mitigated against the public schools. Moreover, always active were socioeconomic determinates, reflecting sectional sensitivities and jealousies, and representing the continuation of residual antebellum attitudes.[2] Thus, for a better comprehension of this study, it appears logical to begin with a description of the state's geography, demographic traits, class, race, and economic and political units.

Known as the "Old North State" and more popularly as the "Tar-heel State," North Carolina is one of "great waters," "great mountains," and vast geographical dimensions. To illustrate, its total land area of 52,712 miles, with 3,615 miles of water included, is some 2,322 square miles larger than England.[3] Roughly a parallelogram in shape, with a total length greater than any state east of the Mississippi, North Carolina extends 507 miles east to west and varies in width from 100 to 185.7 miles north to south. The topography, beginning with a frontage of sea-level land on the eastern shore of the Atlantic Ocean, rises in elevation westward with marked irregularity until it reaches its supreme height and ruggedness in the Appalachians, where it exceeds a height of six thousand feet. Thus, the state is not geographically homogeneous, but actually divides into three natural and clear-cut physiographic regions, a division often mirrored in its historiography. An awareness of the existence of this division is important to this study, for the three regions represent three distinct socioeconomic classes.

One of these regions is the Coastal Plain (also known as the "east," "Black counties," and the "Black Belt"), which covers about 24,200 square miles. It is a part of the eastern seaboard, swept by the Atlantic Ocean, and is an area of great contrasts.[4] From ever-dangerous thundering surfs crashing upon long white beaches, the seafront extends some 320 miles from Virginia to South Carolina and is well marked with inlets, reefs, large bays, and sounds. The region was an extension of the old slavery area and made up a sizeable portion of the Southern Black Belt. Historically, the designation *Black Belt* refers to that part of fertile "black soil," located chiefly in the Central Mississippi Valley, which produced the "Old Cotton Kingdom." In this study I use it to indicate contiguous counties having a large Negro population. It was in the Black Belt that the plantation system, with its economic, social, and political ideals and institutions, developed to its highest degree. After Home Rule it remained a division composed predominantly of Blacks. Figure 1 indicates the eighteen Black counties, so labeled because their Negro population exceeded 50 percent.

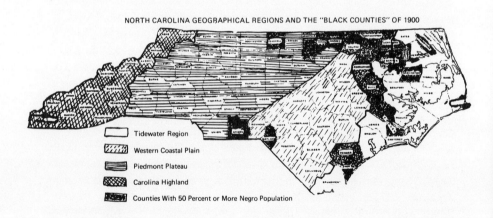

NORTH CAROLINA GEOGRAPHICAL REGIONS AND THE "BLACK COUNTIES" OF 1900

Tidewater Region

Western Coastal Plain

Piedmont Plateau

Carolina Highland

Counties With 50 Percent or More Negro Population

The region in 1900 was much like it is today—rural fairly sparsely populated, with the highest concentration of people located in those areas more suitable for habitation. The economic foundation was centered around the dual crops of cotton and tobacco. It was quite common for the Black Belt oligarchy—planter-merchants, bankers, and absentee landlords—to own land holdings of 250 to 1,000 acres.[5] The tenancy system, embracing both whites and Negroes, was prevalent, and far too many inhabitants were entangled within the webs of the crop-lien system. Only in North Carolina were there more white tenants than black. The records of 1906 show that there were 93,008 landless farmers out of a total of 224,637 adult farmers, 55,785 of the landless farmers being white and 37,223 Black.[6] In proportion to the total Negro population, there was a greater percentage of landless tenants among the latter group, which reflects their deeper state of poverty. During this era the region was severly handicapped by limited railroad mileage of branch lines and by poor roads, most of which were impossible to use in spring and summer. Such isolation certainly promoted problems of excessive individualism and provincialism. It is not difficult to accept the pronouncement of one authority who logically concluded that the region was, "if not the most backward, certainly the most undeveloped area in the state."[7] An investigator could select any pivotal point and traverse the Coastal Plain and encounter extreme variations of poverty and illiteracy among the whites and among practically all Blacks. Thus, it is safe to assume the existence of a close correlation between poverty and poorly financed schools.

The second of the three major regions of North Carolina is the Carolina Highlands, made up of the Blue Ridge counties in the extreme west. This beautiful mountain division was practically unknown to the state and to the Union until roads were cut through Tennessee,[8] for here the "long, curving wall of the Blue Ridge, rising from the foothills like a rampart," once guarded the region beyond it so well that it was "difficult to find an entrance through."[9] Comprising some 6,633 square miles, it is a part of the Appalachian Mountain system, which reaches its climax in western North Carolina. In addition to Mt. Mitchell, the highest mountain of the system, with an elevation of 6,684 feet, there are ninety-two other peaks above 6,000 feet in elevation, "and over a hundred from 5,000 to 5,500 feet."[10] In the mountainous countries the majority of roads made travel "an impossibility in winter" and rendered it "very difficult even in the good summer."[11] As a result of such isolation and poor transportation, denizens of the region were forced to adhere to the economic tenets of Jeffersonian Democracy, which called for the self-sufficent farm. Two factors, among others, that contributed to the necessity of such an arrangement were retarded economic and social development. Here poverty was more notable for such traits as "feud and homicide, gun-toting and moonshining."[12] One of the striking characteristics of the Blue Ridge region in 1900 was the existence of an approximately 100 percent native-born white population, which was plagued with an excessive amount of illiteracy that persisted even after the so-called Progressive era. A paradox seems to be suggested here: racism against Blacks was greatest in some of the mountain counties where there were "scarcely any Negroes at all." This raises a significant question—namely, how does one explain the existence of ethnocentrism in this remote region (the fact that racism and white illiteracy were capitalized upon by the Democrats during the white supremacy campaigns of 1900 notwithstanding)? As will be shown in chapter 6, it was in the Highlands that the Democrats first switched from their theme of "Negro Rule" and "Black Domination" to a promise of universal education.

A traveler crossing the state from either the east or the west would come to the picturesque Piedmont Plateau, the intermediary region lying between the Fall Line and the base of the Blue Ridge Mountains. It occupies 18,265 square miles, roughly 37.1 percent of the state's total area.[13] It is the most progressive region, with the greatest population density. In 1900 its economic core was industrialism (textiles, tobacco, and furniture), and there were signs of rapidly growing towns and cities. Massachusetts had long accepted the principles of taxation for support of schools and established both elementary and high schools. Similarly, in the Piedmont region traces of the Massachusetts school system were discernible. Although segregation was the rule, public school opportunities for the Negro were much superior to those for most whites in both the Coastal Plain and the Blue Ridge regions.

Industrialism had been on the move in North Carolina since the 1870s and had changed the landscape of many previously somnambulant communities. As impressive as this industrialism may sound, it failed to overcome the geographic forces that discouraged the growth of towns, and the particular demographic pattern of the state may be attributed to the many peculiarities of topography. In 1900 there was not a single city of 25,000 people. Wilmington, part of the Black Belt and with a population of 20,963, was the largest city in the state. Only two other cities, Asheville and Raleigh, had populations above 10,000, while twenty-three others had populations between 2,500 and 10,000.[14] The majority of these were located in the Piedmont region and were inhabited by "country folk come-to-town." To analyze the problem more closely, seven towns had populations between 2,000 and 2,499; thirty-one had populations between 500 and 1,999; and over two hundred had populations of less than 500 inhabitants.[15] Of the state's total population of 1,893,810 in 1900, only 186,790, or 17.9 percent, lived in incorporated places. The bulk of North Carolina's population was to be found in numerous scattered villages or was isolated on "solitary farmsteads." "The home sites," wrote Gould M. Hambright, "often appeared to have been deliberately located off the main highways,"[16] and the nearby country villages were characterized by the familiar rural institutions: a blacksmith shop, a post office, a general store, while somewhere nearby on the crossroads were sometimes located the schoolhouse, the church, and the "mournful" little cemetery. Thus, it is a prima facie case that North Carolina, at the turn of the twentieth century, remained a predominantly rural community with numerous names of villages and hamlets on the map. In light of this evidence, one must reach the conclusion that both the state's political and educational philosophy were identified with ruralism, with which racism was inextricably interwoven.

Each of North Carolina's physiographic regions reflected a political dichotomy. In the mountainous counties of the Highlands, a stronghold of intransigent republicanism prevailed; election after election white denizens voted en masse straight Republican, to mirror party loyalty by tradition. For the same reason, the Negro in the Black Belt and elsewhere voted en masse for the party of Lincoln. It is ironic that, though these political factions were irrevocably separated by racism, they were forced together in a "marriage," which, had it been "put asunder," would have meant certain political failure.

To the above must be added the historical rivalry of eastern and western North Carolina. As Professor Collier Cobb, who often lectured to his students on the geology of North Carolina as a determining force in the state's political history, said, in part: "The political questions in North Carolina have always been questions of east and west, of the upcountry against the lowlands, of crystalline schists and granites against unconsolidated clays, sands and gravels."[17] This was essentially a struggle between white men—those of the "Uplands" (Piedmont) against those of the Lowlands (Black Belt)— for supremacy in the House of North Carolina politics. It was the Piedmont whites, with their allied industrial capitalism, greater population density, greater wealth, and higher assessed property, who bore the burden of the state's expenses—including educational expenditures. In contrast, the planter-politicans of the Black Belt, who exercised a powerful legislative veto, were proponents of economy in government, low assessed property, and the continuation of the crop-lien system. They also took a very dim view toward educational progress. Quite understandably, representatives from the Piedmont region logically concluded that political supremacy should be accorded to them. Indeed, they demonstrated their supremacy by taking over the choice elective offices in the state.

The constituents of the Democratic party maintained their loyalty and were of one mind on the concept of white solidarity—especially the white minority in the Black Belt. After North Carolina achieved what is euphemistically called *Redemption,* better known as *Home Rule,* the Redeemers (Bourbon Democrats[18]) initiated the election machinery to maintain party hegemony and to checkmate the formidable Negro vote in the Black Belt counties. These objectives were accomplished basically by such devices as centralization of the state election machinery and intricate, complex election laws.[19]

In the quest for centralization, collaboration was essential in the numerous remote rural towns. The Democratic party line was the medium of communication extending from the General Assembly to the varied courthouse machines. All organs of county government were inextricably interwoven with the "Courthouse Kings" or the "Courthouse Cliques." The county chairman was the key figure, and he received his orders from the state chairman. Meanwhile, he could name the electoral board and could see that only his men were chosen as treasurer, sheriff, and commissioner. The appointment of the county superintendent of schools was always a power of the masters of the court rings, a situation that constantly evoked strong criticism from certain prominent educational leaders.[20]

Tentacles of the Democratic machinery reached down to the municipal levels, notably in the Coastal Plain, embracing the cities where there was a greater Negro than white population. The city of Wilmington, where the Negro voting population was in excess of fourteen hundred over that of the whites, is a typical example. In 1875, an amended charter vested the government to a board of nine aldermen, three to be elected from each of the three wards. Employing the device of gerrymandering, the city was so divisioned as to give the whites a majority in two wards; thus, they were entitled to elect six aldermen. The single Negro Third Ward had three times more voters than the white First and Second Wards.[21] Moreover, the Democrats amended charters in some of the cities in the Piedmont region, which had a sizeable Negro population, including Durham, Raleigh, and Winston. These legal devices were obvious violations of the "fundamental principles of apportionment of representation of the Constitution."

Still more significant was the County Government Act. On the basis of the authority delegated by the Constitution of 1875, the act empowered the legislature to appoint the major county officials, a process that turned out to be "a wheel within a wheel." First, the legislature appointed the justices of the peace, formerly elected by popular vote. The justices were given control over the election machinery of the county, the establishment of voting precincts, and the appointment of registrars and judges.[22] They were also given power to abolish or restore the office of county treasurer. The administrative organ of the county was the board of commissioners, no longer elected by popular vote, but by the justices "acting as a body." The county commissioners also constituted the county board of education, with the registrar of deeds serving as clerk and the county treasurer acting as treasurer of the school fund. They divided the county into school districts, appointed school committees for each district, and appointed a county examiner. Through this medium the Democratic party was able to maintain the administration of public schools in every county.

The underlying intent of the Redeemers' system of centralization was to render impotent Negro political power in the Black Belt counties. Yet by the County Government Act the Carolina Highland region "lost control of its local affairs to a highly centralized party machine," ironically in a region where there were few Blacks and, hence, where there was never a threat of Negro rule. This undemocratic situation, to be sure, evoked considerable opposition, as demonstrated by the fact that thirty members of the 1876–77 General Assembly countered with a signed "solemn protest."[23] The undemocratic county election law would later serve as a catalyst to unite the Republicans and Populists in Fusion politics. Moreover, the extent to which the maze of intricate voting procedures and technicalities deprived Blacks of voting privileges remains to be seen. After viewing the predicament, understandably with dejection, one of the South's foremost Republicans—and also one of its most distinguished literary critics—wrote his party's obituary: "The Republican Party of North Carolina is dead—dead beyond hope of resurrection."[24] Thus, a paradox becomes evident: (1) the Republican party had not met its demise; (2) the party was vigorous, and Blacks were the centrifugal force behind its dynamics; (3) Blacks continued to vote in large numbers; and (4) surprisingly, a number were elected to public office. This historic contradiction merits a brief analogy. A formidable "Black second" congressional district prevailed even after the Redeemers had gerrymandered the counties. Such a situation was not unique, for prodigious Black congressional districts were preponderant in Alabama, Florida, Georgia, Louisiana, Mississippi, North Carolina, South Carolina, Texas, and Virginia. It was in these districts that Blacks continued to vote in large numbers after Reconstruction, thus creating the avenues for Negro officeholders to make their way into the municipalities, state legislatures, federal patronages, and on to Congress. Only seven sat in that august assembly (none from outside the South) from 1880 to 1890, and three of these were from North Carolina. During the next decade the last two Blacks to sit in Congress until 1929 would hail from North Carolina. As is well known, the Black Belt has been the hard core of Southern politics, and the backbone of white solidarity, especially in those counties and sections where Blacks constitute a substantial portion of the population. "In these areas a real problem of politics, broadly considered, is the maintenance of control by a white minority."[25]

Ultimately, the two jealous factions of the "east-west rivalry" compromised their differences, and the wealthy Black Belt planter-merchants identified themselves with the middle classes and the city.[26] They now abetted the leadership of the Democratic party, which inevitably made them the leaders of the lower-class whites. With latent radicalism procreating from the roots of populism, the planter-merchants were apprehensive about an insurgence of the lower-class whites. Most of all they feared the mania of Negrophobia. Both the merchant-planter and the lower-class whites of the Black Belt counties had the strongest feelings about the maintenance of white supremacy. Population wise, they were in a minority and, politically, occupied a most insecure position. Factional politics existed within the ranks of whites. On the contrary, no such factionalism prevailed among the Blacks to enable the white minority to gain a "balance-of-power position." In racial solidarity, the Blacks voted en masse for the Republican party. Likewise, by tradition, the lower-class whites voted en masse for the Democratic party, now headed by the capitalistic oligarchies, which were perpetuating their economic philosophy embracing high interest rates, low wages, long hours, farm tenancy, and the like.[27] It must be amphasized, however, that racism as the core of white supremacy was the only thing the Black Belt whites had in common with the landlords and/or planter-merchants.

By destroying "Black Republicanism," the Redeemers also destroyed the ties that held the poor and middle-class whites together as a political unit. But once the Negro was removed as a political threat, they departed along traditional lines. Industrialism was represented within the plutocracy—by the textile mill owners, the railroad magnates, the bankers, the large landowners, the planter-merchants, and others. These dynamic politico-economic forces controlled the Democratic party under the helm of the attorneys.[28] Accordingly, they were probusiness and antireform, and thus assumed a laissez faire attitude toward vital issues of the day, which involved public education; and, "in many respects," wrote a native historian, "they were apathetic and even hostile toward the introduction of new ideas."[29] At the same time, they created the myth of the "Solid South." They also demonstrated "a fine art" in the use of the race question to maintain their position, while frightening independents and dissenters who occasionally challenged their control.[30] As leaders of the Democratic party, they required utmost loyalty from members. White solidarity was the key, and any political factionalism could be held at bay by converting "latent radicalism" into aggression against Blacks.

But several salient forces were destined to emerge to destroy this very unity, a drama later to be acted out in the Black Belt.

In the 1890s a farmers' movement triggered an outburst of agrarian radicalism, which found expression in the Populist revolt. It was fed by acute economic distress, along with a deep sense of grievance against perpetual shrinkage of agricultural prices, trusts, railroads, banks, and the crop-lien system—the "worst credit system of all." In the face of these adversities, small farmers and tenants alike grew desperately poor. This economic plight opened new wounds between the poor whites and the establishment—whom they suspected of being apathetic, if not inimical, to their interests. Accordingly, they bolted their party and supported populism. The ghost of the Negro past was to walk again. Nevertheless, the initial task of this study is to delineate the status of the public school system as it existed in 1900, along with the causes of that condition.

Notes

1. Horace Mann Bond, *Negro Education in Alabama: A Study in Cotton and Steel* (Washington, D.C., 1939), p. 1.

2. *Raleigh Star,* 20 December 1833.

3. S. Huntington Hobbs, Jr., *North Carolina: An Economic and Social Profile* (Chapel Hill, N.C., 1958), p. 52.

4. Ibid., p. 55.

5. *Twelfth Census of the United States,* 1900, Agriculture, 5: cx, 108–10.

6. Arthur Raper, "North Carolina Landless Farmers," in *Country Life in North Carolina,* University of North Carolina Extension Bulletin no. 3. (Chapel Hill, N.C., 1928), pp. 48, 54, 55; "Forty Years of Progress in Farm Ownership," in Charles L. Coon Papers, Southern Historical Collection, University of North Carolina, Chapel Hill, N.C.

7. Huntington, Hobbs, Jr., *North Carolina: Economic and Social* (Chapel Hill, N.C., 1930), pp. 75–79; see also idem, *Know Your State—North Carolina* (Chapel Hill, N.C., 1924), p. 5.

8. Philander P. Claxton Papers, Special Collection, University of Tennessee Library, Knoxville, Tenn., and Edwin A. Alderman, *A Brief History of North Carolina* (Boston, 1896) in Edwin Alderman Papers, Alderman Library, University of Virginia, Charlottesville, Va.

9. Margaret W. Morley, *The Carolina Mountains* (New York, 1913), p. 103; Cordelia Camp, *The Influence of Geography upon Early North Carolina* (Raleigh, N.C., 1936), p. 3.

10. Hobbs, *North Carolina,* pp. 65–66.

11. "Public School Exhibit for the Year 1900," Claxton Papers.

12. Jonathan Daniels, *Tar Heels: A Portrait of North Carolina* (New York, 1941), pp. 242–43.

13. Hobbs, *North Carolina,* pp. 62–63.

14. *Twelfth Census of the United States,* 1900, Population, pt. 1, pp. 466–67; ibid., p. 2, p. cxxxii.

15. Ibid.

16. Gould M. Hambright, "Transportation and Communication in North

Carolina," in *Country Life in North Carolina,* University of North Carolina Extension Bulletin no. 3 (Chapel Hill, N.C., 1928–29), pp. 24–33.

17. Collier Cobb, "Geology of North Carolina," in *Raleigh News and Observer,* 2 July 1892.

18. Professor Woodward has concluded that the term *Bourbon* is a "much-abused epithet," and strongly believes that it is time that this expression be abandoned since it is a source of confusion. "In the Southern States the term Bourbon has no distinct significance. It is applied indiscriminately by all classes of politicians to anybody who differs from them. It is there a convenient though empty epithet or name of reproach." C. Vann Woodward, *Origins of the New South, 1877–1937* (Baton Rouge, La., 1951), pp. 14, 75 n.

19. Stephen Weeks, "The History of Negro Suffrage in the South," *Political Science Quarterly* 9 (1894) : 692.

20. North Carolina Department of Public Instruction, *Biennial Report of the State Inspector of Public Instruction,* 1898–1900, pp. 6–7 (hereafter cited as *Biennial School Report*).

21. *Van Bokkelen v. William P. Canaday,* North Carolina Reports, vol. 73 (June 1875), pp. 179–92.

22. *Public Laws of North Carolina,* 1876–77, chap. 275, pp. 516 ff.

23. North Carolina *House Journal* (1876–77), pp. 875–76; J. G. de Roulhac Hamilton, *History of North Carolina,* vol. 3, *North Carolina since 1860* (Chicago, 1919), pp. 192–93.

24. Albion W. Tourgèe, The "C Letters", as printed in the *Greensboro North State,* April 18, 1878, University of North Carolina, Chapel Hill, N.C.

25. V. O. Key, Jr., ed., *Southern Politics in the State and the Nation* (New York, 1950), pp. 4–5.

26. Woodward, *Origins of the New South,* pp. 327–28.

27. *Report of the North Carolina Bureau of Labor and Printing 1900* (Raleigh, N.C., 1901), pp. 180–83.

28. Key, *Southern Politics,* pp. 211–15. Lawyers have predominantly controlled North Carolina; in 1948 Kerr Scott became the first governor who was not a lawyer in fifty years, and the state has yet to produce a white spokesman from the "downtrodden".

29. Archibald Henderson, *The Old North State and the New* (Chicago, 1941), p. 272.

30. Dewey W. Grantham, "The Southern Bourbon Revisited," *South Atlantic Quarterly* 60 (1961) : 287.

*Resurgent Politics
and Educational Progressivism
in the New South*

Part I

The Setting of Things to Come

1

North Carolina's Style of Education in 1900

What is the American system of public education? The United States Constitution makes no reference to education as a national or state responsibility. However, a provision of the Constitution reads: "The powers not delegated to the United States by the Constitution nor prohibited by it to the states, are reserved to the states respectively or to the people."[1] In accordance with this principle, the organization, administration, and support of public education are matters of state concern. Although education in each state is completely autonomous, there has currently developed what might be called an American pattern of public education, and Massachusetts originated the trend and provided the guidelines for this pattern.[2] Today, a foreigner visiting the widely separate school systems would, indeed, find little visible evidence that the varied systems are operating under completely independent authorities. Academic leaders and the American people, in general, agree on many of the principles underlying educational policies, theories, and practices.

The development of American education has not always followed this unique trend of unity. Save in a few scattered cities throughout the South, nowhere did the pattern of the Massachusetts school system exist. The low status of public education in North Carolina, to be sure, was a potent issue in the Democrats' white supremacy campaign of 1900. Moreover, it was a galvanizing force that gave impetus to the great public school movement, which followed in its wake. The purpose of this chapter, accordingly, is to describe the status of the public school system in North Carolina as it existed in 1900. Such a plan and approach are essential for two major reasons: (1) the reader will be oriented to the nature and gravity of the problem, and (2) the recorded data will serve as a baseline against which to measure later progress and changes as delineated in chapter 11.

Universal education in North Carolina, constitutionally and politically, meant a four-months school term. There were approximately 450,000 children of school age, of which 17 out of every 18 depended upon the public schools for education. According to the record of the North Carolina state superintendent of public instruction in 1900, the total school fund was listed at $1,018,144.[3] This amount averaged around $4.56 per pupil in daily attendance, as compared to $34.09 in Massachusetts, $38.97 in New York, $21.63 in Ohio, $9.70 in Virginia, and $20.28 for the entire nation. These figures represent an annual expenditure of $.51 per capita of population in North Carolina, as compared to $5.97 in Massachusetts, $4.09 in New York, $3.63 in Ohio, $1.08 in Virginia, and $2.82 for the entire nation.[4]

Educationally, what would have been the observations of Alexis de Tocqueville or Frederick L. Olmsted had either of them visited North Carolina as a stranger at the dawn of the twentieth century? On traveling from the North to the South, our hypothetical visitor would have quickly become cognizant of a prevailing "cultural lag" in North Carolina, as well as throughout the South. Indeed, the state's public schools greatly contrasted with the so-called American school system. Our hypothetical visitor would quickly have become aware of marked disparity in urban-rural education. Attempting to copy the Massachusetts schools, cities and some small towns had established graded school systems. Moreover, they were not a state function or responsibility. Just as self-governing charters emerged out of the feudalistic order, so had the urban schools emerged. Their existence was the result of local initiative, legislation, and taxation. However, the General Assembly did give them legal recognition by a law enacted in 1876, which declared that "in every township of North Carolina having within its limits a city of (5,000) five thousand inhabitants and upwards, and one hundred respectable citizens thereof . . . may apply petition in writing to the board of commissioners of the county . . . that an annual tax be levied . . . for the support of one or more graded schools." This special school tax had to be approved by a majority of qualified voters, and it could "in no case exceed one-tenth of one percent on valuation of property and thirty cents on the poll." It must be pointed out in conclusion that the special tax provision did not apply in the Black Belt counties where were located such cities as Wilmington, Goldsboro, and New Bern.

In making a distinction, the law read: "The application for election shall be made by two hundred of the qualified voters of the said townships who shall be freeholders therein, and at least one-half of the petitioners shall be of the white race."[5]

Hence, independent urban systems were completely autonomous, for the General Assembly granted complete control of them to the local authorities, according to provision of their charters. The entire financial responsibility for the schools' operation, aside from the four-months state school fund, was borne by the cities and towns that founded them. By utilizing the local school tax law and special city charters, they were able to begin the establishment of graded schools in Greensboro in 1876, followed by Raleigh in 1877, Salisbury in 1880, Goldsboro in 1881, Durham, Charlotte, and Wilmington in 1882, and Winston-Salem in 1885.[6] At length, these institutions became the "pacesetters" of the graded school movement. Northern philanthropy, specifically the Peabody Fund, played a notable financial role in abetting the graded school movement.[7] It is of historical interest to briefly sketch this movement. When North Carolina was struggling with the prodigious problem of Reconstruction, a new form of philanthropy came into existence (exemplified by the Peabody Fund and later the Slater Foundation and General Education Board). This type of philanthropy is defined as the legally chartered foundation, whose "large and mobile funds" were administered through a board of trustees, and combined private funds with "public and official" endeavors for the express purpose of helping to promote both public and higher education in the South. The first such organization was the Peabody Education Fund, established by George Peabody, a wealthy merchant and banker of Massachusetts, in 1867.[8] The fund was incorporated by an act of Congress, which at the time appropriated the necessary funds for a gold medal to the donor.[9] This fund of $2.5 million, administered by the board of trustees, was to be employed in behalf of the education of both whites and Negroes. Its general purpose, as the donor expressed it, "was to assist in educational development of the Southern states that had suffered from the ravaging consequences of the Civil War."[10] Dr. Barnes Sears, then president of Brown University at Providence, Rhode Island, became general agent of the Peabody Fund on March 30, 1869.[11]

North Carolina was the first to participate in the distribution of the Peabody Fund, and in 1868 the sum of twenty-two thousand dollars was made available to the state.[12] Requirements were rather generous. For a well-regulated and graded public school that maintained a term of approximately nine months and a teacher for every fifty pupils, a single initial grant of about one-fourth of the annual current expense was given on the condition that a community voted a permanent local school tax. However, two thousand dollars was the maximum amount made available to any city, and such funds were placed in the hands of the proper school official, which in North Carolina was the state superintendent of public instruction.[13]

It should be understood that the major objective of the Peabody Fund was to awaken the public to the needs of voting special and permanent local taxes. This provision proved to be a real bugaboo, for racism soon raised its ugly head. Around the end of the seventies, the whites began to agitate for a racial division of school tax funds. This meant that monies raised from white property and poll taxes would be appropriated exclusively for white graded schools and that such taxes raised from property and polls of Blacks would be applied exclusively for their schools. Moreover, the General Assembly in 1880 approved such an act for the city of Goldsboro.[14] Naturally, the trustees of the Peabody Fund refused to allot money on a racial basis, which was a setback for the state's educational progress.[15] The net results for the decade ending in 1878 showed that the state received only ninety-one thousand dollars in Peabody funds, which was considerably lower than the amounts received by Tennessee and Virginia.[16] Granted, Blacks did receive some financial assistance during the fund's early operation in North Carolina (especially before the Redeemers came into power), but such financial subsidies were meager in comparison to those provided for white education. To a large extent, Dr. Sears summarized the educational situation in North Carolina when he reported to the trustees that the "public mind does not seem to be so well settled here in regard to free schools as in most of the other states."

The graded school movement, notwithstanding, continued at a snaillike pace. By 1900 there were thirty-six white graded school systems, located predominantly in the Piedmont region. Descriptive information on the school buildings is limited, but the available data shows that they were frame and brick structures, the one-story frame structures consisting of half a dozen classrooms. In 1900 there were fifteen such buildings. The remainder were of brick, located in the larger towns, and some were "equipped with the most modern school furniture." We may safely assume that the conditions of the buildings and equipment ran the gamut from poor to fair, since the structures were erected during a time of financial stress, and whatever the original defects were, the conditions were aggravated by the passing of time. The valuation of school property in the special chartered districts may be viewed as an index to the character of school buildings and equipment, and attention is directed to Table 1.[17]

36

TABLE 1

GRADED SCHOOL OPPORTUNITIES FOR THE WHITE POPULATION
OF NORTH CAROLINA IN 1900

Location of School	County	Type of Community	Total Value of Building and Grounds	Number of Grades	Length of School Term in Weeks
Asheboro	Randolph	Rural	$ 2,500	10	36
Asheville	Buncombe	City	57,000	10	36
Burlington	Alamance	City	6,000	10	36
Charlotte	Mecklenburg	City	80,000	10	36
Concord	Cabarras	City	5,000	9	36
Durham	Durham	City	95,000	10	38
Fayetville	Cumberland	City	10,000	10	32
Goldsboro	Wayne	City	12,000	10	36
Greensboro	Guilford	City	50,000	10	36
Guilford College Rural Grade School	Guilford	Rural	60,000		24
Henderson	Vance	City	300	6	32
Hendersonville	Henderson	City	3,000	9	25
High point	Guilford	City		10	40
Kingston	Lenoir	City	30,000	9	32
Lexington	Davidson	Rural	2,500	9	36
Marion	McDowell	Rural	5,000	8	36
Monroe	Union	City	6,000	8	36
Mt. Airy	Surry	City	9,000		36
Mt. Olive	Wayne	Rural	4,400	9	36
New Bern	Craven	City	1,700	9	33
Oxford	Granville	Rural	3,000	10	32
Raleigh	Wake	City	111,000	8	36
Reidsville	Rockingham	City	17,000	7	36
Rockingham	Richmond	Rural	13,582	9	36
Rocky Mount	Nash and Edgecombe	Rural		9	34
Salisbury	Rowan	City	20,000	11	36
Selma	Johnston	Rural	2,500	11	36
Shelby	Cleveland	City	16,000	8	32
Statesville	Credell	City		10	40
Tarboro	Edgecombe	Rural	3,000	8	32
Thomasville	Davidson	Rural		10	36
Washington	Beauford	City	3,000	7	35
Waynesville	Haywood	Rural	10,000	10	32
Wilmington	New Hanover	City		10	36
Wilson	Wilson	City	25,000	8	36
Winston	Forsyth	City	65,000	10	36

A word needs to be said about the curriculum and course of study in the autonomous urban areas. The graded schools, as pointed out earlier, were not a state function, but a responsibility of local officials in special chartered school districts. Accordingly, the course of study was usually determined by the principal and each individual school. The record shows that twenty-five of the thirty-six graded schools provided educational opportunities above the eighth grade. Nevertheless, the completion of eight grades appeared to have been adequate preparation for college. One principal wrote: "Our course of study extends over nine years, prepares for college or university. We give three years of Latin, two in Algebra and Geometry, two in higher English and Rhetoric, one in Physics and other work that is commensurate."[18] These institutions were at best only skeletons of the high schools located in Massachusetts. By the same token, the majority were in reality advanced elementary schools. It should be noted here that Southern colleges maintained preparatory departments that overlapped and competed with the secondary schools. The secondary school curriculum was basically a foundation of the classical course of study that emphasized Latin, Greek, and other traditional subjects. It had only one major function—to prepare youths for college, notwithstanding that many of them would never attend institutions of higher learning.

If one excludes the cities and towns where the graded schools existed, along with the remaining urban towns (Gastonia, Elizabeth City, Salem, Edenton, and Hickory) where they did not exist, it is relatively safe to assume that the "one teacher type common school" furnished the educational opportunities for the state's approximately 82 percent rural population. The so-called common school was an ungraded elementary establishment consisting of pupils of all degrees of advancement from the "beginners through the seven years course of study."

According to the state superintendent's report, there were 5,172 white schools in 1900, but there were only 4,749 schoolhouses owned by the respective counties.[19] This situation leads one to believe that, in all probability, public instruction was provided for the child in some improvised establishment—a rural church, lodge, house, or any suitable place that was loaned to the county for educational purposes. There is a possibility that some children received public instruction in some of the private schools, which at the time were quite numerous and well distributed throughout the state. In the 1890s there were some 500 white private schools, of which approximately 400 were elementary.[20] Employing a plan similar to the English one made famous by William Gladstone, North Carolina made it legal for a child to receive free instruction in private establishments. According to this law, in any district with a private school, annually conducted for at least six months, "the School Committee may contract with the teachers of such private schools to give instruction to all pupils between the ages of six and twenty-one years in the branches of learning taught in the public schools . . . without charge and free tuition; and such School Committee may pay such teachers for such services out of the public school fund apportioned to the district and the arrangement as to such pay shall be arranged between the committee and teacher." However, the private schools were not allowed to receive more per capita of the public fund than they received per capita from the parents in private funds. To illustrate, if the tuition was two dollars per month, and there were forty children in the public school branches whose private tuition was $80, then eighty dollars per month was the maximum the county was allowed to pay for instruction out of the public fund.[21]

The real intent of this law was to solve the problem created by "weak school districts," a description that applied to the widely scattered neighborhoods where there were not enough pupils within a particular area to justify the expense of good school buildings and good teachers. Weak school districts were indeed a real problem. Notwithstanding that the law stipulated that the county boards of education should not create such districts with less than sixty-five children of school age, they had grown up like Jimson weeds in the sparsely settled neighborhoods. For example, 2,427, or 47 percent, of the districts comprised less than sixty-five children of school age, the minimum fixed by law.[22]

Some of the educational leaders were aware of the merits of school consolidation, upon which rested the state's major hope for improving the rural school and changing an ungraded school into a graded school at a saving of expense. They advocated the abolishment of the poor and smaller districts in favor of larger ones through consolidation, a movement that was already gaining momentum in some of the Northern states.[23] As State Superintendent James Y. Joyner explained: "With a small school fund, a sparse, largely rural population, and an immense territory, it (consolidation) is absolutely necessary for the efficiency of the schools and the greatest number of children that there should be the smallest possible number of districts and schools."[24]

The rural schoolhouses, often described as "log houses," "shanties," or "tenant" houses, were truly symbolic of "the very mudsill" of the educational plight. In 1900 none of the rural schoolhouses were of brick structure, and, of the 4,749 white schools, 3,991 were frame buildings and 758 were log structures. The average value of each school was $175, yet in some counties the structure was worth little more than $50. The total value of school property in the counties ranged from $430 in Polk County to $76,570 in New Hanover County. A cursory examination of Table 1 will show that the valuation of the 35 white graded schools was approximately the same as the $839,269 reported for white rural schools in 1900.[25]

It is interesting to describe a typical rural schoolhouse in its environmental setting. The sites of the rural schools varied in size from one to two acres and were generally located on well-traveled roads. The old-fashioned log structures were in the shape of one-room tenant cabins, fashioned with log and clay walls, "stick and clasp" chimneys, and a swayback roof. The majority of the frame buildings were characterized by the old, one-story, boxlike structure and were generally between fourteen by sixteen feet and twenty by twenty-five feet. For the most part, they were shabbily built board structures, one story high, with an overhead ceiling not more than nine feet from the floor. There was one door at the end of the house and six small windows, three on each side. There were no blinds or curtains. The desks were "homemade, with perpendicular backs and seats, all the same size." In many instances, there was no teacher's desk or table, and only one chair. Seldom was there a vestibule or cloakroom; fence nails were driven into the walls for the children's hats and coats. In the center of the room sat the old-fashioned "long John" stove, red with rust and dirt, while a rear corner of the room provided the only storage for fuel to be used against the weather. During the winter seasons, the pupils seldom enjoyed comforts, for they were generally "half warm and half cold," meaning comfortable about the head and shoulders, while their feet and legs were attacked by the cold winds sweeping under the schoolhouse, "which was without proper underpinning." In the rear sat the outhouses, "dilapidated, disreputable and filthy beyond belief." Much too frequently, a bare spot in front of the school at the road was the children's only playground. As a rule, the grounds were unkempt, overflowing with weeds, briars, and honeysuckle vines. And if the teacher attempted to improve the grounds, nature would undo in seven or eight months whatever improvements were made during the short three- or four-months school year. The teacher's lot in the one-room rural schoolhouse was most uninviting. To illustrate, he was expected to do a janitor's work, he could not count on a desk or table to work on, and generally the only educational equipment he was provided with was a small strip of composition blackboard or a patch of painted wall. Comparatively few of the rural schools had libraries or books, save the few textbooks owned by the teacher and some pupils.[26]

The watchword of the American school-building policy has been said to be education, economy, safety, health, and happiness. And yet these concepts were in great contrast to the policy of North Carolina at the turn of the twentieth century. Edwin A. Alderman, then a young teacher, who often campaigned for education before the Farmers' Alliance, after observing a typical, cheerless rural schoolhouse, wrote with compassion: "A school where children never sing, must be a dreary sort of place. In a factory the hands go without ceremony to their joyless work. The school is not that sort of factory."[27] Similarly, Fletcher B. Dressler wrote that "the houses of most American farmers have not resulted from careful planning, either with reference to beauty or convenience, and least of all with due regard to the joys of life," and this habit has fastened itself upon the rural communities that built the public schools.[28]

As for the curriculum of the rural schools the law stated: "The branches taught in the public schools shall be spelling, defining, reading, writing, arithmetic, English grammar and composition, geography, nature and the effects of alcoholic drink and narcotics, elementary physiology and hygiene, civil government, history of North Carolina and of the United States."[29] While the law enumerated the subjects to be taught in the schools, it failed to adopt a formal course of study that would impose any rules for teaching them. The state's educational philosophy, which placed major emphasis on the three Rs, was acquired during antebellum days. Hence, the curriculum was outmoded and certainly not adequate to meet the needs of a child destined to live in twentieth-century America. Such a curriculum did not motivate the child to extend his educational training beyond the seventh-grade course of study in the common schools, or prepare the child for college. It also failed to consider the rural child who was destined to live in an agrarian society.

At this point, it is important to consider such variables as school terms, enrollment, attendance, and illiteracy. Because the legal four-months school term was not compulsory, it varied greatly throughout the state. For instance, the average school term for whites was 14.6 weeks, or 70.5 days. In localities where the graded school existed, the average term was around 33 weeks, while in the counties it varied from 6.3 weeks in Ashe County to 23.6 weeks in New Hanover County. In 1900 some sixty-nine of the state's ninety-seven counties maintained school terms of shorter duration than the four-months constitutional requirement. North Carolina's legal school age extended from six to eighteen years. In 1900 only 270,447 of the total school population of 439,431 were enrolled. This meant that 52.7 percent of school children were enrolled, as compared to 73.03 percent in Massachusetts, 70.03 percent in New York, 67.73 percent in Ohio, 61.8 percent in Virginia, and 68.5 percent throughout the nation. Likewise, the average daily attendance was 51.67 percent in North

Carolina, 64.8 percent in Georgia, 61.8 percent in Virginia, and 71.43 percent in Tennessee. As for the Northern states, daily attendance was 77.3 percent in Massachusetts, 74.3 percent in New York, and 70.3 percent in Ohio, while for the whole South the figure was 67.4 percent and for the nation 68.5 percent. At the same time, in North Carolina 58.8 percent of the children between the ages of five and eighteen were enrolled, as compared to 57.72 percent in Virginia, 61.3 percent in Georgia, and 70.2 percent in Tennessee, while in the Northern states, Massachusetts led with 73.03 percent, followed by 70.03 percent and 67.73 percent, respectively, for Ohio and New York. The enrollment throughout the South was 61.68 percent and throughout the nation 68.53 percent.[30]

Since North Carolina enrolled only 52.7 percent of the school population, it may be concluded that approximately forty out of every one hundred children did not attend school at all. The state's poor school enrollment and attendance record attested to the need for some kind of compulsory attendance law. To be sure, the problem had some influence upon the large degree of illiteracy. The record shows that 28.7 percent of North Carolina's total population aged ten years and above was illiterate, as compared to 24.9 percent in Virginia, 30.5 percent in Georgia, and 20.7 percent in Tennessee. At the same time, the degree of illiteracy in the Northern states was 6.7 percent in Massachusetts, 5.5 percent in New York, and 4.0 percent in Ohio. The figures for the entire South and nation were 23.4 percent and 10.7 percent, respectively. North Carolina's figure of 28.7 percent illiteracy does not paint an accurate picture of the situation, however. As might be expected, the degree of illiteracy was much greater and varied in the rural areas. It was as low as 5.1 percent and as high as 32.9 percent among white adult males in the counties of New Hanover and Stokes, respectively, and the problem was greater among females.[31] Moreover, physiographic factors and racism figured prominently in the problem. It should be pointed out here that approximately 100 percent illiteracy existed in the Highland regions, and a like amount in the Coastal Plain, especially among the Negro population. And we may safely assume that no consideration was given to the problem of "near illiteracy." This category included those persons who could manage to read and sign their names, yet who, for all practical purposes, were as ignorant as the completely unschooled. The mere ability to write one's name or to decipher a few words in a newspaper is of little value for a citizen to function adequately in a democratic society. Thus, the conclusion is that while absolute illiteracy was measured by the hundreds, "near illiteracy could have been measured by the thousands." Accordingly, the educational leaders were faced with the

42

prodigious task of abolishing not only absolute illiteracy, but "near illiteracy" as well.

The Redeemers did not concern themselves with educational philosophies. They made the same commitment to Blacks as to whites, the only exception to this general rule being their stipulation that the schools must be separate. Yet diversified philosophies about education of Blacks prevailed at the close of the Civil War, running the gamut from advocating that Blacks be left in total ignorance to proposing that they be given the opportunity to at least acquire the necessary tools "to read the printed page." At the same time, every outstanding educator agreed that Negroes must be educated. Perhaps the most advanced view was held by Atticus C. Haygood, who would later become the first general agent of the Slater Philanthropy. Haywood was a Methodist clergyman and then president of Emory College in Atlanta, Georgia. In 1881 he published the book *Our Brother in Black*. The title was a most liberal one at the time for a white Southerner. *Our Brother in Black* contained Haygood's social and educational philosophy concerning the Negro. Like many of his enlightened Southern contemporaries, Haygood believed that the Negro was in the South to stay and that the South was the best place for him. But, unlike the dominant majority, he believed that the Negro should be educated for citizenship and enjoy the suffrage. In extolling such views, Haygood declared that this "new citizen (the Negro) is a voter, and unhappily for all, he is not ready for his responsibilities. Voting means intelligence. Woe to the land where those who hold the balance of power are in ignorance. This tremendous engine of political power, the ballot, must be in the hands that know what they are doing. This voter must be educated."[32] For a Southerner, Haygood's social philosophy was so far in advance of its time that one might class him as a radical.

In 1900 the Negro population of 624,469 constituted one-third of the state's total population, and its 208,754 Negro children between six and twenty-one years of age represented one-third of the total school population. Negro education was molded by the same forces that had developed that of whites, and by 1900 the development of public schools for Blacks was a simple process. Evidence indicates that the discrepancy between Negro and white public school opportunities in the state was not so wide in 1900 as it was later, beginning with the public school movement that occurred between 1902–13. Because of the vastness of the subject, my findings will basically be summarized.

In 1889 there were approximately 35 private schools, including those attached to the Negro colleges, with a total enrollment of 5,884 pupils.[33] Although the enrollment at the private schools in proportion to the total school population was negligible, it is germane to point out that early establishment of these schools paved the way for the subsequent development of secondary schools for the Negro population.[34] According to the record of 1900, there were 30 graded schools for Blacks; 9 of them offered some secondary instruction, and all were located chiefly in the Piedmont region. For location, number, type, and other data on these institutions, see Table 2. For the state's rural Negro population, 2,395 schools were conducted in 1900, but there were only 2,118 schoolhouses, of which 1,686 were frame buildings and 432 made of logs. In addition, there were 2,515 school districts; yet 324 of them were without schoolhouses. Needless to say, instruction was given in "some makeshift building loaned to the district"—a rural church, lodge hall or deserted cabin "pressed into service for school purposes."[35]

TABLE 2
GRADED SCHOOL OPPORTUNITIES FOR THE NEGRO POPULATION
OF NORTH CAROLINA IN 1900

Location of School	County	Type of Community	School Population	Number of Grades	Length of School Term in Weeks
Asheboro	Randolph	Rural	951		36
Asheville	Buncombe	City	1,293	8	36
Burlington	Alamance	City	153		
Charlotte	Mecklenburg	City	2,224	10	36
Concord	Cabarras	City		6	32
Durham	Durham	City	1,763	10	38
Goldsboro	Wayne	City	1,136	10	36
Greensboro	Guilford	City	1,666	7	36
Henderson	Vance	City	1,258	8	32
Hendersonville	Henderson	City	191	8	25
High point	Guilford	City	292	9	40
Kingston	Lenoir	City	450	5	32
Lexington	Davidson	Rural	208	6	36
Monroe	Union	Rural	265	7	36
Mt. Airy	Surry	City	312	5	36
Mt. Olive	Wayne	Rural		9	32
New Bern	Craven	City	1,769	7	33
Oxford	Granville	Rural	401	6	32
Raleigh	Wake	City	3,064	5	36
Reidsville	Rockingham	City	834	10	36
Rockingham	Richmond	Rural	155	4	32
Rocky Mount	Nash and Edgecombe	Rural	400		

44

Location of School	County	Type of Community	School Population	Number of Grades	Length of School Term in Weeks
Salisbury	Rowan	City	676	6	36
Selma	Johnston	Rural	276	6	36
Shelby	Cleveland	City	165		
Statesville	Credell	City	313	6	32
Tarboro	Edgecombe	Rural	1,170	7	35
Thomasville	Davidson	Rural	190	6	35
Washington	Beauford	City	807	6	32
Wilson	Wilson	City	1,007	7	36

The average length of school terms countywide was 14.06 weeks. Of the 198,600 rural Negro school children, 127,399 were enrolled, and the average daily attendance was 67,148. In the counties where the Negro population was the greatest (in the Black Belt—see Fig. 1), about one half of the Negro population of school age was enrolled in the public schools in 1900, and about half of that enrollment was in average daily attendance. It was also shown that the length of school term compared favorably with the state's average and in some instances was longer than the white school term in some of the counties.[36]

Furthermore, in the great majority of cases, the number of school-houses balanced with the number of school districts. And yet these schoolhouses were not adequate to meet the needs of the Negro school population. As was mentioned earlier, the one-teacher common school provided the educational opportunities for the rural population, and the size of the average county schoolhouse was twenty by twenty-five feet although in some instances schoolhouses were as small as fourteen by sixteen feet.[37] By using New Hanover County as a typical example and by computing the number of Negro schoolhouses in that county in terms of Negro population, it is possible to ascertain that there were approximately 133 school children per schoolhouse. Concerning the predominantly rural counties of the Black Belt, one authority on Negro education observed and wrote: "Here the Negro population are crowded into one-room county schools, while the more scattered white children are provided with a proportionately larger number of schools."[38] Accordingly, in addition to other problems, there was in 1900 a great need for more, or at least larger, schools for the state's large rural Negro population.

The maxim "as the teacher, so is the school" held true in North

Carolina. Indeed, teacher qualifications, pay, methods of instruction, and teacher-training facilities reflected the status of the entire public school system. By law, all persons employed as teachers in the public schools were required to hold a teaching certificate stating that "the holder was qualified to teach within the jurisdiction of the licensing authority." By 1900 North Carolina honored three types of certificates: (1) the first grade life certificate, issued by the state board of education;[39] (2) the second grade certificate, issued by the county board of education; and (3) the third grade certificate, also issued by the county. In all instances certification was contingent upon the prospective teacher's passing an examination covering the branches taught in the public schools.

Teacher pay was prescribed by law and determined by the type of certificate held; a teacher with a second grade certificate could not receive more than $25 per month, while one who held a first grade certificate received such compensation agreed upon by teacher and county board of education, although the latter had the power to fix a "maximum price for first-grade teachers."[40] Not only did North Carolina pay low salaries, but it discriminated between the sexes, as well as between races. In 1900 the average monthly salary in the state was $26.18 and $23.41 for white male and female teachers, respectively.[41] The average monthly salary in the white graded schools ranged from $40 for males and $30 for females at Hendersonville to $79.50 and $42.50 for male and female teachers, respectively, at Charlotte.[42] Similarly, in the rural areas, the monthly salary varied from $20 for males and $18 for females in Alexander County to $34 for males and $29 for females in Mecklenburg County.[43]

North Carolina kept no record of the academic preparation of teachers. Of the 5,031 white teachers in 1900, some 3,505 held first grade certificates 1,514 held second grade certificates, white only 12 held first grade life certificates.[44] It could be argued that the third grade certificates were created for Black teachers, since no whites held them and since they were very prevalent within the Black ranks. The fact that the greatest percentage of teachers held first grade certificates should not be considered as an index of their qualifications, since it was extremely easy to obtain such certification. Teacher certificate, for instance, was largely a county responsibility, rather than a state function. The county superintendent asked his own questions, graded the papers, and was not obligated to reject an applicant who had failed. Hence, entrance into the teaching profession was almost as easy as a call to the ministry.[45]

Low teacher salaries, it was believed, greatly influenced teacher tenure, as it was estimated that the entire personnel of each corps of teachers changed every four or five years.[46] The greater part of the state's teaching force in 1900 consisted of young people, many of whom had not had twelve months of actual teaching experience. The average age of male and female teachers was twenty-eight and twenty-four years, respectively.[47] In one instance, State Superintendent Mebane stated that he heard of a county board of education employing a girl not "sweet sixteen," but only thirteen, to teach school.[48] Two-thirds of the teachers were men, basically "ungainly country lads who pursued farming for nine months of the year."[49] Therefore, some of the educational leaders logically concluded that the teachers must have followed other occupations in order to make ends meet. This conclusion, in substance, was summed up by State Superintendent James Y. Joyner, who said: "The teacher who does something else for eight months of the year for a living and teaches school for four months for extra money must continue to be something else than a teacher."[50] And quite common was the humorous apothegm: "Even to this day, if you scratch a Southern teacher a preacher will wince." The capricious method of teacher certification in the counties created a vicious circle of incompetence, which easily began to turn on itself. The county superintendent, often a product of the common schools and himself a former teacher, examined teacher prospects for his county, who then returned to the common schools from which they themselves were a product. But the dilemma did not end there. Paternalism and nepotism, as well as local politics, often paved the way for permanent teacher certification. For example, a local politician might use his influence to get his son, his daughter, or a friend into the teaching profession for life.

An educator of the era, Edwin A. Alderman, who between 1889 and 1892 conducted the weekly county teachers' institute through the state, kept two manuscript notebooks during his educational tour of 1889–90.[51] In addition to these original sources there also exist two official reports made by him to Sidney M. Finger, superintendent of public instruction, the first one prepared in 1890 and the other two years later.[52] The two notebooks not only afford a rich view into the history of North Carolina education, but they also "contain penetrating observations on the social, economic and political life of the state." Moreover, they offer insight into teachers practicing pedagogic skills. At the conclusion of the weekly institutes, Alderman and his coworker, Charles D. McIver, conducted examinations to award teacher certificates, which were valid for three years. In the opinion of the two men, the tests were so simple that children of twelve years of age in the city graded school could pass them, "yet only six percent of the teachers were successful."[53]

If we must label these persons as teachers today, then let us recognize that they were products of a static agrarian society. As an institute conductor, Alderman inevitably came face to face with the problem, and was "touched to the heart by the monotonous" lives and lack of mental development of the teachers of that period. For keener insight into them, he would require that, as an exercise, they write a brief autobiographical sketch. "I find that only a small fraction of the teachers," Alderman wrote, "have had the advantages of training other than that offered in the common schools. . . . professional training for their difficult work they have had little. About twelve percent have read a technical work on teaching . . . about eight percent read regularly some school journal. . . . Our teachers do not read much. They do not know books. The reading habit has not fastened itself upon them. The bright and splendid land of fancy and fiction, of poetry and imagination, of history and biography has not revealed itself to their eyes."[54]

Naturally, pedagogic techniques were somewhat of a parody, since most of the teachers had received their entire education in the common schools. There was a great tendency for them to instruct according to the same primitive methods by which they themselves had been taught. Thus, they perpetuated the weaknesses, as well as the virtues, of the system, and many taught whatever their "whims or fancies" suggested.[55] A prevailing method of teaching was oral instruction. In this method the instructor read aloud, and the pupils were required to repeat after him. Consequently, pupil progress was measured by what was memorized and not by what was learned. A child often forgot much that he had memorized, and what he did manage to retain had little meaning; at times the better pupils never knew the parts of speech and were often perplexed "to know what the product of a half of a half referred to."[56] Since the teacher employing this method of instruction was likely to have been an inferior instructor, educational achievement depended, to a large degree, upon whether the student was bright and ambitious. One such student later explained: "I learned nothing from my teacher, except that I could learn algebra, which neither of us had ever seen before, faster than he; but I learned a lot from my friend the bully."[57] To be sure, the greater number of teachers merely "kept school." Charles W. Dabney, an educator of note, referring to instruction in the "square wooden box" rural school, perhaps with a bit of irony, described the situation in the following manner: "Within, it is as bare and cheerless as it is without . . . a tall, thin old maid, with a hard, sad face and a screech voice, is trying to keep some fifty or sixty youngsters of all sexes and ages in the path of virtue, if not of knowledge. It is easy to observe that it is a typical county school of a populous and prosperous neighborhood, where the so-called English branches—may the English forgive us for using that name so profanely—are taught in the usual way. Keeping school defines it better."[58]

In light of the acute shortage of qualified teachers, a relevant question naturally arises: What facilities did the state provide for the training of teachers for the public schools in 1900? A brief description of the history of the development of teacher training will help us better understand the problem as it existed prior to the public school movement. The Redeemers held a dim view of teacher-training facilities for whites. By law, the state board of education, as of March 9, 1877, was authorized to establish a normal school at the University of North Carolina for the training of young white males of the "common schools of the state," and two thousand dollars was thereafter appropriated annually for its support.[59] The state board of education ultimately agreed upon a plan for a summer normal school of six weeks duration, which began on July 3, 1877, at Chapel Hill. Next, the state experimented with an extension of the idea of the summer normal school by authorizing the state board of education to establish additional ones throughout the state. In time, the one at the university was discontinued, but, at a cost of five hundred dollars each, eight new schools were established—at Elizabeth City, Franklin, Newton, Wilson, Asheville, Boon, Washington, and Winston.[60]

The Teachers' Institute was still another novel idea to come into existence. Educational leaders reasoned that instruction could be made more convenient for teachers by sending educational experts into various school districts to conduct teachers' institutes.[61] On March 8, 1889, the state abolished the eight summer normal schools, and created in lieu of them the "county institute." The four thousand dollars formerly used for the summer normal schools was employed to defray the expense of the "institutes" that were to be conducted in each county seat for a week's duration.

On the recommendation of State Superintendent Finger, the state board of education elected Edwin A. Alderman, superintendent of the Goldsboro public schools, and Charles D. McIver, a teacher at the Peace Institute at Raleigh, as full-time institute instructors, at an annual salary of two thousand dollars each. County boards of education were to provide a suitable place and defray all expenses involved in holding an institute. And finally, every white school of the county was to be closed during the weekly session of the institutes, and its teachers were required by law to attend.

Alderman and McIver held the positions of institute conductors for three years. Their major duties involved the training of teachers in (1) scientific methods of instruction; (2) school government, including discipline and punishment; and (3) school organization, including opening exercises, the keeping of attendance, textbooks, and programs. The two educators went beyond their immediate duties and acted as self-appointed evangelists for the cause of public education. Weekly, they appeared before county boards of education, school committeemen, and farmer organizations, pleading for (1) more money through local taxation; (2) more public interest for improving school buildings and grounds; (3) more qualified teachers; and (4) a normal school to train white women teachers.[62] McIver was particularly interested in the development of a permanent normal school for white women. There was a general lack of appreciation for white women teachers, who were "thought of in terms of medieval ideals" as needing no education, since they were intended for housework and the rearing of children.[63] McIver had the support of both the trustees of the Peabody Fund and their new general agent, J. L. M. Curry, who was now pushing for the development of Southern normal schools. The trustees advocated giving special attention to the training of female teachers, for it was strongly believed that the college male was "most likely to teach in the secondary schools for the benefit of the few."[64] Early in 1881, Curry appeared before the state legislature and made a lengthy and powerful address for the establishment of a "high grade normal school." Working toward this goal, McIver believed that the majority of public schoolteachers should be women and converted Alderman to his project at a meeting of teachers at Black Mountain in 1886. Choosing his words with scholarly care and restraint, McIver wrote: "The state appropriates $8,000 to the training of colored teachers, and uses it in helping permanent normal colleges opened to both sexes. . . . Up to the present time our state and leading churches have adopted the suicidal policy of refusing to educate white girls." Delineating the problem further, he stated: "Under our present system of higher education, the white girl, unless her father is comparatively wealthy . . . (has) no place to go. . . . One of the results of this is that two-thirds of our public school teachers are men, whereas two-thirds, at least, ought to be women."[65]

The movement for the institution bore fruit on February 18, 1891. The General Assembly passed an act to establish at Greensboro a four-year Normal and Industrial School for young white girls. Support of teachers' institutes became a county obligation; the four thousand dollars formerly appropriated for them, plus an additional six thousand dollars, became the annual subvention for the maintenance of the college. The institution's curriculum and course of study were geared to Normal, Domestic Science, and Commercial Departments. Tuition was free to those who stipulated that their intention was to teach.[66] The school opened in the autumn of 1892 with McIver as the first president. Alderman taught there only one year, going instead to the University of North Carolina to fill a new chair, professor of

History and Philosophy of Education. In 1896 he was elected president of the university. Meanwhile, the appropriation at Greensboro had increased to twenty-five thousand dollars, largely through Curry's influence, at whose suggestion the name was changed, in February of 1897, from the Normal and Industrial School to the State Normal and Industtrial College.[67]

On February 27, 1893, the General Assembly passed an act to establish a normal department at the Cullowhee High School in Jackson County. This school was placed under the supervision of the State Department of Public Education. Its purpose was to train both male and female teachers for rural and village elementary schools. The curriculum and course of study were divided into both academic and professional subjects. Tuition was free to students prepared to teach, and a person who completed the prescribed course in the normal department was granted a certificate that entitled the holder to teach in any school in the county for three years. After the county institutes became a county responsibility, a law was enacted that gave them permission to hold one or more teachers' institutes jointly at some "convenient and satisfactory point." The institutes were opened also to any teacher of other counties who desired to attend, and in 1900 forty-three institutes were held, attended by 5,891 teachers.[69]

The Redeemers' attitude toward the problem of training Black teachers was quite different from their approach to the training of whites. The Negro had not had the opportunity to acquire any appreciable amount of academic training; thus, the educational authorities deemed it best to establish long-term normal institutions for prospective Negro teachers.[69] The law that made provision for a normal school appropriated an annual $2,000 to defray the expense of the institution, finally established in Fayetteville. It soon became evident that one normal school could not possibly fulfill the prodigious task of training an adequate supply of Negro teachers. Consequently, by 1887 the General Assembly had empowered the state board of education to establish five more schools, with an annual appropriation of $1,250 for each school. They were located at Goldsboro, Franklin, Plymouth, Winston-Salem, and Salisbury. Finally, in 1891 the General Assembly directed the state board of education to establish a seventh normal school at Elizabeth City. For its financial support, the state made no appropriation, but took $500 from the Fayetteville school fund, and $100 each from the other four schools, giving the Elizabeth City Normal School an annual appropriation of $900.[70]

In 1894 General Agent Curry reported to the trustees of the Peabody Fund: "The state does not own a foot of land nor a house

51

for any of these schools; the towns and people where the schools are located furnish the buildings free of charge to the school."[71] The course of study of the Negro normal schools covered three years and "stretched from a crowded room of primary pupils called the model schools" to classes of one or two students in Latin, Greek, and philosophy. But the caliber of work in advanced classes did not surpass that of the public schools of six grades. M. C. S. Noble, one of the state's most outstanding educators, after studying the problem, wrote with constraint: "Candor compels me to say that I regard it as a waste of money to continue the schools under the present system." He concluded that "the present system should be speedily closed so as to obtain better results for the Negro race."[72]

While North Carolina was busy setting up Black normal schools, the Slater Philanthropy came into existence and identified itself with the training of Negro teachers. This fund had its origin in 1882 when John F. Slater, a wealthy textile industrialist of Norwich, Connecticut, founded the philanthropy that bears his name. Slater was disturbed by the "apparent economic helplessness of the ex-slave." He was also motivated by the success of the Peabody Educational Fund. Accordingly, he entrusted $1 million on March 4, 1882, to a group of ten men who were to become the first board of trustees. On February 6, 1883, that trust was incorporated by an act of Congress, which at the time appropriated the necessary funds for a gold medal for the donor. The objective of the Slater Fund, as the donor expressed it, was "the uplifting of the lately emancipated population of the Southern States, and their posterity, by conferring upon them the blessings of Christian education . . . in which the instruction of the mind to the common branches of secular learning shall be associated with the just notions of duty towards God and man"[73] Although the details of the execution of the fund was left to the judgment of the board of trustees, the donor also expressed the idea that "the training of teachers might be the most effective use of the fund." However, no part of the fund was to be employed for the purchase of land or for building construction.

The trustees followed the Peabody Fund closely in administration and practice. In October 1881 they selected Atticus G. Haygood as general agent. While admiring liberal arts studies, Haygood had little use for this type of education for the Southern Negro.[74] Instead, he favored General Armstrong's program at Hampton Institute, later to be made famous by its most outstanding graduate—Booker T. Washington. Haygood believed that the Slater Fund's mission was to appropriate money to each Negro college that would make industrial training a part of its curriculum. He began by traveling, visiting, and talking with college heads about the availability of funds to each

Negro college that included vocational education in its curriculum, with the overall aim of teacher training. Such became both the **guideline and principle upon which Haygood doled out the fund.** In 1880 the fund's initial appropriation was $16,250, and it was distributed among twelve institutions: nine private colleges, two public high schools, and one private school. Shaw University of Raleigh was the only North Carolina school to be so endowed, and it received a grant of $2,000.[75]

By 1883 some thirty-five institutions were on Haygood's list, and five of these were located in North Carolina, at which time they were recipients of $5,700. These meager funds were employed for teacher salaries, industrial education, and equipment. Livingstone College was typical, and the Slater appropriation was used as follows:[76]

Teachers in Carpentry	$320.00
Teachers in Sewing, etc.	280.00
Teachers in preparatory departments	280.00
For appliances and materials	160.00

The subsequent agent of the Slater Fund, in a modified form, continued the policy, as described by one of his beneficiaries, of "dropping nest eggs for a few hundred dollars each in many places," to each Black higher institution that adopted industrial education as a part of its curriculum. As the pendulum of time swung toward the dawn of the twentieth century, the activities of the Slater Fund were merely statistical. This dispensing of $16,500 among fifteen higher institutions for Blacks was an apparent weakness, much too trivial and indirect to effectuate any discernible improvement of public education. Similar to the waste of state money in attempting to maintain seven Black normal schools at a cost of $8,000, this policy was also truly a waste of philanthropic money.

"To the victor belong the spoils" is a political adage originated by William L. Marcy. Indeed, in North Carolina during this era, politics and patronage pervaded the school administration from state to county levels. The school system in 1900 was headed by a state board of education, authorized by the Constitution of 1876. Its principal members were the governor, who was the president, the state superintendent of public instruction, and the state auditors and treasurer. All were elected every four years by popular vote. The state superintendent's name appeared on the party ticket as other state officials. In consequence, he was identified to some degree with active politics and party pledges.[77] (This will be demonstrated in chap. 6, where the gubernatorial campaign of 1900 is described.)

There were no prescribed educational qualifications for the state superintendent of public instruction; the competency of the person who filled the post·depended in general upon his personality and professional training. As to his function, the law declared that he should "direct the operations of the system of public education and enforce the laws and regulations thereto."[78] He was also the liaison agent between the state and local boards of education. For performing such functions, the state superintendent was paid an annual salary of fifteen hundred dollars and allowed five hundred dollars for traveling and additional clerical assistance, and was also authorized to employ a clerk at an annual salary of twelve hundred dollars.[79]

Nevertheless, the powers of the state superintendent did not include the urban systems. As demonstrated earlier, the status of the city schools had not been defined within the state's educational system, for the final control of such schools was not determined by state law or by the state board of education, but by the laws and regulations of the charters of the cities individual where existed the graded schools. It should be remembered that the greater part of the educational expenses of these graded schools was borne by the special chartered districts. In these districts each individual school was free to adopt its own course of study, determine the length of each course, fix the length of the school term, and employ teachers as it saw fit. Further, each school fixed salaries and adopted textbooks without regard to school law or rulings of the state board of education. In describing the situation in 1900, one educator summarized his conclusions in the following manner: "The charters of city districts differ from one another in important details, and along with respective amendments, constitute a mass of special school legislation of which no one knows the extent."[80] And under the above reign of administrative freedom, all kinds of town and city graded schools grew up.

Rural school administration contrasted greatly with that of the autonomous urban systems. To govern and administer the public schools in the rural areas, the General Assembly appointed biannually three men who constituted a county board of school directors, commonly referred to as the county board of education. No educational standards were prescribed for members of the board, save that they be persons of "good business qualifications and known to be in favor of public education." In turn, the county board of education was to appoint biannually in each of the townships of the county "three intelligent men of good business qualifications who were known to be in favor of public education." These three men were to serve as school trustees in their respective townships. The duties of these trustees were (1) to divide the township into school districts as compact as possible, so that every child, white or Black, would be within a radius of three miles of the assigned school; (2) to apportion the school money in the districts in equal amounts between white and Negro schools; and (3) to elect in each of the townships in the county three school committeemen.[81] The general function of the board of committeemen was to maintain and govern the district schools, and, in exercising this function, the board was delegated the powers of a body corporate.

Another major responsibility of the county board of education was the appointment of the county superintendent. The law specified the qualifications to be held by the person who filled this position: "He shall be a practical schoolteacher at the time of his election and have at least one year's experience in teaching school, and shall be of good moral character and liberal education." In most instances, this office was actually a political patronage, or subject to local favoritism or nepotism. Anyone who was fairly educated—a struggling young minister with a family to support, a merchant, a lawyer, a doctor, a real estate agent, or a farmer with a little free time to dispose of—was acceptable for the position. This method of selecting the county superintendent had long been a source of grievance among leading educators. Fusionist State superintendent Mebane complained that in "numerous cases the best men for these places have never had an opportunity to fill the positions." The public schools, he accused, "have been in the galling grasp of the courthouse politicians for twenty years in some of the counties." And the county superintendent owed his election "both directly and indirectly, to the masters of the courthouse ring."[82] The general function of the county superintendent was to supervise the public schools in his respective county. In addition, he served as exofficio secretary to the county board of education.

Just as paltry teacher salaries were fixed by law, so was the pay for the county superintendent. In designating his salary, the law stated: "Compensation of the county superintendent of schools shall not be less than two dollars nor more than three dollars a day," and in no case should compensation be allowed for more days of service during any fiscal year than the average length of school term of the respective county.[83] Accordingly, nine counties paid their superintendents less than one hundred dollars per year, eighteen counties paid less than two hundred dollars, twenty-eight counties less than three hundred dollars, and twenty-five counties less than four hundred dollars per year. In constrast, the pay of the urban school superintendent was an annual average of eight hundred dollars, and was as high as fourteen hundred dollars in Asheville, fifteen hundred dollars in Greensboro, eighteen hundred dollars with a rent-free home in Charlotte, and two thousand dollars in Durham and Raleigh.[84] Moreover, whereas the urban superintendent had a small area to cover and few teachers to supervise, the county superintendent had an extensive area to cover and a large number of teachers under his jurisdiction. For instance, in Alamance County there were ninety-four teachers scattered over 494 square miles. The law required the county superintendent to visit each teacher, but most of the men who ever held that office seldom traveled over the county to "even take a peep" at the schools.[85]

Considering the evidence and judging from the measurable variables, the school system of North Carolina in 1900 was one of the poorest models within the American system of public education. One-teacher common schools, shanties, tenant houses, or log cabins—almost everywhere the picture was the same for North Carolina's approximately 82 percent rural population; they would be condemned by any modern standard of education. The state's varied geographic traits and scattered population indeed compounded the educational problem. Because there was no compulsory-school-attendance law, less than 50 percent of school-age children regularly attended the inadequate schools. Moreover, those in actual daily attendance (the annual school term was less than seventy days) were taught by incompetent and unsupervised teachers, who were isolated from the larger urban community. The educational philosophy of the state emphasized mastery of the three Rs, and this was deemed a good English education. Yet universal education had long been a failure. How else does one explain the fact that for years before the turn of the century almost every white man in the Blue Ridge region grew up in ignorance, and that elsewhere one in five was illiterate? The illiteracy rate among Blacks was approximately 50 percent and assumed to be much higher in the Black Belt counties.

Notes

1. *United States Constitution,* pt. 3, art. 10.

2. As early as 1647 the state of Massachusetts enacted a public school act, which was copied by neighboring states, and, subsequently, throughout the nation. Curtis P. Nettels, *The Roots of American Civilization* (New York, 1963), pp. 487–89.

3. *Biennial School Report,* 1898–1900, pp. xiv, 150.

4. *Report of the United States Commission of Education,* 1900–1901, 1: lxix–lxiii.

5. *Public Laws of North Carolina,* 1876–77, chap. 285, secs. 1, 2, 4.

6. J. G. de Roulhac Hamilton, *History of North Carolina,* vol. 3, *North Carolina since 1860* (Chicago, 1919), p. 364.

7. Charles L. Smith, *The History of Education in North Carolina* (Washington, D.C., 1888), p. 173.

8. J. L. M. Curry, *A Brief Sketch of George Peabody and the History of the Peabody Fund through Thirty Years* (Cambridge, Mass., 1898), pp. 1–11.

9. Ibid., p. 29.

10. Peabody to the trustees of the Peabody Fund, February 7, 1867, and June 29, 1869, in *Three Letters of George Peabody,* published by the Board of Trustees

of the Peabody Educational Fund (Cambridge, Mass., 1910) .

11. Curry, *Brief Sketch of George Peabody,* p. 35.

12. Edgar W. Knight, "The Peabody Fund and Its Early Operation in North Carolina," *South Atlantic Quarterly* 14 (1915) : 168–80.

13. *Biennial School Report,* 1870–72, pp. 52–54.

14. Charles L. Coon, "The Beginnings of the North Carolina City Schools, 1867–1887," *South Atlantic Quarterly* 12 (1913) : 235–47.

15. See chaps. 2 and 7.

16. *Proceedings of the Trustees of the George Peabody Educational Fund,* 6 vols. (Boston, 1875–1916) , 1: 235–36, 297, 6: 636.

17. "Reports of the Superintendents of Graded Schools," in *Biennial School Report,* 1900–1902, part 2, pp. 209–63 (hereafter cited as "Reports of the Superintendents") ; *Biennial School Report,* 1896–98, pp. 369–80; *Twelfth Census of the United States,* 1900, Population, 2: c–cy (Negro population included) .

18. W. C. Allen to Superintendent Joyner, June 14, 1902, in *Biennial School Report,* 1896–98, p. 371.

19. Ibid., 1898–1900, pp. 282–89.

20. Ibid., 1888–90, pp. 89–95.

21. *Public School Laws of North Carolina,* 1901, pp. 23–24.

22. Southern Education Board, *North Carolina Education,* Southern Education Bulletin no. 10 (May 14, 1903) , pp. 134–40.

23. *Report of the United States Commission of Education,* 1900–1901, 1: xxix.

24. *Biennial School Report,* 1900–1902, p. xix.

25. *Biennial School Report,* 1898–1900, pp. 282–88.

26. R. D. W. Connor, *The Women's Association for the Betterment of Public School Houses in North Carolina* (Raleigh, N.C., 1906) , p. 12: Southern Education Board, *Women's Education,* Southern Education Bulletin no. 19 (December 1, 1903) , pp. 390, 401.

27. *Biennial School Report,* 1888–90, pp. 6–7.

28. Fletcher B. Dressler, "Rural School Houses and Grounds," in United States Bureau of Education Bulletin no. 12 (Washington, D.C., 1914) , p. 20.

29. *Public Laws of North Carolina,* 1899, chap. 732, sec. 74.

30. *Biennial School Report,* 1898–1900, pp. 282–84, and *Report of the United States Commission of Education,* 1899–1900, 1: lxvii–lxxxii.

31. *Twelfth Census of the United States,* 1900, Population, 2: c; Clement Eaton, *Freedom of Thought in the Old South* (New York, 1951) , p. 64; Southern Education Board, *Notes,* ser. 1, no. 3, April 7; no. 6, May 19, 1902.

32. Louis D. Rubin, ed., *Teach the Freeman: Correspondence of Rutherford B. Hayes and the Slater Fund for Negro Education, 1881–1887* (Baton Rouge, La., 1969) , pp. xxi–xxiii.

33. *Biennial School Report,* 1888–90, pp. 89–95.

34. Hollis M. Long, *Public Secondary Education for Negroes in North Carolina* (New York, 1932) , pp. 1–2.

35. "Reports of the Superintendents," pp. 209–63; Thomas J. Jones, *Negro Education in the United States* (Washington, D.C., 1916) , pp. 32–33.

36. *Biennial School Report,* 1898–1900, pp. 156–87, 274–78.

37. Southern Education Board, *Education of the Negro,* Southern Education Bulletin no. 20 (December 21, 1903) , pp. 391–400.

38. Jones, *Negro Education,* p. 28.

39. *Public School Laws of North Carolina,* 1899, chap. 108, sec. 3. Earlier, all graduates from the George Peabody Normal College at Nashville were recognized in North Carolina as "certified for life as teachers in any and all public schools" (chap. 372, sec. 1) .

40. Ibid., 1899, chap. 732, sec. 2580.

41. *Biennial School Report*, 1898–1900, p. 160.

42. "Reports of the Superintendents," pp. 214, 116.

43. Ibid., pp. 283–84. This data shows that North Carolina discriminated in the pay of female teachers. As one might expect, discrimination was even greater against Blacks. Racism cut the better-educated ones from other appropriate positions, driving them into teaching, where their salaries were often influenced by farm wages.

44. *Biennial School Report*, 1898–1900, pp. 199–200.

45. Southern Education Board, *North Carolina Education*, p. 162.

46. Edwin A. Alderman, "Reports of the Institute Conductors," in *Biennial School Report*, 1888–1900, pt. 2, p. 1.

47. *Biennial School Report*, 1898–1900, p. 71.

48. Ibid., p. 5.

49. Clement Eaton, "Edwin A. Alderman—Liberal of the New South," *North Carolina Historical Review* 33 (April 1946) : 206–21.

50. *Biennial School Report*, 1902–4, pp. 57–58.

51. These notebooks are entitled "Institute Statistics," but they are really a weekly journal of Alderman's observations and experiences during his educational campaign of 1889–90. They are included in the Edwin Alderman Papers, deposited in the Alderman Library at the University of Virginia, Charlottesville, Va.

52. Alderman, "Reports of the Institute Conductors," p. 2, pp. 1–14; *Biennial School Report*, 1890–92, pp. lii–lv.

53. Eaton, "Edwin A. Alderman," pp. 209–10.

54. Alderman, "Reports of the Institute Conductors," pt. 1, pp. 5–6. While many of the teachers found it difficult to recall three books that they had read, there was an exception, as Alderman discovered—a "simple country girl" who enumerated among the books she had read *David Copperfield*, by Dickens; *The Autocrat of the Breakfast Table*, by Holmes; Scott's *Ivanhoe*; *Ben Hur*; *Little Lord Fauntleroy*; and Charles and Mary Lamb's *Prose Tales*.

55. Edgar W. Knight, *Public Education in North Carolina* (New York, 1916), p. 421.

56. Charles H. Otkens, *The Ills of the South* (New York, 1894), pp. 194–95.

57. John A. Rice, *I Came Out of the Eighteenth Century* (New York, 1942), p. 147.

58. Charles W. Dabney, "The Problem in the South" (Address delivered before the Southern Education Association, Columbia, S.C., December 28, 1901), pp. 3–22.

59. *Public Laws of North Carolina*, 1870–77, chap. 234, sec. 1. Originally, this act was to grant the admission of men only, but the state board of education decided that there were some women who might be invited to attend free of charge; hence, for the first time the doors of the university were thrown open to women. Marcus C. S. Noble, *A History of Public Education in North Carolina* (Chapel Hill, N.C., 1930), pp. 412–14.

60. *Biennial School Report*, 1886–88, p. xxvi. Normal instruction continued at the university until 1889. The school at Boone moved to Sparta in 1886. Knight, *Public Education in North Carolina*, p. 321.

61. Noble, *Public Education in North Carolina*, p. 428.

62. *Public Laws of North Carolina*, 1889, chap. 200, secs. 1, 4, 5. Alderman, "Reports of the Institute Conductors," pp. 10–12.

63. Eaton, "Edwin A. Alderman," p. 214.

64. "Speech of Honorable J. L. M. Curry, Delivered before the North Carolina

Legislature," January 21, 1881, in *Proceedings of the Trustees of the George Peabody Educational Fund,* 4: 330–40.

65. Alderman, "Reports of the Institute Conductors," pt. 2, pp. 21–22.

66. *Public Laws of North Carolina,* 1891, chap. 139, secs. 10–15.

67. *Proceedings of the Trustees of the George Peabody Educational Fund,* 6: 218.

68. *Biennial School Report,* 1892–94, pp. 50–51; 1900, p. 3, pp. 278–85.

69. *Public Laws of North Carolina,* 1876–77, chap. 234, sec. 2.

70. Ibid., 1891, chap. 1414, sec. 2; chap. 234, sec. 1–2.

71. *Proceedings of the Trustees of the George Peabody Educational Fund,* 5: 99.

72. Noble to Superintendent Thomas F. Toon, January 15, 1901, Toon Papers, North Carolina Department of Archives and History, Raleigh, N.C.

73. John F. Slater Fund, *Occasional Papers,* no. 1 (Washington, D.C., 1894), pp. 7–8.

74. Rubin, *Teach the Freeman,* pp. xxvi–xxvii; see also B. C. Caldwell, "The Work of the Jeans and Slater Funds" in *Annual of the American Academy of Political and Social Science* (1913), p. 174.

75. *Proceedings of the Trustees of the John F. Slater Fund,* 1883, p. 20.

76. "Report of the General Agent of the Slater Fund," in ibid., 1887, pp. 3–4, 11.

77. *The General Education Board: An Account of Its Activities, 1902–1914* (New York, 1915), p. 88.

78. *North Carolina Constitution,* art. 9, sec. 8.

79. C. H. Mebane, "Historical Sketch of the Office of Superintendent of Public Instruction," in *Biennial School Report,* 1894–96, pp. 410–415. *Public Laws of North Carolina,* 1899, chap. 732, secs. 10–14.

80. Southern Education Board, *North Carolina Education,* pp. 35, 96.

81. *Public Laws of North Carolina,* 1876–1877 chap. 162, secs. 16, 22, 23.

82. *Biennial School Report,* 1898–1900, pp. 6–7.

83. *Public School Laws of North Carolina,* 1899, chap. 732, sec. 29.

84. Southern Education Board, *North Carolina Education,* pp. 144–45.

85. *Biennial School Report,* 1896–98, pp. 50–51.

2

An Insight into Educational Adversity

No system of public education can be adequately portrayed or interpreted without some recognition of the historical forces that helped to mold its character and determine its line of development. Accordingly, this section of the narrative is devoted to an analysis of a fundamental question: What socioeconomic factors explain or are related to the low status of education in North Carolina as delineated in the preceding chapter? It is difficult to understand why educational forces would resist positive change. One explanation that seems likely is that varied negative social attitudes, fortified by tradition, modes of life, and isolation, persisted and conspired to impede the development of a progressive school system. It is hard to give any one social attitude top priority; however, logically, it seems best to begin with *class distinction*.[1] This term is inextricably related to the old aristocratic concept that education should be left to private enterprise and/or is a family responsibility. It is hard to ascertain the extent to which such a theory prevailed in the late nineteenth century. At least it was not reflected in the literaure. However, there did exist the prevailing notion that one's property should not be taxed to educate the children of the poor class. Accordingly, I commence with the position taken by the Establishment—the economic power structure.

The industrial capitalists and the urban bourgeois—the fountainheads of wealth—to be sure, lacked incentive to support a movement to educate the masses by voting increased taxes. Moreover, free schools were associated in their minds with a "taint of charity," and their educational needs were met by numerous private schools and academies. Edwin A. Alderman, since the early days of the Wataugians, had possessed a strong, sensitive feeling for the educational needs of North Carolina. There was little about the story that he was not aware of, including the attitudes of the wealthy. During his travels through the state as institute conductor for the training of rural teachers (1889–91), he was able to observe firsthand the hostility of influential men of wealth and property to increased taxation and the way in which they stifled impulses leading to educational progress. He recorded these attitudes in two manuscript notebooks entitled "Institutes Statistics." Besides being original sources, they possess valuable data on the state's social history and present a "realistic picture" of the educational conditions of the state—both urban and rural.[2] On his tour of observation he noted the decline of public schools in Lenoir County. "The town of Kinston," he wrote in his notebook, "once had a good graded school but let it die—now the the negroes own the former graded school building and the whites use a hut. In 1883, 500 white children attended school—now in 1890 about 150." He recognized that though the development of industries and railroads was creating wealth by opening up isolated communities, cultural conditions continued to lag. He pointed out that "Concord has the largest factory in the state, streetcars, electric lights and water works, but improvement in schools generally comes last."[3]

Industrialism had a blighting effect upon education in the mill towns. The mill baron felt little compunction about exploiting child labor. The very existence of the textile mills was demoralizing in the Piedmont region, where families of ten to fourteen were quite common. And it was "a rather new thing in Southern life to receive cash payments from week to week."[4] This new wage system did, indeed, invade entire families and affect children early in life; thus, educational advantages for children were an impossibility under the system. According to one source, 18 percent of adult textile workers were illiterate, and so were 32 percent of the children.[5] If a child was illiterate when he entered a factory, he remained illiterate. Furthermore, a child possessing only the rudiments of education had no opportunity to extend this knowledge. Worse still, quite common were instances of a child's forgetting how to read.[6]

The "lords of the acres," it will be recalled, with their crop-lien system, dominated the rural economy of the New Order. They frequently had both the supply merchants and the planters, especially in the Coastal Plain region. Many had moved to the towns and in social outlook were identified with the urban capitalists. Long before 1900, and like the planting aristocracy of the antebellum era, they maintained a land monopoly of "continuous tracts of land of considerable area" in the form of "tenant plantations."[7] Absentee land ownership, with its "multiple evils," was a notable characteristic. This system enabled the large-land proprietary interests to live on the profits of others' labor, which, like that in mill towns, engulfed entire families. To illustrate, when a man was hired out, his wife (who took their children along with her) and every child were also hired. A child began work around six years of age; "by the time he was 10, he was a good worker—girls and boys." A great number of adult male workers did not receive over ten dollars per month.[8] One worker, on farm wages, reported that there was no difference in the prices paid the "black cropper and the white man," the landlords obviously preferring not to disturb their vast supply of cheap labor. Accordingly, they were opposed to progressive school legislation and maintained negative educational attitudes, which, without doubt, retarded school enrollment and attendance. J. W. Brown of Hunterville maintained: "A farmer may grow a crop and that law [compulsory-school-attendance law] would prevent him gathering it, so I would have to pay his debts and lose the cotton. So if we have the compulsory law, we do not want any Negro farmers or poor white people, for it would be better not to have our land worked than to have it done in that way."[9]

Ruralism, to be sure, played an important role in determining the status of public schools in 1900, and there was much about rural life that was obstructive to social progress. North Carolina, as noted earlier, was classified in 1900 as a predominantly agricultural state with a sparse, rural population. Certainly, the natural division of the state into three distinct physiographical regions produced an isolation that affected the people's social outlook. Adequate railroad development is a major step in breaking down the barriers of distance and isolation, yet in 1860 there were only 889 miles of railroads, and by 1890 the mileage had increased to only 2,925 miles. Moreover, as late as 1927 four counties had no railroad facilities, and ten counties had less than 20 miles of railroads. Compounding the problem was the fact that very few roads in 1900 were dependable throughout the entire year. As Professor Holland Thompson described the problem: "Road were universally bad, especially in·the winter, and a visit to town was no small undertaking and association between rural neighbors was not easy." Furthermore, public libraries did not exist in the rural locales so devoted to agriculture, and in some counties there were no newspapers. Rural free delivery, which later became an important factor in rural life, was unheard of during this era. Accordingly, the reading habits of the North Carolina farmers were most deficient, since the majority of farmers took no papers or magazines, save possibly the county weekly.[10] Thus, communication of news and ideas was slow, and there was little social intercourse, other than the regularly attended monthly or semimonthly meetings of the cross-roads churches. In short, agrarian life in North Carolina at the turn of the twentieth century was drab and static, and promoted the development of varied negative educational attitudes.

Evidence strongly suggests that education was viewed by the "rustics" as being of little value. Some farmers, who desired better educational facilities, justifiably complained that their society was not interested in education. Alderman's findings during his travels certainly give credence to that conclusion. In his notebooks he described some western counties as being "dark shadows of provincialism and backwardness." Orange County, site of the university and the famous Bingham Prep School, was marked by mass ignorance. And Alderman observed that in Polk County people were "inert, shoot squirrels, and work about one-third of their time." He also noted that the public took little interest in the improvement of schools and permitted buildings to deteriorate. He described the situation in Pamlico County, an isolated county in the east. The poverty-stricken people had no courthouse. Education was available in "a typical, rickety, cheerless public schoolhouse," where Alderman counted thirteen places where panes of glass were missing from the windows. "These people," he wrote, "know the public schools only to sneer at them as far as I can see and this is not to be marvelled at if a tree shall be judged by its fruits."[11]

Moreover, a jaundiced view of education often existed among the illiterate or semiliterate classes, who were proud of their ignorance of "book-learning," and, consequently, were contemptuous of schools, as well as of the teaching profession, for teaching school was a little less than sitting still and doing nothing. In some circles there had been grumbles that teachers were paid too much by the "state to sit in the school in the summer, or by a good fire in the winter." Consequently, a longer school term was opposed, because it was felt that it would only "mean an opportunity for incompetent teachers to doze in the ill-ventilated schoolrooms and blink at a baker's dozen of lazy boys and girls."[12]

Educational apathy on the part of parents certainly figured prominently in the picture. There was, for example, a lamentable indifference among many parents toward sending their children to school even for the short school terms. Speaking of this situation, Superintendent Mebane in 1896 complained: "In the rural districts we often find boys roaming over the fields, idling away their time, when the Public School Fund is being spent for their benefits."[13] Similarly, A. M. Benton wrote: "I know of children in my neighborhood, ten, fifteen, and eight years old that hunt birds and loaf all winter and have a four months' school within one mile of them and don't go to school for a day. Those are white children. We have seventy children of school age in this school district, the average attendance is about thirty—not half." Benton went on to point out that the blighting effects of illiteracy would be the fate of such children unless they were forced by their parents to attend school, and he warned that "if they have their way . . . they grow up in ignorance."[14]

Educational apathy on the part of parents was not the only reason why children were kept from schools. Many farmers, both white and Negro, strongly felt that they could not adequately work their farms without the labors of their entire family. This attitude made many a farmer a stubborn opponent of progressive school legislation. Believing that they could not dispense with the labors of their children for as much as four months a year, many farmers did not enroll them in school at all or sent them only when farm work was slack, and such practices resulted in poor school enrollment and attendance. One farmer expressed his sentiments as follows: "We lay by our crops in July and August, and from July to the first of September, there is six weeks they could go to school."[15]

But North Carolina's rural educational problem involved far more than public and parental apathy. Farm tenancy and rural poverty also contributed to the problem. Truly, the masses of landless farmers possessed nothing to offer society but their labor. The average tenant was relatively ignorant and habitually in debt and had little or no money to provide the necessary requirements of life for the home or the school. The system certainly mitigated against stability in population, and school attendance was poorest in the counties that had the greatest number of tenants. "In fact," wrote Arthur Raper, "tenancy and illiteracy seemed to be twin-born social ills and each one appeared to be the cause and the result of the other."[16] The farm tenant families added little, if anything, to the srength of the community, as "they sent down no roots to the soil," and formed no real association with the progressive elements of society, for such a family did not make up a part of public opinion, nor feel its restraining force.[17]

The factor of rural poverty, the small farmers of North Carolina, like those of the Southern and Western states, beginning in the mid 1880s suffered one profitless season after another. In the wake of this agrarian distress, many North Carolina farmers in 1900 were desperately poor, lived in wretched houses, and were scantily provided with even the necessities of life.[18] Agriculture as a way of life had failed them. Their plight no doubt had some influence upon educational progress, since it was a factor in creating rural poverty. The situation made it impossible for many parents to provide their children with suitable clothing and books, and the tendency was to let them remain at home.[19]

Despite the fact that North Carolina was very poor during this era, poverty did not justify the diminutive sum of money spent on public education. Some apologist might conclude that the farmers could not have been expected to willingly vote higher taxes for more adequate school support during an era of economic distress, or even to think in terms of the general intelligence and culture of their children. But to be sure, there was a dire need for both a child-labor law and a compulsory-school-attendance law. In the words of one socially conscious citizen: "The tax-payers are taxed to school the poor children of the state, and we are compelled to pay the school tax, so I think that there ought to be a law to make people send their children to the free schools."[20] We make no mistake if we conclude that self-respect and economic progress without education is inconceivable; education is the sine qua non for individual survival in a free society.

Reconstruction left a legacy of public taxation for the support of education, which survived Redemption. "Retrenchment," Professor Woodward wrote, "became the watchword of the Redeemers in their state and local governments." But what does the term mean as it relates to the theme of this narrative? In Texas it meant "strict economies," and in Florida, "spend nothing unless absolutely necessary," while some forces in Virginia "considered the public schools a luxury . . . to be paid for like any other luxury by the people who wished their benefits," and that "taxation to support education was socialistic."[21] "Cheapness, even niggardliness," was the widely accepted educational criterion and characterized the retrenchment policy in North Carolina. The state supreme court, as shall be shown, acted as the guardian of the "property owners against the propertyless and the untaxed masses."

Sufficient financing is essential for the maintenance of a competent public school system, which must be supported through adequate taxation. Massachusetts paid the highest per capita school tax in the world. "It becomes us to find where the secret of this Samsonian strength lies," declared Col. Robert Bingham of the Bingham School in Asheville.[22]

Redeemers in North Carolina, like those in several other southern states, favored special interests—insurance, telegraph, telephone, and railroad companies—in their tax policies. Assessments of the property of these companies, especially that of the railroads, were far below their par value.[23] To secure additional educational funds, the Populists advocated increasing tax on corporate wealth, since the Redeemers had allowed the latter to escape with ridiculously low taxes. (To a large extent, the railroads evaded paying much of their taxes.) A statute of 1897 read: "Every railroad, steamboat or canal company incorporated under the laws of this State, doing business in this State, shall pay to the State a tax on the corporation equal to the sum of one per centum upon the gross receipts of said company." Following a "letter of inquiry" to different states, in order to find out how various railroads were taxed, the Populist state superintendent of public instruction, Charles H. Mebane, wrote: "The gross earnings of the railroads in this State are more than eleven million dollars. Suppose we had a law like Minnesota, taxing the roads 3 percent on gross earnings? What a handsome sum of more than three hundred thousand dollars to give instruction. . . . In addition to this, let us have the same tax on gross earnings of telephone companies, telegraph companies, express companies, insurance companies, and then we will have a school fund from these sources of about four hundred thousand dollars."[24]

In a predominantly agrarian state, land value played a paramount role in determining the extent to which a state could adequately support a public school system through taxation. In 1900 in Massachusetts the average value of a farm of 88.8 acres was $4,348, as compared to 83.5 acres valued at $4,851 in Ohio, and 100 acres valued at $4,727 in New York, while 160.7 acres were valued at $4,016 throughout the nation as a whole. The average value of a North Carolina white farm of 116 acres was $1,209, but this was a statewide average; values varied greatly in the state's three physiographical regions.[25] Land values were extremely low in the mountainous counties of the Carolina Highlands and, likewise, in the Coastal Plain region, where prevailed the highest percentage of farm tenancy. It was in the industrial Piedmont area where one found the highest taxable land, which far exceeded the state average.

Economics related to farm tenancy truly ameliorated against school support from taxation. The problem of farm tenancy, which tended to deplete the soil, certainly depreciated land valuation. For example, the counties that comprised the highest percentage of tenant farmers, in general, had the lowest assessed taxable land and personal property per farm inhabitant.[26] Equally important, the state superintendent's reports for the period 1896–98 show that there were 167,476 registered white voters and 66,674 registered Negro voters, of which 14,430 and 11,752 were insolvent, respectively.[27] The greatest percentage of voter insolvency was to be found in the rural counties dominated by tenant farmers. Considering the fact that poll taxes and property taxes were the major sources of school revenue, the problem was more significant. Lastly, the high percentage of tenancy in the Coastal Plain region suggests a consolidation of wealth among a minority who might have been most reluctant to increase educational taxes for the benefit of a poor majority.

North Carolina, like its neighboring states, had more children to educate per adult male. The state had only 66 adult males to every 100 children of school age, as compared to 135 adult males per 100 children in Massachusetts, 134 in Connecticut, and 128 in New York. There was $6,407 of taxable wealth per child of school age in Massachusetts, as compared to $1,301 in North Carolina.[28] But let us look at the problem more fundamentally. North Carolina, as pointed out previously, was a state of small and landless farmers who occupied the lowest rung of the economic ladder. Speaking of farm income, Professor Hobbs said: "It is the per-farm and the per-family and, even more accurately, the per-farm-inhabitant income that counts. The standard of living is determined very largely by the per-farm-dweller income."[29] Following this trend of thought, the average annual productive power of each farm worker in North Carolina in 1906 amounted to $159.75, as compared to an average of $1,088.11 for each farm worker in Iowa. And when one considers the large percentage of farm tenants in the state, the income figure is seen to be much lower.

The major cause of low valuation of land and property in North Carolina, it would appear, was a defective tax structure and method of assessment. Professor Charles L. Raper maintained that the major defects of the tax structure were largely ones of assessment rather than of taxation.[30] One problem arose from the fact that the state required a uniform tax rate upon all kinds of property, regardless of their "difference in nature, their value to the community or their tangibility to the assessor's eyes." A still greater problem was that assessment of property was controlled by the county, not by state authorities. To illustrate, the task of listing property in the tax books and fixing its valuation was performed by the township assessor. He was appointed by the Board of County Commissioners and was required to be a landholder. Like the county superintendent, he, too, received an insignificant salary—"from $2 to $3 a day for only a few days—25 to 50 working days a year." Also like the county superintendent, he was appointed because he had no other job, or because he was "willing to keep valuation low for the sake of his own property or that of his friends or that of the community."[31] But the problem is more complex. Property value was determined by "self-assessment" by the owner of taxable property, and, as Professor Raper observed, a "premium was placed upon inequality, injustices and even dishonesty."[32] Monies and securities, if assessed at all, were listed in the books at par. One kind of taxable property was penalized, while another escaped the burden of taxation. The more tangible bore the larger share; the less tangible formed a smaller share, or no share at all—taxes on dogs not infrequently produced more revenue than those on the monies, bonds, and stocks. The more conscientious citizen placed higher valuation upon his possessions; the less conscientious, a lower value. The same kind of property was listed on the assessment books at valuations ranging from 3 percent of the real value to 100 percent. Worse still, some tangible property, such as land, was "not assessed at all." On the average, however, lands and other tangibles were "put on the books at from 20 to 60 percent of their value." A good many of the identified "pauper counties" were "really well-to-do."[33] The result was that some counties paid a larger proportionate share of the state's taxes.

Thus the property of a county could be assessed at such a low valuation as to make it impossible to raise sufficient revenue to maintain schools in many counties for at least four months without exceeding the constitutional limitation of taxation. Moreover, the public school law required the county commissioners to levy any additional tax that might be necessary to continue the schools for a period of four months per annum, and such was mandatory under the penalty of indictment for failure to perform this obligation.[34] But the majority of county commissioners merely winked at this law; only a few tried to carry out constitutional requirements. Their attempts resulted in a perpetual struggle between the schools and the taxpayers—a struggle that went before the courts many times, only to reach its climax in the decision of the North Carolina Supreme Court in the case of *Barksdale* v. *Commissioners* of Sampson County in 1885.[35]

In order to understand the significance of the Barksdale decision, it is necessary to review a few factors that set the stage for it. It is worth repeating that there was a constitutional limitation on the taxing powers of the state. It provided that the General Assembly levy a capitation on every male over twenty-one and under fifty years of age, which was to be equal for each to the tax on property valued at three hundred dollars, and the tax was never to exceed two dollars on the head. It also limited the property tax for state and county purposes to sixty-six and two-thirds cents ad valorem on one-hundred-dollar valuation of property.[36] This limitation, in effect, was designed to make the tax on the poll the standard by which the tax on property was to be levied. The combined state and county taxes could never exceed the above limitations.[37]

To bring relief to the schools, the General Assembly of 1881 levied a state tax of twelve and one-half cents on each one-hundred-dollar valuation of property and thirty-seven and one-half cents on each taxable poll for support of public schools.[38] Four years later the General Assembly went further. The property tax of twelve and one-half was retained. The law also stated that "if the tax levied by the state is insufficient to maintain one or more schools for four months in each school district, and without a favorable referendum from the people, then the board of commissioners of each county shall levy annually a special tax to supply the deficiency for the support and maintenance of schools for a period of four months."[39]

In Sampson County in 1885 the state had levied under the revenue law twenty-five cents on property and seventy-five cents on the poll, and for schools under the school law, twelve and one-half cents on property and thirty-seven and one-half cents on the polls—making a total of thirty-seven and one-half cents on property and one dollar and twelve and one-half cents on the poll. This left the county commissioners a levy of twenty-nine and one-sixth cents on property and eighty-seven and one-half cents on the poll for all practical purposes, which in the final analysis was not a sufficient amount to maintain the schools for four months.[40] Aware of this fact, the commissioners of Sampson County disregarded the tax limitation as imposed by section 1 of article 5 of the North Carolina State Constitution and levied enough special taxes to supply the deficiency between the tax levied by the state and the amount of money needed to maintain a four-months school term in every district in the county for the school year of 1885–86. A taxpayer named S. Barksdale sought to enjoin the collection of the tax by taking the controversy to court.[41] The issue was heard the following October in the Sampson Superior Court before Judge A. A. McKay, who sustained the contentions of Barksdale and enjoined the collection of the special tax. At length, the defendant commissioners appealed to the state supreme court, but that court also decided against the collection of the tax. In writing the opinion of the court, Chief Justice W. N. H. Smith declared: "That so much of chapter 174, Laws of 1885, as permitted the commissioners to disregard the tax limitation of Section I of Article V of the Constitution in order to maintain public schools for four months in every school year was unconstitutional and void."[42]

In a democratic society, the courts often manifest the sentiments of the general public. In the Barksdale case, the state supreme court reflected the general public's deep aversion toward increased taxation. County school officials were left with a flat tax rate; consequently, many counties had school terms that fell far short of four months, a situation that was most evident in 1900. No one could be required to pay a special school tax unless such a tax had the endorsement of the majority of the taxpayers and unless the county commissioners no longer levied special taxes. In retrospect, and pointing out the retarding influence of the court on public education in North Carolina, Professor Coon wrote: "Progress North Carolina has made since 1868 toward the beginning of a more efficient public school system has been made in the face of three major difficulties . . . the tragically persistent and continuing indifference of the majority of the people to the blighting effects of illiteracy . . . their consequent indifference to and hatred of public taxation for the extermination of that illiteracy . . . the singularly narrow and reactionary interpretation placed by our highest court upon one section of Article V of our State Constitution."[43]

At this point it is important to consider briefly the educational and religious rivalry that had "been for years simmering" in North Carolina. The leaders of the Missionary Baptists, Methodists and other denominations have been working for years to gain control over education of the state . . . and have recently elected enough members in opposition to aid the State University (Chapel Hill), . . . to embolden them to decide in their late deliberations to oppose all further state aid to the University. About 20 Christian colleges (they call themselves) are united for this purpose."[44] Such church-state rivalry and religious strife were indeed formidable forces that retarded the development of public education in North Carolina. In no other part of the South, or elsewhere in the nation, had such a conflict existed.

Intermittently during each decade following Redemption, the presidents of the denominational higher institutions, notably the Baptist Wake Forest, the Methodist Trinity and the Presbyterian Davidson colleges, had sought to discredit the University of North Carolina with charges of atheistic teachings and "godless" living.[45] They were ably assisted by their press; the *Biblical Recorder* was the most outstanding organ of the Baptists. And one should not forget the preachers these colleges sent among the masses, the "various breeds of empiric dogmatists unable to be mistaken about the infinite hereafter or anything else; men with more piety than brains," according to Edwin A. Alderman.[46]

"The denominational colleges attempted to proselytize that all education should include religious elements, and that the state was prevented by its 'fundamental law' from furnishing religious instruction."[47] Hence, the private colleges were best qualified to impose ecclesiastical principles in education. The *Biblical Recorder* expressed such a sentiment, declaring: "One who is not prepared in a Christian Institution is not prepared for life."[48] Moreover, public taxation to support higher education was, in effect, viewed as socialism. Dr. Charles E. Taylor, president of Wake Forest College, wrote in 1893: "If a state may furnish education below cost to the recipient, because such education is a good thing for the individual to possess, why may it not furnish its citizens blankets, agricultural implements, and other articles of utility and comfort."[49]

Indeed, the crux of the controversy was competition for students and fear of a state monopoly in education. By 1893 the church colleges were becoming desperate, and the Baptists assumed the leadership against the university.[50] At the meeting of the State Baptist Convention in December of the same year, a committee of five was appointed to familiarize the General Assembly on the "friction and competition between the State schools and the denominational schools."[51]

It must be pointed out that the twenty-thousand-dollar appropriation for the university was not "the smallest sum given by any state to its University."[52] Between 1893 and 1895 a number of resolutions that affected the university were introduced in the legislature. Some went beyond jeopardizing the institution—they would actually destroy it. For instance, one measure called for its annual appropriation of twenty thousand dollars to be given to the public schools, and for every cent of money raised by taxation available for educational purposes to be spent on public schools.[53] Even if the legislature had abolished the twenty thousand dollars in favor of the cause of schools, no benefits would have accrued. It must be pointed out here that these outlandish agitations arose during the era of populism. Nevertheless, university alumni held key positions in the legislature, and prominent among them was Marion Butler, Populist publisher of the *Caucasian,* who threw his influence in support of state aid, much to the "delight of the University." Others giving support to the state schools were William A. Guthrie and future Republican governor Daniel L. Russell.[54]

The Baptists carried the religious controversy from the higher institutions into the rural counties. Numerous factional quarrels and religious dissension in the little communities certainly impeded public school development. Baptists predominated in Transylvania County, in which was located the town of Brevard, which had a school enrollment of less than forty, classes being conducted in a building used by the Baptist Church and the Masonic Lodge. The town was torn by intense religious discord. An identical situation prevailed in the town of Jefferson, the disharmony stemming not from the matter of a schoolhouse—the town had a good one—but from the failure of the school committee to agree on a teacher, "owing to local friction."

In Cabarrus County, church dissension had the effect of acting "against the welfare of children." "Politics and religion never fail to *draw*," Alderman commented caustically after observing how the Montgomery County teacher-training institute was injured by a large "revival"; he concluded that "hard-shell Baptists were opposed to all education."[55] This conclusion was not necessarily accurate; Baptists were in favor of education if *they* could provide it. In their effort to identify the schoolhouse with the "church-house," they would later oppose the public school movement, especially on the secondary level. As pointed out earlier, in 1890 there were more than five hundred private schools and academies. During the next decade, the Baptist Association established more than twenty preparatory schools, and eight more in the single year of 1900.[56] It seems likely that these schools were established to train future students for Wake Forest College (Baptist). One thing is certain, the private and denominational schools could not possibly replace public schools. It should be mentioned here that private colleges maintained preparatory departments and "competed among themselves and with the high schools for the only revenue available—tuition fees."[57]

Racism was another weighty factor to interfere with educational progress in North Carolina, and the existence of a large Black population, estimated at one-third of the total population in 1900, made it a major problem, especially in the Coastal Plain of the east, where the Black Belt counties predominated. It is much too simple to equate *racism* with *prejudice* and *discrimination,* as social scientists and others have done. The term logically suggests a theoretical umbrella, broken down into analytical components leading to an intransigent set of racist attitudes harbored by all whites. But one must be aware that there are varying degrees of racism—from negligible racism to racism of venomous proportion—and I am faced with the problem of assigning any one degree top priority. However, I shall begin with the racial attitude of the Redeemers as it related to public education for Blacks.

The Redeemers were former Whigs and members of the Conservative party, and comprised the "best people of the South." By law they made no discrimination between Blacks and whites in offering educational opportunities, except to say that the schools must be separated. Governor Vance in his message before the legislature in January of 1877 perhaps expressed public sentiment on the matter when he reminded the members to live up to their pledge to make no racial discrimination between children in matters of public education, but to deal justly and equitably with all school children of the state with a thorough North Carolina spirit.[58] But even as he spoke there were forces in operation that soon caused the conservative leaders to shift over to an alliance with the reactionary poor whites.

A residue of negative educational sentiment identified with the Reconstruction era still prevailed in the 1890s. In the wake of the Union victory and the decision at Appomattox, Yankee "schoolmarms" came to uplift the newly emancipated Blacks through educational and spiritual guidance. Northern enthusiasm, engrained with humanitarism, was great as hundreds of young men and women made their way into the South, bringing with them "slates, pencils, spelling books, readers, blackboards and chalk." Notwithstanding the region's poor educational facilities, Negro children attended schools in larger and larger numbers, while in many cases the educational opportunities for poor whites languished. Naturally, for any number of reasons, these educational endeavors on the behalf of Blacks met with strong opposition from whites.[59] This legacy was perpetuated, along with memories of Reconstruction. Alderman possessed the acumen to analyze the political-educational situation in the eastern town of Washington. He recorded in his notebook: "The negroes are the great bug-bear here. The place was once garrisoned by colored troops. Hence the aversion. They need a graded school there and if they can rise above the negro hindrance and prejudice, will get it. Party necessities and race prejudice keep all this feeling fresh."[60]

When political leaders opposed Negro education, they unconsciously sacrificed the interests of whites, and the Blair bill was a classic example. The measure was introduced into the Senate on December 14, 1883, by Henry W. Blair of New Hampshire. It provided for the distribution of ten annual appropriations, beginning at $15 million and diminishing by $1 million annually, to be determined by the degree of illiteracy in each state. Because of the large rate of Southern illiteracy, it was estimated that $11 million out of the initial $15 million would have to be accrued by the South, an amount more than the entire South spent on public schools in 1880.[61] While the bill permitted segregation of the races, there was to be no discrimination between white and Black children in the use of the funds. However, each individual state was required to vote permanent school taxes to receive the desirable educational funds. For most of the decade the Blair bill lingered in Congress, but it passed in the Senate on three occasions, with the majority of the Southern senators voting for it. The bill was debated furiously in the House both on constitutional grounds and on the grounds that it weakened opposition to the tariff. The Blair bill never actually came to a vote in the House. Jabez L. M. Curry suspected that Southern racism was to blame—for the reason that some whites felt that an educated Negro would be less subordinate to whites, and the "fear that the educated Negro could be less easily manipulated in elections had more influence on adverse action than had constitutional scruples."[62]

A dominant racist view nourished by the propertied classes was that education would vitiate the Negro's effectiveness as a laborer in the Southern socioeconomic order. Education spoiled a good field hand or created an "insolent cook." The *Wadesboro Intelligencer* warned: "Nothing is so surely ruining Negroes of the South as the accursed free schools." It concluded that "they should be wiped out of existence instead of having their capacity increased."[63] From one farmer came the absurd prediction that cultural training of Blacks would surely destroy the labor system and "consequently impoverish the country."[64]

To the aforementioned racist attitude must be added those of a more general nature, arising in part (1) from the traditional apathy of poor whites, who, to some degree, were in competition with Blacks on the labor market; (2) from the mores and folkways emerging from master and slave relations; (3) from political antagonism as a result of the Negro's persistent ambition for political offices; and (4) from his continued efforts to obtain a socioeconomic status that was identified with social equality. These are in addition to the suspicion that Black children of North Carolina, and of the South in general, were more eager to get an education than whites, and, not being deterred by poor clothing, and so on, would go to school in larger numbers than the poor white children and would acquire the ability to read and write more rapidly.[65] It was more than a suspicion, for education was the only avenue away from the hot fields and hot cooking stoves. "Blacks like white collars too."

The results would elevate the Negro socially, economically, and politically to run afoul of the doctrine of white supremacy. Accordingly, there was a strong temptation to keep Blacks in perpetual ignorance, to keep them out of politics, and to keep them from becoming dissatisfied with their subordinate status in the social order.[66]

Finally, many whites, aware that their schools were altogether inadequate to meet the needs of the white children, were strongly convinced that it was folly to support Negro schools when the educational opportunities of the white children were so limited. They did not necessarily oppose Negro education, but strongly believed that the Negroes should support their own schools and that taxes paid by the white population should be retained for the advancement of white schools. R. H. Privot expressed public sentiment when he said: "We need more free schools for the white people, their taxes to go to educate their children and the Negro taxes to educate theirs."[67] His attitude is probably more fundamental in explaining white opposition to Negro education. Behind it is the philosophy that each race should be held responsible for the education of its children. Then too, there was ample reason to believe that many whites would not have been indifferent to education or opposed to local taxation if they could have been assured that Blacks would not be educated with funds derived from white taxation. Such sentiment early generated a graded school movement, a struggle that is of historical interest.

As shown earlier, graded schools were not a state function. They

74

were autonomous and existed in towns and cities as a result of special taxation, which was granted first by the General Assembly, followed by approval by local voters. On March 29, 1880, the legislature, for the first time, granted the city of Goldsboro the right to establish graded schools on the principle of racial division of taxation. According to this law, "taxes raised from the property and poll of white persons shall be appropriated exclusively to a graded school for white persons and the taxes raised from the property and polls of colored persons shall be appropriated exclusively to a graded school for colored persons." After suffering an initial setback, Goldsboro successfully passed a bill based on this law in 1881, with the leadership of the editor of the *Goldsboro Messenger,* and similar action was soon taken by the city of Durham.[68]

The success of these two cities generated an educational awakening, especially in the eastern part of the state, where a graded school movement ensued. Between 1881 and 1883 the towns of Statesville, Newbern, Monroe, Fayetteville, Wilson, Edenton, Guilford County, Lenoir, Shoe Hill (now Maxton), Lumberton, Rocky Mount, Battleboro, Washington, and Magnolia had established graded schools. It should be recalled that this was the period when the Peabody Fund was still available for promoting graded schools. Moreover, to give the movement a greater impetus, the General Assembly on March 8, 1883, passed a statute authorizing the principle of a racial division of school taxes on a statewide basis. This law is commonly known as the Dortch Bill, named after Senator William T. Dortch of Goldsboro, who sponsored it in the Senate.[69] It provided that upon receipt of a petition signed by ten white voters of any school district for white children, or by a like number of Black voters of any school district for Black children, the county commissioners were required to call an election on the question of local assessment not exceeding twenty-five cents ad valorem on a one-hundred-dollar valuation of property and seventy-five cents on the polls in the white or Black district that had petitioned for the election. And if a majority of the qualified voters voted in favor of the assessment, a special tax was to be levied and expended in the district voting such taxation.[70]

The local assessment act restricting the school revenue pro rata to the race paying the taxes was assailed by certain prominent leaders, in and outside the state. In disgust, J. L. M. Curry, general agent of the Peabody Fund, declared that the practice was "weak demagogism and unworthy of Christian statesmen or wise patriots," and, if successful, would result in consigning Blacks to hopeless ignorance, which would have had an incalculable effect upon the white race. His views were shared by the state superintendent of public instruction, the governor, and other leading educators, and he made it a policy to withhold all Peabody Funds from any school where such practices were in force.[71]

Naturally, the assessment act resulted in litigation by both white and Black citizens. The white property owners feared increased taxation, while the Black leaders feared retarded public school opportunities for their children. In 1886 the state supreme court in two astounding decisions declared taxation by racial division unconstitutional. In *Puitt* v. *Commissioners of Gaston County*, the court held that a law that allowed a tax on the property and polls of persons of the same color to be applied exclusively to the education of children of that color violated the last clause of article 4, section 2, of the state constitution, which maintains that there "shall be no discrimination in favor of or to the prejudice of either race." in *Riggsbee* v. *The Town of Durham,* the court ruled that "a law which directs the tax from the polls and property of white persons to be devoted to sustaining schools for white persons, and that raised from polls and property of Blacks to be used for the support of their schools" was unconstitutional and void.[72]

The two supreme court decisions had a tremendous impact on the graded school movement. Those towns contemplating the establishment of graded schools scrapped their plans. At the same time, some —notably Goldsboro—abandoned their white schools. The town of Wilson defied the court's ruling for several years, and Durham continued its schools with private subscriptions, while Kinston transformed its public schools into private institutions. However, after emotions had been tempered, the whites reestablished their schools and concomitantly made provisions for schools for Blacks.[73]

Evidence strongly suggests that the greatest obstacle to Negro education in North Carolina in the eighties arose from the notion that Blacks paid little or no taxes. Thus, thousands of whites refused to vote special educational taxes that would have brought about better schools for their children, as well as for Blacks. But not everyone was of the opinion that the Negro was practically a nontaxpayer. In defending Blacks' right to education, Professor Coon sought to debunk the concept that whites bore the entire "cost of Negro Public Schools in the South," and that Blacks were truly the "white man's burden when it comes to paying the bills for public education." He suggested that whites "look the question in the face." In 1900 he pointed out: "The states of Virginia, North Carolina, Georgia, Alabama, Mississippi, Texas, Louisiana, Arkansas and Tennessee contained 81.4 percent of all the Negroes then living in the United States. These states are now spending $32,068,851 for public schools." He went on to say that this total expenditure for all school purposes— the sum of $23,856,914, or 74.4 percent of the total—was expended for teaching, $20,038,204 being paid white teachers and $3,818,705 being paid Negro teachers. In other words, the white teachers who served 60 percent of the population received 62.4 percent of the total school expenditures, while the Negro teachers who served 40 percent of the population received only 12 percent of the money expended.[74]

On the same subject, Superintendent Joyner came up with some interesting conclusions, which were more specific than Professor Coon's findings and related directly to North Carolina. Using figures taken from the "Official Report of the State Auditor for 1908," he listed the total assessed valuation of Negro real estate and personal property at $21,253,581, or 3.7 percent of the general property tax for schools. He estimated that Blacks represented 27 percent of registered voters. Since they constituted one-third of the total population of the state, he logically concluded that they paid one-third of the revenue derived from forfeitures, penalties, and liquor licenses. As for special appropriations from the state treasurer, he estimated that Blacks paid the same proportion of this as they paid for other property taxes, which was 3.7 percent. Following a most liberal estimate, Superintendent Joyner summarized the results as follows:

Total general property and poll tax	$149,313.17
Total special property and poll tax	37,207.12
Total part of special state appropriations	9,065.00
Estimated part of fines, liquor licenses, etc.	58,394.29
Total	**$253,979.58**

From the Report of the State Superintendent of Public Instruction, Superintendent Joyner showed that the state expended the following for education of the Negro in 1908:

Teacher Salaries	$313,913.94
Schoolhouses	52,820.34
Supervision, supplies, furniture, fuel oil, and other administration expenses	93,281.21
Total	**$460,015.49**

According to the above results, Superintendent Joyner concluded that the white population paid directly or indirectly two dollars for every one dollar paid by Blacks for educaion.[75] Superintendent Joyner's findings, analyses, and conclusions are to be appreciated, but it is well to point out that by 1908, the public school movement had just about crested, and whites, as shall be seen in chapter 9, were voting enormous amounts of educational taxes. But even if this phenomenon had not occurred, there still existed an economic chasm of great magnitude between Negro and white wealth. Black economics was too much identified with what Professor Woodward labeled "Mudsills and Bottom Rails." Blacks, economic status in Georgia can be used to illustrate the point. Blacks made up about half the state's population in 1880, yet owned only $1.5 million of the $88 million in total land value, some $2 million of the $23 million recorded on cattle and farm animals, and a little more than $163,000 of the $3.2 million in agricultural tools.[76] This economic picture was mirrored throughout the South. Across from the railroad tracks of most cities was the ghetto, with its "two-room shanties" of the Black proletariat. The latter's community was cursed with perpetual unemployment, which turned men into loafers. Here and there were houses of the "Negro bourgeoisie," conspicious symbols like museum pieces. Too many social scientists and others have perpetuated the erroneous idea that a Negro middle class existed during this era. The far greater percentage of Negro professionals were identified with teaching, and it has already been shown that teachers generally were paid bare subsistence wages. Thus, it is needless to point out that the existence of a viable black middle class based on occupation, income, and wealth was a myth.[77]

On the threshold of the twentieth century, Blacks made up the mass of North Carolina's untaxed and propertyless. Such was a natural status, and if they had been allowed to achieve any other condition, this would have proved them industrially superior to the Southern white man, considering their short experience with freedom. Blacks certainly did not have a monopoly on poverty, for its variants were ways of life among most rural whites. "A marginal farmer," wrote Professor Woodward, "could well pose as the Forgotten Man." The same was true of the urban classes, who were unable to afford homes and were forced into "squalor and isolation . . . [and] gaunt barracks . . . huddled around the factories."[78]

Nevertheless, in terms of race relations the middle- and upper-class Southern whites were always their less-fortunate brother's keeper. For instance, they voted with the smaller landholders for laws alloting school funds proportionately to the taxes paid by each race. One might surmise that such laws would have meant no education for the Negro. Indeed, it is sobering that some leading educators, always the apologists for the better class of white Southerners, did not subscribe to this brand of racism. The same may be said of the North Carolina Supreme Court, which declared the racial-division school tax laws unconstitutional.

For over two hundred years the "Black slave codes" had proscribed the education of slaves, and a strong tradition against the education of Blacks had persisted. Since Blacks had enjoyed less than forty years of freedom, it did seem natural to some that, through no fault of their own, most blacks were too poor to pay taxes. For the most part, however, whites unwillingly paid the greatest part of the taxes and thus assumed the burden of the education of Blacks. To the advocates of a racial disvision of taxes, State Superintendent James Y. Joyner said: "The weaker [and] the more helpless, the louder the call for the strong to help. The humbled and more helpless, the more binding the duty to elevate." Continuing along the same line of thought, Joyner stated: "We have made many and grievous mistakes in the education of the Negro. We can correct these mistakes in not decreasing the quality of his education, but rather by improving the quality of it—not by destroying the means of his education, but rather by directing it in proper channels. There is danger in ignorance, whether it be wrapped in a white skin or a black one."[79]

It might be argued that there were many middle- and upper-class Southerners whose heritage and life-style prevented them from seeing the school problem in a twentieth-century perspective. They also seemed to be suffering from a lack of peripheral vision, which obscured their awareness of the experiences and needs of those with whom they came into little contact. Little value can be placed on the stigma of Southern poverty as a rationalization for educational negligence, for how does one explain the marked educational changes that occurred after 1902? By finding ways to prevent the Negro from sharing in the benefits, did North Carolinians cease to oppose increased taxes for better schools? These challenging questions will be tackled in chapters 7 and 9. The next stage of the narrative focuses on political developments and concommitant pervasive racism, which ultimately gave impetus to the marked educational transformation that took place between 1902 and 1913.

Notes

1. Elwood P. Cubberly, *History of Education in the United States* (New York, 1920) , p. 122.

2. Clement Eaton, "Edwin A. Alderman—Liberal of the New South," *North Carolina Historical Review* 33 (April 1946) : 208.

3. Edwin Alderman "Institute Statistics," December 16, 1889, Edwin Alderman Papers, Alderman Library, University of Virginia, Charlottesville, Va.

4. George H. White, testimony of February 8, 1900, in *Reports of the United States Industrial Commission,* vol. 10 (1900) .

5. *Report of the North Carolina Bureau of Labor and Printing* (Raleigh, N.C., 1900) , pp. 75, 183.

6. Holland Thompson, *The New South,* Chronicle of America Series, vol. 42 (New Haven, Conn., 1919) , p. 115.

7. *Thirteenth Census of the United States,* 1910, Agriculture, 5: 878.

8. William A. Graham (farmer of Mackpelah, North Carolina), testimony of March 13, 1900, in *Reports of the United States Industrial Commission*, vol. 10 (1900).

9. J. W. Brown to B. R. Lacy, September 7, 1900, in *Report of the North Carolina Bureau of Labor and Printing*, p. 263; *Raleigh News and Observer*, January 12, 1902.

10. Thompson, *The New South*, p. 107; Gould M. Hambright, "Transportation and Communication in North Carolina," in *Country Life in North Carolina*, University of North Carolina, Extension Bulletin no. 3. (Chapel Hill, N.C., 1928), pp. 25–26.

11. Edwin Alderman, "Institute Statistics," p. 88 n.

12. *Raleigh News and Observer*, August 4, 1897.

13. *Biennial School Report*, 1896–98, pp. 47–49.

14. A. M. Benton to Lacy, September 26, 1900, in *Report of the North Carolina Bureau of Labor and Printing*, p. 256.

15. William A. Graham, testimony of March 13, 1900.

16. Arthur Raper, "North Carolina Landless Farmers," in *Country Life in North Carolina*, University of North Carolina Extension Bulletin no. 3 (Chapel Hill, N.C., 1928), pp. 48–58.

17. Holland Thompson, *From the Cotton Field to the Cotton Mill* (New York, 1906), pp. 169–70.

18. Paul W. Wagner, "North Carolina Farm Homes," in *Country Life in North Carolina*, University of North Carolina Extension Bulletin no. 5 (Chapel Hill, N.C., 1930), p. 34.

19. *Biennial School Report*, 1889–90, p. xiv.

20. Wilson Hensley to Lacy, September 15, 1900, and Joseph W. Terry to Lacy, October 10, 1900, in *Report of the North Carolina Bureau of Printing and Labor*, pp. 240–45.

21. C. Vann Woodward, *Origins of the New South, 1877–1913* (Baton Rouge, La., 1951), pp. 58, 60–61.

22. Robert Bingham, "The New South" (address delivered before the Superintendent's Department of the National Education Association in Washington, D.C., February 15, 1884), pp. 7–8. University of North Carolina Library, Chapel Hill, N.C.

23. George E. Barnett, "Taxation in North Carolina, *Studies in State Taxation with Particular Reference to the Southern States*, in *John Hopkins University Studies in History and Political Science* ed. V. H. Hollander (Baltimore, Md., 1900), pp. 77–114.

24. Charles H. Mebane, "$400,000 More for Public Schools Attainable," in *Biennial School Report*, 1898–1900, pp. 32–84.

25. *Twelfth Census of the United States*, 1900, Agriculture, 2: cx.

26. Raper, "North Carolina Landless Farmers," p. 47.

27. *Biennial School Report*, 1896–98, pp. 302–5.

28. Charles L. Coon, *Facts about Southern Educational Progress* (Durham, N.C., 1905), pp. 67–70.

29. S. Huntington Hobbs, Jr., *North Carolina: An Economic and Social Profile* (Chapel Hill, N.C., 1958), p. 90.

30. Charles L. Raper, "North Carolina Taxation Problem," *South Atlantic Quarterly* 14 (1915): 1–3.

31. Ibid., pp. 6–7.

32. Ibid., pp. 8–9.

33. Charles L. Coon, "Our Taxation Problem," *South Atlantic Quarterly* 12 (1913): 314–26.

34. *Public Laws of North Carolina,* 1876–77, chap. 162, sec. 11.

35. Charles L. Coon, "School Support and Our North Carolina Courts, 1868–1926," *North Carolina Historical Review* 3 (July 1926): 399–412.

36. *North Carolina Constitution* art. 5, secs. 1, 3.

37. Fred W. Morrison, *Equalization of the Financial Burden of Education among the Counties in North Carolina* (New York, 1935), p. 4.

38. Samuel H. Thompson, "The Legislative Development of Public School Support in North Carolina," (Ph.D. diss. University of North Carolina, 1936), p. 271; *Public Laws of North Carolina,* 1881, chap. 200.

39. *Public Laws of North Carolina,* 1885, chap. 174, sec. 23.

40. *Biennial School Report,* 1884–86, pp. 7–8.

41. Thompson, "Legislative Development of Public School Support," pp. 287–88.

42. Coon, "School Support," pp. 409–10.

43. Ibid., p. 399.

44. Edwin Alderman, "Facts about the University," in a scrapbook of clippings dated 1896, Edwin Alderman Papers, Alderman Library, University of Virginia, Charlottesville, Va.

45. Luther L. Gobbel, *Church-State Relationships in North Carolina since 1776* (Durham, N.C., 1938), pp. 3–63 passim.

46. *Raleigh State Chronicle,* August 31, 1890.

47. David L. Smiley, "Educational Attitudes of the North Carolina Baptists," *North Carolina Historical Review* 35 (July 1958): 318.

48. "The Education Issue and the Public," in *Biblical Recorder,* October 24, 1894.

49. Charles E. Taylor, *How Far Should a State Undertake to Educate; or, A Plea for the Voluntary System in the Higher Education* (Raleigh, N.C., 1894), p. 9.

50. Gobbel, *Church-State Relationships,* pp. 132–33. "The state," the author explains, "which before 1890 was competing with the churches in two institutions, the University and the Agricultural and Mechanical college, chartered a third in 1891, the State Normal and Industrial institute, bringing competition to the women's college and adding them to the opposition."

51. Alderman, "Facts about the University," Alderman Papers.

52. *Report of the United States Commission of Education,* 1900–1901, 2: 1688–1707. Some southern institutions received no appropriation, while some received between ten thousand and fifteen thousand dollars.

53. Gobbel, *Church-State Relationships,* pp. 143, 154–55.

54. Ibid., p. 144 n; Josephus Daniels, *Editor in Politics* (Chapel Hill, N.C., 1941), pp. 102–11.

55. Eaton, "Edwin A. Alderman," p. 212.

56. Smiley, "Educational Attitudes," p. 320.

57. Woodward, *Origins of the New South,* p. 438.

58. Frenise Logan, "The Legal Status of Public Education for Negroes in North Carolina, 1877–1894," *North Carolina Historical Review* 32 (July 1955): 346–47.

59. John Hope Franklin, *From Slavery to Freedom* (New York, 1967), pp. 276–77.

60. Eaton, "Edwin A. Alderman," p. 213.

61. Hugh T. Lefler, *History of North Carolina* (New York, 1956), 2: 684–50. Residents of North Carolina "seemed to favor the measure," as did many of the newspapers. However, the *Wilmington Star* expressed the conservative attitude on May 6, 1886: "It [the Blair bill] would kill our schools and kill our educational spirit. Woe if it passes" (quoted on p. 648).

62. Merl Curti, *The Social Ideas of American Educators* (New York, 1935), p. 272.

63. *Charlotte Democrat,* October 21, 1897.

64. Joe Humphrey to Lacy, July 28, 1900, in *Report of North Carolina Bureau of Labor and Printing,* p. 248.

65. Josiah W. Bailey, "Popular Education and the Race Problem in North Carolina," *Outlook,* May 11, 1901, p. 116.

66. Ibid., p. 114.

67. R. H. Privot to Lacy, *Report of North Carolina Bureau of Labor and Printing,* p. 43.

68. Charles L. Coon, "The Beginning of the North Carolina City Schools, 1867–1877," *South Atlantic Quarterly* 12 (July 1913) : 244–45; Logan, "Legal Status of Public Education," p. 347.

69. Marcus C. S. Noble, *A History of Public Education in North Carolina* (Chapel Hill, N.C., 1930) , pp. 407–8.

70. *Public Laws of North Carolina,* 1883, chap. 148, secs. 1–3.

71. Abraham Flexner, *Funds and Foundations* (New York, 1952) , p. 22.

72. *Pruit* v. *Commissioner of Gaston County,* 94, N.C., 709, and *Riggsbee* v. *the town of Durham,* 99, N.C., 34.

73. Coon, "Beginning of North Carolina City Schools," p. 246.

74. Charles L. Coon, "Who Pays for Negro Education?" July 1909, Charles L. Coon Papers, Southern Historical Collection, University of North Carolina, City?, N.C.

75. James Yadkin Joyner, "Negro Taxes," 1908, James Yadkin Papers, Southern Historical Commission, University of North Carolina, City?, N.C.

76. Woodward, *Origins of the New South,* p. 206.

77. White historians, consciously or unconsciously, when referring to a Negro middle class in this era meant according to Negro economic standards, and not according to those of white American society. My argument here is that a Black middle class reflecting wealth did not exist. However, a true Black middle class, located predominantly in the South, has emerged since World War II, and has far outdistanced those Black middle classes in the North. This is especially true in the area of home ownership, including the numerous suburban communities in cities like Atlanta, Ga., Houston and Dallas, Tex., Nashville, Tenn., Durham, Greensboro and Charlotte, N.C., Louisville, Ky., and Norfolk, Va. It is also true in regard to professions, enterprises, and educational values.

78. Woodward, *Origins of the New South,* p. 227

79. Quoted in Elmer D. Johnson, "James Yadkin Joyner, Educational Statesman," *North Carolina Historical Review* 33 (July 1956) : 368.

Part II

Farmers and Politics:
The Historic Theme of Racism, the Trump Card of White Supremacy

3

Populism and the Ascendancy of Fusion Politics

When people of a region or state exhibit inertia during one decade, what forces move them to action during another? Southern politics was the answer in the case of North Carolina. Southern politics was no "comic opera;" it revolved around white supremacy, rested upon political solidarity, and was maintained through the machinery of the Democratic party. Yet during the 1890s, politico-economic forces emerged in North Carolina to destroy that very unity. A latent agrarian movement, appearing first in the West and then in the South as a third party, triggered the Populist revolt, but only in North Carolina did it move into a multidimensional stage—Fusion politics. No historical movement can be adequately understood without a knowledge of its immediate history, the events progressing forward, the forces propelling it, and the historical background from which the movement emerges. Thus, the purpose of this chapter is to describe and analyze the political atmosphere of racism as an underlying force of the issue of universal education—one that ultimately gave impetus to the public school movement. I shall begin by identifying the depressed economic situation that drove the farmers into the Farmer's Alliance and ultimately into the Populist party, where they found their fullest expression in fusionism. The Black man, whose voting power had been lying dormant but who always constituted a formidable element within the Republican party, reappeared on the scene as a potent political force to be reckoned with.

As the eighties lumbered on, the so-called American land of

opportunity witnessed the rise of two "plight" groups—discontented farmers and the urban laboring class. Smoldering with a spirit of revolt and fed by acute economic distress and a deep sense of injustice, these socioeconomic forces, crossing sectional, class, and racial lines, were destined to consolidate under the banner of populism. Nevertheless, the farmers (tenants, small landholders, and a "surprising number of large landholders") were the centrifugal force underlying the Populist revolt. Their leadership included an elite of interests—educators, ministers, physicians, editors, and elected officials.

Populism also called for a "united front between Negro and white farmers." Thomas E. Watson of Georgia was perhaps the "first native white Southern leader of importance" to advocate a Populist policy toward Blacks. He logically concluded that the Negro was in the South to stay and was an integral part of its economy. At the same time, he recognized that the Black tenant and laborer were in the same boat as their white counterparts.[1] He well understood the way of post-Reconstruction politics, that the charge of "Negro Rule" was heard only at election time to perpetuate race antagonism and to divide the races. "You are kept apart," he wrote in the *Arena,* "that you may be separately fleeced of your earnings. You are made to hate each other because upon that hatred is rested the keystone of the arch of financial depotism which enslaves you both."[2] Watson was advocating Negro political equality, but within the framework of white supremacy. This called for "something that no American party had achieved before or since—a political coalition of the poor whites and the poor Blacks of the South."[3] Yet it remained to be seen whether the walls of sectionalism and racism could be surmounted to achieve political harmony.

The story of populism has been told many times; yet it varies somewhat from region to region and, more specifically, from state to state. The agrarians of North Carolina, like those of the South as a whole, had grievances against the monetary system (echoed in the Greenback movements), the railroads, and the monopolies. Monopolies had recently sprung up in the state, and what they were "the farmers hardly knew," but they did believe that they controlled prices. They punctuated their arguments by pointing out that the price of cotton bagging soared from $.07 to $.14 a yard within a few weeks following the formation of the Southern jute-bagging corporation. There was also a sudden rise in the price of commercial fertilizer from $2.50 to $5.00 a ton.[4] Their grievance against the railroads was not imaginary. In 1888 the *Progressive Farmer* ran the following exposé of discrepant freight charges for two railroad routes:[5]

TABLE 3

DISPARITY IN FREIGHT RATES PER HUNDRED POUNDS

	Chicago to New York 1040 miles	Charlotte, N.C. to New York 582 miles
Grain	$0.25 per 100 lbs.	$0.32 per 100 lbs.
Flour	0.25 " " "	.38 " " "
Bacon	0.35 " " "	.39 " " "
Leaf Tobacco	0.35 " " "	.61 " " "

In the spring of 1887 the *Progressive Farmer* stated with some accuracy what the farmers of North Carolina and many of the other agricultural states had been thinking for some time: "There is something wrong in our industrial system. . . . There is a screw loose. The wheels have dropped out of balance."[6]

Worst of all, farming was no longer a profitable enterprise. Southern farmers were prisoners of the one-crop system, and North Carolina farmers were locked into a two-crop system, the crops being cotton and tobacco, which both had been declining steadily in prices. The price of cotton dropped from an average of $.20 a pound in the seventies to $.09 in the eighties, and to $.058 per pound in the nineties.[7] There it "remained at a level below production cost." The price of tobacco followed the same trend; it was ironic, though, that Americans were purchasing more and more tobacco products, but prices were controlled by the trust—the American Tobacco Company—which meant more farm tenants.

Far too many North Carolina farmers found themselves increasingly at the mercy of the supply merchant, who advanced credit in the form of supplies—the cash prices. The credit prices (including interest) were always higher, never less than 30 percent and frequently as much as 70 percent higher. But when a tenant farmer, white or Negro, signed a lien to be redeemed by a future cotton or tobacco crop, he had, in effect, actually "sold" himself and members of his family into peonage. In North Carolina, the crop-lien system operated under and was protected by the Landlord and Tenant Act.[8]

Under the system, the majority of farmers, so goes the adage, "failed to pay out" at the end of the year. Not understanding the economic law of supply and demand, the farmer continued to drive farm prices down by overproducing, thus glutting the market in an effort to surmount his indebtedness, and much too often remaining the "unredeemed farmer."

"Few farmers anywhere," wrote historian John D. Hicks, "were in a more strained circumstance than those of North Carolina." Too many farms were encumbrances with mortgages carrying excessive interest rates. Every tax acre bore a mortgage of $.53, and from 1880 to 1890 the total of these mortgages increased from $21,471,428 to $55,832,062. Unable to pay mortgages or taxes, farmers often lost their property.[9] Concomitantly, their dreams of economic independence vanished. In despair, many migrated to cities and became family proletariats, while others became trapped within the quicksands of the oppressive crop-lien system. Each year it trapped entire families and sank its victims deeper in debt to the point of no return. It may be surmised that farm indebtedness helped to swell the teeming ranks of North Carolina's landless farmers.

"Let us organize," Western farmers told their Southern brethren. The Granges made their appearance in North Carolina, where much rhetoric was heard on scientific farming and diversified crops, along with other promises that were not likely to be kept. With the decline of the Granges, the agrarian political grievances were channeled into the Farmer's Alliances, which served as the nexus between Granger movement the Populist revolt and what? The demise of the Granger movement left a vacuum for capable agrarian leadership, and the aggressive Dr. C. W. Macune of Waco, Texas, came forward and filled it. Under his leadership the Southern Alliance became national in scope, secured a national charter in Washington, and, armed with this charter, sent forth missionary teams into all Southern states.[10] In April of 1887 an organizer appeared in Robeson County, North Carolina, and set up the first suballiance. Within a few days eleven more suballiances were organized. From this point they spread rapidly, and by the next summer there were 1,018 local branches in sixty-two counties, with a membership of 42,000. By 1889 there were 1,600 suballiances, with a total membership of 72,000.[11]

Paralleling the rise of the Southern Alliance was the Colored Farmers' National and Cooperative Union. The formation of the latter was only natural since the former drew the color line. However, some whites, like Richard Manning Humphrey, recognized early the wisdom of enlisting Negro farmers in their struggle. Founded by Humphrey in Houston County, Texas, in 1886, the Negro Alliance soon spread into all Southern states, claiming a membership of 1.2 million in 1891. North Carolina reported fifty-five thousand members.[12] Indeed, this could have been a frightening prospect for the Democrats, if the Alliance forces had induced the Colored Alliance to vote almost to a man for third-party nominees. However, there is no evidence to support the claim made by some historians that close cooperation existed between the two organizations. According to the recent findings of Professor William F. Holmes, a serious division—a "black-white division," an unbridged chasm—prevailed from the outset, and racism proved to be a strongly divisive issue with which the agrarians never learned to cope effectively. Many articulate Blacks believed that the Alliance movement was not in "accord with their interests." Black Alliance spokesmen, accordingly, demonstrated a commendable zeal in working only for improvement of the economic lot of their people, and they did not ignore public education.[13] This is not to suggest that similar situations prevailed in all Southern states. Among the reluctant Black spokesmen who ultimately joined the Populists' ranks were Melvin Wade and John Rayner of Texas, Rev. H. S. Doyle of Georgia, and W. A. Patillo of North Carolina. Rayner was the most outstanding one. His background included school teaching and political speaking, and he often encountered hostile audiences. He was "ranked as an orator only behind two nationally known Texas third party men"—Harrison S. P. "Stump" Ashby and James H. "Cyclone" Davis.[14]

No Southern state gave rise to a more dynamic and colorful group of agrarian leaders than North Carolina. They included: Marion Butler, editor of the *Caucasian,* an influential paper in Sampson County; Frank Skinner, originator of the controversial subtreasury scheme; Dr. Cyrus Thompson, physician, but known to audiences as a poet, orator, and politician; Elias Carr; and Syndenham B. Alexander. The foremost figure was Leonidas L. Polk, whose star was already on the ascendancy and was ultimately to eclipse that of Dr. Macune on the national scene. He was born in Anson county on April 24, 1837, of inconspicuous parents, who died while he was still a child. He attended Davidson College for one year, served with two regiments during the Civil War, was a member of the state legislature in 1860 and 1864, and was elected to the Constitutional Convention in 1865. Establishing the *Progressive Farmer* the next year, he became well known for his publications and was named the first commissioner of agriculture in 1877.[15] Polk deserved chief credit for the organization of the Alliances in the state, chartered under the title North Carolina Farmers' Union. This organization's program called for the repeal of the crop-lien laws, limits on the rate of interest, the establishment of a land-grant college, and greater support to public schools.[16]

It is important to mention that the great majority of Alliance men put aside the thought of a revolt until the strategy of working within the Democratic party had been given a fair trial. The reason is quite clear. Party lines were fashioned by racial attitudes, and any rivalry to the Democrats—the white man's party—was criticized as a threat to white supremacy. Whether Polk harbored this ideology is questionable. He gave the Alliance program his approval in the *Progressive Farmer,* while enthusiastically endorsing the controversial subtreasury scheme.

Historians have credited the ubiquitous Dr. Macune with the conception of the subtreasury idea, but the North Carolinian Harry Skinner was its originator. Skinner had made the Southern farmer, whose cotton was nonperishable, the chief beneficiary. Macune broadened the scope of the plan to include all those products of Westerners and Southerners that could be stored successfully.[17] The projected idea called for the establishment of a subtreasury system to enable farmers to store nonperishable crops—cotton or grain—in government warehouses or elevators at 2 percent interest and to receive treasury notes up to 80 percent of the local value of the crop deposited. When the market was glutted, a farmer could hold his produce until prices rose, while the government loan was secured by the crops and repaid after they were sold. The subtreasury idea was adopted at the first national meeting of the Farmers' Alliance, held in St. Louis in December 1889.

On the eve of the 1890 election, Alliance leaders began a movement to impose their demands upon the various state legislatures by requiring all candidates to support the Alliance program as drawn up in the St. Louis platform of 1889, which included the subtreasury project and other state measures. All candidates for election were compelled to sign pledge cards in support of the program. In actuality, they were being asked to stand up and be counted. Accordingly, practically all the Democrats, half the Republicans, state legislators, and eight out of nine members elected to Congress proclaimed Alliance views.[18] Nonetheless, the conservative strategy of the North Carolina Alliance to work within the Democratic party was "reported to be going to the rocks." It can be surmised that some candidates, including the veteran Senator Zebulon B. Vance, had agreed to Alliance demands only for members' political support. Senator Vance, who had reluctantly presented the measure in the United States Senate at the insistence of Polk, soon turned against it even at the risk of being defeated in the next election. Later he wrote Elias Carr, president of the Alliance, that he was unable to support it in the form in which it had been presented, believing that it was unconstitutional.[19] Even the Negro Alliance considered the subtreasury plan to be "economically unsound."

While the subtreasury scheme resulted in disruption of the Alliance-Democrat accord, outside forces came into play to indirectly abet it. In June of 1890 Congressman Henry Cabot Lodge introduced a measure that became popularly known as the "force bill." Like a similar bill of 1870, designed to enforce the Fifteenth Amendment, the enactment of the measure. Following the Ocala convention, the National Alliance met at Omaha the next year and released a disclaimer that the Alliance would take no part "in a political struggle by affiliation with Republicans or Democrats."[25] But the next year it was a different story.

The stage was now set for the St. Louis Conference, convening on February 22, 1892. Here, the radical element, a motley group of delegates including farmers, Knights of Labor, "single taxers," Greenbackers and others who officially founded the People's party, rapidly moved toward the direction of populism. One reporter wrote that "all the second and third class hotels are crowded to overflowing."[26] the Lodge bill, in effect, called for complete federal supervision of state and local elections. No federal measure since Redemption had caused more alarm and ramifications. The *Greensboro Patriot* predicted that the force bill precluded all possibility of a third-party action by the North Carolina Alliance.[20] During the debate over the Lodge bill in 1890, a group of Southerners, in a volume of 452 pages entitled *Why the Solid South?* gave their answer to the measure in one word: "Reconstruction." "State by state they described" in familiar terms federal troops with bayonets, images of reconstruction surely to be revived by the force bill.[21]

The annual Alliance Convention met in Ocala, Florida, in December 1890, where dissident forces (radicals versus moderates) tended to divide the delegates. Third-party projects and the force bill were the main topics of discussion. Western delegates were ready for revolt and for formation of a third party and made it their mission to convert the South to populism.[22] The Black Alliance, meeting separately in Ocala, was ready to revolt and endorsed the force bill with enthusiasm. In contrast, with a spirited frenzy, the Southern Alliance adopted a protest against the Lodge measure. As the radical delegates pushed on toward a third party, they were to realize that Southern agitation over the force bill prevented such a movement at this time. Furthermore, the conservative views of Dr. Macune prevailed, for he had steadily maintained that the Alliance and third party must be kept separate, "that the Party and Order could not be supreme over the same subject at the same time."[23] Polk had been named president of the National Alliance. Emotionally, it appears, he sided with the radical delegates, but perhaps was a bit frightened at both the conservative and insurrectionary tones, and he chose to remain silent. The delegates did endorse the Ocala platform, with the subtreasury scheme taking top priority among its demands.[24] Meanwhile, in North Carolina, forces quickly aligned against the force bill, as a large number of prominent Alliance men were persuaded to sign an appeal to Democratic solidarity against

It was "truly a thrilling spectacle as the banners of the different states rose above the delegates throughout the hall, fluttering like flags over an army encamped."[27] Marion Butler, Carr, and Skinner headed the North Carolina delegation. They, like the majority of those from the South, rebelled against the idea of any third-party action. The St. Louis platform was adopted, and plans were laid for a convention to nominate candidates for president and vice-president. Polk, as head of the National Alliance, was in constant contact with Populist leaders and speedily came to share their views. Indeed, he identified himself with the third-party movement and "could be definitely counted within its ranks," for it was common knowledge that he was willing to carry the Alliance into the new party. When the radicals successfully elected Polk as permanent chairman, they "likewise scored a victory for the third-party men."[28] Finally, the convention heartily endorsed a decision to vote only with the political organization that represented its principles.

Immediately upon returning from St. Louis, Polk decided to canvass a group of fifty Alliance men assembled at Raleigh to determine independent party sentiment. The result of the poll showed them anxious to "avoid secession from the Democratic Party except as a last resort." Disappointed, but undismayed by that turn of events, he planned a strategy to "almost single handedly lead the North Carolina Alliance into the Third Party movement." In the meantime, he employed his *Progressive Farmer* to echo the views of the People's party and "to display the Populist banner."[29] In an attempt to establish friendly relations between the Alliance forces of North Carolina and the Western Populists, he arranged for "Sockless" Jerry Simpson, "the only American to achieve immortality by being accused of going without stockings," to tour the state in the interest of the new party.[30] Likewise, he was to pay a return visit to Kansas, perhaps "to stiffen up the backbone of Kansas Populists," who were about to concede that there would be no third party in the South.

The Republican party, to be sure, was also split over the race issue, as evidenced by the factionism between the "Blacks and Tans" —the term used by the *Raleigh News and Observer* to describe Negro allies and white Republicans. The "lily-whites" were led by Jeter C. Pritchard, "the foremost Republican in the state." They desired to purge the party of Black members and reorganize it from the ground up. Some leaders, like Daniel L. Russell and J. J. Mott, advocated no Republican tickets in the field as a means of "breaking the race issue." Russell, who would later need Negro support for both his nomination and his campaign in the 1896 gubernatorial race, ironically, was the most vocal against the Negro.[31] This racism ultimately caused a number of prominent Republicans—including Francis D.

Winston and Neill McKay—to desert the party. Nevertheless, self-interest prevailed. The Republican stronghold—the Carolina Highland counties—demanded party unity for attacks on the Democrats' election and county government laws.

Blacks, meanwhile, were becoming disenchanted with the Republican party over its lily-white proclivities. In North Carolina, as shall be seen, they were always at odds with the Republicans over the number of public offices allotted to them. For example, on April 9, 1890, a Black convention of three hundred met in Greensboro and formally denounced the Harrison Administration for failure to accord them due recognition for their long and constant support of party leaders. An executive committee was appointed for each township with the view of defeating the incumbents of the Republican party in the coming election. Aware of their powerful voting power, the Black voters were advised to "remain at home and to let the White Republicans do their own voting."[32]

Notwithstanding discontentment over race policy or for ideological reasons, the political salvation of the year of 1892 demanded that all parties field their candidates. The Alliance state president, Butler, expressing party loyalty and white supremacy in one breath, wrote in his newspaper: "Whatever, differences may exist among North Carolinians over a question of national policy, there should be none in the State where Anglo-Saxon rule and good government is the paramount issue."[33] A few weeks later he lead a bolt from the Democratic party. This movement should not have come as a surprise, however. Under his leadership, an Alliance Convention had already met in Raleigh on May 8, 1892, at which time delegates from seventy-five counties had taken preliminary steps to organize the Populist party and to select delegates to attend the national convention scheduled for Omaha. The state Republicans watched this movement with undisguised pleasure and very cleverly lost no opportunity to encourage Alliance discontent. Moreover, the Democrats repeatedly charged that the Republican national committee assisted materially in financing the third-party campaign in North Carolina.[34] Many Republicans were visible within the Populist ranks, but were really there as wolves in sheep's clothing. They had little in common with the Populists except hostility toward the Democrats, generated by a desire to return to political power. Their biggest point of contention with the Democrats', understandably, was their undemocratic local and county election laws. Accordingly, when the third party was in the making, a considerable body of Republicans joined it and devoted their energies toward the promotion of a new party, seeking ultimately to uproot the entrenched Democrats. "It was the case of building a fire under the Democratic Party to get even, which might also prove to be the salvation of the Republicans in the election of 1892."

The Populist forces, both in North Carolina and across the nation, suffered a heavy loss by Polk's untimely death on June 11, 1892.[35] They had expected to nominate him as the first Populist candidate for president at the third-party convention at Omaha. Instead, the nomination fell to James B. Weaver of Iowa.

Butler, who was president of the state Alliance and chairman of the Populist National Committee, assumed the leadership. He also moved his paper, the *Caucasian,* from Clinton to Raleigh and continued to champion Populist views. However, being an apostle of white supremacy, he showed a strong proclivity to remain in the Democratic party. In the meantime, the Populist cause was picking up momentum with the support of many former Democrats. These included J. L. Ramsey, who became editor of the *Progressive Farmer*; Hay Ayer, another newspaper man; Charles H. Mebane, outstanding educator and the party's choice for state superintendent; eloquent scholar and orator Dr. Cyrus Thompson; William H. Worth, a future state auditor; and William H. Mark of Guilford County. Among the Republican notables was Col. William A. Guthrie, an attorney from Durham County.

Under Butler's leadership a convention was held on August 16, 1892, in Raleigh to organize a People's party. It was attended by 495 delegates, almost equally composed of "Alliance men," Blacks, and Republicans, and representing seventy-two counties.[36] Indeed, political opportunism was evident. Butler served as both temporary and permanent chairman. The majority of Republicans had not left their party, but were present "primarily to assist in the defeat of the Democratic Party." By acclamation Skinner was nominated for governor, but the spirit was soon dampened when he agreed to accept only on condition that he could later withdraw if it appeared that the creation of a third party would result in a Republican victory. "I do not believe," he said in defense of his decision, "I ought . . . to act in such a way as to turn your government over to the Republicans." The nomination then fell to Dr. Wyatt P. Exum of Wayne County.[37] The remainder of the ticket consisted of R. H. Cobb, lieutenant governor; L. N. Durham, secretary of state; W. H. Worth, treasurer; E. G. Butler, auditor; R. H. Lyon, attorney general; and V. W. Woods, superintendent of public education. The platform favored, among other things, the taxation of all railroad property, a legal rate of interest of 6 percent, an eight-hour workday in the factories, and the "fullest development of the educating system in all of its departments."[38]

The Democratic leaders were visibly alarmed over the emergence of the Populist party, which struck terror in their hearts at the prospect of a split in the white vote. Meeting in convention at Raleigh a day after the Populists' convention, with their party greatly weakened by defection, they hastily made efforts to sway the farmers to remain in the party. On the other hand, a sizable number of radical members vehemently demanding that the party "purge itself of reactionary leadership and champion the interests of the masses." At the same time, the radicals urged the proponents of the St. Louis platform to "control the Democratic primaries and convenion." In retaliation, many conservatives sought to exclude from primaries and conventions all members who favored the St. Louis platform and who would not agree to abide by the decision on nominees and the platform in the state and nation. In the end, the wiser heads prevailed and "searched anxiously for nominees who would appeal to those who clamored for reform, even opposing the nomination of Cleveland for the presidency." They passed "over all the old party 'wheel-horses' and gave the gubernatorial nomination to the former Alliance President and 'dirt' farmer—Elias Carr of Edgecombe." Lastly, they conceded to the farmers every possible point and included in the Democratic platform every Alliance demand."[39]

In light of the ugly racial situation, it appears that leaders of the Republican party sought an understanding with their Negro allies. Assembling their convention in Raleigh on August 26, 1892, delegates from eighty-five counties attended; and several outstanding Blacks were among these delegates, including James H. Young, James H. Harris, E. E. Smith of Wayne County, John S. Leary of Cumberland County, and V. S. Lusk of Buncombe County. The convention leaders scoffed at the idea of Negro domination and proceeded to give recognition to their Black members. John H. Eaves, chairman of the state executive committee, appointed as temporary chairman Smith, who courteously counseled the delegates for harmony. Other articulate Blacks made rousing speeches. Lusk, "a forceful speaker," was the most outstanding. The convention was brought to its feet in mirth when he declared that "Democrats claim everything but the right to 'Hades'. . . . they thought they would finally come into it by inheritance." Leary's name was placed for nomination of chairman, and Lusk was nominated for associate justice, but he lost to W. T. Fairchild, 115 to 83.[40] The Republicans finally fashioned a platform, endorsing fair election laws and local self-government. For governor, they nominated David M. Furchess of Iredell County, former superior court judge.

While no Republican campaign events merit comment, such is not the case in regard to the other two parties. For political strategy, the Democrats resorted to propaganda, employing the force-bill scare, the return of federal bayonets, and "Nigger rule." Voters were warned of a sinister secret society known as Gideon Band, ready to invade North Carolina and turn the state over to Blacks and the Republican party. Furnifold M. Simmons of New Bern, a comparatively young and thoroughly able political leader, was placed at the head of the party. In this position he immediately exerted aggressive leadership. First, he arranged a systematic program of public speaking throughout the state and concomitantly distributed copious amounts of propaganda literature. Secret instrucions were issued to his election officials to employ all legal means to exclude Populist and Republican voters from registration. At the same time, Simmons sought to coax Populists to return to the fold by "compromises and conciliation," excluding, however, those Populists who refused to "recant."[41]

A major highlight of the 1892 campaign was the visit to North Carolina by the Populist presidential condidate, Gen. James B. Weaver. He was accompanied by Mary Ellen Lease of the six-volcanic-words fame—"Raise less corn and more hell." And according to Josephus Daniels, both celebrities were enthusiastically received, especially in Raleigh. "I do not recall ever," he later wrote, "to have seen so many horses and buggies and wagons and carts bringing county people to town. Farmers came from a dozen counties, some of them traveling all night over rough roads." There was no hall adequate to hold the crowds. While Weaver's speeches were greeted with some criticism and ridicule, he did possess an excellent voice and had a fine presence. Of Mary Lease, Daniels wrote: "She was a hummer . . . [and] carried the farmers by storm," and the North Carolina Populists "hailed her as a sort of Joan of Arc." There was, however, adverse reaction. Southerners were not ready for political speeches by women, who were reported as "simple disgusting, and as degrading womanhood to the level of politics."[42]

The tour of the Populist gubernatorial candidate, Exum, did more harm than good, and his almost infamous activities proved to be more of a liability than an asset to the campaign. He was accused of having little tact and a quick temper and was indicted for "carrying a concealed weapon and threatening the life of one Arnold Broden." On another occasion, he was allegedly arrested for using "profane language . . . in the presence of ladies." After the postmaster of Goldsboro testified that "certain remarks were made by Exum," which he denied, he was fined and left for Raleigh, reportedly with a warrant of perjury awaiting him if he ever returned to Goldsboro.[43] However, his gravest offense was a personal attack with a knife upon Charles B. Aycock, Democratic candidate for elector-at-large, and the state's future governor. Ill feelings had been brewing between the two men. During a political performance at

Greenville, Exum and Butler debated Aycock. Each engaged in personalities, and feelings became strained. A fight broke out between Aycock and Exum, but the two were separated. Continuing the political presentation, Aycock's forensic remarks at one point angered Exum, who called him a liar. Aycock demanded an apology, which Exum refused to make. Aycock retorted, "I'll see you later." Following the end of the debate, the three men set out in separate buggies for the thirty-five mile trip to Goldsboro. Exum rode alone, while Butler and Aycock rode together. Intermittently, the buggies would come to a halt, and the two men exchanged heated words. Exum asked Aycock to ride with him, which he refused to do, still demanding an apology from Exum. Finally, they arrived at Exum's home, and here Aycock asked Exum if he would retract his accusation. Exum lunged at him with a large knife. Aycock snatched a stick from Butler and struck his foe, and, while walking backward, stumbled and fell. With this advantage, "Exum jumped on him, struck him in the face and cut him in the arm and side of the head." Butler hastily parted them. Cursing, Exum threatened to kill Butler "if he did not stand back." Meanwhile, Mrs. Exum had run out of the house and importuned the two men to cease the fracas; they "yielded to her entreaties."[44]

Such action is not to be condoned, but one is reminded of the violence sometimes generated at political rallies. Ironically, rallies were often opened with readings from the Bible, followed by prayer. Yet the men who attended them often had shotguns and Winchester rifles hidden in their wagons and buggies, or else their pockets bulged with concealed weapons, sometimes to be used to avenge an insult to their leaders. The Populist era, especially, was one of heated tempers and intense passion. Candidates were often insulted, smashed with rotten eggs, and physically attacked by angry crowds.

The Democrats carried the 1892 election, but emerged as a minority party. For a young party, the Populists made a good showing, gathering 47,840 popular votes, with 94,684 and 135,519 votes for the Republicans and Democrats, respectively.[45] Immediately, the Democrats were charged with fraud and other irregularities at the polls. According to the *Progressive Farmer,* many persons were denied the right to vote because of unnecessary requirements in registration, or many votes were thrown out "without good reasons," and at many polls the number of votes counted was greater than the voting population. It also claimed that some Democratic judges deliberately placed Republican votes in the wrong ballot box, that some cities—most notably, Charlotte—made employment a condition of voting, and that "inmates of the poor house" voted the Democratic ticket by coercion. And Blacks, who were unanimous in their support of the

Republicans and deemed "solid" in many places, such as Winston and Charlotte, were not allowed to vote.[46]

The Negro held the balance of power, which the Populists obviously needed for success at the polls. Aware of this power, many Populist leaders, including those of Georgia, Texas, and South Carolina, had courted the Negro. Evidence strongly suggests that no Populist-Negro combination ever existed in North Carolina, a fact that calls for some analysis. Historically, there antagonism always existed between Negroes and poor whites.[47] The latter were fervent Democrats and were implacable foes of the Republicans. Notwithstanding the race dissension among the Republicans, Blacks remained Republicans and would oppose any third-party movement to "unseat Republican incumbents," viewed as a threat to their party's power.[48] Black farmers, like their white counterparts, it could be theorized, showed an emotional interest in the Populist program—especially concerning the proposed repeal of the crop-lien laws and improvement of public education for both races. Moreover, it could be argued that they hesitated to identify with third parties, unless the programs were espoused by the "party of Lincoln."

The talk of Fusion politics filled the air in the wake of the 1892 election. What was the attitude of Negro political leaders toward it? Black conventions were quite common from the time of Redemption through the Populist era, and county delegates constituted the greater part of them. Most of the militant speeches were given by county politicians opposing fusionism. They logically doubted that the Populists (Democratic apostates) could be trusted and would permit Negroes to hold office. This sentiment was expressed by a prominent Republican, who said that "Populists are like 'jack-o-lanterns in the swamps and marshes.' They spring up and shine but when you go to find them, they are not there."[49] In the same vein, the Negro chairman of the Republican party in Wilson County agreed that whites would vote a Fusion ticket with Blacks on it, but would take all offices, leaving the Negro with nothing but fuse. "We can't trade that way," he contended. "There is not much in fuse if you take all the offices."[50] Succinctly stated, Blacks who were identified with the Populists were an abnormality, and any Populist-Negro combination in North Carolina might be considered a forced marriage. Yet such a marriage was already destined.

Between elections, the last cord snapped, driving dissident Democrats into the Populist fold. Progressive legislation extolled by the Farmers' Alliances met with defeat after defeat. Moreover, the Democrats had already committed a serious blunder by amending the charter of the Farmers' Alliance so as to make it possible to annul it at the least excuse and, at the same time, render the organization powerless.

Greatly chagrined, the Populists became more determined to capture the state government from the Democrats, but how to do this certainly posed a paramount question. The answer was to be found in Fusion politics, which was nothing new. Earlier, the Redeemers had collaborated with Negro politicians (Republicans) against lower-class whites in the Black Belt. It was a case of simple mathematics; the 1892 election had demonstrated clearly that the Populists and Republicans together had polled a sizable majority of votes.

It is safe to assume that "owl meetings" (secret night sessions) took place. In any event, on the eve of the 1894 election at Raleigh on July 30, a group of prominent Republicans and Populists met in a secret caucus. The Republicans were John V. Mott, Virgil S. Lusk, Maj. Hiram L. Grant, G. Roberts of the *Asheville Register*, Claude M. Bernard, Abraham R. Middleton (a Black), R. S. McCall, and Richmond Pearson. The Populists were Butler, Skinner, and William W. Kitchen. The next day, the *Raleigh News and Observer* informed its readers that the Republicans and the Populists had fused their interests and decided on candidates and division of public offices.[51] Political positions at the state level were for state treasurer, chief justice, three associate justices, and a number of judges and solicitors, besides members of Congress and the legislature. The legislature that was chosen would elect two United States senators, one for a short term as a result of the death of Senator Vance. Basic party ideologies were subordinated to the main objectives: (1) capture the election, (2) repeal the County Government Act, and (3) divide the offices between the two parties. Hiram L. Grant of Wayne County, a successful businessman and maunfacturer who had formerly been a carpetbagger, had the confidence of the solid people of Goldsboro and, according to Josephus Daniels, was responsible for fusion between the two parties. He regarded the Negro as equal to the white man and was "hated and feared by the Democrats" of eastern North Carolina. However, Butler and Jester G. Pritchard were the chief advocates of fusionism on the Populist and Republican sides, respectively. Ironically, Skinner, who in 1892 "had been denied the nomination for Governor on the Populist ticket because of the announcement of his firm belief in white supremacy, had now taken a front seat on the Fusion Band Wagon and was ready to become a Republican and swallow his former declaration."[52]

The three parties held their respective conventions in August, with the Populist party convening first on August 1, 1894. As to platform, the Populists reaffirmed the principles of the national party, and on state matters favored—among other things—a four-months school year for both the white and Negro population. Meeting a week later, the Democrats ignored a state plank and endorsed that of their national party. The Republicans assembled on August 30. The repeal of the County Government Act and a fair election law were the paramount items that composed the Republican platform.[53] In the past the Democrats had been known for their "flattering predictions," but as the campaign lumbered on toward election day, fear of defeat was very evident in some quarters; their chances of carrying the state became dubious for the first time in many years. Thousands seemed to have "crossed the Rubicon." "Big Democratic Losses," announced the *Raleigh News and Observer* the day after the election. Gleefully, the Populists boasted that the Democrats had resorted to widespread fraud and "had stolen 40,000 votes and were still defeated."[54] The outcome stunned most Democrats, and hard feelings prevailed among some die-hard party members.

When the *Raleigh News and Observer* admitted that the Fusionists had carried the state, Capt. Nathan O'Berry, chairman of the Democratic party of Goldsboro County, sent Josephus Daniels a telegram saying: "Please never let the *News and Observer* darken my doors again. Any Democratic paper that will give up an election before the official count is made is not the Democratic paper I want to subscribe to."

The General Assembly of 1895 was politically divided: the ratio of Populist-Republicans to Democrats was 69 to 49 in the House; 41 to 9 in the Senate.[55]

It has been stated that the Democrats had predicted the return of the Negro as a political force. Since Blacks constituted a large segment of the Republican party, the Populist-Republican fusion inevitably meant the return of the race question in state politics, and this became a discernible fact when the General Assembly convened on January 19, 1895. This former lily-white assemblage was now spotted here and there with a Negro face. Fusion politics had sent James Young of Wake County and William H. Crews of Granville County to the House of Representatives. Their presence immediately evoked the race question in politics. Beginning with the opening day, Abraham "Abe" Middleton of Duplin County, an ebony Negro, replaced one-legged Confederate veteran V. Reitzel of Catawba as assistant doorkeeper. This conspicuous position was a modest political patronage. Reitzel, who held the position during the former Democratic General Assembly, had joined the Populist party but failed to be reelected. Middleton was a very shrewd politician—and a key member of the triumvirate of Butler, Grant, and Middleton—who had made fusion possible in the counties of Sampson and

Duplin.[56] He was also Butler's first lieutenant in charge of keeping the Blacks organized without offending the Populists, who had all their lives been opposed to Negro participation in politics. His appointment to the post of assistant doorkeeper drew fire from several quarters, most notably from the *News and Observer*; it accused the Fusionists of showing preference for Negroes over whites. Indeed, this was an insignificant position, but it was conspicuous enough to ignite racial incidents.[57]

It was on the state level of government that Blacks made their first and most conspicuous impression on American historiography. Evidence strongly suggests that the caliber of Black political leadership greatly improved in North Carolina between Reconstruction and the era of Fusion politics. A few lines here on Congressman Crews might be of historical interest. (Congressman Young was more astute, and a character sketch of him will appear later.) Born in slavery in 1844, Crews attended the public and private schools of the city of Oxford. His public offices included committee member, justice of the peace, deputy sheriff, and constable for twelve years in Granville County, and prior to the Fusion era he served four successive terms in the state legislature.[58] His political career might have passed unnoticed had he not introduced on February 21, 1895, a resolution to adjourn in honor of Frederick Douglass, famous Negro abolitionist, statesman, and orator, who had just died. The resolution was adopted. But February 22 was George Washington's birthday and no official action had been taken to pay respect to his memory. The Democrats thus charged that a Negro had been honored but that the legislature had failed to honor the birthdays of Lee and Washington. The fact that Douglass's second wife was white added flame to the controversy, and the respect paid to Douglass was seen as an endorsement of marriage between the races. Josephus Daniels denounced the adjournment in honor of Douglass as the "climax of infamy," with cartoons in his paper pillorying the whole affair. One of them showed the Fusionists ignoring the ladies who begged them to honor the Confederate dead and obeying the demand of the Blacks by honoring Frederick Douglass. The legislature quickly appropriated ten thousand dollars to women's organizations to erect a Confederate statute, in the hope of mitigating wide criticism stemming from the Douglass resolution.[59] Earlier, the appropriation had been voted down.

The Abe Middleton affair and the Crews resolution were merely emotional events involving racism. To be sure, the 1895 legislature was faced with several key problems.

Most importantly, the Fusionist-dominated legislature faced the difficult task of satisfying both Populists and Republicans. It had earlier elected Zebulon V. Walser, a Republican, as Speaker of the

House. It also chose Butler to fill the regular seat, and Republican Pritchard to complete the unexpired term of Senator Vance. Utmost on the Republican agenda was the County Election Law, and the Fusion legislature embarked upon the task of dismantling the Democratic election machinery as created by the Redeemers. A new county election law was carefully designed to restore to the people of North Carolina local self-government and home rule. Succinctly stated, it abolished the Democrats' policy of appointment of local offices and made them all subject to popular election. A number of the larger municipal charters—notably Wilmington, Raleigh, Goldsboro, New Bern, Greenville, and Elizabeth City—subject to the Democrats' same policy of control, were revised for more Democratic elections. The Republicans, in particular, knew that the intricate provisions of the old registration and voting requirements were barriers against Blacks. Hence, registration and other practices at the polls were made as simple as possible. For example, each party was to have a judge and registrar at each precinct, appointed upon the nomination of each party chairman. The Democrats required white ballots. However, the Fusion election law permitted ballots of different colors, so that the illiterate voter could identify his party ticket by color. It also permitted the counting of votes placed in the wrong box.[60] The Democratic features of the Fusionist election laws, indeed, were destined to regenerate the formidable Black vote, lying dormant since 1877 but soon to be revived in the 1896 election.

The 1896 campaign was one of emotion on the national scene, but on the state level was an alignment more of parties and personalities than of issues. After the enactment of the Fusionist County Election Law, the reconstructed Negro voters made up a sizable proportion of the Republican party. Meanwhile, the party had split: one wing, constituting a large minority, was "tired of truckling to the Populist forces," and of continuing an identity with Black voters and politicians. This lily-white element nutured the hope of conducting the ensuing campaign on the issues of the tariff, free silver, and white supremacy. Earlier, a Republican organ had declared that Free Silver at a ratio of 16 to 1 and White Supremacy would be the platform and that "Anglo-Saxon supremacy is necessary and must be preserved in the Old North State." It also warned that "no colored man need apply, not even James H. Young."[61] The other wing, perhaps realizing that a split party had little chance of victory in the ensuing election, preferred to endorse both Populists and Negro cohorts.

The Republicans held their convention on May 14 at Raleigh. Prominent Negro delegates included Middleton; John C. Dancy of Wilmington; Dr. James E. Shepard of Raleigh; L. A. Scruggs; Edward

A. Johnson; Dr. Aaron McDuffie Moore; Loge Harris; Professor Copehard of Shaw University; W. G. Pearson of Durham; and V. O. Nixon, Alderman of Wilmington, Rev. W. H. Leak of Raleigh; L. B. Berry of Iredell County; and, of coursee, James H. Young. As might be expected, the convention opened amid strife and dissension. Ten counties sent in two delegations to throw the convention into an uproar at the outset. After a furious dispute over the seating of delegates, the convention was next confronted with the task of selecting a state ticket, beginning with the nomination of a gubernatorial candidate, for which the contest centered tensely around two men—Daniel L. Russell and Oliver H. Dockery. Specifically, the conflict involved the color line—white versus black—being expressed as anti-Russell and pro-Dockery forces. Russell had come under attack in some Negro quarters for his alleged racist remarks, uttered when he was not active in politics. The one most frequently quoted was: "All Negroes are natural born thieves. They steal six days a week and go to church on Sunday and shout and pray it off." Allegedly, on another occasion he remarked that Blacks "were no more fit to govern than their brethren in the swamps of Africa."[62] Russell categorically denied ever having said such a thing. And since no evidence existed, the charge was strictly speculative. Thus, one can surmise that the Democratic presses started the rumor to create discord within the Negro ranks.

A total of 117 of the 232 delegate votes was necessary for the gubernatorial nomination, and the struggle for that majority began thunderously. Dancy, amid great excitement, mentioned Dockery's name. All the pro-Dockery forces formed a solid phalanx behind him, and a series of anti-Russell speeches commenced.

Dr. Shepard declared Russell to be "the meanest judge that ever sat on the bench in North Carolina" and stated that "no self-respecting Negro would vote for him." The pro-Russell forces greeted this address with hisses and howled down the speaker. Young, truly an experienced politician and also a member of the 1895 legislature, led the Black forces for Russell. "I wish we could get nine Russells on the Supreme Court," Young told his audience. "He is the only judge who ever sat upon the bench who had the courage and audacity to say the Constitution doesn't know the difference between the colored man or the white man. If you nominate Russell, fusion is assured."[63] A rousing ovation by the Russell forces followed, the party machine already set on their candidate. After seven separate ballots, Russell won with 119 3/7 votes to Dockery's 112 4/7. The Russellites greeted the results with cheers. Some Black delegates, reported the *Raleigh News and Observer*, "took possession of the stage and danced a break down." Recalling the event years later,

Josephus Daniels wrote: "This skulduggery began in Wake County, where Parson Leak and the bulk of the other Negro Republicans, who were advocating Dockery, were out-generalled by Jim Young and Loge Harris, Russell leaders."[64]

In his acceptance speech, Russell sought to allay the fears of the Black delegates by saying: "I entertain a sentiment of deep gratitude to the Negroes. I stand for the Negroes' rights and liberties. I sucked at the breast of a Negro woman. I judged from the adult development the milk must have been nutritious and plentiful. The Negroes do not want control. They only demand, and they ought to have it, every right a white man has." Later in the campaign he was to promise them a full share of the spoils, or, as he phrased it, "oats and fodder."[65] In the attempt to secure disciplines before the campaign got underway, Russell was introduced in Wilmington to mass meetings of Republicans, including Blacks and others, as a man who destroyed white supremacy. To the number of men who called themselves Democrats, he denounced the Democrats as traitors and hypocrites and prevailed upon them to desert their party.

After the fervor over the selection of gubernatorial condidates subsided, the Republicans proceeded to complete their state ticket. While some delegates desired cooperation with the Populists, the question of fusion was kept in the background. There were anti-fusion forces led by John B. Eaves, Republican state chairman, and Russell, who was quite vocal in his opposition. The platform, among other pledges, gave some recognition to education by agreeing to support "an efficient state superintendent of public education regardless of party." The delegates completed their slate of candidates, but they released a skeletal ticket by not nominating anyone for secretary of state, treasurer, or superintendent of public instruction as an incentive for the Populists to fuse with them.[66]

Two days after the Republican Convention closed, a Black caucus, composed primarily of pro-Dockery forces, met on May 19 at Raleigh. Members of the caucus believed strongly that their favorite should have won the gubernatorial nomination but that the Russell forces had resorted to highway robbery to defeat Dockery. They claimed that Dockery had had the endorsement of four-fifths of the Republicans but that the Russell forces had secured control of the committee on credentials and, by shrewd manipulations, selected the delegates. Angered at both Young and United States Senator Pritchard for outfoxing them, but knowing that the former could not be intimidated, the Black caucus set out to get Senator Pritchard. Hence, it was decided that they would promote Dockery for the Pritchard seat, and it was declared that they would support no one for the seat or the legislature who refused to pledge for Dockery. Finally, they

104

agreed to hold a second convention on July 2 at Raleigh to promote the pro-Dockery movement.

The second Black caucus, representing sixty-five counties, met as scheduled and was comprised almost completely of Negro voters. Prominent delegates were Dr. Aaron Moore, Professor Copehard, W. G. Pearson, and V. O. Nixon. Rev. W. H. Leak and L. B. Berry were elected chairman and secretary, respectively, of the conference, which organized itself under the title of State Convention of Colored Republicans. An opening resolution censored the anti-Russell Republican forces and the "cowardly insults uttered against the race by Hon. D. L. Russell." Another resolution adopted conscientiously called upon every Black in whose heart there was "still a spark of self-respect, manhood, honesty, and integrity of the race to do all in his power to defeat the election of Russell, whose "name has become a stench" to honest and intelligent Blacks "throughout the land, and whose election would be a blot upon the fair name of North Carolina." The platform reiterated demands for honest election laws, improvement of public education, and longer school terms for both whites and Negroes. A new state executive committee of nine men, including two whites, was created from the nine congressional districts. And finally, W. A. Guthrie of Durham County was endorsed as the gubernatorial candidate.[67] These developments represented a definite schism within the Republican ranks, in which the Negro vote was a potent factor.

Meanwhile, the Democrats had held their convention on June 25 at Raleigh amid all the discord and spontaniety generating from dissident factions. Some delegates suggested a Democrat-Populist fusion strictly to attract the Populist vote. Searching for a well-known gubernatorial candidate, overtures were made to noted educator Charles D. McIver. Declining, McIver "declared [that] his chief interest was in education . . . [and that] he could not permit his name to be used for any public office." The Democrats finally settled on Cyrus Watson.[68] If public education were to become the cornerstone of the Democrats' interest, their platform was completely barren of it, the concentration being solely on national issues. The nomination of William Jennings Bryan for president may have given some hope to "silverbugs," but silver oratory and rhetoric, for which Bryan was nationally known, were to prove of little value to the Democrats in North Carolina, the South, and the nation. Moreover, with the Populist defection, the Negro vote being rejuvenated en masse, and the fusion of Populist-Republican forces, the chance of a Democratic victory on the state level was very slim.

The Populist Convention assembled on August 13 in Raleigh, with every county represented except small Chowan in the Black

Belt. The Populists had the distinct advantage of knowing what the Black caucus, the Republicans, and the Democrats had already accomplished. The question of fusion with the Democrats was raised, but the issue deeply divided the Populists. Like their Southern brethren, North Carolina Populists desired a separate Populist presidential ticket and, having been at odds with the Democrats for years, wanted no fusion with them in state politics. At the same time, State Chairman Skinner and his forces wanted no compromise with the Republicans, while the Butler faction would collaborate with the Republicans if there could be an agreement on free silver. It seems safe to conclude that the Populists did not want to divide their platform, which would certainly blur their own party identity. Completely disregarding the Republican slate of candidates, they proceeded to choose their own, beginning with the endorsement of Guthrie as gubernatorial candidate. Definitely bidding for Negro support, Dockery, who had been defeated by the Russell forces as Republican candidate and who was now the choice of the Black caucus, was nominated for lieutenant governor. When the complete slate was released, the Republican Executive Committee quickly filled in the vacant spots on their ticket with candidates the Populists had named. Hence, the Populist nominees—Dr. Cyrus Thompson for secretary of state, William H. Worth for state treasurer, and Charles H. Mebane for superintendent of public instruction—were now accepted in "good faith" by the Republicans.[69] Fusionism was tacitly approved by parties of different ideologies, but American politics has strange bedfellows, as history has so often shown.

The Raleigh News and Observer, in trying to widen the breach between Blacks and whites in the Republican party, employed the talents of the young gifted cartoonist, Norman E. Jennett, whose first cartoon mocked the change that took place in Russell's attitude toward Blacks before his nomination as governor. Russell denied ever having referred to Blacks as savages and stated that he merely had said that there were "black savages and white savages." He declared that John Brown was one of the heroes of the world's history and that his picture should hang in every Negro home.[70]

There were moves, countermovements, and maneuvers, right down to the final stages of the campaign, to create some sort of Populist-Democratic fusion. Moreover, in some Populist quarters, pressure was exerted to cut Guthrie loose. Believing that he had been repudiated by his party, Guthrie exploded an eleventh-hour bombshell, declaring that the Populists should fuse with the Democrats. Russell, too, was having his problems. There was the outrageous allegation of his being a mulatto. Rumors were circulated of a tacit understanding that Russell would come off the ticket, "presumably in favor

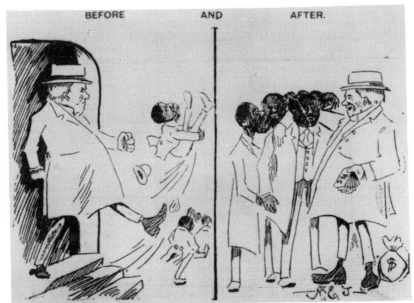

Raleigh News and Observer, *May 17, 1896*

of a Populist candidate."[71] Despite the political vicissitudes, all three gubernatorial candidates stayed in the race. When the campaign ended and the results were tabulated, Russell emerged victorious and became the first Republican governor since Reconstruction. He carried forty-nine counties with 153,787 votes, in contrast to Democrat Watson, who carried forty-six counties with 145,266 votes and Populist Guthrie, who carried one county, polling 31,143 votes.[72] Russell scored heavily over Watson in the Black Belt region. There factionalism had cracked the walls of white solidarity. Nevertheless, the underlying factor was the resurrection of the formidable Black Republican vote. The 1897 General Assembly stood as follows: thirty-nine Populists and fifty-four Republicans to twenty-four Democrats in the House; twenty-five Populists and eighteen Republicans against only seven Democrats in the Senate.[73]

Three Blacks were added to the assembly—John T. Howe in the House and William L. Person and W. B. Henderson in the Senate. Fusion politics also elected the controversial, courageous, and somewhat militant George Henry White to the United States House of Representatives. A tall, broad-shouldered ebony man from Edgecombe County, born a slave on December 18, 1852, of a mixed lineage of Negro, Irish, and Indian, White was the last former slave to serve in Congress. He had worked his way through Howard University, become a teacher and principal, and, at the same time, studied and read law under Superior Court Judge William J. Clark of Craven County. He had been admitted to the bar in 1879. At this time he had already begun to take an increasing role in politics. Now a lawyer-politician, he served in both the state Senate and the House of Representatives and from 1886 to 1894 was solicitor and prosecuting attorney for the Second Judicial District of North Carolina.[74] White was well known for his forceful oratory and relaxed speaking style. He served two terms in Congress, ironically the sole and last Negro spokesman of the era in that august body. Keenly aware of being the only Negro representative in Congress, he became more race-conscious than ever. It was said of him that "no matter what the topic under discussion might be, White, like Cato of Rome, could always bring it around to a discussion of Negro rights."[75] The purpose of such deviations was to call to the attention of his colleagues in the House, along with the citizens in the gallery, the plight of American Blacks—with mob rule and violence, job discrimination, Jim Crow, and lynching being common.

With the exception of James H. Young, no other Black politician suffered more unjust condemnation than White. It is needless to point out that editor Daniels led in the casting of aspersions. In the *Raleigh News and Observer* appeared the affront: "It is bad enough that North Carolina should have the only nigger congressman, [which] is sufficiently humiliating to the white Second District." The paper went on to emphasize the need for making an "end of him and his kind to show the absolute necessity of permanent rule in this state."[76]

Earlier historical interpretations have characterized the Fusionist era as one of "Black Domination," especially in the Black Belt. History books relate that following the election of the Republican Daniel L. Russell, the Fusion majority in the legislature was maintained. "As a consequence, more Negroes were appointed to office than ever before; there were at least a thousand Negro office-holders in the State after the complete Fusion victory in 1896."[77] In 1951 a very different position was taken by Black historian Helen G. Edmonds, who offered a new interpretation of the Fusion era.[78] It appears, nevertheless, that other historians have not taken a positive stand to set the record straight; indeed, the injustice done to the Fusion era by historians has been perpetuated for too long.

It is interesting to consider what the masses themselves believed during this era. The ubiquitous tales of "Negro Rule," as propagated by the Democrats, came to be regarded as the gospel truth, considering how white racism went on the rampage taking on a momentum like that of a religious crusade. It would be a mistake, however, to imply that everyone was fooled by the Democrats' antics. "The Democrats want offices, is the long and short of the whole matter," exclaimed *Star of Zion,* the official organ of the African Episcopal Zion Church. The *Zion* warned its readers that the Democrats' cry of "Negro Domination" was a 'scare crow' and a "false alarm" and the "last and only trump card that they can play in their diabolical game." Domination by Blacks was an impossibility in a state where whites outnumbered them three to one, and "those who believe to the contrary should instantly have their family physicians examine their mental condition."[79]

Under the doctrine of white supremacy, the holding of any public office by Blacks inevitably produced a smoldering fire of resentment. To be sure, the Democrats well knew how to utilize to the fullest the "nigger racket" at election time. Judge Robert W. Winston, who lived in Oxford and who was very involved in politics during the 1880s, later wrote: " 'Nigger, nigger, nigger' is its only cry. The nigger is the Democratic stalking-horse. Down in Hell—and Hell's where the Democrats belong—down in Hell you can tell a Democrat every time. There he sits holding some little skinny-headed Negro between him and the fire."[80] Dr. Cyrus Thompson, a Populist of note, called the Democrats hypocrites. He recalled that the "campaign of 1876 was largely waged upon the issue . . . of Negro equality." Contrary to their campaign pledge to remove the Negro from politics, the Democrats inaugurated a fusion policy of appointing Black magistrates, postmasters, policemen, and school committeemen. In the appeal for white supremacy, however, the Democrats always found it expedient to draw the color line, and racism retained its rallying point when identified with the charge of Negro officeholding. In support of this point, Dr. Thompson accused the Democrats of leaving a few Blacks in offices for the "purpose of future campaigns." He emphasized that the Democrats needed the "nigger issue" for their propaganda and declared: "When the Democratic Party in North Carolina removes the Negro from politics . . . the Democratic Party goes out of existence in North Carolina."[81]

Blacks holding positions involving federal patronage could always draw fire from whites. The postal system, involving postmasters, mail clerks, and route agents, provided the most conspicuous jobs. The pay of postmasters ran the gamut from about three hundred dollars (fourth class) to the first-class positions paying eighteen hundred dollars annually in cities like Fayetteville and Wilson. Whites coveted even the poorest-paying ones. It should be remembered that the paying of low wages was a major element of the economic doctrine of the New Order. Low-paying postmaster positions may have carried prestige in the rural areas; at any rate, evidence strongly suggests that whites held on to them for dear life. There was always apprehension that Black Belt Republicans would remove them. Senator Matt

Ransom's office was constantly badgered by people asking him to use his influence to retain Democrats in these occupations, or to secure potential jobs for them, especially the more lucrative ones.[82]

The number of Negro postmasters is not known. However, the Democrats charged "that there were from 15 to 25 Negro postmasters in Eastern North Carolina."[83] Whites made Blacks in this occupation their prime targets. For example, a poor white woman in Fayetteville addressed a letter (on cheap paper and without a heading) to the Senator as "Mr. Ransom," and, judging from the syntax of her letter, she possessed about a fourth grade education, based on North Carolina's standards. She reminded Senator Ransom that he was a "Southerner and how it make our blood boil to see a negro P.M.," and in the next breath she asked him to use his influence to help her get the position. Earlier, a friend of hers had tried to intercede in her behalf. That she was "a widow with four or five children," the wife of a late sheriff, and a good Democrat formed her credentials for the first-class postal position at Fayetteville.[84]

During this era, the triumph of one political party inevitably meant changes in federal patronage. Postmasterships took top priority because of the "hungry demands" for the offices "from this section." Whites, in their eagerness to get control of such offices, were not content to await the expiration of the officials' terms but, by extraordinary pressure, forced incumbents to resign. Such was the case of the competent Samuel H. Vick, Negro postmaster at Wilson. Born during the Civil War on April 3, 1862, and graduated from Lincoln University in 1884, he taught school for four years and in 1889 was appointed postmaster by President Harrison.[85] During the white supremacy campaign of 1898, whites of the city sought to obtain his position and were eventually successful.

Shepard of Durham and Dancy of Wilmington were the most prominent Black federal appointees in North Carolina. James E. Shepard the son of a distinguished theologian, was born in 1875.[86] He was graduated from Shaw University (Department of Pharmacy) at the age of nineteen. Like many of the young men of his age and intelligence, he fell under the sway of politics, while still a student of theology. As has already been mentioned, Dr. Shepard was active in politics, and in 1899 he was appointed deputy collector of the United States Department of Internal Revenue. Remaining there until 1905, he was the first and last Negro to hold that position in North Carolina. He later founded and became president of what is now North Carolina Central University in Durham.[87]

John C. Dancy was one of the giants among the Black political figures of North Carolina. Born in slavery at Tarboro in 1857, he studied at Howard University and later became a competent theolo-

John C. Dancy. Courtesy of Livingstone College

W. H. R. Leak (From Josephus Daniels, Editor in Politics, *Copyright 1941 The University of North Carolina Press. Reprinted by permission of the publisher.)*

James H. Young (From Josephus Daniels, Editor in Politics, *Copyright 1941 The University of North Carolina Press. Reprinted by permission of the publisher.)*

gian, college professor, journalist, and one of the nation's foremost public speakers, acquiring an international reputation. During the tenure of President Harrison, he served as minister to Haiti for three years.[88] It was President Harrison who, in 1889, appointed him collector of customs at Wilmington. Grover Cleveland, who was elected in 1892, did not retain him; but upon the defeat of Cleveland in 1896, Dancy was restored to his post by President McKinley. His position, allegedly paying some four thousand dollars annually, gave him economic status far above most people in the city, which was greatly resented by many whites. The editor of the *Wilmington Messenger* slandered this magnificent man by referring to him as the "Sambo of the Custom House."[89]

A representative sketch of Edward A. Johnson should offer additional insight into the caliber of Negro politicians of the Fusion era. Johnson achieved distinction as a lawyer, as an alderman of Raleigh, and as dean of the Law School of Shaw University. Moving to New York City in 1907 to practice law, he became the first Negro to be elected to the New York legislature. A leading historian and author, he wrote such work as *History of the Negro Race in America; History of the Negro Soldier in the Spanish-American War; Lights Ahead for the Negro;* and *Negro Almanac and Statistics.*[90]

James H. Young of Wake County was the most astute Black politician of the Fusion era. His adroitness in politics has already been noted as being the major force behind the Fusion strategy to help maneuver the gubernatorial nomination of Daniel L. Russell over the pro-Dockery forces in 1896. The white president of Shaw

James E. Shepard

112

Henry B. Cheatham (From Josephus Daniels, Editor in Politics, Copyright 1941 The University of North Carolina Press. Reprinted by permission of the publisher.)

George H. White (From Josephus Daniels, Editor in Politics, Copyright 1941 The University of North Carolina Press. Reprinted by permission of the publisher.)

University, Dr. Charles F. Meserve, praised Young as possessing "a marked degree of quality of leadership as important as it is rare." Born on October 26, 1858, in Henderson, he attended Shaw University from 1874 to 1877 and later rose "step by step" from the position of laborer to that of collector of Internal Revenue in the Fourth District and finally to chief clerk and cashier, a position he held for five years. Later he served as register of deeds in Wake County and in 1893 became editor of the *Gazette*, proving himself to be a "strong, forceful and versatile newspaper man." Meanwhile, he had become a dominant personality within the Republican party of the state. He was a delegate-at-large in 1884 and a delegate to the Republican National Convention in 1892.[91] Governor Russell, who held Young in high esteem, appointed him in 1897 as chief fertilizer inspector for the state. Leading Democrats, led by the *Raleigh News and Observer,* censured Governor Russell for the appointment of "the position aforestated . . . with a big fat salary and with white men working under him."[92] And when the Spanish-American War broke out the next year, the governor appointed him a colonel to command all Black regiments. This act also evoked strong criticism of Governor Russell from the state's white supremacists, who were preoccupied with the task of reducing the status of the Negro.

In every sense of the word employed in American historiography, Young was a progressive. Fór example, he led the struggle to amend the undemocratic charter the Redeemers imposed upon Raleigh.[93] To increase the beauty of that city, he successfully promoted a measure to have the streets paved around Capitol Square. Meanwhile, he fought for increased taxation for school support, longer school terms, and higher pay for teachers. To no avail, he sought to have a reform school established for juveniles.[94] He was in the forefront of the successful movement for the founding of the Deaf, Dumb, and Blind Institution in Raleigh, at a total cost of fifty-six thousand dollars. Naturally, Governor Russell appointed him to the board of directors of that institution. Young's name was among the names of the founders inscribed on the cornerstone of the building. This act was condemned throughout the state, with Young and Governor Russell bearing the greater burden of the disapprobation from the *News and Observer.*

One might expect that Daniel L. Russell, being the first Republican governor since Reconstruction became a prime target in Daniels's paper. The governor was a "rare character." A member of a large slaveholding family, an ardent Confederate captain, and an excellent student at the University of North Carolina, he was later a successful lawyer. While a Republican in the Black Belt, he seemingly did not ascribe to the harsh racism so prevalent among white men of this era.

It is apparent upon examining the evidence more objectively and inclusively that the governor was sincere, intelligent, and well qualified for the position, but historians—unjustly—have been unkind to him. One portrayed him "as a man full of bitterness who had made an unenviable record in the Confederate Army and had carried the stigma all his life." The *Raleigh News and Observer* inaugurated a smear campaign under the rubric of "Russellism." With an augmentation of racial incidents, charges of misgovernment, extravagance, and corruption, plagued his entire administration. Historian J. G.

de Roulhac Hamilton has recorded that "burglary, robbery and murder were offenses of increasing frequency and Negro juries made convictions practically impossible" in the eastern Coastal Plain.[95] Such accounts received wide press coverage throughout the South and parts of the nation and were viewed as the gospel truth. It was also reported that some cities in the Black Belt had been willfully turned over to Negro rule, and Wilmington was cited as the classic example. The *Literary Digest* wrote: "The Negroes had control of the city government, not by virtue of election, but through the connivance of the [Fusionist] legislature and the Governor, Daniel Russell, who desired the humiliation of decent people among whom he had lived prior to his elevation."[96] Relying heavily on data from the Democratic press, headed by the *Raleigh News and Observer*, well-trained historians, ironically, had not subjected their sources to external and internal criticism. Truth and probity are accepted axioms of the historical method. "Historians," observed a noted British scholar, "have such great opportunities to do good or evil."[97] In light of the glaring omissions and distortions, it appears that the Russell Administration needs to be reevaluated. The progressive legislation enacted by the Populists was clouded by editor Daniels's smokescreen —"Russellism." Like the Progressives of the next decade, the Populists believed that the lot of the masses could be bettered permanently through education. Acting on this belief, they made the first attempt to deal constructively with the public education problem. An account of their efforts is presented in the next chapter.

Notes

1. C. Vann Woodward, *Tom Watson, Agrarian Rebel* (New York, 1938), pp. 218–20.

2. Thomas E. Watson, "The Negro Question in the South," *Arena* (1892): 458.

3. Eric D. Goldman, *Rendezvous with Destiny* (New York, 1956), p. 39.

4. John D. Hicks, "The Farmers' Alliance in North Carolina," *North Carolina Historical Review* 2 (April 1925): 165–67.

5. *Progressive Farmer*, July 31, 1888.

6. Ibid., April 28, 1887.

7. John D. Hicks, *The Populist Revolt* (Minneapolis, Minn., 1931), pp. 5–7, 54–56.

8. Congressman George Henry White, testimony of February 18, 1900, *Reports of the United States Industrial Commission*, vol. 10 (1900).

9. Hugh T. Lefler, ed., *North Carolina History Told by Contemporaries* (Chapel Hill, N.C., 1934), p. 322; J. G. de Roulhac Hamilton, *History of North Carolina*, vol. 3, *North Carolina since 1860* (Chicago, 1919), pp. 222–23.

10. Hicks, *The Populist Revolt*, pp. 109–10.

11. Hicks, "Farmer's Alliance in North Carolina," pp. 170–72.

12. Article 7 of the Alliance Constitution restricted membership to white males over sixteen years of age. *National Economist,* March 14, 1889. Hicks, *The Populist Revolt,* pp. 114–115, and idem, "Farmers' Alliance in North Carolina," p. 182.

13. William F. Holmes, "The Demise of the Colored Farmers' Alliance," *Journal of Southern History* 41 (May 1975) : 186, 189–91, 193–94.

14. Lawrence Goodwyn, *Democratic Promise: The Populist Movement in America* (New York, 1976), pp. 300–4.

15. Stuart Noblin, *Leonidas Lafayette Polk, Agrarian Leader* (Chapel Hill, N.C., 1949), pp. 28–31, 51–56, 124–25, 149–56; idem, "Leonidas Lafayette Polk and The North Carolina Department of Agriculture," pt. 1, *North Carolina Historical Review* 41 (April 1943) : 113–14.

16. *Raleigh News and Observer,* January 27, 1887.

17. *National Economist,* December 28, 1889. Dr. McCune contended that if warehouses were built for the benefit of Southern cotton growers, then the Western farmers would desire a similar system.

18. Hicks, "Farmers' Alliance in North Carolina," p. 174.

19. Zebulon B. Vance to Carr, June 29, 1890, in Clement Dowd, *Life of Zebulon B. Vance* (Charlotte, N.C., 1897), p. 284.

20. *Greensboro Patriot,* January 29, 1891.

21. George B. Tindall, "Strategy: A Historical Perspective," *North Carolina Historical Review* 48 (April 1971) : 126–41.

22. Hicks, *The Populist Revolt,* pp. 207–209. Kansas left the West and joined its Southern rivals for the express purpose of supporting a third-party movement.

23. *National Economist,* February 28, 1891.

24. The Ocala Demands, December 1890. See *Proceedings of the Supreme Council of the National Farmers' Alliance and Industrial Union* (1890), pp. 32–33, and Hicks, *The Populist Revolt,* app. B, p. 430.

25. *National Economist,* February 28, 1891. Dr. McCune consistently maintained that the Alliance and the third-party movement must be kept separate. The Order (Alliance) could not be supreme over both at the same time.

26. Hicks, *The Populist Revolt,* pp. 210–12.

27. *National Economist,* March 5, 1892.

28. Hicks, *The Populist Revolt,* p. 226.

29. Hicks, "Farmers' Alliance in North Carolina," pp. 180–81.

30. Goldman, *Rendezvous with Destiny,* p. 49.

31. *Raleigh News and Observer,* September 18 and 21, 1892.

32. Ibid., April 10, 1890.

33. *Caucasian,* July 2, 1892.

34. Hicks, "Farmers' Alliance in North Carolina," p. 182.

35. *Greensboro Daily Record,* May 30, 1892.

36. Simon Delap, *The Populist Party in North Carolina,* Trinity College Historical Papers, ser. 24 (Durham, N.C., 1922), pp. 51–52.

37. *Greensboro Patriot,* August 24, 1892.

38. *Progressive Farmer,* August 23, 1892.

39. Theron Paul Jones, "The Gubernatorial Election of 1892 in North Carolina," (Master's thesis, University of North Carolina, 1949), p. 13; *Raleigh News and Observer,* August 13, 1892.

40. *Union Republican,* September 4, 1890.

41. William A. Mabry, "Negro Suffrage and Fusion Rule in North Carolina," *North Carolina Historical Review* 12 (April 1935) : 83–85.

42. Josephus Daniels, *Tar Heel Editor* (Chapel Hill, N.C., 1939), 455; *Greens-*

boro *Patriot*, September 30, and October 15, 1892.

43. *Caucasian*, September 8, 1892.

44. *Union Republican*, November 3, 1892.

45. Hamilton, *North Carolina since 1860*, p. 241.

46. *Progressive Farmer*, December 13, 1892.

47. See Prologue.

48. Holmes, "Demise of the Colored Farmer's Alliance," p. 193.

49. *Raleigh News and Observer*, October 3, 1898.

50. Ibid., October 31, 1898.

51. *Raleigh News and Observer*, July 31, 1894.

52. Josephus Daniels, *Editor in Politics* (Chapel Hill, N.C., 1941), p. 123.

53. *Caucasian*, August 8, 1894; *Raleigh News and Observer*, August, 9 and 31, 1894.

54. Hamilton, *North Carolina since 1860*, pp. 245–46.

55. *Appleton's Annual Cyclopaedia*, new ser. (New York, 1894), p. 553.

56. Daniels, *Editor in Politics*, p. 126.

57. On March 12, 1885, the Speaker of the House strongly urged all members to remain throughout the last day and invoked the House rules. Accordingly, Middleton, acting under the order of the Speaker was not to let anyone in or out. Later, two members, Capt. R. B. Peebles and W. T. Lee, approached the door and demanded to be let out; however, Middleton held the door fast with both hands. A struggle ensued when several whites sided with Peebles and Lee, and several Blacks rushed to the aid of Middleton. In the midst of the strife, which lasted about a minute, the door flew open. The next day Josephus Daniels featured the incident as "The Crowning Infancy," in the *Raleigh News and Observer*, March 13, 1895.

58. Collins and Goodwin, *Biographical Sketches of the Members of the General Assembly of North Carolina 1895* (Raleigh, N.C., 1895), p. 36.

59. North Carolina *House Journal* (1895), p. 479; *Charlotte Observer*, February 26, 1895; Daniels, *Editor in Politics*, p. 134; Hamilton, *North Carolina since 1860*, p. 242.

60. Florence E. Smith, "The Populist Movement and Its Influence in North Carolina," (Ph. D. diss. University of Chicago, 1929), pp. 127–30. Copy in Library of Congress; on film in University of North Carolina. For a propaganda discussion of the law, see the *Democratic Party Handbook* (Raleigh, N.C., 1898), pp. 84–92.

61. *Union Republican*, February 27, 1896.

62. *Raleigh News and Observer*, October 30, 1896.

63. Ibid., May 16, 1896.

64. Daniels, *Editor in Politics*, p. 153.

65. *Caucasian*, July 9, 1896.

66. Ibid., May 26, 1896.

67. Ibid., July 2 and 3, 1892.

68. Daniels, *Editor in Politics*, p. 155.

69. On educational matters the Populists continued to favor a four-months school term. The Democrats and the Republicans included mild endorsements for educational improvement in their platforms. *Caucasian*, August 20, 1896; Delap. *The Populist Party in North Carolina*, 62–63.

70. Daniels, *Editor in Politics*, pp. 153–55.

71. *Raleigh News and Observer*, September 11, 1896.

72. Philip J. Weaver, "The Gubernatorial Election of 1896 in North Carolina," (Master's thesis, University of North Carolina, 1937), pp. 63–72, 78–79.

73. Hamilton, *North Carolina since 1860*, p. 263.

74. *Biographical Directory of the American Congress, 1774–1927*, (Washington,

D.C., 1928), p. 1690.

75. Samuel D. Smith, *The Negro in Congress, 1870–1901*, (Chapel Hill, N.C., 1940), pp. 125–26.

76. *Congressional Record,* 56th Cong., 1st sess. (1899–1900), p. 1507.

77. *Raleigh News and Observer,* October 20, 1898.

78. Helen Edmonds, *The Negro and Fusion Politics in North Carolina, 1894–1901,* (Chapel Hill, N.C., 1951), pp. 97–134.

79. *Star of Zion,* October 27, 1898.

80. Robert W. Winston, *It's a Far Cry* (New York, 1937), p. 157.

81. Dr. Cyrus Thompson, "Dr. Cyrus Thompson's Great Speech" (Delivered at Clinton, opening of the Populist campaign, August 19, 1898), University of North Carolina Library, Chapel Hill, N.C., pp. 20–21.

82. C. W. Wooley to Ransom, February 19, 1889; James T. Barrett to Ransom, December 14, 1894; R. O. Holt to Ransom, February 18, 1889; Matthew W. Ransom Papers. Southern Historical Collection, University of North Carolina, Chapel Hill, N.C.

83. *Raleigh News and Observer,* October 30, 1898.

84. Nannie G. Fisher to Ransom, December 14, 1894, and B. G. Sedbury to Ransom, December 13, 1894, Ransom Papers.

85. A. B. Caldwell, ed., *History of the American Negro,* North Carolina ed., vol. 4 (Atlanta, Ga., 1921), pp. 851–53.

86. Shepard's father, Dr. August Shepard, was a graduate of Shaw University, a noted minister, founder of an orphanage asylum for Blacks at Oxford, and for twenty years state missionary of the American Baptist Society. Ibid., pp. 425–26.

87. *Who's Who in America,* vol. 23 (1924–45), p. 1921.

88. John Campbell Dancy Collection, Private Papers and Correspondence, Andrew Carnegie Library, Livingston College, Salisbury, N.C.

89. *Star of Zion,* November 10, 1898.

90. Daniels, *Editor in Politics,* p. 337.

91. Collins and Goodwin, *Biographical Sketches,* pp. 52–53.

92. *Raleigh News and Observer,* October 30, 1898.

93. Ibid., February 9 and 22, 1895.

94. North Carolina *House Journal* (1895), p. 140, and (1897), pp. 237, 489; *Public Laws of North Carolina,* 1897, chaps. 142, 197, 207, 321, 348, 492, 778.

95. Hamilton, *North Carolina since 1860,* pp. 274–75.

96. *Literary Digest,* November 26, 1898.

97. George K. Clark, "The Critical Historian," in *The Dimensions of History,* ed. Thomas N. Guinsbury (Chicago, 1971), pp. 9–11.

4

Populism and Public Education

Traditionally, farmers have been portrayed as indifferent and even hostile toward progressive educational ideas. Trapped within a labyrinth of steadily declining agricultural prices, debts, a growing number of farm mortgages, and the deplorable crop-lien system, North Carolina farmers naturally concluded that education had little to offer them in the way of aid with their daily work or solutions to their financial problems. But one thing is clear—such an attitude, together with inadequate schools, certainly serves to encourage and perpetuate an American caste system. This fact was recognized early by socially conscious individuals, both inside and outside the farmers' ranks, who saw illiteracy not only as the foe of a full life but also as the chief cause of poverty. This viewpoint, along with the militant agrarian movements of the eighties and nineties, stirred a demand for better schools for the debt-ridden farmers. Ignatius Donnelly of Minnesota inaugurated the movement on the national scene and favored, among other things, federal support for Southern schools.[1]

The pioneering of the educational cause for farmers in North Carolina began with Charles D. McIver, Edwin A. Alderman, Walter Hines Page, and Leonidas L. Polk. The first three men began their careers while members of the Watauga Club, organized in Raleigh in May 24, 1884.[2] The name *Wataugians* was adapted from the Watauga Association, a group of pioneers who settled in the western part of the state long before the American Revolution. The name had significant meaning to the members, who felt like the early pioneers, struggling to build a new state out of chaos. This unique organization was composed of intellectuals whose social consciences were deeply moved by the poverty and illiteracy that prevailed among the masses. Among the club's charter members were W. J. Peele, Raleigh attorney, civic leader, and founder of the club, and Walter Hines Page, founder and editor of the *State Chronicle* at Raleigh, who later became nationally known as the editor of the *Forum* and the *Atlantic Monthly* and was appointed by Woodrow Wilson to the influential post of ambassador to England. Other outstanding members were John W. Thompson, judge in Wake County and in the Panama Canal; Alfred D. Jones, Democratic leader and consul general to Hong Kong and Shanghai; and Charles W. Dabney, noted educator and later president of the University of Tennessee. Later members included James Y. Joyner, a mainspring of the North Carolina public school movement and future superintendent of public instruction; Philander P. Claxton, a prominent figure of the Tennessee public school movement; and Josephus Daniels, owner and publisher of the *Raleigh News and Observer* and later a member of President Wilson's cabinet. Others were W. E. Ashley, Joseph Brown, Alfred D. Jones, and Edgar Leach.[3] From the Watauga Club sprang that centrifugal group of educators who gave credence to universal education, although at the time North Carolina showed little interest. They believed that educational and industrial training are essential to modern economic development. As youths demanding something new to replace a "perpetual dry rot in education," they placed in the forefront the necessity of founding an agricultural and industrial college and actively campaigned for it. Although the movement lagged, interest was sustained and picked up momentum when farmers became more militant and politically involved during the eighties.[4] This crusade for an agricultural and industrial college was to have a negative impact on the liberal arts state university in North Carolina and elsewhere. In South Carolina, for example, the fiery Ben Tillman rancorously assailed the state university as being a haven for privileged classes and concomitantly demanded that the majority of the state's money available for higher education be appropriated to the newly established agricultural college at Clemson. And when Tillman was governor he deliberately crippled the state university by reducing its appropriations and cutting its faculty from twenty-five to thirteen.[5] A storm of agrarian opposition was to hit the University of North Carolina, but not with such malicious intent as identified with the University of South Carolina.

In North Carolina, the movement toward the establishment of an agricultural and mechanical college was given the necessary momentum with the organization of the Farmers' Alliance. Polk joined forces with W. T. Peele and Alfred D. Jones and promoted the idea in his *Progressive Farmer*. The University of North Carolina enjoyed an annual income of $7,500 (with its meager $20,000 annual appropriation, it certainly needed it) from federal land-scrip fund acquired from the Morrill Act of 1862 for the endowment of agricultural schools. In 1867 this fund of $125,000 was lost in the postwar crash. To compensate the loss of the income, the General Assembly assumed the responsibility of paying interest representing $7,500 to the university. This was done on condition that the institution grant each county the privilege of sending one student free of charge for tuition and room rent. In 1881 there were 166 students, and 89 of them paid no tuition.[6] Nevertheless, Polk accused the university's authorities, headed by President Kemp P. Battle, of perverting the Morrill Act. It should be remembered that this controversy took place during the time the church colleges were leading their attack upon the university. When the Farmers' Alliance met in Raleigh in January 1887, Polk enlisted its forces behind him, which included Elias Carr, Sydenham B. Alexander, and others.[7] Resolutions on the subject were successfully introduced into the legislature. The last land-scrip income of $7,500 was taken away from the university and given to the North Carolina College of Agriculture and Mechanical Arts, established in 1889 at Raleigh.

Alderman and McIver were the two Wataugians, particularly, who stood in the forefront of the educational awakening, beginning with the Farmers' Alliance and continuing during the Populist era.[9] "No two such evangelists of education," Josephus Daniels declared, "have appeared in America, certainly not since the days of Horace Mann." But were forceful speakers, yet contrasted greatly with each other physically and in oratory techniques. Alderman was born May 15, 1861, of "plain middle-class" parents of English and Scotch-Irish stock. He graduated from the University of North Carolina in 1882, where he acquired the art of public speaking. Physically, he was slim, handsome, urbane and "looked every inch an aristocrat." Compared to McIver, it was said that Alderman was "a man of finer culture, quieter in his methods, and an orator of finer restraint."[10] His diction was elegant, careful, and slightly formal, and he had an extraordinary degree of power to charm an audience, formal or informal. After he became president of the University of Virginia, the students nicknamed him "Tony," because the name carried an Italian connotation. The name was given him because of his modish and even sporty clothes.[11]

On the other hand, McIver was shorter and heavier than Alderman. As an orator he was much closer to Stephen A. Douglas, "a steam engine in breeches," or, as characterized by some, a little less than an "unwinding tornado." He was born in Moore County, September 27, 1860. He graduated from the University of North Carolina in 1881, where he was awarded a Greek medal and won honors in French and Latin. He taught in the public and private schools of Durham and Winston-Salem. From 1886 to 1889 he was a professor of English at Peace Institute at Raleigh.[12] McIver was not only a forceful talker, but also a politician and his own personal lobbyist for the causes he advocated. While in Raleigh, he made it his business to know every one of the legislators, and "spent his evenings and nights at the hotels talking to them. . . . He loved to talk, which included telling humorous stories and "had more of them than you can imagine." He was not concerned with the way he formed his sentences and was definitely not in Alderman's class as a polished orator. His greatest assets were his zeal and enthusiasm, which attracted and held the attention of all manner of men. Though very different in their approaches, McIver and Alderman were two influential leaders, and, as a team, "they complemented each other."[13]

North Carolina witnessed the beginning of an educational awakening and revival following their appointment as state conductors of the weekly county Teachers' Institute (1889–92), which has already been noted. "Holding the teachers' institutes," it was said, "was the smallest thing they did." In reality, the two became self-appointed evangelists for North Carolina. Both young crusaders "in their travels, found ignorance in its natural setting—rural poverty, isolation, racial tension." At the same time, they saw the educational problem in a larger context than did most of their colleagues. Yet they "refused to allow its enormity and complexity to discourage them from their efforts to cope with it."[14]

In 1889 Alderman traveled 3,199 miles, conducting thirty institutes that served 1,548 teachers, while McIver did the same.[15] The first four days of the institutes (five hours each day—three in the morning and two in the afternoon) were devoted to teachers. On Friday the institute conductors would hold meetings with the school committeemen of the county, hoping to promote better schools by persuading them to levy local taxes for more school support, longer terms, and better and more women teachers.[16] Saturday, in a special sense, was the "People's Day." The two young men broadened their educational drive and turned each Saturday session into a public school rally. And "on that day one theme only was discussed, the Gospel of Popular Education in all its relations."[17] These educational rallies were something new, and reports spread from county to county about the zeal and eloquence of the two young "Horace

Manns of North Carolina." During his first year as institute conductor, Alderman spoke to approximately twelve thousand people, using the local chapters of the Farmers' Alliances as instruments to stimulate public school sentiment.[18] On October 4, 1889, he spoke to his largest audience, some seven hundred people, in the Union County Courthouse—a meeting that the Farmers' Alliance attended in a body. He addressed similar Alliances in Lincoln and Alexander Counties, and his efforts soon began to bear fruit. For example, one farmer expressed the conviction of many farmers when he said: "We must educate or we must perish." Another farmer, named J. M. Finger, expressed his dissatisfaction with public schools when he wrote: "We pay the sum of $3,000 out of our school fund to support the Superintendent of Public Instruction, why cannot the Board of Education attend to our school needs?"[19] And a delegate to the State Alliance told Alderman, following a large 'educational rally in Alexander County, that the Alliance wanted an increase of 50 percent in school appropriations and that the Democratic party had better shoulder some of the responsibility.[20] While public education was not a major issue among the farmers, Alderman and McIver had made it a lively subject to convince many of them of the need for improvement of educational facilities. Farmer organizations had already placed their support behind the establishment of an agricultural and mechanical college for white males. Education was included among the pledges politicians had to make in order to get Alliance support during the campaign of 1890.[21] The next year the General Assembly was largely controlled by Farmers' Alliance members, whose first important act was the creation of the Railroad Commission. The same legislature also passed a law to increase school taxes 25 percent, which exceeded the constitutional limitations, and the State Supreme Court promptly declared the law unconstitutional.[22] Educationally, the most significant act enacted in 1891 called for the establishment of the Normal and Industrial School for White Women at Greensboro.[23] The following year both Alderman and McIver concluded their careers as conductors of the weekly Teachers' Institute. And, as noted earlier, McIver became president of the women's school, while Alderman went there as a professor for one year.

As pointed out in the preceding chapter, the year 1892 marked the emergence of the Populist party as an independent political party. Included within its platform was a pledge calling for a four-months school term in all counties, as required by the state constitution. The Populists were the first to include such a pledge in their party platform. However, they had not the numbers or the influence necessary to bring about any changes in the school law.

Again in the 1894 campaign, the Populists pledged a four-months school term. With the triumph of Fusion politics, and with a Populist-Republican majority in the legislature, the Populists became the first to attempt to deal constructively with the public education problem. enacting the most progressive legislaion since Reconsruction. A revenue act of 1895 was passed to bring all school terms up to four months. By law, the poll tax remained at $1.29, and the property levy was increased from $.43 to $.46, thus making available an increase of from $.18 to $.20 for education, which was adequate for a state-wide four-months school term.[24] True to its conservative precedents, the state supreme court invalidated the law, because the "constitutional equation between property and poll was therefore destroyed."[25]

Another notable educational law enacted by the Populists was one that sought to remedy the problems of the county school systems by destroying almost completely the administrative organization as it existed under the Democratic regime. To illustrate, the county board of education was abolished and its powers transferred to the chairman of the county board of commissioners. Another law enacted empowered a county examiner to test teacher's qualifications and to select textbooks. These changes, like the new County Election Law, were intended to place responsibility for the above school functions in the hands of the county commissioners, who were elected by the people. Yet their actions constituted a step backward. As one writer concluded, "The Populists must have had good intentions in regard to this law, but their knowledge of school administration was limited." They lacked at this time sufficiently experienced, intelligent leaders able to draw up an efficient and effective public school law.[26]

It should be recalled that the Republicans later filled in the three vacant spots in their 1896 slate with Populist condidates, who endorsed Charles H. Mebane as state superintendent of public instruction. The Fusion triumph in this year swept this competent Populist educator into office. He was born in Guilford County on October 21, 1862, and attended both common and private schools. After teaching for six years, he enrolled at Catawba College at Newton, where he "cut wood, swept floors and did any honorable work to pay his way in school." He finally graduated in 1892—at the age of twenty-nine—with an outstanding academic record. He was appointed to the faculty and the following year elected professor of Greek and history.[27] Mebane was not a politician nor had he had previous experience as an educational lobbyist. "I have taken no active part," he wrote, "in any campaigns." In this respect, he differed from some of his predecessors. It was his special objective, true to Populist equalitarian credo, to bring the office "closer in touch with people and remove the office and its duties as far as possible from partisan politics."[28]

Mebane was a progressive educator. He knew that the duties of the superintendent extended far beyond furnishing forms to local school officials for records and for the preparation of statistics. He was definitely acquainted with the county educational problems, and some of his recommendations cut deep into old abuses. He proposed radical changes in local school administration, and was especially adamant in his denunciation of the rigid economy practiced by the county board of education.[29] A progressive and a reformer at heart, he argued cogently that local taxation was the soul of the public school system.[30] And concomitantly, he argued for some form of compulsory attendance law to combat poor school attendance and the abuse of child labor. Superintendent Mebane also recommended the establishment of a state textbook commission with the power to adopt a list of texbooks, and the consolidation of seven Negro schools concluded earlier to be a waste of state money, into three.[31]

The progressive educational talents of Mebane were demonstrated during the 1897 session of the legislature. He was the chief architect behind the Populists' outstanding educational statutes. Under his leadership, the Populists sought to repeal all educational measures of the 1895 session that had "proven to be boomerangs" by passing on March 6 "an act to revise and improve the public school system of North Carolina." This act,' in effect, restored the county school system to its former organization.[32] Still trying to secure enough money to operate a four-months school term in all counties, and again testing the old Barksdale decision, Mebane and public school friends successfully pushed through a law to increase property taxes beyond the constitutional limitations—of $.46 per one hundred dollars of property. Basing its decision on the Barksdale doctrine, the state supreme court declared the act unconstitutional.[33]

Dismayed and concluding that the court would not budge, some educational forces were strongly in favor of making a one-hundred-thousand-dollar appropriation to the public schools, but this measure brought opposition, especially from Alderman and McIver. They suggested an appropriation based upon local taxation.[34] Since 1892, Alderman had become president of the University of North Carolina. His and McIver's major concern, naturally, was to obtain increased appropriations for their institutions. Nevertheless, they did promise friends of the public schools and legislators that they would work for a bill designed to stimulate school districts to willingly vote taxation beyond state constituional limits.

Accordingly, the educational forces began to fashion an appropriations act based upon the principle of local taxation. State Superintendent Mebane wrote the original bill. In its final form, it required an election to be held in the subsequent August in every school district of the state to determine whether a special tax, of at least $.10 on each one-hundred-dollar valuation of property, should be levied for the purpose of prolonging the school term. It also required the county commissioners to hold an election every two years in the districts that failed to vote the tax until a special school tax was levied, and the special tax could only be repealed after three years by a majority vote of qualified voters. Finally, none of the provisions of the act applied to any city, town or school district that was already levying a special tax of as much as $.10 on each one-hundred-dollar valuation of property and $.30 on every poll, and all laws in conflict with the act were repealed. The sum of fifty thousand dollars was appropriated to the state board of education to match the special tax collected each year until the sum was exhausted, but no district was to receive more than five hundred dollars annually.[35]

To push the proposed bill, Mebane spoke before the committee and at one time saved it when neither Alderman nor McIver was present. At this time they were pushing for the appropriation for their own institutions. The bill passed easily in the Populist-dominated House, but in the Senate it met rough sailing. For several days its fate was doubtful in the Senate. "While Mebane and other friends of the public schools struggled to get the measure to a vote, Alderman and McIver came down from Chapel Hill and Greensboro respectively to lend their rare oratorical skills and "stayed until this bill was passed."[36] Ironically, it was finally carried almost unanimously in the Senate. The "Act to Encourage Local Taxation" became a law on March 9, 1897, and, in Alderman's opinion, "was one of the wisest laws ever passed in North Carolina, for which no one can claim credit."[37]

To give impetus to the act, its proponents planned an extensive educational campaign to promote local tax elections scheduled in August. McIver's thoughts turned to Walter Hines Page, one of his greatest sources of inspiration since their Watauga days. He recalled the urbane and erudite Page, then editor of the *Atlantic Monthly*, to be a long champion of universal education and a forceful speaker. Accordingly, he wrote, urging him to come home and deliver the commencement address at the women's college at Greensboro. "We are just going into a great educational campaign," McIver told Page, ". . . [and] no people on earth have ever become an educated people without a local tax for school purposes." He also asked him to emphasize in his address "what North Carolina has missed because of her illiteracy and . . . what she has to gain by adopting a liberal educational policy.[38] Later he informed Page that such an address would make a "very effective appeal to the institution's four hundred students, representing every nook and corner of the state" and urge them to unite in this patriotic effort by championing the principle of local school taxation in their respective communities.[39] McIver had the notion of giving the campaign an early stimulus and wide publicity by identifying it with this controversial figure.

"Walter Hines Page! The very name was exclamatory!"[40] In 1883 Page established the *State Chronicle* at Raleigh, first as a weekly and later as a daily. He nurtured a dream of "infusing a breath of fresh air into North Carolina's rich resources in climate, soil, materials, and sound population, which he maintained should be devoted to creating an agricultural and industrial self-sufficient state. Concomitantly, he prevailed upon the people to turn their backs on a past with which they had been too preoccupied, for Page could not consider as "lost" a war that had preserved the Union. Thus, he severely criticized men who thought and talked of nothing but things before the Civil War. He referred to "before-the-War" things as "mummies." Likewise, he dubbed the old ladies who spent their time writing poetry and organizing societies to build monuments in honor of Confederate heroes as "the little sisters of the dead." As might be expected, his beratement "wounded some very sacred cows." Page later concluded that three "ghosts" were responsible for preventing Southern progress: "the Ghost of the Confederate Dead; Ghost of Religious Orthodoxy; and the Ghost of Negro Domination."[41] Southern romanticism during the era was indeed a powerful ideal; in fact, it was a cult. Naturally, whites did not enjoy being reminded of their defeated heroes. Their vanquished era had become a mirror that reflected the recent Civil War. In the final analysis, "Page made people mad—with him and themselves."[42] He soon found himself in conflict with his environment, for he was not a part of its "Bonds of Mind and Spirit." Moreover, the Southland, as others were to discover, was not a fertile ground for literary figures. After his flirtation with the role of critic of Southern romanticism, Page became a forerunner of the writers who later deserted the New South.

The *State Chronicle* failed to be a profitable enterprise. So Page deserted his native state, "dead broke," to look for a paying position on a New York paper. He soon became a successful "transplanted Yankee" journalist. Within ten years he put the *Forum* on its feet and later became editor of the *Atlantic Monthly*. By this time he was a nationally known figure within literary circles. When the news of his proposed visit to North Carolina began to circulate, "tongues wagged"—some most apprehensively over what this controversial individual might say.

As the principal commencement speaker at the Normal and Industrial College for Women at Greensboro, and having an editorial gift for coining unique titles, Page called his address "The Forgotten Man"; it was full of touches of "very high eloquences."[43] The "Forgotten Man" was the neglected and illiterate white man; one out of every four who was wholly forgotten, because he was unable to read and write (while Page did not mention him, the Black man was included). Even more tragic, he reminded his audience, were the "forgotten women," who existed by the thousands—"thin and wrinkled in youth from ill-prepared food, and without warmth or grace, living in untidy houses, working from daylight to bedtime at dull, weary duties, the slaves of men of equal slovenliness, the mothers of joyless children—all uneducated if not illiterate."[44] He told his audience that the state was controlled by a little aristocracy, which had failed in its social and economic philosophy. He also assailed the aristocratic idea of education as an old relic of the past that had bypassed both the forgotten man and woman. He went on to charge the stump and pulpit as the chief backward influences, since both the politician and the preacher had failed to improve the conditions of the masses after a century of unobstructed opportunities. In conclusion, he emphasized that it was time for wiser statesmanship to take the leadership in educational matters and develop a "public school system supported by public sentiment and generously maintained by both state and local taxation." Such was the only effective medium, he assured his audience, "to develop the forgotten man and even more surely, the only means to develop the forgotten woman."[45]

Page's eloquent and provocative address lasted one hour, while his audience gave rapt attention. It was followed by a standing ovation of some three minutes. "Thus Page nailed his thesis upon the doors of his native state," wrote his biographer. Newspapers printed it word for word, and great were the repercussions. Page was "damned and praised" and excoriated in some circles as a "renegade," a "Southern Yankee," and a sacrilegious intruder who had dared to visit his home state and desecrate its traditions and religion.[46] In contrast, the more intelligent citizens accepted his candid description of education as an unquestionable social ill, to be eradicated only by constructive management. From the *Raleigh News and Observer* came this eloquent editorial: "Mr. Page owes his position to the fact that he has made himself a leader among leaders. . . . It took him fifteen years to write the speech. It was the result of many years of reflection. . . . He believes so firmly that the doctrines he expounded are based on eternal truth that, having sown the seed, he will await with confidence the day of harvesting."[47] Meanwhile, the Greensboro address made its way across every Southern state, welcomed by educational leaders who were to employ its spirit and philosophy in future campaigns for the redemption of the "Forgotten

Man." Moreover, the local newspaper carried long extracts of the address in the places where local campaigns were scheduled.[48]

Despite the pros and cons of this "great speech," Page had indeed played his role of educational statesman well and returned to the North. An educational awakening was in the making, engendered by forces set on redemption of the "Forgotten Man." And the first objective was promotion of the recent Populist election law. An extensive educational campaign was planned for local tax elections scheduled for August. Early in July the friends of the public schools organized a local tax committee, with Superintendent Mebane as chairman. Members included such individuals as Josiah Bailey, editor of the *Biblical Recorder*; McIver; editor Daniels; ex-Superintendent John C. Scarborough; and Professor Hugh Marson. Subcommittees were sought in the respective counties, and political figures—as the future Governor Aycock, ex-Governor Thomas J. Jarvis, and Republican Jeter C. Pritchard—agreed to serve. Finally, some fifty leading citizens signed their names to an address on behalf of the tax.[49]

In this campaign, Bailey had charge of the propaganda literature, which was widely circulated. Meanwhile, Jarvis and others went on a campaign tour to drum up local stump speakers for the cause. Speaking before an enthusiastic assembly at Chapel Hill, McIver informed his listeners of the public apathy on the eve of the August election. Speaking from experience, the veteran campaigner ventured to lecture on the negative educational sentiments one could encounter: "I don't," he listed first, "believe in the principle of taxing one man to educate another man's children." He went on to cite other familiar arguments, which included "poverty of the people," the Negro question, and "the unconstitutionality of the act."[50] It was not long before these negative seniments began to echo through the press.

The *Raleigh News and Observer* wrote auspicious editorials at the beginning of the campaign, but, as Bailey later recalled, many papers that were advocates of the tax suddenly changed fronts.[51] *The News and Observer* reflected its change in policy by featuring opposition Letters to the Editor. From the Black Belt of Hertford County echoed an adamant voice: "No need of an educational revival." Thomas A. Boone of that county claimed that the local tax was to educate the Negro race, while white people paid the taxes and urged that "we must vote against the tax."[52] Naturally, the large landholders who depended upon Black labor looked upon the tax with abomination. Then there were inquiries as to whether white districts might vote the tax on a racial division. There were also those who opposed taxation on general principles. Finally, the constitutionality of the 1897 local tax law was called into question. Opponents hoped that the state supreme court would declare it unconstitutional and "asked for a speedy decision."[53] But this time the court remained neutral.

The campaign did, however, bring forth voices defending the tax. Z. V. Welser of Davidson County believed it to be "the greatest piece of legislation put on the statute books in the present century." Some people opposed an increase in taxes, but supported this tax to give the back country an equal chance for education. In campaigning, ex-Governor Jarvis emphasized: "Educate All the People."[54] In the meantime, Superintendent Mebane on July 19 sent a special circular to all county superintendents requesting them personally to do all that they could "to carry the coming elections for schools." "We have had a considerable space devoted to show our ignorance, etc.," he wrote, "but our zeal rises with opposition . . . for the local tax."[55]

According to the laws of 1897, the special school taxation elections were held on the Tuesday after the second Monday in August. Despite the educational significance of Page's "The Forgotten Man" speech, the wide circulation of propaganda literature, and the extensive campaigns for local taxation, only eleven districts voted for the special tax, raising a mere $2,260 in revenue.[56] Ironically, the campaign itself cost between $12,000 and $15,000. Democrats and other critics of the local tax bill went around the state asserting it cost $65,000. Bailey blamed this dismal result on racism. While he did not say it, such opposition paralleled earlier negative reaction to the Blair bill. Whites, while opposing education for Blacks, inevitably denied it for their own children. Bailey explained: "The reason universally given for refusing to vote this tax was that it would help the Negroes as much as the whites. I may cite the instance of one man with six children to educate, whose extra tax would not have amounted to fifty cents, who refused for this reason to vote for it."[57] There were many persons, especially in the counties controlled by Democrats, who undoubtedly did not understand the act. Democrats withheld their support or discouraged the movement because the measure was enacted by the Fusion parties and because the schools were made a "football of politics."

Nevertheless, at the turn of the twentieth century, forces in operation opened the way for educational progress. In 1902 a great educational movement, "A Crusade against Ignorance," exploded throughout the South. Ironically, its origin, impetus, and leadership came from North Carolina. While the Populists were promoting the futile educational campaign of 1897, the Democrats were concentrating on the approaching election of 1898 and on strategies for returning their party to power, and to this theme our attention is now directed.

Notes

1. Merle Curti, *The Social Ideas of American Educators* (New York, 1935), pp. 213–14.

2. Burton J. Hendrick, *The Life and Letters of Walter Hines Page* (New York, 1923), pp. 46–47, and Charles W. Dabney, *Universal Education in the South* (Chapel Hill, N.C., 1936), 1: 182–89. A year earlier, a young group of intellectuals, including George Bernard Shaw, Henry G. Wells, and Sidney and Beatrice Webb established the Fabian Society. It could be logically argued that they were the English counterpart of the young Wataugians. They adopted their name from the ancient Roman general Quintus Fabius Maximus. While their ultimate goal was different from that of the Wataugians, they championed social and economic measures that would bring political democracy for the dispossessed masses. Edward R. Pease, *A History of the Fabian Society* (London, 1925), pp. 14–55.

3. Josephus Daniels, *Tar Heel Editor* (Chapel Hill, N.C., 1939), p. 465.

4. David Lockmiller, *History of the North Carolina State College of Agriculture and Engineering of the University of North Carolina* (Raleigh, N.C., 1939), pp. 21–49.

5. Francis B. Simkins, *Pitchfork Ben Tillman: South Carolinian* (Baton Rouge, La., 1944), pp. 93–95, 176–77.

6. Luther T. Gobbel, *Church-State Relationships in North Carolina since 1776* (Durham, N.C., 1938), pp. 92–98.

7. Clarence Poe, "L. L. Polk: A Great Agrarian Leader in a Fifty Year Perspective," *South Atlantic Quarterly* (October 1902): 409–15.

8. *Public Laws of North Carolina*, 1889, chap. 105.

9. Henry M. Wagstaff, *Impression of Men and Movement at the University of North Carolina,* ed. Louis R. Wilson (Chapel Hill, N.C., 1950), p. 67.

10. Hendrick, *Life and Letters of Walter Hines Page*, p. 74.

11. Dumas Malone, *Edwin A. Alderman* (New York, 1940), pp. 79–81.

12. Rose Howell Holder, *McIver of North Carolina* (Chapel Hill, N.C., 1957), pp. 80–113; Charles L. Coon, "Charles Duncan McIver and His Educational Services, 1886–1906," in *United States Bureau of Education* (Washington, D.C., 1908), p. 339.

13. Daniels, *Tar Heel Editor,* pp. 457–58.

14. Louis R. Harlan, *Separate and Unequal: Public School Campaigns and Racism in the Southern Seaboard States, 1901–1915* (Chapel Hill, N.C., 1958), p. 46.

15. Edwin A. Alderman, "Reports of the Institute Conductors," in *Biennial School Report,* 1889–90, pt. 2, p. 1.

16. Ibid., pp. 7–11.

17. Harlan, *Separate and Unequal,* p. 48.

18. Daniels, *Tar Heel Editor,* pp. 370–71; Alderman, "Reports of the Institute Conductors," pp. 3–4.

19. *Progressive Farmer,* September 9 and 16, 1890.

20. Clement Eaton, "Edwin A. Alderman—Liberal of the New South," *North Carolina Historical Review* 23 (April 1946): 213.

21. See chap. 3.

22. Samuel H. Thompson, "The Legislative Development of Public School Support in North Carolina" (Ph.D. diss., University of North Carolina, 1936), p. 309.

23. *Public Laws of North Carolina,* 1891, chap. 139, secs. 1, 5, 7. During this legislative session, provisions were made for the establishment of the Agriculture

and Technical College for Blacks at Greensboro.

24. Ibid., 1895, chap. 116.

25. Thompson, "Legislative Development of Public School Support," p. 318; Harlan, *Separate and Unequal*, p. 52.

26. Simon Delap, *The Populist Party in North Carolina*, Trinity College Historical Papers, ser. 24 (Durham, N.C., 1922), pp. 58–59.

27. David K. Eliades, "The Educational Services and Contributions of Charles H. Mebane, Superintendent of Public Instruction 1897–1901," (Master's thesis, East Carolina University, Grenville, 1963), pp. 8–10.

28. *Biennial School Report*, 1896–98, pp. 47–49.

29. Amory D. Mayo, "The Final Establishment of the Common School System in North Carolina, South Carolina and Georgia, 1863–1900," in *Report of the United States Commission of Education*, 1903, 1: 1905, 1017–18.

30. *Biennial School Report*, 1896–98, pp. 13–14, 46–47.

31. Ibid., 1898–1900, pp. 11–13, 16–17.

32. *Public Laws of North Carolina*, 1897, chap. 108.

33. Edgar W. Knight, *Public Education in North Carolina* (New York, 1916), p. 325, and Thompson, "Legislative Development of Public School Support," pp. 325–27.

34. Gobbel, *Church-State Relationships*, p. 194 n.

35. *Public Laws of North Carolina* 1897, chap. 421, secs. 3, 4, 5.

36. *Raleigh News and Observer*, March 10, 1897.

37. "Facts About the University," an editorial in Alderman's scrapbook, Edwin Alderman Papers, Alderman Library, University of Virginia, Charlottesville, Va.

38. McIver to Page, April 15, 1897, Walter Hines Page Papers, Houghton Library, Harvard University, Cambridge, Mass.

39. McIver to Page, April 27, 1897, Page Papers.

40. Peter M. Wilson, *Southern Exposure* (Chapel Hill, N.C., 1927), p. 171.

41. Hendrick, *Life and Letters of Walter Hines Page*, pp. 40–44, 91.

42. Holder, *McIver of North Carolina*, p. 62.

43. Hendrick, *Life and Letters of Walter Hines Page*, pp. 74–75.

44. Walter Hines Page, *The Rebuilding of Old Commonwealths* (New York, 1902), pp. 11–24.

45. Ibid., p. 26.

46. Hendrick, *Life and Letters of Walter Hines Page*, pp. 79–83.

47. *Raleigh News and Observer*, May 19, 1897.

48. McIver to Page, July 22, 1897, Page Papers.

49. *Raleigh News and Observer*, July 2, 1897.

50. Ibid., July 10, 1892.

51. Josiah W. Bailey, "Popular Education and the Race Problem in North Carolina," *Outlook*, May 11, 1901, pp. 114–15.

52. *Raleigh News and Observer*, July 27 and 28, 1897.

53. Ibid., July 14, 1897.

54. Ibid., July 11 and 28, 1897.

55. Superintendent Charles H. Mebane, "To the County Supervisor of Public Schools," July 19, 1897, in *Biennial School Report*, 1896–98, p. 74–75.

56. Ibid., pp. 42, 134.

57. Bailey, "Popular Education," p. 115.

5

White Supremacy Drama of 1898: Theme—"Black Domination"

The North Carolina political campaign of 1898 was unparalleled in American history. It was not a' gubernatorial election, but rather a roaring crusade for the choice of a new General Assembly with a Democratic majority, which adds an interesting dimension to the drama. There were numerous giant political rallies, parades, and sometimes mammoth picnics and fireworks spectacles; it was, indeed, a study in rustic politics and pageantry. The Democrats fielded the most picturesque "Red Shirt" brigades. Even the fiery "Pitchfork" Benjamin Tillman came up from South Carolina to address thousands of North Carolinians. Moreover, this was the year of the Spanish-American War. "Remember the Maine," reflected an enthusiastic and jingo spirit throughout the nation. If the famous Compromise of 1877 were the "politics of reconciliation," generally historians are in agreement that American patriotism toward the Spanish-American War truly demonstrated that the South had finally accepted the decision handed down at Appomattox. In North Carolina, nevertheless, the war occupied a secondary place to the white supremacy campaign of 1898. Especially was it relegated to that position by the *Raleigh News and Observer* and by many leading Democrats. Perhaps ex-Governor Jarvis expressed public sentiment when he said: "Imperialism, it will cut no figure whatsoever, we are too much interested in home affairs to discuss the fate of the Philippines."[1]

The Populist revolt of the nineties presented the Democratic party of North Carolina with its greatest crisis since Reconstruction. It was demonstrated in chapter 3 how a combination of Republicans and Populist forces (fusionism) abetted by a formidable bloc of votes by Blacks captured control of the General Assembly in 1894 and topped the feat by electing a Republican governor in 1896. This political upheaval resulted in a Democratic resurgence aimed at returning that party to power, with Democrats employing all means politically expedient to accomplish this objective. In pursuit of this goal, they were forced to improvise machinery for reaching the voters and consolidating their support, while tapping all centers of influence within the electorate, including private, nonpartisan associations, which could be attracted to their cause. At the same time, they realized that they had to create a star candidate with enough public magnetism to attract en masse admirers and dedicated followers. The Democrats successfully put all these forces together and inaugurated the emotional white supremacy campaign of 1898. It was aided by a press carrying sensational articles and racist cartoons of vilification, while the political orators fulminated from the rostrum and stumps the clichés "Negro Domination," "Negro Rule," and "Fusion Corruption." There also appeared White Supremacy Clubs and the "Red Shirts," a Southern symbol of terrorism—mounted men attired in red shirts, and armed with Winchesters, shotguns, and even pistols.

The political drama of 1898, as the Democratic leaders resolved, was one of redemption, calling for the restoration of good government and white supremacy in North Carolina. This weighty task fell upon the shoulders of the adroit, shrewd, and calculating Furnifold M. Simmons, chairman of the State Democratic Executive Committee. One of his contemporaries spoke of him as the grandest statesman that North Carolina has produced in half a century.[2] He was recognized as "a genius in putting everybody to work—men who could write, men who could speak, and men who could ride—the last by no means the least important." He was author of both the white supremacy drama and its theme song, and also stage manager. Simmons was born on January 20, 1850, in Jones County, near Pollocksville, on an ancestral estate of more than one thousand acres and more than one hundred slaves. He entered Wake Forest College in 1868 and early became a college dropout. In 1870 he enrolled at Trinity College, then located near High Point in Randolph County, and graduated three years later, the youngest and the second best student in the class. He studied law privately, assisted by his brother's attorney, Albert Gallatin Hubbard, described as "a man of great learning." Young Simmons was admitted to the bar in 1875, some seventeen days before he reached the legal age of twenty-one. He set up practice in New Bern and was successful in both civil and criminal cases.[3] He entered politics as early as 1874 and was elected to Congress in 1886, but failed in his bid for reelection in 1888, against his Black opponent—Henry P. Cheatham. The Democrats were forced to drop him as a candidate for Congress in 1890 because he refused to sign a pledge of the Farmers' Alliance to support their demands. In expressing his opposition, he explained: "Gentlemen, I am sorry I cannot sign your pledge. Some of your demands are unconstitutional; others are unwise, even dangerous."[4] In 1892 he was a delegate to the State Democratic Convention, and in the summer of that year, to his surprise, he received a telegram notifying him of his appointment as chairman of the State Democratic Executive Committee.

Chairman Simmons was fully aware that his party faced defeat in the ensuing 1898 election unless the campaign was waged on some issue that would cut through party lines. Southern political history had long demonstrated that the question of Negro participation in politics was a "smoldering flame which could easily be fanned into a full one." Accordingly, he decided to make "Negro Rule" and "White Supremacy" the watchwords upon which to return the Democrats to power. Concomitantly, charges of corruption, scandals, and extravagance were to be leveled against the Republican-Populist regime, but these were to be given secondary consideration. The campaign was to be centered around the issue of Blacks sharing in government. The color line would be so sharply drawn that finally little else would be talked about politically. All the charges made against Fusion rule were made dependent upon the participation of the Negro in politics.[5] All whites were expected to take sides, particularly the Democratic side, in the coming campaign. The only middle ground was confidential conversation and, best of all, silence.

Simmons bypassed the old Democratic personalities and recruited an aggressive, colorful, and dynamic group of young actors from each of the state's two extreme sections—the Carolina Highlands and the Coastal Plain. They included editor Josephus Daniels of the *Raleigh News and Observer,* later appointed secretary of the navy in President-elect Wilson's cabinet, and future governors Charles B. Aycock, 1900–1904; Robert Glenn, 1904–8; William W. Kitchin, 1908–12; and Locke Craig, 1912–16, from the mountain city of Asheville, whose racism was engendered by a "boyhood on a Black Belt farm." Other outstanding members were Claude Kitchin, brother of William; Henry G. Connor, speaker of the State House of Representatives, 1900–1902, and later associate justice appointed by President Taft; Walter Clark, associate justice on the state supreme court, and candidate for the United States Senate in 1912; Cameron Morrison, the champion of the distillers and, according to Chairman Simmons, "the grandest statesman that North Carolina has ever produced"; George Rountree, outstanding legal attorney; and Francis D. Winston, judge and lieutanant governor, 1904–8. In essence, the older leadership of the party was rejected and now replaced with a "younger and more progressive" group of leaders who "talked of a new day in North Carolina."[6] The majority of the young men were lawyers, representing diversified economic views. For example, the State Democratic Executive Committee was comprised of thirty-six members, and thirty-three of them were lawyers, of which twenty-four were retainers for the railroad interests.[7] But one thing was certain: all were apostles of white supremacy, prepared to rebuild the Democratic party on the "basis of a middle-class appeal."

Excluding Simmons, at this time the most outstanding actor was editor Daniels of the *Raleigh News and Observer*. The entire state of North Carolina was the stage for the Democratic drama of 1898. The *News and Observer* not only was the stage impromptu, but also its voice and publicity organ, and it was relied upon to carry the Democratic theme and "to be the militant voice of White Supremacy and it did not fail in what was expected." At the same time, there were volunteer correspondents, vigilantes who were keen to watch every movement in every county and district and telegraph or telephone Daniels of a Republican or Fusionist conference that was in progress. Moreover, he planted spies in Republican and Fusionist meetings, thus, whatever the Fusionists did leaked out and the *News and Observer* would print it the next morning. "Day and night we worked," Daniels later recalled. "I rarely went home until two or three o'clock in the morning, getting news and writing the editorials and conferring with Democratic leaders."[8] He was ably assisted by other Democratic papers, such as the *Charlotte Observer,* the *Greensboro Patriot,* the *Wilmington Morning Star,* the *Fayetteville Observer,* and others. Frequently, he even printed supplements for the Democratic papers of the state. He had already established a weekly newspaper at Raleigh, *The North Carolinian,* and it had played an active role in the Democratic victory of 1892. However, the paper was losing money.[9] Nonetheless, he employed it to a greater extent in the 1898 campaign. On one occasion he printed one hundred thousand copies of one issue and sent them to County and State Democratic Committees to influence white people toward the Democratic theme. And whenever there was an attack upon the Republican party or the Populist party for any gross crime on the part of Blacks, Daniels printed it in yellow journalism style.

While the stage was being set for the drama of 1898, its theme was publicly advertised after the meeting of the Democratic Executive Committee in Raleigh on November 30, 1897. In "an eloquent address," Francis D. Winston of Bertie County called upon all whites to unite and "reestablish Anglo-Saxon rule and honest government in North Carolina." He reported that evil times had followed as a consequence of turning over local offices to Blacks: "Homes have been invaded, and the sanctity of woman endangered. Business has been paralyzed and property rendered less valuable. The majesty of law has been disregarded and lawlessness encouraged." Such conditions were "wrought by a combination of Republican and Populist leaders." The Democratic party promised to correct these abuses and to restore security once more to the "white women of the state." To accomplish these ends, a clarion call to action was sounded: "Let every patriot rally to the white man's party. To your tents: Oh Israel."[10] Hence, the heroes of this drama were to be the Democrats, the saviors and new redeemers, who would rescue the state from the villains, the hordes of corruptionists,—namely, the Republican-Fusionist regime.

In answer to such allegations as the ones listed above, the Populists warned the people that "the Democratic machine is crying 'nigger' with the purpose of diverting the attention of the people from it. Do you see?" In the meantime, the Populists were the first to stage a convention for the political alignment of 1898, assembling on May 17 at Raleigh. It quickly became evident that two factions were at work over what course to take in the ensuing campaign. Harry Skinner, leader of the "bolters" in 1896, along wih A. S. Pease and Otha Wilson, favored fusion with the Republicans, despite the charge of "Negro Rule." Seeking to avoid identification with the Republicans, the "regulars," led by Marion Butler, Dr. Cyrus Thompson, and Hal W. Ayer, desired to proclaim white supremacy and fuse with the Democrats. The Butler faction triumphed, "with overtures to be made to the Democrats."[11] Meanwhile, the Populists proceeded as an independent party, fashioning a platform somewhat identical to the previous one, which included the "demand" for improving, broadening and revising the present school system to increase its efficiency.[12]

When the Democrats met for their convention in Raleigh on May 26, they were well aware of the rumor of a Populist-Democratic Fusion. Many prominent Democrats, including editor Daniels, favored cooperation with the Populists. White-supremacy advocate ex-Governor Jarvis gave support to the movement when he presented a letter from the Populist Conference Committee, which gave details for cooperation between the Democratic party and the "People's Party" in the coming campaign. The proposition for fusion submitted by the Populists was "respectfully declined," which no doubt embarrassed Dr. Thompson, sitting in the gallery as a spectator.[13] Next, the Democrats proceeded to fashion a rather progressive platform, which included a clause for the improvement of public schools. It is needless to point out that the platform was a declaration of white supremacy and a condemnation of the Republican party and Negro domination.[14]

Blacks' continued disillusionment with the Republican party merits mention before we look into the Republican Convention. As one malcontent put it, "We are not getting enough of the pie." Black Republican leaders objected to the giving of the majoriy of offices to white Republicans, who represented only 30,000 voters, compared to 120,000 Negro voters. Their discontentment led to the calling of a Black caucus at Raleigh on November 3, 1897, at which time the Lincoln Republican League was formed. Its purpose was "to promote the interests of the Republican Party and secure to Colored Republicans their just and proper recognition." Outstanding delegates included Dr. Aaron McDuffie Moore of Durham, who opened the convention, and Rev. W. H. R. Leak of Raleigh, elected chairman of the Executive Committee. An invitation was not extended to James H. Young, for it was feared "to do so would have been a special invitation (to him) to take a prominent seat in the convention."[15]

During the conference militant speeches and resolutions were made and radical measures adopted. "There is a great fight in the world between capital and labor," declared one radical delegate, "and both white and black must recognize it and take steps accordingly." Nurturing a view similar to that presented earlier by Tom Watson to the Georgia Populists, he emphasized that the interests of the poor white and the Negro were the same and that both should come to recognize that fact.[16] The most militant speech was delivered by J. F. Koger of Reidsville. He told the delegates that the Republican party had betrayed its principles and promises and "drawn the color line." He called upon his Black brothers to vote for no man who was opposed to giving the Negro full recognition. As at the Southern Alliance in 1890, resolutions were finally adopted avowing that in the future, before any man was nominated, Blacks should exact a written pledge that he would "give half his clerical force to the Colored Republicans, and all nominees must give a pledge in favor of Negro education." "We shall see," Blacks warned, "that those colored men who are willing to trade their offices off for offices shall not be nominated by us."[17] To sum up, Black political leaders were demanding more public offices. The paradox here was that, at the same time, Democratic leaders were claiming that Blacks held too many positions, leading to the charge of "Negro Rule."

Thus, when the Republican Convention finally met on July 20 in Raleigh, the party had to reckon with dissident Black delegates, attending in larger numbers "than any other time," while the Democratic orators were already fulminating from rostrums and stumps the clichés "Negro Rule" and "Black Domination." "Negroes Exalted," wrote Daniels in his paper. He also called the assembly a variegated crazy quilt, from the "red face" of Charles A. Cook to the "black face" of Abe Middleton and from the "white face of James H. Young, dressed out spic and span in his fall regimentals of social equality, to the ginger cake color of John C. Dancy." The Negro delegates were demanding "more of the pie," meaning a fairer distribution of the offices.[18] By this time the *News and Observer* had already saturated the state with its propaganda. Second Congressional District Negro Congressman George H. White, a most effective speaker, took the *News and Observer* to task and brought the Negro delegation to its feet when he said: "I am not the only Negro who holds office. There are others. There are plenty now being made to order to hold offices. We don't hold as many as we will. The Democrats talk about the color line and the Negroes holding office. I invite the issue."[19] To be sure, this burst of eloquence offered no comfort to the conservative white Republicans, especially the lily-white faction, already cringing from the identification of their party with Black politicians. Ignoring the Democrats' charges, the party proceeded to formulate a platform, while making no reference to fusion with the Populists.[20]

With the close of the Republican Convention, three separate parties had entered the campaign of 1898. The Democrats had the advantage not only of a cast of talented campaign orators but also of finances from powerful business and industrial interests. To secure the necessary campaign funds, Democratic Chairman Simmons had ex-Governor Jarvis visit the bankers, railroad officials, and manufacturers of the state to solicit contributions. These commercial and industrial leaders were informed of the intolerable conditions prevailing under the Fusion regime, ant it was stressed to them that the Democrats possessed no penchant for populism. Jarvis also promised that in the event of a Democratic victory, "their taxes would not be increased during the next biennium." "From these economic leaders and Democrats of lesser means," Simmons later wrote, "I obtained all the campaign funds I needed."[21] Secret trading was also carried on by Simmons and Jarvis with religious figures of commanding influence, including John C. Kilgo, president of the Methodist Trinity College; Josiah W. Bailey, editor of the Baptist organ, the *Biblical Recorder*; and Rev. John E. White, the influential secretary of the Baptist State Convention. An agreement was reached that called for these religious leaders to "throw their influence toward victory for white supremacy." For their support, Simmons promised to see that the legislature of 1899 did not increase the biennial appropriations for the state university and colleges.[22] As a result of this behind-the-scenes diplomacy, the white supremacy campaign renewed the rivalry between the denominational and state higher institutions, which up to this point had been moving toward a modus vivendi.[23] Leaders of the Democratic party expected ministers to do their share, in the traditional manner, to redeem North Carolina from the sins of Fusionism and to help restore Anglo-Saxon rule to government. They logically reasoned that two of "the cardinal principles of Democracy" were the "Christian religion" and "white supremacy."[24] However, the degree of enthusiasm with which the clergy would "meddle in politics" varied from silence and reluctance to active participation. The giant political rallies in many instances opened and closed with a prayer by a local minister.[25] As in slavery times, Rev. T. H. Leavitte of Fayetteville "resurrected the Biblical arguments" to justify white supremacy. Likewise, Rev. V. L. Stringfield supported Daniels's racist propaganda. Speaking to the King's Mountain Baptist Association, he contended that "not one twentieth of the horrors of negro domination had been published in the papers."[26] It is safe to assume that many ministers, behind the smoke-screened rhetoric of their sermons, used the pulpit to urge their congregation to vote for the Democratic party.

Attention is directed now to the early stages of the campaign and to the Democrats, who were thoroughly organized down to the last precinct, with an able group of orators for the political circuit. From headquarters Simmons had scattered a large amount of racist propaganda that preceded every speaker throughout the state. Notably active during the early stages of the campaign were Aycock and Craig, the latter having come down from the west to campaign in the eastern counties, the Black Belt. Aycock was also campaigning in these counties, and his star was slowly on the ascendancy. At Laurinburg he was introduced as the "idol of the East," and on another occasion as the "next governor of North Carolina." His addresses picked up momentum and were often compared to "religious gatherings." His speeches including "amusing jokes, but always centered around the Democratic theme song, Negro rule, white supremacy, reverence for white womanhood, while pleading for white solidarity by urging the Populists to return to the Democratic party."[27]

Meanwhile, Simmons lent his oratorical skill to the campaign, moving into the Carolina Highlands in the west. He made speeches at major locales, but he had trouble with the Democratic theme in these remote mountain counties. A case in point was the city of Wilkesboro, where his audience remained unconvinced of "humiliation and suffering" endured by whites in the Black Belt. Moreover, as pointed out earlier, this physiographical region was plagued by white illiteracy. Here, the literature had not accomplished its objectives. Suddenly, Simmons conceived the idea of a racist cartoon movement, for those who could not read would certainly learn what they were supposed to know from lurid pictures. He carried his scheme to Daniels, who immediately contacted young and talented cartoonist Norman Jennett of New York to return and help out by drawing cartoons for the *News and Observer*.[28]

On August 6, Daniels's paper announced the return of Jennett, "our Sampson Huckleberry," so named because he was a native of "Sampson County, famous for its big berries." He had once worked on the *News and Observer* for four dollars a week. Later he had studied in New York, where his drawing had improved and where he had begun to rise professionally. On August 13, Jennett launched his sensational cartoon campaign with front-page coverage in the *News and Observer*. The cartoons were to continue for the duration of the campaign. A few illustrations of them are included. Now and then, he depicted Fusion corruption and made attacks upon Governor Russell, but it was most often the Negro was pilloried. During the same period, a Democratic sheet called *Facts about Negroes* was circulated anonymously throughout the state, with big black headlines, "Negro," "Negro," "Negro" and with ugly Negro cartoons cunningly drawn and bearing sensational captions. The Black who bore the brunt of this enmity was the progressive and civic-minded James H. Young of Raleigh. As the *Caucasian* justly complained: "They would have us believe that Jim Young is running the whole thing at the State Institution for white and colored, and that negroes have about taken several of our big cities and soon will have the whole country in their charge."[29] Other Democratic papers soon got in on the act, especially the *Wilmington Morning Star*. Late in October the *Caucasian* began to counterattack with its own cartoons, but it was at a disadvantage from the beginning since it had no artist with Jennett's talents. And the paper did not have nearly the circulation of the *News and Observer*.

The Democratic leaders soon added another act to their white supremacy drama by organizing White Government Union (white supremacy)· Clubs. These local grass-roots clubs were the brainchild of Francis D. Winston of Bertie County, clubs were designed to engender a patriotic loyalty in every community to the gospel of white supremacy. The Democratic papers carried notice of the meetings, place, and time, while urging every white man, regardless of former party affiliations, to identify himself with the Union.[31] Becoming unique Democratic cliques, the clubs experienced an accelerated growth in both the Piedmont and Black Belt regions. Rabid speeches were made before these clubs "with the deliberate purpose of inflaming the white man's sentiment against the Negro."

Raleigh News and Observer, *August 13, 1898*

Raleigh News and Observer, *August 19, 1898*

Raleigh News and Observer, *October 15, 1898*

Raleigh News and Observer, *October 18, 1898*

Caucasian (Raleigh), October 20, 1898

Caucasian (Raleigh), October 20, 1898

144

THE LAOCOON UP TO DATE

Raleigh News and Observer, *October 29, 1898*

On one occasion the tirade was so wrought with "white heat" that the club members were ready to leave immediately to kill all Negro officeholders.[32]

Mudslinging, name-calling, and waving the "bloody shirt," as might be expected, were major propaganda techniques of the Democrats to divide and conquer. Moreover, by the end of August, every Democrat who could speak "was on the stump;" every Democrat who could write was "writing;" and every Democrat who could ride was riding to enthusiastically sway the voters. And these forces had emotion on their side. By this time the Populists had become most sensitive to their plight as an independent party. In a speech at Clinton, Dr. Cyrus Thompson, executive secretary of the Populist party, asked some fundamental questions: "What course shall we pursue in this campaign? Shall we go in the middle of the road for a straight .fight, or shall we fuse with the Republicans?"[33] In light of their gloomy prospect, both parties realized that fusion was advantageous; thus, on September 1, "the Populists and Republicans reached a unanimous and harmonious" agreement for collaboration in dividing county offices.[34]

Meanwhile, the Democrats had stepped up their propaganda attacks on Black politicians, carrying them to a new level. These politicians were now accused of harboring designs to make North Carolina into a Black commonwealth. A cartoon released by Jennett showed a high North Carolina state official struggling to keep Blacks from migrating into the state via water from Virginia and South Carolina. And in September of 1898 a staff correspondent of the *Atlanta Constitution* wrote from North Carolina: "It is no secret that colored leaders, ambitious for their race, have matured in their minds a plan by which they hope to obtain absolute control of the legislative, judicial, and executive machinery, and then to rapidly carry out a scheme of colonization by which this will become a thoroughly Negro sovereign state, with that population in the majority and furnishing all officials in the public service, from United States Senators and Governors down through judges, legislators, and solicitors, to the last constable."[35] This article received wide coverage and caused grave concern in other states.

Naturally, the Republicans and Populists struck back at the Democrats' red journalism. They pointed out that the lurid description of Negro rule was the "basest hypocrisy," an exaggeration and misrepresentation of facts, and an insult to the intelligence of the voters. They also contended that Blacks had long held offices under Democratic appointment and furnished a list that indicated that the Negro postmasters in Warren County—J. M. Tilman, J. H. Howard of Weldon and Edward Cheek—were all bonded by uncompromising white Democrats.[36] In an editorial in the *Caucasian,* a small farmer expressed quite adequately the sentiments and arguments of the Republicans and Populists.[37] "Negro Domination a Blind," he declared. According to him, it was an attempt to sidetrack the real issue. "I am very disappointed indeed," he wrote, "that the farmers, as a class, are so unwatchful of their enemies. If they only would devote a little more time to reading and watching the acts of those fellows and their agents, they would not be fooled so easily, and would know just for what men and measures to vote on election day." He reasoned that Negro domination was a small evil, compared to domination of the money power, and that it was "bad legislation foisted upon" the farmers by these "white-shirted" money-thirsty lords that should be replaced. "Through their very efforts and cunning," he continued, "the 99-year lease of the State's railroad was made for their advantage, and to the detriment of the people. They are known to have worked and fought against most every bill introduced in the legislature in behalf of the farmers, viz: reduction of freight and passenger rates, free passes and the six percent interest bill, etc., and all of which they opposed, and still oppose. Why? Because these bills interfered with their dollar grabbing." The Democrats, he accused, "snatched up a few planks of the Populist platform and hollered themselves hoarse in praise of said platform . . . (and when) they thought they could pull through without further aid of the Populists, they changed their tune of praise to that of denunciation and abuse. Now, they are asking you, fellow citizens, in the face of all this, to help them save the State from Negro rule." In conclusion, he cautioned his fellow farmers to "watch these fellows and see if they are kicking up this Negro dust for anything but to blind you to the real facts."[38] This was a cogent rebuttal to the Democrats' propaganda attacks, but, unfortunately, neither the Republicans nor the Populists had an adequate campaign theme to counter that of their opponents.

Public persuasion (political oratory) from rostrums and stumps was the major artillery of each party. Beginning with the Democrats, there was the fiery Alfred M. Waddell of Wilmington, sometimes dubbed an "American Robespierre." He called for violence against Blacks, Republicans, and Populists, and his "defiant utterances were quoted by speakers on every stump."[39] Definitely superior was the heavyset and vigorous Robert B. Glenn, a perfect rough-and-tumble, "give them hell" type of speaker. He was a political revivalist whose speeches contained little or no logic. He often began speaking slowly with a deliberate cadence, and gradually his words came faster and faster. Employing every muscle in his body, and with dramatic emotion, he spoke in a "voice that could be almost heard in the next county." He was a crowd pleaser and rarely spoke less than two hours. One of his antics was to "take off his coat and collar and when he would get half through, if he hadn't taken off his collar, the people having heard that at some other place he had done so, would cry out: 'Bob, take off your collar and give 'em hell,' which he proceeded to do to the cheers and hurrahs of the great body of people."[40] The Democrats had other effective speakers who could excite their listeners. They were the veteran ex-Governor Jarvis, Simmons, Cameron Morrison, and Winston. The king of oratory, nevertheless, was Charles B. Aycock, the Democratic "Moses" who would lead North Carolina out of the chaos and darkness of "Negro Domination" and restore peace and security to rest permanently upon the foundation of white supremacy.

Aycock was born on November 1, 1859, in Wayne County near Nahunta (now Fremont), son of Benjamin Aycock and an illiterate mother whose legal signature was a mark. He graduated from the University of North Carolina in 1881, winning the Bingham Essay and Willie P. Mangum medals for best graduation oration.[41] He studied law under A. K. Smedes of Goldsboro, a lawyer of marked "ability and learning," and was admitted to the bar, entered into a law partnership with Arthur Daniels, and made only $144 the first year. As was typical of young struggling Democrats, he served as a county school superintendent for two years and as a member of the Goldsboro School Board from 1887 to 1901. The first public office he ever held was that of United States district attorney for the Eastern District of North Carolina, 1893-1897, a position to which he was appointed by President Cleveland.[42] As a campaign orator, Aycock had mastered and employed all the skills of the craft. He appeared on the stump before his urban or rural audiences without manuscript or notes. He would cunningly switch from graceful, eloquent expressions in the cities to the vernacular of agrarian audiences, using a language that was simple and direct. At the same time, his moods were numerous and varied: he could plead, scold, be humble, gentle, rough, humorous, admirable, or tempestuous. Choosing his style on the basis of the occasion or moment he delivered his speeches with the mannerisms that his audiences liked and remembered. From their deep sockets, his eyes would twinkle when he told a humorous anecdote, or flash in indignation, while his mouth twisted in scorn, and when he deemed it necessary, as sometimes for effect, he cupped his hands into the form of a megaphone. Like the ending of a symphonic overture, he "strode about waving his arms, while his voice, high and nasal," crescendoed to the forte climax.[43] His audience, rising to its feet in a spontaneous ovation, acted as the clash of the cymbals, which brought the dramatic ending.

The outstanding Republican orators were all Black; James H. Young, James Y. Eaton, and George H. White, the last an astute politician, were very eloquent and shrewd in debate. However, John C. Dancy of Wilmington, known throughout the state and the nation and also abroad for his eloquence, had no equal—white or Black—as an orator.[44]

The Populists, too, had their big guns—Marion Butler and Dr. Cyrus Thompson, both dangerous in debates. Butler, who was versatile in abilities, was tall, imposing, angular, well-groomed, with thick, gently waving hair.[45] Comparing Butler with Glenn, Josephus Daniels wrote much later: "Whenever it was announced that Glenn and Butler were to have a joint speaking engagement, as often happened, the crowd was measured by acres and it was an all-day contest. Butler was more adroit . . . (and) had much of insinuation and invective . . . but no matter how deep a hole Glenn thought he had dug for him, Butler was able to keep from falling in. Glenn said that in a debate with Butler he had to be on his guard in order not to let Butler get the best of him . . . and a less skillful debater than Butler would have been annihilated by Glenn."[46]

As a debater, Dr. Thompson of Onslow County was superior to both Glenn and Butler and equally as skillful as Aycock on the stump. A well-educated man who had studied the "Greek Poets," he was known to audiences throughout the state as a scholar and as an orator of eloquence. He did not speak like anyone else, for his voice was polished and had an "originality and a quintessence that was attractive . . . even in private conversation." Moreover, he possessed a touch "of humor that Butler did not have" and could enthuse an audience with his whimsical stories.[47] And, if not possessing the physical build of Daniel Webster, perhaps, to some degree, he might have awed his opponents in debates. Indeed, one historian tells us that "he appeared to be frail . . . but his looks were deceptive."[48]

For some time the Populists had been hounding the Democrats to meet them and debate the issues. In truth, since the origin of their party the Populists had been debating the Democrats. After Dr. Thompson was billed to speak at Concord on September 12, the county Populist committee challenged the Democratic committee to get the strongest Democratic speaker in the state to meet him in joint discussion. The Democrats accepted and telegraphed Chairman Simmons to send Aycock. The Populists were elated over the prospect of turning their biggest gun—the "politician physician" Thompson— on Aycock. With great fanfare, they distributed one thousand posters announcing the great debate. It was well covered by correspondents from the leading Democratic presses: *Wilmington Morning Star, Raleigh News and Observer, Raleigh Post, Charlotte Observer, Charlotte News, Lexington Dispatch, Concord Times,* and *Concord Standard.* F. T. Reed of the *Salisbury Watchman* was the only Populist representative present. The townspeople constituted the bulk of the Democrats present, for few people came in from the country. Many had declared earlier that they were "not coming to hear Cy Thompson abuse the Democrats." The Populists accused the Democratic leaders of deliberately keeping away as many of the rank and file as they could to prevent them from hearing the truth.[49]

Aycock spoke first, and his speech was devoted largely to repeating previous ones (he always gave basically the same address). He made charges of Republican-Populist corruption and extravagance, claiming that the parties had spent three hundred thousand dollars more for the three years 1895, '96, and '97, than for the three years of Democratic rule 1892, '93, and '94. He ended up playing the Democratic theme song of Black rule in the "East . . . and the viciousness of their race in meting out justice." He closed with a climactic appeal for "white supremacy on behalf of Democracy and the white womanhood of the State." Dr. Thompson arose, faced his audience, and graciously said: "We have listened to a speech presenting the other side of this question . . . such as no man will or can make in North Carolina, except the man that made it." In his reply, Dr. Thompson was "cool as ever." He accused Aycock of being a tool of the Democratic machine, headed by Simmons and backed by A.

B. Andrews (a wealthy railroad Democrat) and his gang, which was trying to return to a position of power. According to Dr. Thompson, they could not fuse with the Populists because Populists insisted on legislation to which Andrews was opposed. Next, he charged Aycock with avoiding entanglement with the convention, since it was to run him for governor in 1900. Dr. Thompson then "took up Aycock's nigger racket," and, dropping his graciousness, he shouted: "In the name of God, are we never going to hear anything in North Carolina except the Negro?"[50] He denounced as malicious and slanderous the cartoons of the *News and Observer*, especially the one of "Jim Young visiting the bedroom of two white women."[51] Calming down a bit, he pointed out that Democrats had long supported Negro officeholders and cited the fact that "Warren County has had a colored Register of Deeds for 25 years and bonded by white Democrats, which made hypocrisy out of their claim of white supremacy."[52]

Thunderous applause followed as Dr. Thompson took his seat. He had dealt his opponent some heavy blows. Aycock trembled visibly when he rose for rebuttal, and in "his agony, while trying to read a portion of a letter of Charles M. Cooke replying to Dr. Thompson's charges," his hands shook as if they were afflicted with palsy. His rejoinder was "furious and tempestuous," and in his anger he lost his head completely and shouted to Dr. Thompson: "Sir, the hour has come, when you can no longer go about over North Carolina villifying and abusing men." When the smoke of the battle cleared away, it was a "study to observe the faces of the local Democrats." The Populists gleefully claimed the victory, as the *Caucasian* wrote: "Aycock held to ridicule." And even a leading Democrat was inclined to agree that the "Democrats were as blue as they were just after election two years ago."[53] Nevertheless, these two oratorical giants were never to meet again in the political arena.

It seems safe to say that Dr. Thompson was more adroit and soundly defeated Aycock, but Aycock's reputation as an orator did not suffer, while his popularity grew, picking up momentum as the campaign lumbered on. At the rallies, it was Aycock who was the magnet used to attract immense crowds. To illustrate, at Leesville he addressed one of the largest multitudes ever assembled in Wayne County, comprised "of men, women, and children twelve hundred strong, who came in buggies, in carts, in carriages, in wagons, on horseback and on foot." The Leesville performance, however, was greatly outdone by the Raleigh rally held in the Metropolitan House, where the people had early "filled all seats, the windows and occupied every inch of standing room in the rear of the hall." Aycock spoke for one and one-quarter hours and swept the audience off its feet with his magnetism.[54] As pointed out earlier, he echoed strains of the Democratic theme song throughout his address, centered on Negro Rule, while drawing his audience gradually and skillfully toward the dramatic climax, with an earnest plea for white supremacy and white womanhood. Like a skilled evangelist, entreating backsliders and sinners to come forward and be saved, he would ask the Democrats if they would come and rescue the state from "Russellism, Fusionism, and Black Domination." Rising and cheering, they shouted, "Yes, we will!" Since the days of William L. Yancey of Alabama, no political orator had possessed such audience appeal, certainly not in North Carolina. In the meantime, the less influential, yet still forceful, Democratic orators, like "one-armed" Frank Ferrell of Wake County, Capt. Charles M. Cooke, the three Kitchin brothers, Edward W. Pou, Thomas Mason, and others widened their range by fanning out in all directions. They rode the country by day and night, summoning their followers to go to the polls ready to meet force with force. State Executive Chairman Simmons thought the Democratic papers kept the public informed of speaking engagements with eye-catching announcements about the "grand political rally" or the "big rally and barbecue.

With the campaign moving into high gear, we now return to the Democrats' strategy of mudslinging and the waving of the "bloody shirt," particularly against Black leaders. Around mid-October, they exploded an eleventh-hour bombshell with the "Manly Editorial." This was a classical example of stirring up racial hatred for partisan purposes. To fully appreciate this issue, a look backward is necessary. From the beginning of the 1898 campaign, the Democratic papers, led by the *Raleigh News and Observer,* had carried on a smear campaign against Black males, claiming that crimes of rape and attacks upon white women had increased under the Fusion administration. Moreover, the Democrats perpetually used the charge of rape by Blacks as propaganda against Negro candidates, concomitantly upholding the doctrine of white supremacy. Such inflammatory news releases and cartoons, understandably, embarrassed and infuriated the Black leaders. Even more galling to them was the fact that the cartoons were accompanied by lurid captions and featured on the front page, a practice that was intensified as the campaign continued.

The intrepid Black editor Alexander L. Manly employed his paper in Wilmington, the *Record,* to rebut the Democrats' defamation of Negro males. The *Record* was launched around 1892 but did not amount to very much as a newspaper until it came under the management of the enterprising Manly. It was perhaps the only Negro daily in the nation, and its editor used it to champion the cause of Wilmington's Black citizens, which included the promotion of progressive legislation. Manly's militant pen did not enhance his popularity with some "whites who thought him too *high strung, bold and saucy,*" while some Black leaders were a "bit shaky over his many tilts with editors of the white papers." According to Black writer David Bryant Fulton, Manly was "sitting in his office one evening in August reading a New York paper, when his eye fell upon a [column] from a Georgia paper from the pen of a famous Georgia white woman, whose loud cries for the lives of Negro rapists had been widely read and commented upon during the past year." The article referred to the exposure of and the protection of white girls in the isolated districts of the South and called for the lynching of "lustful black brutes." Manly meditated: "White girls in isolated districts exposed to lustful black brutes. Colored girls in isolated districts exposed to white brutes: what's the difference?" Infuriated over the calumination of a "defenseless people," he took up his pen and wrote the "retort which shook the state from the mountains to the sea."[55]

Thus emerged the Manly editorial, one of the most famous in North Carolina's history. Through certain omissions, it was distorted from the beginning by the Democratic news media; scholars have perpetuated the distortion by using the Democratic papers as their sources, and, of the works of authorities sampled, not one has seen fit to include reasons why Manly wrote that editorial.[56]

Manly entitled his editorial "Mrs. Felton's Speech." "A Mrs. Felton from Georgia," he began "makes a speech before the Agricultural Society, at Tybee, Georgia, in which she advocates lynching as an extreme measure. This woman makes a strong plea for womanhood, and if the alleged crimes of rape were ,half so frequent as is oftimes reported, her plea would be worthy of consideration." And, like many "so-called Christians," Manly contended, she "loses sight of the basic principles of the religion of Christ in her plea for one class of people as against another. If a missionary spirit is essential for the uplifting of the poor white girls, why is it? The morals of the poor white people are on a par with their colored neighbors of like conditions, and if anyone doubts the statement let him visit among them." He went on to point out that papers were frequently filled with reports* of rapes of white women and the subsequent lynchings of the rapists. The editors "pour forth volleys of aspersions against all Negro males, because of the few who may be guilty. If the papers and speakers of the other race would condemn the commission of crime because it is crime, and not try to make it appear that the Negroes were the only criminals, they would find their strongest allies in the intelligent Negroes themselves, and together the whites and blacks would foot the evil out of both races."

This section of Manly's editorial was intentionally omitted by Democratic presses, which began their account of his article at this point. The *Raleigh News and Observer* reported that Manly had written:

> We suggest that the whites guard their women more closely, as Mrs. Felton says, thus giving no opportunity for the human fiend, be he white or black. You leave your goods out of doors and then complain because they are taken away. Poor white men are careless in the matter of protecting their women, especially on the farms. They are careless of their conduct toward them, and our experience among poor white people in the country teaches us that women of that race are not any more particular in the matter of clandestine meetings with colored men than the white men with colored women. Meetings of this kind go on for some time until the women's infatuation or the man's boldness, brings attention to them, and the man is lynched for rape. Every negro lynched is called "a Big Burly Black Brute," when, in fact, many of those who have thus been dealt with had white men for their fathers, and were not only not "black and burly," but were sufficiently attractive for white girls of culture and refinement to fall in love with them, as is very well known to all.

The Democratic presses terminated the article at this point; nevertheless, Manly had more to say.

He recommended that "Mrs. Felton should start at the 'fountain head' if she wishes to 'purify the stream'." Further on, he stated: "Teach your men purity. Let virtue be something more than an excuse for them to intimidate and torture a helpless people. Tell your men that it is no worse for a black man to be intimate with a white woman than for a white man to be intimate with a colored woman." Moved emotionally, he wrote in conclusion: "You set yourselves down as a lot of carping hypocrites; in fact, you cry aloud for the virtue of your women while you seek to destroy the morality of ours. Don't think ever that your women will remain pure while you are debauching ours. You sow the seed—the harvest will come in due time."[56]

The indignation that this article aroused among whites of all classes can be easily understood. Threatening letters were sent to the editor's office: "Leave (town) on the pain of death"; "Stop the publishing of that paper"; "Apologize for that slander." The *Progressive Farmer* urged all Blacks with a "scale of decency" to drive Manly from the states, "never to return."[57] Manly stood his ground, however; even in the face of a mass meeting of white citizens, who advised him to retract, he "was obdurate and 'refused to apoligize.' " In time, the excitement abated, while the *Record* continued its publication. Later, during the Wilmington race riot, the destruction of the Manly press would be the mob's first objective. In the meantime, the Democrats resurrected the article, originally written in August, to sling more mud and to generate more white heat for the political campaign. It reappeared in the *Morning Star* on October 18 and again two days later, the "most horrid slander" and the "most infamous assault upon the white women of the state." The *News and Observer* wrote of the "vile and villainous" attack on white women by a Negro newspaper published in Wilmington.[58] "Every white man in the state," wrote the *Fayetteville Observer,* "having any regard for the purity of his mother, sisters and daughters, must take this matter into consideration." Doubters were invited to the office of the paper "to see the original copy of the slanderous sheet."[59] Meanwhile, the article was circulated inside and outside the state and went like "wildfire from house to house," especially in the rural communities, while the Democratic orators added it to their theme song.

What was the reaction of Black leaders to the Manly editorial? As whites "blazed their indignation," Frank Denham, a member of a prominent Black family of Raleigh, wrote in the *Raleigh News and Observer*: "Not a word of Manly's editorial expresses the sentiments of the colored people in North Carolina. I was never so shocked in my life. I shall not be surprised to hear that violence has been done Manly by either whites or Negroes."[60] In contrast to Denman, many Black spokesmen, some quite prominent in and out of the state, supported Manly's conclusion. One Negro minister braved ostracism by contending that there was no repugnance of marriage between Black and white persons of the "same financial, educational and social levels."[61]

More to the point, the theme of Manly's editorial had been voiced earlier in the House of Representatives. For example, Congressman Thomas E. Miller was the most distinguished of South Carolina's Black political leaders. He was a graduate of Lincoln University and an astute attorney and politician.[62] He had fought courageously against Benjamin Tillman's effort to write a grandfather clause into South Carolina's constitution of 1895. While a member of Congress in the 1890s he had become particularly incensed at Georgia Congressman Alfred Colquitt's charge that white men in the South must constantly worry about the chastity of their women. Before this august body of representatives, and expressing a sentiment similar to that of the Manly editorial, Miller arose in indignation and spoke these words: "My God," "is there no limit to the slander and malignant utterances of these self-constituted friends of a toiling . . . portion of the American people?" Miller continued: "Stand up and indict a race of males as the invaders of the sanctity of Caucasian home ties, as the brutal destroyer of that in woman which is her very existence. The charge is groundless, mean, slanderous, and most damnably false." He informed Congress that there had been no cases of assault or rape by Blacks against white women—those "walking emblems of American purity," as he called them—in his district since emancipation. He maintained that the records of Southern courts would prove that such charges were usually untrue; generally, it was a matter of mutual consent. "Whenever it [a rape charge] is hurled at him [the Black man] the crime is laid in a locality where the numbers of the whites and the Negroes are nearly equal, where the whites and the Negroes are equal in morals; and, even after the poor unfortunate victim has been lynched and his spirit gone to the eternal world, letters or verbal admissions coming from the supposed victim of licentious brutality invariably absolve the innocent dead man from the crime charged."[63]

There followed close in the wake of the Manly controversy the "Red Shirt" Movement. This sinister, klanlike organization wore the "red-shirt badge of Southern manhood." Unlike the hooded Klansmen, the Red Shirts wanted Republicans, Populists, Blacks, and the entire white population to know who they were and what they stood for—rule by the Democratic party and white supremacy. The Red Shirts made their first appearance at Fayetteville on October 21, accompanied by the fiery "Pitchfork" Benjamin Tillman, the "one-eyed, grim-faced figure from Edgefield, South Carolina."[64] A little background on Tillman is interesting and instructive. He was born on August 11, 1847, at Chesterfield in Edgefield County and grew up in a family pervaded with violence. To illustrate, Thomas, the oldest, was killed at Churusos in 1847. Another brother, Oliver, was killed in Florida. The third brother, John, "wild, dissipated and handsome," was murdered by two brothers in 1860. George, the sole surviving brother besides Benjamin, killed a mechanic named Henry Christian during a drunken quarrel over a faro game. This brother later became a successful politician and was ultimately elected to Congress. Tillman possessed only a rudimentary education. He had been a Red Shirt leader in 1876 during South Carolina's Redemption, when Wade Hampton was elected governor.[65] He rose to power during the Populist Movement in his state, when hatred of President Cleveland was preached with evangelistic fervor. He achieved a prominent place in American historiography with these words: "He (Cleveland) is an old bag of beef, and I am going to Washington with a pitchfork and prod him in his old fat ribs." He was close to the soil, resembled a farmer in personal appearance, and looked at life from the farmer's angle expressing his ideas in a passionate manner that rural classes could fully appreciate.[66]

It is shrouded in mystery who sent the "Macedonian cry" over the South Carolina borders to identify Tillman with the North

Carolina white supremacy movement. We have all heard the theatrical maxim, "The show must go on." When Tillman appeared in Fayetteville, according to the local papers, from seven thousand to ten thousand stood in a heavy rain to see the parade and hear him speak. Such figures, no doubt, are an exaggeration, but it is safe to assume that the crowd was large and enthusiastic. The procession was led by over two hundred Red Shirts, followed by a float drawn by four fine horses and occupied by twenty-two beautiful young ladies in white, representing the twenty-two precincts of Cumberland County. Next came the carriage containing Mayor Cook, County Chairman Huske, Major E. J. Hale, and Senator Tillman. Then followed a long line of carriages and other vehicles. On either side marched the White Government Unions escorting their guests, the visiting delegations from Wilmington, Bennettsville, and other points in Lumber Bridge, Red Springs, Maxton, and Lumberton. The rally was held at the fairgrounds, and the Wilmington white brass band furnished the music. Tillman was introduced as the "liberator of South Carolina." Several times during the hour-and-one-half address, he attempted to conclude it, but the audience urged him on, enthralled by his ringing voice and imperious gestures. His sentences were well constructed, containing picturesque illustrations and bearing the "flavor of wholesome country life . . . (and) running into great rapidity of utterance at the climaxes," but hitting the mark every time. His main theme was how South Carolina, in which state Blacks outnumbered whites three to one, had risen up against Negro rule and succeeded in denying Blacks the ballot by constitutional amendment.[67] Tillman spoke next at a rally in Red Springs and received a similar ovation.

Largely as a result of Tillman's visit to North Carolina, the Red Shirt idea took on momentum, spreading like a wild forest fire throughout the Black Belt counties.[68] "These men rode horses, carried Winchester rifles, shotguns and even pistols. While the organization was tinctured with hoodlumism, it included wealthy farmers, schoolteachers and bankers of both young and old men. With pants tucked in their boots, they were cloaked in red shirts of calico, flannel or silk, according to the taste of the owner and the enthusiasm of his womankind."[69] Jonathan Daniels has left us a keener insight and has described them as a "terrifying spectacle." Just before sunset to see "three hundred red-shirt men riding towards the sunset with the sky red and the red shirts seemingly to blend with the sky . . . it looked like the whole world was carmine." Another reported: "They rode out of the dawn and into the light of sunsets as red as their shirts into the Negro sections, and by the houses of Negro farmers . . . leaving terror in their wake." The more militant members of the party rode the county by day and by night, "a yelling file of horsemen, galloping wildly. They were men who meant violence if fear was not enough."[70]

The Red Shirt movement was immediately adopted as a regular feature of the white supremacy drama. While Aycock did not wear a red shirt, as we shall soon see, he quickly became identified with both Tillman and the Red Shirts. Meanwhile, as October drew to a close, a sort of "Reign of Terror," to borrow a phrase from the French Revolution, prevailed. It had its origin in political malice, fed from racism, fiery speeches, vitriolic writings, and cartoons, which created an explosive state of public feeling. Accordingly, it was inevitable that violence would erupt somewhere, especially against non-Democrats. At some places Fusion speakers were belted with rotten eggs or rocks. Increasingly, it became unsafe for Republicans, including Governor Russell and Senator Pritchard, to make campaign speeches. All canceled their engagements to prevent disturbances.[71] Anticipating violence in certain counties, the Republican committee withdrew the Fusion ticket.[72]

A well-organized movement by whites to take over Black jobs added fuel to the political fire. For example, the Democratic Club of Winston-Salem passed resolutions demanding that white establishments replace Black employees with whites. A small racial clash became imminent at Ashpole, near Lumberton. Here whites were trying to forcefully take over the lumber camp jobs. The Blacks naturally armed themselves as a gesture of resistance. Newspapers throughout the state carried warnings of the potential time bomb when threats were made to burn the place down.[73] This caldron boiled over into a small riot on October 24, when a large group of white men suddenly appeared at the camp and demanded that the Blacks leave. In the face of overwhelming odds, the Blacks retired, but shooting began and three white men were hit. The *News and Observer* compared the Ashpole affair "to the first shot fired at Lexington, by making it a political issue."[74] "The incendiary speeches of radical leaders," it explained, "had borne their logical fruit and the welfare of the State was at stake in the election to be held in November." It pointed out further that "there was a limit to the forebearance of even the law-abiding Anglo-Saxon, and that if pushed beyond certain limits then the responsibility rests upon the heads of the White scalawags and the ignorant and vicious Blacks."[75]

Another foreboding racial incident was to occur after Capt. William H. "Buck" Kitchin, his son, son-in-law, and three other whites, during the night, broke into the home of B. B. Steptoe, a Negro registrar, and forced him at gunpoint to resign. At the urging of Republican State Chairman Holman, the Negro politician brought charges, and Justice W. W. Montgomery of the state supreme court issued a warrant for the arrest of Kitchin and his associates. Tension built up during the interim before the trial, as indignant whites rallied around Kitchin, denouncing "his arrest as a highhanded piece of Jeffreyism." A sense of uneasiness prevailed on the day of the trial, as scores of Kitchin sympathizers came with him from Halifax County. Many of them filed into the courtroom, allegedly with pistols in their hip pockets, while others milled outside, denouncing Judge Montgomery with all types of invectives. In this volatile atmosphere of intimidation, naturally Kitchin and his associates were exonerated.[76] This state of racial unrest prevailed more or less throughout the Black Belt.

Democratic leaders claimed that the Steptoe controversy "was a conspiracy hatched out in order to furnish a pretext for bringing Federal troops into the State." An editorial headline in the *News and Observer* exclaimed: "To Invoke Bayonet Rule."[77] The paper warned its readers of the confidential two-page letter Senator Pritchard had written to President McKinley briefing him on the threatening conditions in North Carolina. His letter expressed grave anxiety over the intense racial feelings instituted by the Democrats. Whites were arming and Blacks were buying weapons wherever purchasable, and the most serious trouble could be expected "in counties where colored people predominate." Here the whites displayed weapons in great numbers to frighten colored voters and to keep them away from the polls. Pritchard asked the president: "Will you send deputy United States marshals to preserve the peace?"

On October 24 cabinet Chairman Babcock called an informal cabinet meeting that included Attorney General Griggs, and Secretaries Alger, Long, and Hay. President McKinley broached the subject of the possibility of having to send federal troops into North Carolina during the November election. Meanwhile, through authentic media, Daniels knew of the content of Pritchard's letter and of its discussion in the cabinet.

To allay the Democrats' fears of federal intervention, the *News and Observer* quickly provided the answers. "Of course the President has no power to send Federal troops into the State until the Governor has made requisition for them and shows that he is unable to handle the situation with the forces at his command." And also, Governor Russell could not call for federal troops until the supposed rioting had actually occurred and he was able to show that he had exhausted all the efforts of the state to suppress it. Then too, the President could not send in troops unless the United States mails were interfered with.[78] Pritchard's letter was branded as a ghost story, which soon threw him on the defensive. In his explanation, he denied asking for troops and merely described the state of affairs in certain of the eastern counties, which was the result of incendiary and inflammatory Democratic speeches. At the same time, he counseled the Republicans to abstain from violence or from entering into any discussion that might lead to a disturbance.[79]

On returning to the campaign, we find preparations being made for large final rallies, soon to mushroom in many cities. The first of these gigantic assemblages convened on October 28 at Goldsboro, after careful preparation and good advertising.[80] For this giant rally, the Atlantic Coast Line, the Seaboard, and the Southern Railroads reduced the rates to one fare for round trip to this meeting; they also ran special trains from Greensboro.[81] Some "8000 white supremists were represented, representing delegates from nearly every county in the east and some westerners." The meeting was given wide coverage by the Democratic presses, which included the *Raleigh News and Observer, Raleigh Morning Post, Wilmington Morning Star, New Bern Journal, Winston Journal,* and the *Goldsboro Argus.*[82] Among the prominent speakers were Simmons, Aycock, Waddell, and Guthrie. The last had run the gamut from a former Republican to a Populist candidate for governor in 1896, and was now temporary Democratic chairman.[83] Simmons opened the conference and soon surrendered the chair to Maj. William A. Guthrie of Durham. As Major Guthrie advanced, he was met with thunderous applause from the multitudes. He immediately called upon the Methodist minister N. M. Jurney to pray. Reverend Jurney prayed briefly, but fervently and devoutly. "Let us feel this day," he entreated God, "the vibrations of our coming redemption from all wicked rule and the supremacy of the race destined . . . to rule this country."

Afterward, Major Guthrie said to his audience: "We have met, by common consent to lay aside our former partisan differences and come together, breast to breast, and man to man as patriotic white men [to] settle for ourselves, for our state and for posterity knotty questions." He then alluded to the conditions in the eastern part of the state under Fusion rule and Negro domination and asked: "Is there a good white man in North Carolina who loves his state and his race?" He then censured the Democratic apostates, calling them "bolters," whom he accused of having sold the party's flag. Then he asked: "What have they received for it?" Immediately answering his own question, he replied: "Negro magistrates!" "Negro legistators!" "Negro postmasters!" "Negro deputy marshalls!" and Negro revenue officers all over eastern North Carolina, and in some counties in western North Carolina. "Nor were these bolters forgotten." He told his audience that "they received their pay for the party's flag in federal offices. It was with these federal offices that Pritchard and

Holton and the other McKinleyites bought the flag from these traitors, and now they have turned that flag over to the one hundred and twenty thousand Negro voters in North Carolina." Raising his voice to an intense volume, Guthrie promised: "I shall find the flag of the white man's party." Pressing the point, he further promised that the 120,000 blacks would be forced "to surrender back the flag of the [white] people's party." In the tone of a zealot, he continued: "The Anglo-Saxon planted civilization on this continent and wherever this race has been in conflict with another race, it has asserted its supremacy and either conquered or exterminated the foe . . . This great race has carried the Bible in one hand and the sword in the other, and say to the nations of the world, resist our march of progress and civilization and we will wipe you off the face of the earth."

As the audience listened to his lengthy speech as if hypnotized, he dramatically raised a copy of the Bible and shook it several times in the direction of the crowd and declared: "This is the only document I care for in this campaign. I am going to read from the Holy Scriptures, and I hope that no Fusionist will go off and say that Guthrie read at Goldsboro a lot of Democratic lies."

He then read from the Book of Nehemiah how the Persian army, under Cyrus, had torn down the walls and burned the gates of the Jewish city, and how the young Jewish leader, Nehemiah, had come with his followers to retake the city and rebuild its walls. Major Guthrie read the story with powerful effect, comparing and contrasting points as he went along. He also drew a parallel between the rebuilding of the walls of Jerusalem by Nehemiah and his faithful followers and the rebuilding of the broken walls of the Anglo-Saxon race in North Carolina. He climaxed his speech in a stentorian voice by calling on every white man to join in rebuilding North Carolina's "broken wall."[84] Thus, as it was with Nehemiah, Major Guthrie assured his listeners that there will be "much gladness and rejoicing. [Tremendous cheers and applause.]" This was the kind of speech the audience wanted to hear.

A preamble and eight militant resolutions, enthusiastically adopted, best explain the purpose of the Goldsboro rally. "We the citizens of Eastern North Carolina," the preamble read, "in a mass meeting assembled, being mindful of the obligations we are assuming, and . . . desirous of informing our fellow citizens of the conditions of affairs in our section of the state do publish to the world the following statement of facts." The preamble explained that "in many counties, cities and towns of Eastern North Carolina," the local government had "been turned over wholly or in part to the Negroes." It also asserted that blacks were "wholly unfitted" for administering a government or for holding public offices. The preamble included

160

the list of alleged offices filled by Negroes: "Register of Deeds, Deputy Sheriffs, Constables, Justices of the Peace, School Committeemen, Town Commissioners, Policemen, Postmasters, Collectors . . . nearly one thousand Negroes, . . . [and] nearly three hundred Negro magistrates alone."

The first of the eight resolutions contended that the "Republicans leaders had for a second time clearly demonstrated their inability and their unfitness to govern North Carolina." Another one affirmed the determination to restore to "capable white men" in the "East" the "management and control of government in county, city and town." Still another one warned Blacks that whites will and must rule and that white government was best for them. Finally, the "President and Secretary" of the meeting was directed to publish in "all the papers of the state" the eight resolutions as "statements of facts," and the Democratic Executive Committee was "requested to give them the widest possible circulation among the people."[85]

It is worth restating the problem. In the Black Belt, where Negroes constituted a substantial portion of the population and, in some counties, the majority of the population, the problem had always been the maintenance of political control by a white minority. Hence, a clarion call was sounded to close the division of white men and reunite them to zealously "use all proper means to free ourselves of *this negro domination.* which is paralyzing our business, and which hangs like a dark cloud over our homes." But it was the fiery Alfred M. Waddell of Wilmington whose speech electrified the convention. After vividly describing, the conditions in his city, he declared: "We are going to protect our firesides and our loved ones or die in the attempt." He concluded with a thunderous, defiant promise that the white people of Wilmington would drive out the "Manlys and Russells" and the hordes of corruptionists if they have "to throw" enough negro dead bodies into Cape Fear to choke up its passage to the sea.[86] To be sure, we have not heard the last of Waddell.

After the Goldsboro conferences, the political rallies picked up momentum, exploding throughout the Black Belt counties, as if set off by remote control. The next day, October 29, despite a cold and drizzling rain, several thousands listened to Locke Craig address a rally at Weaverville.[87] On the same day, another grand all-day affair, with dinner on the grounds, was held at Tarboro. Here three or four thousand people braved a downpour of rain to hear Aycock and Simmons. On November 1, a still larger one was held at Laurinburg near the South Carolina border. The Red Shirt Clubs of Maxton, Laurel Hill, and Gibson Station, four hundred strong, formed a "procession nearly a mile long." Thousands of people had come into town in wagons, buggies, carriages, on horseback, and on foot to hear Claude Kitchin of Halifax County.[88] Describing the event, a Northern reporter wrote: "For ten miles through pine-forests and cotton plantations these men rode, singling out the Negro hamlets as the special object of their *visitation*; while in the afternoon they listened to an impassioned address in which they were advised to win the election—peaceably if they could, forcibly if they must."

It must be pointed out that figures on the attendance at the rallies were reported by Democratic papers. Often, they were exaggerations. But one fact is certain: the crowds were large, as well as enthusiastic.

Meanwhile, Aycock was on the circuit in the Black Belt, some-times teaming with the tempestuous Ben Tillman. Both spoke at Hamlet and Sanford.[89] Aycock later spoke at Lumberton. He was met at the depot by a procession, including one thousand mounted Red Shirts, while a crowd of four thousand witnessed the parade and heard him speak.[90] The largest of the rallies was held at Burling-ton, where "seven thousand enthusiastic white people gathered under the auspices of the Democratic County Executive Committee. It closed the doors of twenty cotton mills in Alamance County for the entire day (and) stopped the activity on countless farms." The mile-long parade, was led by five hundred marshals on horseback, riding four abreast, and the "great volume of moving humanity" marched to the music of a band of fifty-four pieces, made up of cornet bands of Burlington, Haw River, and Liberty. The featured speakers were A. L. Brooks of Greensboro and Lee S. Overman, with Guthrie delivering the major speech, telling the enthusiastic crowd to "take council for white supremacy on Tuesday next." During this political oratory the greatest "barbecue" spread ever attempted took place. One hundred forty-two lambs and pigs were roasted "with not a black one among them" for this vast throng. It was a great banquet spread upon a table 516 feet long and 4 feet wide. More or less the same scenes were witnessed at New Bern, Concord, Roxboro, Reidsville, Tuckahoe, and other towns.[91]

Conditions in Wilmington, especially, were already bordering on a state of anarchy. In fact, the city was sitting on a racial powder keg. Thus, it is most significant to say a few words about its rally. It was held on November 3, and the whole city turned out to see the large Red Shirts parade. It "electrified" and created enthusiasm among the whites, but caused consternation among the Blacks. Thousands of cheering white women waved flags and handkerchiefs as the long column of armed and menacing-looking horsemen rode by. Waddell was the pivotal figure. On the night before the election, "in the Opera House to a rather full house," he told the madly cheering horde: "You are Anglo-Saxons. You are armed and prepared, and you will do your duty. Be ready at a moment's notice. Go to the polls tomorrow, and if you find the Negro out voting, tell him to leave the polls and if he refuses kill him, shoot him down in his tracks. We shall win tomorrow if we have to do it with guns."[92]

"Do you think the election will pass off peacefully?" On the eve of the election many persons throughout the state asked or pondered this question apprehensively. As in frontier days, many men carried concealed pistols. The fiery and passionate writings of the newspaper editors, along with the inflammatory oratory flowing from the stump, and the doctrine of white supremacy being preached from the pulpits in the same breath as the story of Christ's love, had galvanized many people toward anticipation of violence. These impetuous forces prevailed within the ranks of the Red Shirts. There were rumors of threats to assassinate Governor Russell, and a race riot in the state appeared imminent. Against the activities of the Red Shirts and other groups with a predeliction for violence, Governor Russell issued the following proclamation on October 26, 1898:[93]

NOW, THEREFORE, I, DANIEL L. RUSSELL, GOVERNOR OF THE STATE OF NORTH CAROLINA, IN PURSUANCE OF THE CONSTITUTION AND LAWS OF SAID STATE, AND BY VIRTUE OF AUTHORITY VESTED IN ME BY SAID CONSTITUTION AND LAWS, DO ISSUE THIS, MY PROCLAMATION, COMMANDING ALL ILL-DISPOSED PERSONS, WHETHER OF THIS OR THAT POLITICAL PARTY, OR OF NO POLITICAL PARTY, TO IMMEDIATELY DESIST FROM ALL UNLAWFUL PRACTICES AND ALL TURBULENT CONDUCT, AND TO PRESERVE THE PEACE, AND TO SECURE ALL THE PEOPLE THE QUIET ENJOYMENT OF ALL THEIR RIGHTS OF FREE CITIZENSHIP.

AND I DO FURTHER COMMAND AND ENJOIN IT UPON ALL GOOD AND LAW ABIDING CITIZENS NOT TO ALLOW THEMSELVES TO BECOME EXCITED BY ANY APPEALS THAT MAY BE MADE TO THEIR PASSIONS AND PREJUDICES BY THE REPRESENTATIVES OF ANY POLITICAL PARTY WHATSOEVER; BUT TO KEEP COOL HEADS, AND USE THEIR GOOD OFFICES TO PRESERVE THE PUBLIC PEACE AND TO PROTECT EVERY, THE HUMBLEST CITIZEN IN ALL HIS RIGHTS, POLITICAL AND PERSONAL.

The Red Shirts, however, had no respect for either the proclamation or the august status of the chief executive of the state.

Governor Russell had gone to Wilmington to vote. He first intended to return to the state capital at Raleigh by way of Goldsboro. He learned, however, that there was a mob of several hundred men at Goldsboro waiting to give him a reception, so he changed his route and went via Maxton. But word got to Maxton ahead of the governor that he was going that way, and when the train arrived at Laurinburg a swearing, howling mob of Red Shirts, heavily armed, were awaiting him. The train was surrounded and boarded by Red Shirts shouting: "Where is Russell?" "Where is the governor?" "Bring him out!" Their cries were accompanied by vulgar language. Anticipating that some violence would be inflicted on the governor, one of his friends had already moved and hustled him out of the coach into a boxcar, which was locked behind him, and the conductor and his friends stood guard until the train pulled out. Governor Russell reached his home in Raleigh, over the Seaboard Air Line, very badly frightened. The *New York Herald* reported that his friend "did not have a button on his coat and his clothing was in tatters."[94] Led by the *Raleigh News and Observer,* few if any of the North Carolina papers reported this incident. It is pathetic, indeed, when the chief executive of a state is subjected to such crass humiliation. This incident made a mockery not only of the two-party tradition but of the democratic process as well.

What was the general attitude of Blacks on the eve of the election? The Black editors displayed a spirit of resoluteness. Manly's *Wilmington Record* published an article by an organization of colored ladies with resolutions telling every Negro to vote. They were resolved to teach their "children to love the party of manhood's rights and liberties, trusting God to restore order out of the present confusion." Another newspaper, the *Kinston Searchlight,* wrote: "You can look for the burly Negroes on the eighth of November at the ballot box in a solid phalanx animated by the Negresses." It urged every Negro "to stick to the Republican Party because it had freed him."[95] Nevertheless, it is safe to conclude that the majority of Blacks lived day by day in great distress amounting to a state of terror.

Meanwhile, the Democratic papers had been daily reminding: "White men, do not fail to see that your names are on the Registration Books."[96] Some department stores carried large advertisements of their merchandise along with statements telling prospective customers to vote the Democratic ticket so that "white People of North Carolina would rule, make and administer all its laws." And on November 3, Simmons published a final plea for white supremacy in the form of an address. Editorially, he wrote: "In the midst of all this din and conflict, there came a voice from the East like the wail of Egypt's midnight cry. . . . claiming not to be a voice of despair." He reminded his readers that a "proud race which had never known a master had been placed under the control and domination of that race which ranks lowest . . . in the human family." He boasted that "North Carolina is a *White Man's* state and the *White Men* will rule it, and they will crush the party of negro domination beneath a majority so overwhelming that no other party will ever dare to attempt to establish negro rule here."[97]

Election day finally dawned, and in the storm centers preparations had been made to meet any emergency. Red Shirts milled around many precincts, armed with Winchester rifles and shotguns. They stalked about, frightening Republicans, Fusionists, and Blacks away from the polls by intermittently shooting into the air throughout the day and into the night. The Negro was advised to "lay low." In general, that advice was followed. Anticipating victory, the *News and Observer* announced "BIG MEETING TONIGHT," and had arranged for a mass meeting at the Raleigh Metropolitan Hall. In anxiety, a throng of "upturned faces" watched the results come in from the precincts on a screen in front of the *News and Observer* office. By 8:00 P.M. results from most of the counties showed a Democratic landslide. Pandemonium and exhilaration broke loose; "tin horns . . . and pans took up the chorus until the street was an inferno of noise," all followed by a torchlight procession.[98] This celebration was merely the prelude to the prodigious victory jubilee to be held in Raleigh on November 15, a week later. Daniels immediately began to make plans for it, and the *News and Observer* carried daily announcements of the coming event.[99] The next day the *News and Observer* reported that "the Great Victory and the state has gone Democratic by 25,000 majority." Earlier, the *Morning Post* had announced that the state had been redeemed and rescued from the evils of Negro domination and that Russellism and fusionism were "smitten, beaten, slain" and buried under an avalanche of indignant and disgusted white 'men's ballots.[100]

The Republicans and Populists charged the Democrats with employing illegal and devious methods to secure Democratic majorities in some counties, in addition to intimidation and fraud. Overawed, the Republicans and Populist forces disintegrated in every section of the state, while in the Black Belt many Negroes did not dare to vote. And in most instances, the Populists either abstained from voting or cast their ballots for the Democrats. Voting irregularities occurred statewide. Some ballot boxes were stuffed, and one man (who later became a prominent newspaper editor in Richmond, Virginia,) admitted that he voted nineteen times in a little town in the Piedmont region. In Alexander County the Democrats were accused of polling more votes than people registered. In the city of Wilmington there was widespread suppression of Negro votes. At one Black precinct some whites "held pistols in the faces of Negro" pollsters, while kerosene lights were extinguished, "some bowled over, the others blown out by gunfire." A Northern reporter charged that "in the Wilmington district a Republican majority of 5,000 in 1896 gave place to a Democratic majority of 6,000—a gain for the Democrats of 11,000 votes."[101] Thus, the Democratic victory in many parts of the state was not the result of a free and untrammeled ballot.

The Wilmington race riot was the bloody sequel to the 1898 campaign. Leading Democrats had clandestinely prepared and instigated the rebellion. While the riot was in full blast, the Reformers used it as a smoke screen to take over the city's government by forcing the resignation of the mayor, the chief of police, and the entire board of aldermen. Next, they inaugurated a forceful policy of banishment. A militia with "fixed bayonets" amid jeering crowds banished from the city forever leading white Republicans and Negro leaders. When the massacre was over, the streets were dotted with dead Negro males. Newspapers and historical sources differ in their estimation of the number of casualties, listed variously as eleven, twelve, and twenty, while some contend that there were "more than one hundred Negroes slain in the conflict."[102] From a moral viewpoint, I must take the stand that the tragic Wilmington event was not a riot but a white massacre of defenseless Blacks. It was justifiable at no point," correctly concluded a noted historian, "a riot directly due to the white man's campaign."[103]

Attention is now directed to the finale of the white supremacy drama of 1898. The major interest of editor Daniels was not the Wilmington event but, rather, plans for celebrating the victorious return of the Democrats to power, and preparations for this event went on for a week. Daily, the *News and Observer* reminded the public: "Great Celebration and Torchlight Procession Next Tuesday Night," and stressed—"EVERYBODY INVITED."

At Raleigh on November 15, Daniels staged a great jubilee in commemoration of the triumph of white supremacy and the rescuing of the state from "Negro Rule." It rivaled, or perhaps surpassed, the gala English Restoration of 1660, restoring Charles II to the throne and symbolizing the end of the "rule of the Saints." Multitudes flowed into the city from all parts of the state, coming early, carrying white supremacy placards, while white supremacy badges were "glowing on many coats."[104] They filled every hotel and rooming house, no doubt at inflated prices. "It was a clear, cold, autumnal day—crisp . . . just enough sunshine to make it comfortable." Intermittently, that comfort was interrupted by currents of fresh, cold wind. Great and elaborate preparations had been made for the event. A triumphal arch of gleaming white had been erected in front of the city hall. All the principal buildings and others along the streets were decorated with long tapestries of the national colors and illuminated by lights in red, white, and blue. And add to this picturesque scene celebrating people, shouting joyously. Tin horns blew, "bells rang and men yelled like mad."[105] And finally, it is safe to conclude that there were many "fountains running with wine" (North Carolina moonshine).

By nightfall this setting had taken on a new dimension of dramatic proportions. "Eastside, westside, all around the town" crackling bonfires blazed, "making the horizon like a little sunset in full bloom." "All over the city were barrels of blazing tar, as moltenly fierce as the inner core of a blast furnace. From them rolled upward a maze of varied colored smoke printed in gorgeous hues by the consuming fires that lit the landscape and silhouetted the heads of the passing throng against the surrounding darkness." Through all this, fireworks of all types exploded, reminding one "of a night of shooting stars."

A grand parade and speeches were the highlights of the event, and it was 7:00 P.M. before the procession was formed and ready to start. The parade was headed by a bandwagon filled with "fine musicians." Following them were 40 mounted marshals. Behind them came a score or more of people carrying placards. A number of bicyclists with gaily decorated wheels came next, and immediately behind them were some 150 horsemen; every rider "had a torchlight which gleamed and blinked like the eye of some mighty Cyclops, through the murky atmosphere." Finally came the carriages containing the speakers and distinguished visitors, then more mounted men carrying torchlights and banners and brooms and pitchforks and transparencies. Among the transparencies were noted the following:[106]

1. "There is retribution in politics."
2. "The same old Solid South."
3. "Simmons is just the thing."
4. "Down with Negro rule."
5. "Pitchfork Brigade—The Manure Pile must be scattered."
6. "Hurrah for Wilmington."
7. "White Supremacy—means work for all."
8. "No more crucifixion on colored crosses."

Joseph Blake, elected surveyor of Wake County, carried a transparency proclaiming his victory, and on his staff were a full-grown possum and a huge sweet potato.

The procession meandered through the major streets, and "through the swirling mist blinked the lights of the city and above the general bank of color rose the white dome of the Capitol, never out of sight. "The streets were filled with spectators, a moving, shouting mass of humanity." The destination of the procession was a rostrum in front of the *News and Observer* building, whose center was illuminated with crossed brooms, symbolic of the white man's victory. Daniels, who presided, had previously extended speaking invitations to prominent people. Letters and telegrams of regrets came from Aycock, Glenn, Waddell, ex-Governor Jarvis, Tillman, and others. One response best expressed the sentiments of those absent: "I will be there with you in spirit if not in flesh." Daniels read all replies with a patriotic fervor, and all were greeted with thunderous applause.

Representing the Democrats were Francis D. Winston, Locke Craig, and Furnifold Simmons, and some lesser-known figures, including Capt. W. P. Snow, whose short address compared the uprising of white men to that of the Greeks when Helen of Troy had been carried away. Craig's address emphasized that "self-preservation demands that the Negro be eliminated as a disturbing element in politics." In time, Daniels introduced State Democratic Executive Committee Chairman, Simmons, who received an ovation that rose above the boom of explosives and the strains of the bands as he mounted the stand. His speech electrified the crowd. In defense of the campaign as conducted by him, he said: "I did not send out a single statement that has not been verified." The Democrats did not need to "resort to falsehood." In conclusion, he promised: "For corruption we will substitute incorruption; for extravagance we will give economy and replace incompetence with competence. What shall we do with the Negro? We will do what is just and fair. The Democrats intend that the Negro shall know his place."

In the midst of the celebration were some unscheduled excitements. A little flurry was caused when the draperies caught fire from the colored lights on top of the arch. The fire alarm was turned in, and the first company responded, but before it had a chance to put a stream of water to it, the fire had been contained by a party of men who hastened to strip off the burning cloth. However, there was one infamous, premeditated incident of racism. During the heat of the white supremacy campaign, orators had declared that the last vestige of Negro direction of white institutions would end when the Democrats came into power. While the speaking and celebrating were in progress, a group of white men marched to the Blind Institution, taking with them a skilled stone mason who cut from the cornerstone of the institution the name of the Negro leader, James H. Young.[107]

The gala day and night of pageantry and jubilation inevitably came to an end. By midnight the streets were deserted, and the city was once again silent. On every street the still-flickering fires burned out, dying one by one, leaving only heaps of ashes. But the spirit of enthusiasm that inspired this demonstration was to live on. William Gaston was able to capture this mood in his poem "The Old North State Forever."[108] Thus, the curtain was lowered on the first act of the Democratic white supremacy drama of 1898. Behind the curtain the stage was hastily being reset for the second act—Black Disfranchisement—to be enacted in 1900.

Notes

1. "Governor Jarvis Talks," an editorial, *North Carolinian* (Raleigh), July 14, 1898.

2. Pocahontas W. Edmunds, *Tar Heels Track the Century* (Raleigh, N.C., 1966), p. 209.

3. Fred Rippy, ed., *Furnifold M. Simmons, Statesman of the New South: Memoirs and Addresses,* (Durham, N.C., 1936), pp. 3–8.

4. Ibid., pp. 17–19.

5. Josephus Daniels, *Editor in Politics* (Chapel Hill, N.C., 1941), pp. 283–84, 410 ff.

6. William A. Mabry, "Negro Suffrage and Fusion Rule in North Carolina," *North Carolina Historical Review* 12 (1935): 44.

7. Joseph Flake Steelman, "The Progressive Movement in North Carolina, 1884–1917" (Ph.D. diss., University of North Carolina, 1955), p. 171.

8. Daniels, *Editor in Politics,* p. 295, 284–85.

9. Joseph L. Morrison, *Josephus Daniels; The Small-d Democrat* (Chapel Hill, N.C., 1966), p. 22.

10. *Wilmington Morning Star,* December 2, 1897.

11. *People's Party Handbook of Facts* (Raleigh, N.C., 1898), pp. 37–38; J. Gide Roulhac Hamilton, *History of North Carolina,* vol. 3, *North Carolina since 1860* (Chicago, 1919), pp. 280–82; *Raleigh News and Observer,* May 19, 1898.

12. People's Party Platform, adopted May 17, 1898.

13. *Raleigh News and Observer,* May 25, 26, and 27, 1898. The Populist Conference Committee (Ayers was out of town) sent five resolutions with a letter that favored cooperation with the Democrats, while maintaining "headquarters at Room No. 19, Park Hotel." See *Is the Democratic Party Honest? A Statement of Facts Issued by the People's Party State Control Committee,* University of North Carolina Library, pp. 17–20.

14. *Democratic Party Handbook* (Raleigh, N.C., 1898), p. 41.

15. *Raleigh News and Observer,* November 4, 1897.

16. Ibid.

17. Ibid.

18. Ibid., July 21, 1898.

19. Ibid., August 26, 1848.

20. Republican Platform, adopted July 20, 1898; *Democratic Party Handbook,* pp. 195–96.

21. Rippy, *Furnifold M. Simmons,* p. 23.

22. This deal was not exposed until the meeting of the 1899 legislature, and it did much to strain relations between the Democrats and the two educators—Charles P. McIver, president of Normal and Industrial School for white women, and Edwin A. Alderman, president of the University of North Carolina. Alderman showed his disgust with the legislature by resigning to become president of Tulane University at New Orleans. Daniels, *Editor in Politics,* pp. 318–23.

23. Luther T. Gobbel, *Church-State Relationships in North Carolina since 1776* (Durham, N.C., 1938), pp. 205–28.

24. Frederick A. Bode, "Southern White Protestantism and Crisis of the New South, 1894–1903" (Ph.D. diss. Yale University, 1969), pp. 297–98.

25. *Raleigh News and Observer,* October 29, 1898.

26. Bode, "Southern White Protestantism," pp. 302–3.

27. *Raleigh News and Observer,* May 13 and August 4, 1898.

28. Ibid., August 6, 1898.

29. *Caucasian*, September 22, 1898.

30. Ibid., October 20, 1898.

31. *Fayetteville Observer*, September 8 and October 20, 1898.

32. George Rountree, "Memorandum of My Personal Recollection of the Election of 1898," Henry G. Connor Papers, Southern Historical Collection, University of North Carolina, Chapel Hill, N.C.

33. Dr. Cyrus Thompson, "Dr. Cyrus Thompson's Great Speech" (Delivered at Clinton, opening of the Populist campaign, August 19, 1898) , University of North Carolina Library, Chapel Hill, N.C., pp. 22–23.

34. Steelman, "Progressive Movement in North Carolina," p. 175; *Fayetteville Observer*, September 3, 1898.

35. *Appleton's Annual Cyclopaedia* 3d ser., (New York, 1898) , 509. The correspondent's letter was printed in all the newspapers in the state. Its arguments were approved or ridiculed according to the political views of the editors. The Democratic papers published it "as a startling revelation of facts."

36. *Caucasian*, October 20, 1898.

37. The Populists presented evidence to show that the Democratic party was a "lawyers' machine" and had for years been controlled and dominated "by one profession of people, viz: Lawyers." The Democratic Convention of 1896 was called the "Great Lawyers' Convention." Out of the seventy-four delegates, there were fifty-seven attorneys, six merchants, four doctors, one editor, and a drummer, with five occupations unknown. The legal machinery was accused not only of stealing from the Populists' platform but also of acting in the interest of the "great syndicate, or railroad corporations or trusts." *Is the Democratic Party Honest?* pp. 21–24.

38. Thomas Meade, "Negro Domination a Blind," an editorial, *Caucasian*, September 28, 1898.

39. Evelyn Underwood, "The Struggle for White Supremacy in North Carolina," (Master's thesis, University of North Carolina, 1943) , p. 49.

40. Ibid., pp. 296–97, *Raleigh News and Observer*, September 18 and November 1, 1904.

41. R. D. W. Connor and Clarence Poe, *The Life and Speeches of Charles Brantley Aycock* (New York, 1912) , pp. 7, 24.

42. Ibid., pp. 44–48.

43. Oliver H. Orr, *Charles Brantley Aycock* (Chapel Hill, N.C., 1961) , pp. 117–20.

44. *Star of Zion*, September 22, 1898.

45. Orr, *Charles Brantley Aycock*, p. 91.

46. Daniels, *Editor in Politics*, p. 297.

47. Ibid., p. 298.

48. Orr, *Charles Brantley Aycock*, p. 122.

49. *Caucasian*, September 22 and 29, 1898.

50. *Raleigh News and Observer*, September 13 and 14, 1898.

51. *Caucasian*, September 22, 1898. The cartoon in the *Raleigh News and Observer* depicted Young inspecting the living quarters of a frightened white woman.

52. Ibid., *Raleigh News and Observer*, September 13 and 14, 1898.

53. *Caucasian*, September 22, 1898.

54. *Raleigh News and Observer*, October 21, 1898.

55. David Bryant Fulton, *Hanover; or, The Persecution of the Lowly* (New York, 1969) , p. 13. Among the older works consulted were Hamilton, *North Carolina Politics since 1860*; Daniels, *Editor in Politics*; William A. Mabry, *The*

Negro in North Carolina Politics since Reconstruction Trinity College Historical Papers, ser. 23 (Durham, N.C., 1940); and more recent works sampled were Helen Edmonds, *The Negro and Fusion Politics in North Carolina, 1894–1901* (Chapel Hill, N.C., 1951), and Steelman, "Progressive Movement in North Carolina."

56. Thomas W. Clawson, "The Wilmington Race Riot of 1898," in the Louis T. Moore Collection, North Carolina Department of Archives and History, Raleigh, N.C. Throughout this source, Mrs. Felton's name is incorrectly spelled as Mrs. Fellows."

57. *Progressive Farmer*, August 30, 1898.

58. *Raleigh News and Observer*, August 24, 1898.

59. *Wilmington Morning Star*, October 18 and 20, 1898, and *Fayetteville Observer*, October 27, 1898.

60. Quoted in Daniels, *Editor in Politics*, p. 286.

61. *Wilmington Morning Star*, October 9, 1889. This was a reprint allegedly taken from Manly's Paper (the *RECORD*).

62. *Biographical Directory of the American Congress, 1774–1929* (Washington, D.C., 1928), p. 1315.

63. *Congressional Record*, 51st Cong., 2d sess. (1891), p. 2693.

64. *Fayetteville Observer*, October 22, 1898.

65. Francis B. Simkins, *The Tillman Movement in South Carolina* (Durham, N.C., 1926), pp. 27–31.

66. Ibid., pp. 95–96.

67. *Fayetteville Observer*, October 22 and 27, 1898; *Raleigh News and Observer*, October 22, 1898.

68. The Red Shirt idea originated with the first Mississippi Plan in 1874 and was designed to generate "enthusiasm among the Democratic masses." Whites, attired in "the red-shirt badge of Southern manhood," organized rifle companies and drilled and marched in public unmasked. The Red Shirts often fired cannons in the vicinity of Republican rallies, "staged torchlight processions, made nocturnal raids against some carpetbaggers and whipped Blacks who were politically active." They put the state "under a kind of martial law." See R. G. Randall and David Donald, *The Civil War and Reconstruction* (Lexington, Mass. 1969), pp. 684–85.

69. Alexander J. McKelway, "North Carolina Suffrage Amendment" *Independent* 2 (August 1900): 2978.

70. Jonathan Daniels, *Tar Heels: A Portrait of North Carolina* (New York, 1941), p. 72.

71. Rountree, "Memorandum of My Personal Recollection," pp. 5–7.

72. *Wilmington Morning Star*, October 29, 1898.

73. *Raleigh Morning Post*, October 23, 1898; *Wilmington Morning Star*, October 25, 1898.

74. *Asheville Morning Gazette*, October 24, 25, and 30, 1898.

75. There are other theories as to what ignited the Ashpole violence. Daniels wrote in his paper that the trouble originated as a consequence of the registrar's failure to allow a Negro to register on the day he applied. Another theory was that a storehouse was robbed and burned and a certain Black was suspected of the crimes. Rumors flowed that Blacks were securing arms and storing ammunitions, while threatening to burn down the town and murder the white citizens. In each racial clash of this nature, the press always charged a Negro with firing the first shot—always against greatly superior numbers. In this situation, a Negro supposedly fired first during ambush upon the whites. *Raleigh News and*

Observer, September 25, 1898; *Pittsboro Chatham Record*, November 3, 1898. See also *Appleton's Annual Cyclopaedia*, 3d ser., vol. 3 (New York, 1898), p. 510.

76. Daniels, *Editor in Politics*, pp. 304–7.

77. *Raleigh News and Observer*, October 25, 1898.

78. Ibid., October 28 and 30, 1898.

79. *Asheville Daily Gazette*, October 28, 1898.

80. *Goldsboro Argus* special to the *Raleigh News and Observer*, October 21, 1898; *Fayetteville Observer*, October 20, 1898.

81. *Raleigh News and Observer*, October 22, 1898.

82. Ibid., October 29, 1898.

83. *Raleigh Morning Post*, October 29, 1898.

84. *Raleigh News and Observer*, October 29, 1898.

85. Ibid.

86. Rountree later recalled that Colonel Waddell made the same statement in Wilmington and "used some rather violent language about choking the Cape Fear River with the bodies of dead negroes." See "Memorandum of My Personal Recollection," p. 9, and *Pittsboro Chatham Record*, November 3, 1898.

87. *Asheville Daily Gazette*, October 30, 1898.

88. *Charlotte Daily Observer*, November 2, 1898.

89. *Raleigh News and Observer*, November 4 and 5, 1898.

90. *Charlotte Daily Observer*, November 4 and 5, 1898.

91. *Raleigh News and Observer*, November 6, 1898.

92. *Outlook*, November 19, 1898.

93. Daniel L. Russell, *Letter Book*, 1897–1901, North Carolina Department of Archives and History, Raleigh, N.C., p. 49.

94. *New York Herald*, November 20, 1898.

95. *Wilmington Morning Star*, November 8, 1898.

96. *Charlotte Daily Observer*, November 8, 1898.

97. Rippy, *Furnifold M. Simmons*, pp. 83, 86.

98. *Raleigh News and Observer*, November 9, 1898.

99. Ibid., November 12, 13, and 14, 1898.

100. *Raleigh Morning Post*, November 9, 1898.

101. Harry Hayden, *The Story of the Wilmington Rebellion* (Wilmington, N.C., 1936), p. 8. See also the *Progressive Farmer*, November 29, 1898.

102. H. Leon Prather, Sr., "The Day the River Ran Red: The Wilmington Racial Massacre, November 10, 1898" (Paper delivered at the annual meeting of the Association for the Study of Afro-American Life and History., Inc., Philadelphia, Pa., October 25, 1974).

103. John Spencer Bassett to Herbert Baxter Adams, November 15, 1898, in *Historical Scholarship in the United States, 1876–1901*, ed. W. Stull Holt (Baltimore, Md., 1938), p. 256.

104. *Charlotte Daily Observer*, November 16, 1898.

105. *Raleigh News and Observer*, November 16, 1898.

106. *North Carolinian*, November 17, 1898.

107. Daniels, *Editor in Politics* (none of the newspapers consulted carried an account of this incident), p. 311.

108. *North Carolinian*, November 17, 1898.

6

Black Disfranchisement and the Origin of Universal Education

The Democrats, defeated in 1894 and 1896, reappeared as the dominant party after the 1898 campaign. Restoration of their former power was their goal in that election. Circumstances demanded that they find some means to permanently entrench their party in North Carolina. Disfranchisement of Black voters was the logical mechanism for achieving this objective. In time, there would appear a suffrage amendment, uniquely designed to extirpate the political power of the Negro voter, while permitting the illiterate white to vote. It also had great educational significance, for section 4 of the document made clear that after 1908, only literate persons could vote.[1] The suffrage amendment thus became an accompaniment to the elimination of illiteracy among the younger generation after 1908. But education was no concern of the Democrats, who had fashioned the document with the perpetuation of white supremacy in ·mind. Since they were bent on capturing the governorship and controlling the legislature in 1900, their uppermost concern was to persuade the voters to approve the amendment by a large majority. There were, however, more dissident factions within the white electorate to be pacified than in the last campaign. Employing their stratagems of 1898, with a few variations introduced, the Democrats launched the second white supremacy movement. It was abetted by a propaganda press carrying articles of vilification and racial cartoons. White supremacy clubs and Red Shirts appeared in greater numbers, with "their range wider and their influence greater than in 1898." At the same time, strains of the "nigger racket" continued to dominate the Democratic theme song, which retained the same melody and pattern of rhythm, but the lyrics were modified somewhat from allegations of "Negro Rule" and "Black Domination" to promotion of the suffrage amendment, necessary to assure the perpetuation of white supremacy. The campaign that follows was intense. It is the purpose of this chapter to chart and follow these salient developments and to observe how an embryonic educational question emerged and rode the political storm to give rise to the issue of public education in 1900.

Our main attention at this point falls on the General Assembly of 1899, in which there were ninety-four seats held by Democrats in the House, a clear majority over the Republicans, who held only forty; twenty-three Democrats to seven Republicans in the Senate; and only three Populists in each house.[2] This predominantly Democratic legislature proceeded to ignore all Republicans, Populists, and Blacks on committee assignment. It elevated Henry G. Connor to Speaker of the House and Charles A. Reynolds to president of the Senate. At the same time, a spirit of revenge permeated the body, a mood best exhibited by Don Hugh McIver of Harnett County, who desired to repeal all Fusion laws at one stroke."[3] However, the calmer heads were emphatically opposed to extreme measures and moved cautiously like skilled surgeons, cutting away the laws that posed a threat to their future security, leaving only those they deemed innocuous. The legislature of 1899 passed a law "to restore good government to the counties of North Carolina." The Democrats repealed the Populists' democratic .features of popular election of local officials and reverted to the practice of appointment, the system set up by the Redeemers in 1876. However, the law was drafted with great ingenuity, in effect applying in totality in the Black Belt, with cunning and deceptive variations wherever the Negro was a political force. Fusion popular election laws were left intact in thirty-two counties, embracing the Carolina Highlands—the Republican stronghold.[4]

With suffrage confined to minority whites of Black Belt counties, principles were pushed aside for expediency. To this end, the legislature created the new county of Scotland out of Richmond and Robeson Counties, counties in which six out of ten people were Black. Here the Red Shirts' influence had "made a terrorist peace." They asked the Democratic legislature of 1899 for a county and got it. "It was a white man's county which is black still."[5] And finally, the Democrats were able to control the municipalities by abolishing the Fusion charters in such places as Wilmington, Raleigh, New Bern, Greenville and Edenton, in addition to returning to the old technique of gerrymandering.[6] Thus, in effect, the reactionary legislature of 1899 had restored the old regime of the Redeemers.

On the question of public education, the Democrats expunged the statute books of all the progressivism enacted by the Fusion legislature of 1897. Their answer to the public school problem was an appropriation of "the first hundred thousand from the state treasury." This sum was to be distributed among the counties on a per capita basis of school population, and its purpose was to bring the school term up to the constitutional requirement of four months. Despite the fanfare given this piece of legislation, leading educators like Alderman and McIver knew that it would add only a few hours to the school term. Concomitantly, it reduced the educational tax on real and personal property from $.20 to $.18, but permitted the poll tax to remain at $1.29 per adult male. The Democrats were determined to eschew the subject of local taxation at this time, for it was too closely identified with fusionism and the futile local tax campaigns of 1897. In abolishing the tax law that allowed automatic or intermittent election, they fell back upon the old law that allowed one-third of the qualified voters to petition the county commissioners for a special school tax to be levied by the latter if approved by popular vote.[7] In criticizing this action, Superintendent Mebane wrote that "one of the serious mistakes of the legislature of 1899 was the repeal of the Acts of 1897. "Instead of repealing laws," he pointed out, "it would have been wiser to legislate to encourage and make it easier to have the special tax. The future citizens of North Carolina will look upon this as a backward step."[8]

Beginning with Tennessee in 1881, the color line had made its way across the South, and capitulation to Jim Crowism became the Southern way. However, as late as 1898 North Carolina had avoided the Jim Crow movement; but with the triumph of white supremacy, it became necessary to institutionalize by legalization the subordinate status of Blacks to fortify the creed of white supremacy. Beginning modestly in 1899, the legislature gave legal sanction to the racial doctrine of providing separate but equal accommodations for passengers on the railroads. The law was entitled "An act to promote the comfort of travellers on railroads, trains and for other purposes" and required separate accommodations for the races in trains and railway stations. Faced with the prospect of providing dual accommodations, the railroads demonstrated stiff opposition to the law.[9] Other Jim Crow laws were destined to sweep the entire state, as the signs For White and For Colored became familiar symbols in waiting rooms, transportation facilities, ferries, restaurants, and courts, where there was even a "Jim Crow Bible for colored witnesses to kiss." In time, residential segregation, the "all-white and all-Negro blocks," evolved. Winston-Salem designated city streets according to the racial majority, proscribing whites and Blacks from living in any block where persons were "forbidden to intermarry."[10] Other cities drew the color line by ownership as well as by occupancy. Finally, in 1913 Clarence Poe, editor of the *Progressive Farmer,* carried the apartheid to an extreme by leading a movement for the segregation of farmlands. And he successfully marshaled the unanimous endorsement of the North Carolina Farmers' Union.[11]

Considering the historical existence of shades of color, running all the way from brown, copper, and "through the cream of white mulattoes," Francis D. Winston promoted a most unique Jim Crow law. On January 21, 1890, he introduced a cohabitation bill (commonly dubbed "bed law") into the House to "punish fornication between negroes and whites by imprisonment of not less than four months or not more than five years" and to make it a felony. Acrimonious debates followed, with the majority of the Democrats against the measure. "It will not pass," predicted Historian Bassett, and he was right.[12]

In spite of the white supremacy orators, the propaganda literature embracing Negrophobia, and white chauvinism, violence, and fraud, the Democratic triumph of 1898 was not decisive. Later figures revealed a majority of less than eighteen thousand instead of the projected twenty-five thousand—a margin much too narrow to leave the Democrats with a feeling of comfort. Obviously, total Black disfranchisement was the permanent solution. Certain prominent Democrats during the late campaign had promised that there would be no disfranchisement of illiterate voters.[13] Notably, this sacred pledge was made by Furnifold M. Simmons, chairman of the State Democratic Committee, and he truly meant it. What he did not say, however, was "white only." The rally cries of the Democrats, worth repeating here, were "Black Domination" and "Save the State from Negro Rule." The 1898 victory was logically interpreted as a mandate from the people to make innocuous the political power of the Negro. Hence, within the Democratic ranks of the 1899 General Assembly, almost every man was for Black disfranchisement, and, if it should "prove unconstitutional . . . it would be better to abrogate the Fourteenth Amendment."

To legally accomplish their objective, the 1899 General Assembly faced the problem of surmounting constitutional obstacles on both the state and federal levels. North Carolina had been "Reconstructed" under the Presidential Plan in June of 1868. In compliance with the provisions of the Reconstruction Acts, a clause provided "that the constitutions of the said States shall never be so amended or changed as to deprive any citizen or class of citizens of the United States of the right to vote in said States."[14] On the constitutionality of the suffrage amendment, the legalist George Rountree expounded that if section 5 of the document was void, leaving section 4 in full force was not worthy of serious consideration. "If one portion of the law is unconstitutional the whole law is void."[15] Moreover, in 1898 the United States Supreme Court validated the Mississippi literacy tests by ruling that the state's constitutional suffrage requirements did not "discriminate between the races."[16] Thus, the road was opened for the legal disfranchisements of Blacks. How to create a legal method of Negro disfranchisement compatible with the United States Constitution posed a serious dilemma. Negro suffrage was assured by the Constitution, which stated: "The rights of citizens of the United States to vote shall not be denied or abridged by the United States or by any State on account of race, color, or previous condition or servitude. . . . The Congress shall have power to enforce this article by appropriate legislation."

Mississippi, with its Second Mississippi Plan of 1890, invented the standard devices for circumventing the restrictions of the Constitution on a racial basis. It pioneered the movement and was the only state to take such action prior to the Populist revolt. "Disfranchisement was accomplished by a Constitutional convention in 1890."[17] For illiterate whites the Second Mississippi Plan provided the "understanding clause" which mandated that after 1892 qualified voters would have to be able "to read any section of the constitution; or to be able to understand the same when read to him, or give a reasonable interpretation thereof." It is needless to point out that in administering the clause, the registration officers were tacitly expected to discriminate against Black voters. In addition, varied devices were set up to trap Black voters, who were required to pay a two-dollar poll tax and, if requested, to present their tax receipts at the polls. The assumption was that they were inclined neither to pay the tax nor to preserve the record of their payment. A two-year residence requirement was imposed, on the theory that Blacks were more migratory than whites. Conviction for bribery, burglary, theft, arson, obtaining money under false pretenses, perjury, forgery, embezzlement, murder, and bigamy would disqualify a person from voting.[18]

Other states, including South Carolina in 1895 and Louisiana in 1898, employed Mississippi's original system but modified it to fit their own formula for Black disfranchisement. Louisiana invented the "grandfather clause" which fascinated the Democratic leaders of North Carolina. The clause read: "No male person who was on January 1, 1867, or at any date prior thereto, entitled to vote under the Constitution or statutes of any State of the United States, wherein he then resided, and no son or grandson of any such person not less than twenty-one years of age at the date of the adoption of this

Constitution . . . shall be denied the right to register and vote in this State by reason of his failure to possess the educational or proper qualifications."[19]

Prior to the meeting of the 1899 General Assembly, Josephus Daniels, at the request of the Democratic Executive Committee, had visited Louisiana "and observed at first hand the working of the suffrage plan recently adopted in that State. Upon returning to North Carolina, he turned in a favorable report on how the Louisiana suffrage amendment had eliminated Blacks from politics, yet still guaranteed every white man the right to vote. Meanwhile, he published in substance all of the constitutional laws of Mississippi, South Carolina, and Louisiana in the *News and Observer,* and when the legislature met, its members had all the data from these states.[20]

We have already encountered Francis B. Winston, originator of the white supremacy clubs of 1898 and sponsor of the ill-fated "bed law." It was he who introduced into the House on January 6 a suffrage bill, which was in essence a duplication of the Louisiana franchise law. The measure was referred to a special joint committee of prominent lawyers of both houses, under the chairmanship of George Rountree of Wilmington. The bill remained in committee for eleven days, where it was debated and underwent considerable revision.[21] Meanwhile, the pros and cons of the measures were debated throughout the state.

Despite the Democrats' use of intimidation and violence against Black voters, Populists, and Republicans during the white supremacy campaign of 1898, five Blacks were elected to the General Assembly. Seated in the 1899 House of Representatives were W. C. Coates of Northhampton county, James Y. Eaton of Vance county, Isaac Smith of Craven county, and O. H. Wright of Warren county, while Thomas O. Fuller, elected from Warren and Vance counties, which constituted the Eleventh District, was the sole representative of his race in the Senate. All of these legislators took a strong stand against the amendment. Soon after the document was sent to the constitutional amendment committee, Smith requested a hearing of a Negro committee before that body.[22] Anxious to listen to their arguments, the amendment committee granted his request by "unanimous consent." On January 13 Smith and a group that included Rev. R. H. W. Leak of Raleigh and Professor John Crosby of Shaw University assembled before the constitutional amendent committee. Rountree took the initiative by explaining to them that the amendment was necessary because the illiterate Negro was unfit to exercise the ballot, and the franchise must be curtailed for the welfare of the state. Reverend Leak was inclined to believe that the masses of Blacks were probably unqualified to formulate intelligent opinions on political questions. Crosby also agreed that the great number of Blacks tended to vote blindly for the Republican party. At the same time, he urged the legislature to deal with the problem fairly. "You want," he pleaded, "to disfranchise enough Negroes to make it certain that good government will prevail. Do that and stop. Do not go to the extent of persecution."[23]

A few days later a Black caucus of some eighty-nine delegates, chiefly from the Black Belt counties, met in Raleigh to discuss the impending amendment. Prominent among the delegates were United States Congressman George H. White, John C. Dancy, Dr. A. A. Scruggs, and Reverend Leak. Congressman White presided over the body, and Dancy served as secretary. White, along with several other delegates, led a movement, to no avail, for the adoption of a resolution that advised Blacks to emigrate in case the Democrats made their stay in North Carolina "intolerable." This Negro State Council, as the conference named itself, sent a message to the legislature asking it not to pass any laws that would "blunt our aspirations, ruin our manhood and lessen our usefulness as citizens, but guarantee us equal chance with other men to work out our destiny."[24]

Naturally, Fuller, being the only Black member in the state Senate, led the fight there against the proposed amendment. He contended that it was unnecessary, unconstitutional, impractical, impolitic, unwise, unjust, and contrary to the spirit of American democratic institutions.[25] Meanwhile, "Ike" Smith had circulated an open letter among the members of the legislature that began with a biblical text, Proverbs 29:14, saying: "The king that faithfully judgeth the poor, his throne shall be established forever!" Employing Black psychology, he admitted that "the great and good white race is king" and reminded the Democrats: "Remember your word and your promise made during the campaign, that if the Democrats won, the colored man would not be disfranchised."[26] Speaking against the amendment, Wright called it a "great sledge hammer of political death." And referring to the charge that ignorance disqualified Blacks as voters, Eaton took the white members of the General Assembly to task when he asked: "Why is the Negro ignorant? Is it not your fault? Wasn't there a law on the books in 1831 making it a crime for a Negro to learn to read and write? This law was in force until 1865. Now thirty three years afterward, you are making the result of your own wrong the pretext for disfranchising the Negro."[27] Momentarily, silence prevailed following Eaton's speech. But the overwhelmingly Democratic legislature was caught in its own web—Black disfranchisement; there was no turning back, for it had reached the point of no return.

The original Winston bill underwent considerable revision in the hands of the committee. While it was being amended, a vocal minority in the legislature advocated not submitting it to the people. They were afraid that any debate on a suffrage amendment might arouse such suspicion among the illiterate white voters as to doom it to defeat. Like the promoters of the Mississippi suffrage law, they preferred that a constitutional convention be called to enact the bill without submitting it to the people. This procedure was strongly opposed by such prominent Democrats as Chairman Simmons, Connor, Rountree, Daniels, Aycock, Craig, and others. The House passed the suffrage amendment on February 18 by a vote of seventy-nine to twenty-nine, and bedlam broke loose in the crowded galleries. The next day the bill steamrolled through the Senate, crushing the opposition by a vote of forty-two to six. "The People Will Speak Next," declared the *News and Observer,* meaning that the amendment would be a major issue in the 1900 gubernatorial election.[28]

The main provisions of the amendment in its final form were: (1) every person presenting himself for registration must be able to read and write any section of the Constitution written in the English language, and have paid his poll tax; (2) no male person entitled to vote on January 1, 1867, or prior thereto, and no descendant of any such person shall be disfranchised by the amendment; (3) voters shall have registered prior to December 1, 1908; and (4) all persons so registered thereafter have the right to vote in all elections, if they have paid their poll tax.[29] The first clause standing alone would confine suffrage to persons able to read and write English. The second clause added to it would extend the right of suffrage to partically all white males in the state, and would also have the effect of disfranchising all illiterate Blacks and enfranchising all illiterate whites. The third clause modifies the other two and excludes all illiterate whites who became twenty-one years of age after 1908, and after this date, no white could vote unless he could read and write the English language and pay the poll tax. In defense of the grandfather clause, Aycock voiced public sentiment when he said: "We permitted him (the white man) to vote by reason of his inherited qualification, white supremacy."[30]

During the time between the passing of the suffrage amendment and the gubernatorial elections, comments and discussions (basically opposed to the measure) were echoed in the press in parts of the Piedmont and Highland counties and even in the halls of Congress. To be expected, the Democratic papers, led by the *Raleigh News and Observer,* the *Charlotte Observer,* the *Wilmington Messenger,* the *Wilmington Morning Star,* and the *Asheville Citizen,* were the most enthusiastic champions of the amendment. Prominent among the opposition were the *Caucasian,* the *Progressive Farmer,* and the formerly Democratic *Asheville Gazette,* which came out against the amendment and reflected the same sentiment in Western North Carolina. An embittered Ramsey, editor of the *Progressive Farmer,* now joined hands with Governor Russell, United States Senator Pritchard, Populist Marion Butler, and Dr. Cyrus Thompson. In denouncing the amendment, Butler wrote: "The last words of a dying man tell whether he is a saint or a sinner. So with the present legislature. . . . The election law is a plumb humbug. The law is made in the interest of the Democratic Bourbon machine." He continued with the warning that suffrage measures "disfranchise more whites than Negroes. There is no differences between a Negro and a white man with an office hunting Democrat."[31]

In examining the opposition toward the amendment, one point should be made clear: neither the Republicans nor the Populists were concerned about the Negro's political future; the major theme of their argument was that the suffrage bill discriminated against and would ultimately disfranchise the illiterate white man. Both Republicans and Populists quickly lined up to defeat the disfranchisement bill, but it was the Populist leaders who represented themselves as the sole champions of the illiterate whites. Resolutions adopted by the Populist Executive Committee on January 18, 1900, warned: "This amendment will disfranchise approximately as many white men as it will Negroes in this state, and will leave the Negro still a factor in politics." Another cogent argument was that the document would leave the vote in the hands of Blacks in the cities, where they had the advantages of education, while it would disfranchise the country farmhands. This class of literate Blacks would hold the balance of power in close elections, and white politicians would continue to appeal to Negro voters. Furthermore, poor people unable to pay the poll tax would be disfranchised. And finally, the unfortunate "white boys" who would come of legal age after 1908 and who could not read and write would be disfranchised and placed on the same level as Blacks.[32] The conclusion, here, was that "the political conditions of the state would, in no sense, be improved by the adoption of the Suffrage Amendment."

The unconstitutionality of the grandfather clause was the main theme of the Republican's arguments. The Populists also did not omit this point. "I find without much surprise," Butler wrote, "that it (the amendment) is clearly in conflict with the provisions of the Constitution of the United States."[33] During a Republican conference held in Statesville in November of 1899, Senator Pritchard pointed out that the amendment violated the 1868 Act of Congress and was also in conflict with the Fourteenth and Fifteenth Amendments to the federal Constitution. Moreover, rumors were circulated in the Democratic presses that Governor Russell and other Republicans contemplated testing the amendment in the courts.[34] Case in point, the Republican state chairman, during his party's conference, was authorized to employ counsel to test the document. Such gestures certainly generated a feeling of apprehension within the ranks of the Democrats.

However, the Democratic leaders had some comfort, since more than 150 state lawyers had read and reported favorably upon the amendment. But, indeed, the responses would have been different if they had petitioned the opinion of non-Southern constitutional lawyers. For example, the *Outlook* concluded: "If the amendment should be brought before the Supreme Court, it would be declared unconstitutional." This prospect created other fears, the general fear among the white voters being "that while the educational clause would be sustained by the courts, the 'grandfather-clause' protecting white voters, would be overthrown, and thus the white illiterates would suffer disfranchisement together with the colored."[35] For better or worse, the Republicans never got around to testing the constitutionality of the amendment.

Nevertheless, Senator Pritchard carried the controversy into the halls of Congress. On January 8, 1890, he introduced in the United States Senate a resolution declaring that the suffrage amendment being considered in his state was unconstitutional. He logically concluded that "any state which conferred the right to vote upon certain citizens because of their descent from certain persons . . . and excluded other citizens because they are not descended from certain persons . . . in the opinion of the Senate" was in clear violation of the Fourteenth Amendment and Fifteenth Amendment.[36] The resolution met with defeat; some days later he reintroduced it. Pritchard's resolution was an indirect challenge to other states with similar amendments. Naturally, it occasioned vehement protests from other Southern Democrats, namely, Senators Hernando de Soto and H. D. Money of Mississippi, Samuel D. McEnery of Louisiana, and John T. Morgan of Alabama. Senator D. McEnery reminded Pritchard that Congress had no authority to pass a resolution declaring the amendment to be unconstitutional and that the issue was one to be decided by the Supreme Court.[37] In defense of the North Carolina amendment, Senator de Soto contended that states in regions other than the South had educational qualifications. He also maintained that representation in Congress could not be affected by the amendment because it was based on population and not on votes cast.[38] Senator Morgan took the floor and, in a fiery speech, defended the Southern states' right to rid themselves of Negro rule; and "no body of white people in the world could be expected to quietly accept a situation so distressing and demoralizing as is created by Negro suffrage in the South."[39]

On January 23, Senator Pritchard took the floor in rebuttal to the attacks made against the resolution. He rejected the allegation that the Republican party had forced Negro suffrage upon the South. He emphasized that the race issue had been injected into politics "to blind the Southern people to the splendid results of Republican legislation which had brought prosperity to the nation" and was solidifying a Republican unity in the South. Accordingly, he warned that the Republican party could not afford to fold its hands and permit the Democratic party to again secure political ascendancy "by resorting to unconstitutional method." This august body took no significant action on the Pritchard resolution, for there was no real interest in the fate of Black voters. This was in keeping with the spirit and temper of the age and nation, which was rapidly capitulating to "the Mississippi Plan as the American Way."[40]

Every political figure and the public at large knew that the suffrage amendment would be the major issue in the gubernatorial election of 1900. It is needless to point out that the Democrats were looking forward to it with great expectation. Their top priorities were to recapture the governorship from the Republicans and to secure public approval to write the new suffrage amendment into the state constitution. Nineteen hundred was also the year of the national elections. Anticipating the possibility of federal interference with the North Carolina elections, the Democrats took no chances; they adroitly changed the time of the state elections to Thursday, August 2, 1900.[41]

The Democratic State Convention, meeting on April 11, 1900, at Raleigh, "was the greatest and most enthusiastic political convention that men of that generation had ever seen." The people poured into Raleigh more like "crusaders than partisans." Even the *Caucasian,* the main organ of the Populists, admitted that it was the largest political gathering ever assembled in the city.[42] Many of the stray sheep (Populists) and others had returned to the fold. Prominent among these was Charles H. Mebane, present Fusionist state superintendent of public instruction. He made it known that he was again a candidate for that office and had the backing of all the leading educators and some outstanding Democrats, including editor Daniels of the *News and Observer.*[43] Moreover, Mebane supported the suffrage amendment. Nevertheless, educational qualifications were not important, for the Democrats were determined to make a clean sweep of the "Fusion Crowd"; they passed over Mebane and nominated Thomas F. Toon, then sixty years old, frail and sickly. His only

183

qualification for the office was an honorable record as a Confederate soldier.[44]

Toon was born in 1840 in Columbus County, graduated from Wake Forest College, and later rose to the rank of colonel in the Confederate Army. He had devoted his life to teaching public school and farming but was more successful at the latter occupation. In extolling his qualifications, the *News and Observer* boasted: "One farmer who could make a living at teaching and farming brings to the office vigor of body and intelligence of mind, experience in life and good common sense. He is clean, honest, upright. His elevation to the high office is an example of the office seeking the man."[45]

The nomination of Charles B. Aycock as the Democratic gubernatorial candidate was no surprise, and the applause and shouts of elation following the announcement was deafening. The platform denounced Negro rule, glorified Democratic accomplishments since 1876, and stressed the necessity of adopting the suffrage amendment. In regard to public education, it reminded the voters: "We heartily commend the action of the General Assembly of 1899 for appropriating one hundred thousand dollars for the benefit of public education of the state, and pledge ourselves to increase the school fund so as to make at least a four months school term in each year in every school district in the state."[46]

In his keynote speech before the convention that nominated him, Aycock seized the opportunity to identify public education with the ensuing campaign. Among his opening remarks, he declared: "The fight is on . . . we unfurl anew the old banner . . . we inscribe thereon white supremacy and its perpetuation. . . . Life and property and liberty from the mountains to the sea shall rest secure in the guardian of the law . . . to do this we must disfranchise the Negro. This movement comes 'from the people." He then ventured to lecture on the value of education as the foundation of white supremacy and denounced anyone who sought to perpetuate illiteracy in the state as a "miserable demagogue." He called attention to section 4 of the suffrage amendment, which mandated that after 1908, only literate persons would be enfranchised. "The man," Aycock declared, "who seeks in the face of these provisions to encourage illiteracy is a public enemy and deserves the contempt of all mankind." In conclusion, and speaking directly to the numerous Democratic orators soon to hit the campaign circuit, he said: "In your speeches to the people, in your talks with them on the streets and farms and by the firesides, do not hesitate to discuss this section . . . speak the truth, 'tell it in Gath, publish it in the streets of Askalon' that universal education of the white children of North Carolina will send us forward with a bound in the race with the world."[47]

The Populist Convention met on April 18 at Raleigh and warned that those who had been saying that the People's party was dead were "either mistaken, or will see the grandest insurrection they have ever seen."[48] Condemining the suffrage amendment, it proceeded to draw up a straight ticket, headed by Dr. Cyrus Thompson as the gubernatorial candidate.

The Republican Convention, meeting on May 2 at Raleigh, nominated Spencer B. Adams for governor. Its platform denied the Democrats' charge of Negro rule and criticized the suffrage amendment as being unconstitutional. On the question of education, the platform declared: The Republican party has always fostered education. That party engrafted in the organic law of the state the mandatory requirements providing public schools for both white and Black, but this "party will never accept ignorance as a crime, whose penalty is disfranchisement, so long as the cause of that ignorance is the neglect of the state."[49]

From the very beginning, Simmons and other Democratic leaders had set the stage for an aggressive and offensive campaign, keeping the Republicans and the Populists on the defense throughout the 1900s. As a forerunner of other campaign orators, Winston traversed the state reorganizing his white supremacy clubs.[50] Meanwhile, the Red Shirts were being activated to stalk about and spread their terror among non-Democrats. And with them, Ben Tillman, by their invitation, was in the state to abet the cause with speeches that included his familiar tirades against the Negro.[51] In the meantime, Norman J. Jennett returned to the state to draw his lurid propaganda racist cartoons. Already in circulation was the *Democratic Catechism,* designed to answer all questions that might arise over the suffrage amendment. Its purpose was to convince whites that the amendment would disfranchise the Negro and not a "single white man." The *News and Observer* gave wide coverage to the catechism.[52]

The official *Democratic Party Handbook* of 1900 was the most systematic campaign document. It included the catechism and other pertinent data, all centered around the doctrine of white supremacy.[53] As pointed out in the preceding chapter, the success of this election depended upon the ability of the Democrats to groom a key candidate having enough public magnetism to attract en masse admirers and dedicated followers. Indeed, as has been demonstrated earlier, they created their star in Aycock. Thus, at this time, let us succinctly follow his campaign itinerary.

On April 16, the Democrats inaugurated their gubernatorial campaign with a big rally at Burlington. Aycock was the main speaker. Early in the address he told his audience that the issues of the campaign "amount to one thing—the negro question. The Democratic

185

Caucasian *(Raleigh)*, *June 28, 1900*

Raleigh News and Observer, *July 3, 1900*

Raleigh News and Observer, *July 4, 1900*

Caucasian *(Raleigh), July 12, 1900*

Raleigh News and Observer, *July 14, 1900*

Caucasian *(Raleigh), July 15, 1900*

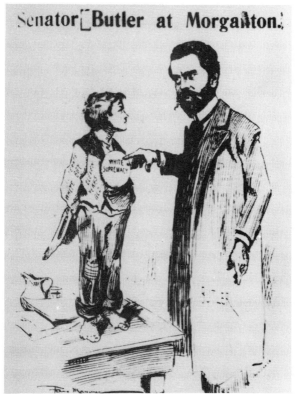

Senator Butler at Morganton.

Caucasian *(Raleigh), July 28, 1900*

party for years," he continued, "has been fighting this issue until at last it has made up its mind that it must be settled, and settled once and for all. We are going to win this fight, and we want to win it with practical unanimity. I've sort of got used to the unanimous way of doing business, and I'm in favor of it." Turning his attention to the suffrage amendment, he closed by declaring: "This amendment was drawn with great skill after long thought, and with full knowledge of the end to be attained . . . [and if it would] deprive one white man, however ignorant or humble, of his suffrage, I would not support it."[54]

After the Burlington rally, the Democratic orators began to stump the state. They included Locke Craig; Robert B. Glenn; Alfred M. Waddell; ex-Governor Thomas J. Jarvis; Julian Carr; William A. Guthrie, the Populist candidate for governor in 1896; the veteran educational campaigner Charles D. McIver; and the current Fusionist state superintendent of public instruction, Charles H. Mebane.[55]

Meanwhile, for the remainder of April, Aycock traversed the central part of the state, moving westward in a zigzag fashion, speaking at central cities such as Winston-Salem, Greensboro, Hickory, Asheville, Murphy, Waynesville, and Charlotte.

Throughout the campaign, he often made short, impromptu speeches to groups of curious people gathered at small stations and railroad crossings. About the beginning of May, he was touring the Black Belt cities, which included Fayetteville, Wilmington, New Bern, Elizabeth City, Washington, and Edenton.[56] It should be emphasized at this point that neither Aycock nor his campaigning cohorts made any educational promises during the first two months of the 1900 campaign. Centering their theme on the "Negro question," the Democratic orators stressed to their audiences the necessity of adopting the suffrage amendment.[57] For example, in Winston-Salem, Aycock made an emotional appeal to white voters to lift the state from the "disgrace of negro rule," while at Hickory he declared that the "negro shall not rule." And on another occasion he told the crowds that the negro "was a curse to the state and the Democrats were tired of the Negro in politics." At the same time, he urged white voters not to allow "the destinies of this great state to be harnessed by this great black crowd."[58] Such phrases he repeated countless times.

While the Democratic orators were busy haranguing their audiences with racist spleen, the Republicans and the Populists had organized themselves in a solid phalanx to campaign against the suffrage amendment. They concentrated their efforts in the Highland counties, the Republican stronghold, where there was a high rate of white illiteracy. Most active were Senator Pritchard; Spencer B. Adams, the Republican gubernatorial candidate; and Marion Butler. In touring the mountain counties, Butler repeatedly warned the illiterate whites of the danger of disfranchisement that the amendment held for them in the event that the grandfather clause was not sustained by the court.

Then too, the Republicans and Populists played upon the apprehension of illiterate whites by pointing out the inadequate and poorly maintained schools. Thus, white parents became fearful about voting for anything that could exclude their sons from the ballot boxes. Meanwhile, the *Asheville Gazette,* formerly a Democratic organ, changed fronts by becoming antiamendment and emerged as the Republican-Populist voice of the region.[59]

The Republican-Populist forces were rather successful in arousing suspicion against the amendment especially among illiterate whites, who soon began to voice strong opposition toward the document. Many parents logically concluded that it would work a hardship on white children who would come of legal age after 1908. As the 1900 gubernatorial campaign progressed, Democratic leaders were thrown into a quandary by this unexpected opposition. Resistance was so strong that some prominent Democrats desired to delete the 1908 provision from the amendment. In view of this development, a special session of the General Assembly was called during the heat of the campaign for the purpose of obtaining a "declaration that the entire amendment must stand or fall together."[60] The resolution was passed. But Aycock, it was claimed, had threatened to withdraw from the campaign if his party modified the amendment; he regarded the entire document as a pledge to the people to be submitted as adopted.[61]

Around the beginning of June Aycock again stumped the Highland counties, where strong opposition had solidified against the amendment. Many parents were openly expressing fears that they might not be able to educate their sons, who would stand then on the same footing as illiterate Negroes in 1909. Aycock did not take these fears lightly. His speeches gradually shifted from the Negro issue to a sudden emphasis on universal education for whites. He explained the problem to mountain whites in the Highlands: "We recognize and provide for the God-given and hereditary superiority of the white man and all white children now thirteen years of age, but for the future, as to all under thirteen, we call on them to assert their superiority of which we boast by learning to read and write."[62] Aycock prevailed upon the white parents to send their children to school, in order to prepare them for the progressive age in which the rising generation was to live. Likewise, he admonished the apprehensive parents by pointing out that it was not the answer to say: "I am afraid I will not be able to educate my boy, and therefore cannot vote for this amendment." Aycock also sought to make the suffrage amendment more palatable by promising that no white child would be disfranchised by 1908 because of the lack of educational opportunity. "If you vote for me," he said in the western town of Waynesville, "I will want you to do so with the distinct understanding that I shall devote the four years of my official term to the upbuilding of the public schools of North Carolina." In another western town, he declared: "If I am elected, my administration pledges itself to abolish illiteracy."[63]

To what extent does Aycock's early career identify him as a progressive educator? There is no precedent that would relate him as a friend of public education, and he only became a strong advocate during the time of his gubernatorial campaign. His contemporary, Alderman, later recalled: "I lived in the town with Aycock, of course, during those days from '82 to '89. At that time he was not particularly interested in public education. He was a young lawyer not particularly, entirely consumed with law, and I do not think terribly eager about the whole idea of compulsory education. In fact, I would imagine he would be against compulsory education."[64] Professor Helen E. Edmonds offers deeper insight into Aycock's educational background. "It is doubtful" she wrote, "if his interest in educational improvements was evolutionary. His record at the University of North Carolina after his first year is hardly average." She has also made a careful study of his early campaign speeches and discovered that no pledges had been made in support of universal education.[65] Political expediency was clearly a weighty factor in Aycock's "stand upon the two planks of disfranchisement and universal education."

While Aycock was echoing the new theme of universal education in the western part of the state, Democratic orators in eastern North Carolina were still beating the drums to the refrain of the "nigger racket." Here the campaign in its final days was picking up momentum. To give it greater impetus, Ben Tillman again appeared. The Democrats at Concord advertised that a feast would be provided for ten thousand people.[66] If the Democrats had now made public education the cornerstone of their campaign, it maybe safely assumed that Tillman's speeches would not reflect it. He continued to make speeches unrelated to education, while popularizing his racist views as follows: "The great mistake . . . Yankees made is that they think that a negro is a black white man . . . the negro may become as white as the fairest lady in the audience and he will be no nearer the white race than a mule is to the fastest racehorse."[67] Another orator promised: "We will all be in line August 2nd for White Supremacy if the Lord lets us live and have health and strength that day." Lee S. Overman, candidate for the Senate in 1895, spoke eloquently of a new era, with "appeals to the white people to stand together, and forever lift the black shadow from old North Carolina." Only State Superintendent Mebane's speeches voiced the sentiments of a friend of education.[68]

Aycock returned to the Black Belt counties during the final stages of the white supremacy drama of 1900 and stepped up his campaign. The Red Shirts reappeared in greater numbers than in 1898; they swarmed around him everywhere he appeared like bees seeking nectar. The same was true of the enthusiastic crowds, abetted by the railroads, which featured reduced excursion rates. The *News and Observer* and other Democratic papers carried daily notices of his itinerary, as follows:

1. Wake County—Fuquay Springs, Friday, July 13th
2. Wayne County—Goldsboro, Saturday, July 14th

3. Chatham County—Pittsboro, Monday, July 16th
 4. Moore County—Carthage, Tuesday, July 17th
 5. Montgomery County—Wednesday, July 18th
 6. Robeson County—Lumberton, Thursday, July 19th
 7. Bladen County—Elizabethtown, Friday, July 20th
 8. Columbus County—Whiteville, Saturday, July 21st
 9. Hertford County—Winston, Monday, July 23rd
10. Bertie County—Aulander, Tuesday, July 24th
11. Nash County—Kenansville, Thursday, July 26th
12. Pender County—Burgaw, Friday, July 27th
13. Sampson County—Clinton, Saturday, July 28th
14. Carteret County—Beaufort, Monday, July 30th
15. Morehead City—Monday, July 30th (night)
16. Jones County—Trenton, Tuesday, July 31st

The above agenda does not include the many impromptu speeches Aycock made between stops. A chronicle of his campaign from this point is truly a study in rustic pageantry. He was greeted at Pittsboro by "some 3000 people—ALL IN PURE WHITE"; in the procession that followed the first float was a huge white swan drawn by four white horses and filled with thirty young factory girls in pure white, wearing white supremacy badges and banners. Upon his arrival the next day at Carthage, he was met by the Seaboard Air Line Band and by hundreds of Red Shirts who later doffed their "splendid red uniform and donned spotless white." An estimated three thousand people lined the streets and cheered as the parade passed. First came the chief marshals with lady escorts on horseback. Next came an immense float drawn by six mules containing the thirty-eight members of the band. Following the float was the carriage in which Aycock rode; then came a huge white float filled with white women with the inscription "White Supremacy," "Protect Us." There were also horsemen carrying banners of the national colors and white flags with such inscriptions as "No Negro Rule"—"Our Women Shall Be Protected" and "White Rule for Tarheels." Such scenes were duplicated more or less for the remainder of the campaign. The largest of these, however, occurred at Lumberton. Thirteen railroad carloads of excursionists, and among them many Red Shirts from Rockingham and other counties, accompanied Aycock and Glenn to the Lumberton rally. En route, the train stopped at Laurinburg, where a large crowd had assembled to hear a ten-minute speech. Aycock "mounted a box" and said in part: "North Carolina . . . was the birthplace of the first white child born to English parentage, and that child was a girl. It has always been our proud boast that whatsoever things we undertook it was in the name and with the benediction of our glorious womanhood." He also predicted that the Democrats would win by fifty thousand votes. This projection was followed by a mighty roar of cheers and applause, which continued for several moments, coming and going "in waves." As the slow train pulled off, Aycock stood on the rear platform, visibly elated over the demonstration, and, with a broad smile engulfing his countenance, waved back at many white handkerchiefs moving in unison. And at every station "people piled on"; men, women, children, and even Croatan Indians got aboard.

When the Aycock-Glenn train came in sight of Lumberton, strains from the brass band were quickly drowned out from "a sound which grew and swelled into deafening roars of thousands of human voices." Hundreds of Red Shirts, a "perfect jam of men on foot and horse-back," could be seen lining the street as far as the eye could reach. Some streamed up to the car, carrying high above their heads two large armchairs. Aycock was seated in one and the corpulent Glenn in the other. In time, the seething mass of humanity began to move, and high above it the chairs and their occupants "bobbed and danced like corks on the waves." Glenn sat back dignified and solemn. In contrast, Aycock considered the situation a bit ridiculous, as he "sat grasping the arms of his chair, with his derby far back on his head," and managed to force a broad grin. The procession that followed was similar to others described previously. In it, however, was a new addition. The Red Shirts had brought along the rapid-fire gun that was displayed at Wilmington prior to the riot. And during the rousing reception and throughout the day, a cannon was fired every few minutes.[70]

Before we look at the results of the election, a word needs to be said about the intimidation and violence resorted to by members of all parties. Both the Populists and the Democrats invaded their opponents' political meetings. The Populists were accused of making personal assaults on prominent Democrats in Columbus and Sampson Counties.[71] The pelting of opposition speakers with rotten eggs was a common practice. Charles M. Gold, editor of the *Wilson Times,* was "egged" while discussing the suffrage amendment at a meeting composed entirely of Populists.[72] There were other instances of humiliation. At Winston two registrars were "arrested and assaulted" for refusing to register some Blacks. Likewise, four men—three Blacks and one white—forced an official at gunpoint to open the book for registration.[73] To be sure, the Democrats were not idle. A hoodlumish mob of Democrats attacked a rival speaker at Smithfield, and the Republican chairman telegraphed Governor Russell for troops, a request with which he complied. However, the sheriff of Johnston County countermanded the appeal, and the troops were ordered back to Raleigh.[74] The activities of the Red Shirts were most evident; they employed various types of intimidation to deprive Republicans and

194

Populists, including Marion Butler, of the right to speak publicly. The *New York Post* reminded its readers of the "terrorizing by the "Red Shirts," "while the United States shuts its eye to North Carolina government maintained by force."[75]

It is a foregone conclusion that violence would have erupted had Blacks been politically active in this election. Governor Russell and others counseled Blacks to refrain voluntarily from voting. In all probability, this advice was needless in view of Red Shirt activities on the eve of the election. As in 1898, Red Shirts carrying all types of guns could be seen throughout the Black Belt loitering around the polls in a riotous manner. Finally, election day of August 2 dawned. Surprisingly, all proceeded in a quiet and organized manner. The elections were most gratifying to the Democrats. Aycock won the governorship against his Republican rival, Adams, by a decisive vote of 186,650 to 126,296, the largest majority ever attained by a gubernatorial candidate. Likewise, the suffrage amendment won by a margin of 53,932 votes in a vote of 182,217 to 128,285.[76] The jubilant *News and Observer* referred to the Democratic victory as "the political revolution of 1900."

"But fraud and rascality have reigned supreme," complained Butler. He reported that in Fayetteville the Democrats had won by the mere margin of 350 votes in 1898, but that in this election they won by a margin of 1,100 votes, which meant that all Blacks voted for the amendment. The Democrats, charged the *Caucasian*, "stole everything in sight on the 2nd, election day," along with resorting to other illegalities. Blacks who were brave enough to vote against the amendment and for the Fusionist ticket were counted as voting the straight Democratic ticket, or their votes were thrown out. And only two votes were cast against the amendment in the predominantly black New Hanover County.[77] In addition, intimidation and physical terror were employed against Blacks throughout the Black Belt regions, which strongly suggests an almost complete elimination of Black voters. The city of Wilmington was a typical example. In 1900 "only 30 voted out of 3000 entitled to vote." On February 23, 1901, on the floor of Congress, George H. White of North Carolina, and the only Black member, called his colleagues' attention to the alleged supression of Negro votes in his native state. He pointed out that in the general election of the previous August for the adoption of the Constitutional amendment with the grandfather clause, Scotland Neck had a registered white vote of 395, mostly Democrats, and a registered Black vote of 534, virtually all Republicans. When the count was announced, however, there were 831 Democrats to 75 Republicans; but in the town of Halifax (same county) the result was much more pronounced. In that town the registered Republican vote was 345, and the total registered vote of the township was 539, but when the count was announced it stood 990 Democrats to 41 Republicans, or 492 more Democratic votes counted than were registered votes in the township. Comment here is unnecessary. "The claim is made that the Constitution followed the Flag," wrote Butler. "Perhaps it has gone to the Philippines or China—it certainly has departed from North Carolina during this election."[79]

Statistics on the impact of the new suffrage amendment on Negro voting are not available. The Union League of New York City conducted a study in December of 1903 and noted a decrease of 34 percent in the number of Black voters.[80] Thus, the Negro population being one-third of the state's total population, the inference here is that the North Carolina suffrage amendment destroyed the voting power of the Black man. More important, the grandfather clause of 1908 was a gate that white registrars could arbitrarily swing open for white men and close on Black men. To be sure, this gave whites a tremendous lead in the electorate. It was a tacit conclusion that the Negro was told to catch up if he could, but, with the poor substandard educational facilities soon to be offered him, he would never catch up.

Whatever the major issues are during any significant election, it follows that in a Democratic society the officials who are elected generally reflect the sentiment of the people whose votes placed them in office. The movement to disfranchise the Negro, commonly recognized by authorities and others, became a fait accompli. The real impact of it on Black voters is difficult to determine, in light of inadequate registration statistics. However, the so-called revolution of 1900 terminated the issue of the Negro as a political force in the state. But the question of race continued to emerge as a political issue. Why? As in the story in Greek mythology, the whites refused to give it a decent burial. Moreover, the Negro served as a scapegoat to carry the amendment, which certainly would have failed without him, along with his being held accountable for the ills of North Carolina politics. Thus, Black disfranchisement has been identified with Southern progressivism and well documented to support the claim. Nevertheless, it is ironic how scholars and informed citizens could conceive of any community surviving in a democratic society without political power.

"During the August campaign of 1900," wrote the "Lame Duck" Superintendent Mebane, "we heard many glorious promises as to the education of the rising and the future generations of children of this state. Some of these pledges came from honest, sincere hearts, and the men who made those promises did so in good faith, but others were playing to the grandstand."[81] When the Democrats began to promulgate universal education as a campaign pledge, an unequivocal promise was made to improve the neglected public schools by providing a four-month school term throughout the state. This was to assure that the white child would not suffer disfranchisement after 1908 for lack of educational opportunities. These promises were absolutely necessary, for without them, one contemporary concluded, "the amendment would have been defeated."[82]

In consideration of this statement, we return once again to Aycock and the Democratic legislature of 1901, beginning with a brief description of the pomp preceding the governor's inaugural address as it related to education. The mood and setting of Aycock's inauguration on January 18, 1901, were auspicious. The day was perfect, with "a cloudless sky—and the air like crystal," and a gentle breeze blew across the city. The Raleigh streets had on their holiday dress, the buildings being draped with the American flag and with red, white, and blue buntings. Thousands of visitors had crowded into the city for this Democratic triumph. Conspicuously absent were the Red Shirts. In their stead was a military procession, the largest ever witnessed in the city. It was comprised of fifteen hundred state guards, soldiers, cadets, out-of-town battalions, and naval reserves, along with bands.[83] As the parade passed through the principal streets, the spectators cheered loudly. It may be safely assumed that these cheers included the familiar "Rebel Yell." In time, the procession reached the Capitol Square, where the immense throng had gathered. The people jammed around the erected stage, with the legislators seated in a reserved section in the square.

Francis D. Winston was the master of ceremonies. Silence prevailed as Justice Walter Clark of the state supreme court administered the oath of office. Thunderous applause and cheers broke the stillness, and when they subsided Aycock began his address, this time using notes. After a short introduction, he said to his audience: "This year we meet under extraordinary circumstances—one party goes out of power and another comes in; one policy ends and a new one begins; one century passes away and a new century claims our service; a new constitution greets the new century." Quickly changing his mood and with his voice reaching a crescendo, he charged the·vanquished party with a "ruinous . . . stamp of Republicanism." "Under their rule [his words now moving in a rhythmic crescendo to sway the crowd], lawlessness stalked the State like pestilence-death stalked about at noonday . . . the sound of the pistol was heard more frequently than songs of mocking-birds—the screams of women fleeing from pursuing brutes closed the gates of our hearts with a shock."[84]

Beginning a new theme, he exhibited ·a marked change in temper. As to education, his words were cautious. But he reminded his

197

listeners that on a "hundred platforms" he had "pledged the State, its strength, its heart, its wealth, to universal education," for the illiterate poor man and the "education of his children." Turning and focusing his eyes upon the legislators, he spoke these words: "Gentlemen of the General Assembly, you will not have aught to fear when you make ample provision for the education of the whole people. Rich and poor alike . . . and pledge ourselves to increase the school fund so as to make at least a four months' term in each year in every school district in the State. . . . For my part, I declare to you that it shall be my constant aim and effort, during the four years that I . . . serve the people of this state, to redeem the most solemn of all our pledges."[85]

The General Assembly had already convened since January 4, 1901. Evidence strongly suggests that it was not "an educational legislative body," as it was labeled by the *News and Observer*. There were, however, a few sincere and honest friends of education in the assembly. For instance, on January 11, State Representative Simms introduced in the House a bill to appropriate $250,000 annually for the benefit of the public schools. At the same time, Senator Justice introduced a measure to amend the law so as to increase Governor Aycock's annual salary from $3,000 to $4,000. Introduction of this bill resulted in a heated debate, along with instances of humor. Senator Crisp said: "Judging by Governor Russell's appearance he has been very extravagant in his living," the inference being that Governor-elect Aycock could live in a grand style on his current salary.[86] A Senator Thomas explained that he opposed any increase in salary until the school term was lengthened. The measure finally passed by an almost strictly party vote, 35 to 12. Only three Democrats voted against the bill. In the House the measure passed by a slim margin, in a vote of 55 to 53. The Simms bill to provide a $250,000 appropriation for schools was lost in the wrangle over increasing the governor's salary.

A general feeling of unanimity and fellowship characterized the final meeting of the 1901 General Assembly. Early in this session, Senator Yarborough moved that the rules against smoking be suspended, but Senator Patterson preferred that they remain in force until Judge Allen supplied the members with cigars. Judge Allen protested vigorously against smoking, and asked: "What will the gentleman from Wayne county furnish those who do not smoke?" Yarborough replied: "I'll tell the gentlemen in private." The members lighted their cigars but soon called a halt after Speaker Moore "spied a lady in the gallery." New bills were passed almost unanimously with a modicum of discussion. During the mirthful final hours, the governor's older brother, Senator Benjamin F. Aycock, was elected "Educational Agitator for the State of North Carolina." In this capacity, he was to conduct at least five agitations per week, opening each meeting by singing vociferously the "Old North State" and continuing to agitate until the entire state was "fully agitated from mountains to the sea." Senator Aycock was empowered to ride on all common carriers, lodge at hotels, and eat at public establishments free of charge. The amount of his salary was contingent upon the number of educational agitations given.

Joyous singing and farewell speeches followed the last action. Senator Winston called upon senior member John W. Jenkins of Granville County to say a few parting words, and Jenkins boastfully declared: "We pledged to the people that no white man should be deprived of an education, and we have done our duty. Now go forth with a lion's heart, an eagle's wings, a serpent's wisdom, doing all things good for North Carolina." Afterward, Speaker Moore ordered the curtain drawn and the doors thrown open so that the numerous spectators who had assembled in the gallery might witness the adjournment of the Senate. The Senators struck up "Auld Lang Syne," singing lustily as the Speaker kept time with his gavel. "Tenting on the Old Camp Ground," "Home Sweet Home," and "The Old North State" followed. The women in the gallery were invited to come down to the floor and assist in the singing. However, "they were bashful and merely lent sweet strains to the melody from their lofty point of vantage."[87]

To what extent had the Democrats fulfilled their promise of universal education? An examination of the educational legislation enacted by the 1901 General Assembly reveals that the most significant law was "An Act to Carry Out the Constitutional Requirements of the Public Schools." Under the provisions of this act, a "Second Hundred Thousand Dollars" was appropriated the public schools for the purpose of bringing all school terms up to four months.[88]

Along with the Democrats' "First Hundred Thousand" in 1899, the schools now realized a total of two hundred thousand dollars. "The Second Hundred Thousand" was a joke, since it was inadequate for a four-months term in every school district. This legislature also passed a law that provided for the appropriation of five thousand dollars for the establishment of rural libraries. Third, it created a textbook commission that was empowered to select a series of textbooks to be used in all public schools for a period of five years. Fourth, it enacted a law designating one day each year as "North Carolina Day" in the public schools.[89] The purpose of this day was to awaken in the rising generation interest and pride in the history of North Carolina and confidence in the future.

It is interesting to note that the 1901 legislature adjourned without making provisions for the "Second Hundred Thousand Dollars." For the first time in many years, the legislature was confronted with a treasury deficit. Editor Daniels wrote: "Let no tax payer escape! Property that can not be seen will continue to escape until its owners are forbidden to ignore payment unless it is listed." People were not paying taxes, and in support of his claim against the "Tax Dodgers," he singled out one man who owned property valued at from $4,500 to $5,000, but who only paid taxes on $500![90] Worse still, the railroads were not paying their share of taxes. Furthermore, the state had never adequately assessed railroad property. On two occasions, Superintendent Mebane recommended to the General Assembly that this excellent source of revenue be utilized for support of public education. He asserted: "The railroads in North Carolina now net five million dollars annually," and that a fair assessment of their property and taxation of gross earnings would give to the public schools $700,000 and leave to the railroads $4.3 million to carry out of the state.[91] In light of the substantial contributions made to the Democratic campaign, Aycock naturally reached an understanding with the railroads.[92] The schools, nevertheless, did receive the "Second Hundred Thousand Dollars" for the 1901–2 school term, but appropriation for the 1903 session was to become an acute problem.

The Democrats, contrary to their campaign promises, made no significant improvements in public education during the Aycock administration, and as we shall see, such was the case during the subsequent decade also. In light of this evidence, it is clear that the Democrats' sacred pledge of universal education was a political hoax. The campaigns, did, however, stimulate a graded school movement in some urban areas, including Goldsboro, Henderson, Oxford, Kingston, Gastonia, Durham and Mt. Airy. These cities scheduled educational rallies to generate enthusiam for the approaching bond elections, and the proper school officials called upon Governor Aycock to speak as an added impetus to the pro-school forces. He obliged them and was accompanied by Superintendent Toon. But the tour was too much for the aging superintendent, who soon became ill, and Governor Aycock was forced to assume his speaking commitments as a one-man crusader for education. To be sure, his popularity as an orator had not diminished. In Mt. Airy, the largest political assembly yet crowded into the opera house to hear him.[93] This scene was typical. Moreover, the special tax elections were being carried; people were talking education in every town of importance, where graded schools were already constructed, or under construction. The one exception was the city of Washington, located in the Black Belt. The paramount question at this time was, "what is being done to ameliorate conditions in the rural school districts?"

The educational sentiments of the urbanites failed to pervade the rural areas where dwelled the masses, and there was almost complete silence on the educational question. Benjamin Aycock, the elected educational agitator, like Superintendent Toon, also became ill.[94] Furthermore, Governor Aycock's one-man crusade did not convince anyone that he was fulfilling his campaign pledge to provide universal education. It is worth repeating that universal education in North Carolina, constitutionally and politically, meant a four-months school term. As late as June 30, 1902, twenty-seven counties still failed to provide such terms for their white schools. Thus, more than one thousand districts maintained school terms of less than four months, while forty counties did not support four-months terms for the Negro schools.[95] Obviously, Governor Aycock needed all the proeducational forces, both inside and outside the state, to effect an educational renaissance. The Conference of Education in the South had already met at Winston-Salem in April of 1901. An educational crusade soon to explode throughout the state, was in the making. This movement will be traced in chapter 7.

Notes

1. *Charlotte Daily Observer*, February 10, 1899.

2. *Appleton's Annual Cyclopaedia*, 3d ser., vol. 3 (New York, 1898), p. 511.

3. John F. Jones, ed., *Memoirs and Speechs of Locke Craig, Governor of North Carolina, 1913–1917* (Asheville, N.C., 1923), pp. 32–33.

4. *Public Laws of North Carolina*, 1899, chaps. 127, 145, 167, 301, passim.

5. *Raleigh News and Observer*, November 4, 1898; Hugh T. Lefler, ed., *North Carolina History Told by Contemporaries* (Chapel Hill, N.C., 1934), p. 398.

6. *Public Laws of North Carolina*, 1899, chaps. 16, 30, 48, 82, 115, passim.

7. Ibid., chap. 11, p. 35 ff; chap. 637; chap. 732.

8. *Biennial School Report*, 1898–1900, p. 11.

9. *Public Laws of North Carolina*, 1899, chap. 384; *Raleigh News and Observer*, January 25, 1899.

10. C. Vann Woodward, *The Strange Career of Jim Crow* (New York, 1966), pp. 97, 101–2, 67 ff.

11. Clarence Poe, "Rural Land Segregation between Whites and Negroes: A Reply to Mr. Stephenson," *South Atlantic Quarterly* 13 (1914): 207–12.

12. *Union Republican*, January 26, February 2 and 9, and March 23, 1899. John Spencer Bassett to Herbert Baxter Adams, February 19, 1899, in *Historical Scholarship in the United States, 1876–1901*, ed. W. Stull Holt (Baltimore, Md., 1938).

13. *Raleigh News and Observer*, October 25, 1899; *Charlotte Daily Observer*, October 25, 1899.

14. *Asheville Gazette*, October 19, 1898.

15. George Rountree, "Great Speech of George Rountree" Delivered in the House of Representatives of North Carolina on the subject of the Constitutional Amendment, June 1900), University of North Carolina Library, Chapel Hill, N.C.

16. *Williams* v. *Mississippi*, U. S. 213 (1898), in Thomas D. Clark, ed., *The*

South since Reconstruction (New York, 1973) , p. 170.

17. C. Vann Woodward, *Origins of the New South, 1877–1913* (Baton Rouge, La., 1951) , p. 321. The first Mississippi Plan was devised in 1876 and was a shotgun policy of intimidation and violence, against Republicans and Blacks who were politically active; Randall and Donald, *Civil War and Reconstruction*, pp. 684–85.

18. Clark, "The Mississippi Plan" in *The South since Reconstruction*, pp. 149–51.

19. "The Grandfather Clause," in ibid., pp. 152–54.

20. William A. Mabry, "White Supremacy and the North Carolina Suffrage Amendment," *North Carolina Historical Review* 13 (193) : 3; Josephus Daniels, *Editor in Politics* (Chapel Hill, N.C., 1941) , pp. 324–26.

21. *Union Republican*, January 12, 1899; *Caucasian*, January 19, 1899.

22. North Carolina *House Journal* (1899) , p. 83.

23. *Charlotte Daily Observer*, January 14, 1899.

24. Ibid., January 19, 1899. ,

25. Thomas O. Fuller, *Twenty Years in Public Life, 1890–1910* (Nashville, Tenn., 1910) , pp. 80–91.

26. *Charlotte Daily Observer*, February 16, 1899.

27. *Raleigh News and Observer*, February 18, 1899.

28. Ibid., February 19 and 20, 1899.

29. Proposed Suffrage Amendment, in Platform and Resolution of the People's Party, 1900, University of North Carolina Library, Chapel Hill, N.C., pp. 2–5.

30. "Views of Distinguished Statesmen of South and North Carolina on White Supremacy," *Atlanta Journal* (undated) , University of North Carolina, Chapel Hill, N.C.

31. *Raleigh Caucasian,* January 4 and March 2, 1900.

32. *Asheville Gazette,* October 19, 1899.

33. *Raleigh News and Observer,* October 8, 1899.

34. Ibid., April 5, 1899; *Wilmington Morning Star,* April 5, 1899.

35. *Outlook,* August 11, 1900, pp. 843 44.

36. *Congressional Record*, 56 Cong., 1st sess. (1899–1900) , pp. 1027–38. Jeter C. Pritchard, "On the Proposed Amendment to the Constitution of North Carolina" (Speech delivered before the United States Senate, Washington, D.C., January 22, 1900) .

37. H. D. Money, "Right of Suffrage in North Carolina" (Speech delivered before the United States Senate, Washington, D.C., January 25, 1900) .

38. *Congressional Record,* 56 Cong. 1st sess. (1899–1900) , pp. 1161–73.

39. John T. Morgan, "Negro Suffrage in the South" (Speech delivered before the United States Senate, Washington, D.C., January 8, 1900.

40. For a stimulating discussion that supports this conclusion, see Woodward, *Origins of the New South*, pp. 321–49.

41. William A. Mabry, *The Negro in North Carolina Politics since Reconstruction* (Durham, N.C., 1940) , p. 63.

42. *Caucasian,* April 11, 1900.

43. *Raleigh News and Observer,* April 10, 1900.

44. R. D. W. Connor, *North Carolina: Rebuilding an Ancient Commonwealth, 1584–1925*, 3 vols. (New York, 1929) , 2: 467.

45. *Raleigh News and Observer,* January 15, 1900.

46. Lefler *North Carolina History*, p. 405.

47. R. D. W. Connor and Clarence Poe, *The Life and Speeches of Charles Brantley Aycock* (New York, 1912) , pp. 84–85, 221–24.

48. *Raleigh Caucasian*, April 19, 1900.

49. *Appleton's Annual Cyclopaedia*, 3d ser., vol. 5 (New York, 1900), pp. 444–45.

50. *Raleigh News and Observer*, May 16, 1900.

51. *Ibid.*, July 13 and 19, 1900.

52. *Democratic Catechism* (Raleigh, N.C., 1900), University of North Carolina Library, Chapel Hill, N.C.

53. *Democratic Party Handbook* (Raleigh, N.C., 1907), University of North Carolina Library, Chapel Hill, N.C.

54. *Raleigh News and Observer*, April 17, 1890.

55. *Ibid.*, May 20, July 18, and July 25, 1900.

56. *Ibid.*, April 18, 19, 20, 22, 27, 29, 30, and May 1, 3, 5, 6, 8, 10, 19, 1900.

57. *Independent*, August 9, 1900.

58. *Raleigh News and Observer*, April 18, 19 and 20, 1900.

59. *Asheville Gazette*, May 16, 29 and 31, 1900.

60. Rippy, ed., *Furnifold M. Simmons, Statesmen of the New South: Memoirs and Addresses* (Durham, N.C., 1936), p. 28.

61. Connor and Poe, *Life and Speeches of Charles Brantley Aycock*, p. 86.

62. Charles Brantley Aycock Papers, North Carolina Department of Archives and History, Raleigh.

63. *Ibid.*

64. Alderman to Charles W. Dabney, December 31, 1929, in Dennis Malone MS notes, Alderman Library, University of Virginia, Charlottesville, Va. Quoted in Louis R. Harlan, *Separate and Unequal: Public School Campaigns and Racism in the Southern Seaboard States, 1901–1915* (Chapel Hill, N.C., 1958), pp. 64–65.

65. Helen Edmonds, *The Negro and Fusion Politics in North Carolina, 1894–1901* (Chapel Hill, N.C., 1951), p. 216 n.

66. *Raleigh News and Observer*, July 13, 1900.

67. *Ibid.*, July 19, 1900.

68. *Ibid.*, August 2, 1900.

69. *Ibid.*, July 13, 1900.

70. *Ibid.*, July 17, 18, 19, 20, and 26, 1900. The largest of these demonstrations was held a day before the election at Burlington. A crowd of from ten thousand to fifteen thousand lined the sidewalks as some five hundred Red Shirts, a half dozen floats containing girls in white, and hundreds of farmers in wagons, carts, and buggies passed by, creating a parade nearly one mile long. *Ibid.*, August 2, 1900.

71. *Charlotte Observer*, July 20, 1900.

72. *Raleigh News and Observer*, July 20, 1900.

73. *Ibid.*, July 11 and 15, 1900.

74. *Asheville Gazette*, August 2, 3, 1900, and *Raleigh News and Observer*, August 2, 1900.

75. *Union Republican*, August 9, 1900.

76. R. D. W. Connor, ed., *A Manual of North Carolina* (Raleigh, N.C., 1913), pp. 1006, 1018.

77. *Caucasian*, August 9 and 30, 1900.

78. *Congressional Record*, 56th Cong. 2d sess. (1901), p. 1635.

79. *Independent*, August 16, 1900; *Outlook*, August 11, 1900.

80. Francis G. Cappey, "Suffrage Limitations in the South," *Political Science Quarterly* vol. 20 (March, 1905): 60.

81. *Biennial School Report*, 1898–1900, 31.

82. Josiah W. Bailey, "Popular Education and the Race Problem in North

Carolina," *Outlook*, May 11, 1901, p. 115.

83. *Raleigh News and Observer*, January 16, 1901.

84. Connor and Poe, *Life and Speeches of Charles Brantley Aycock*, pp. 229–30.

85. *Public Documents of North Carolina*, 1901, pp. 4–7.

86. *Raleigh News and Observer*, January 12 and March 14 and 16, 1901.

87. Ibid., March 16, 1901.

88. *Public Laws of North Carolina*, 1901, chap. 543.

89. Ibid., chaps. 1, 164, and 662.

90. *Raleigh News and Observer*, February 20 and 23, 1901.

91. *Biennial School Report*, 1896–98, pp. 38, 34–35.

92. *Raleigh News and Observer*, January 29, 1901.

93. Ibid., April 7, 9, 28, and May 4, 8, 9, 10, 1901.

94. Ibid., April 6, 1901.

95. *Biennial School Report*, 1902–4, pp. 102–6.

Part III

*The Crusade for Redemption
of the "Forgotten Man":
Men and Measures of the Forces
That Propelled the Movement*

7

The Public School Movement: A Crusade Against Ignorance

The educational promises made by the Democrats during the gubernatorial campaigns of 1900 boomeranged as the new officeholders were unable to fulfill them. However, the Democrats did create an educational vacuum, and leading educators and other forces came forward to fill it. What social (humanitarian) forces were behind this movement? In what ways did these forces pervade North Carolina to give momentum to the educational spirit generated by political leaders? The purpose of this chapter is threefold: (1) to identify the outside educational forces that invaded the state to help stimulate educational support in 1901; (2) to identify the way in which the educational leaders unified their forces to inaugurate a great educational revival; and (3) to describe the agencies and methods they employed to promote a great educational movement beginning in 1902.

In the same year (1898) that the Democrats launched the white supremacy campaigns, the Conference for Education in the South was established at Capon Springs, a small resort town in West Virginia. Here had ensued a private discussion of the deplorable state of education in the South and ways of decreasing the rate of Southern illiteracy. The discussion was led by Dr. Edward Abbot, an Episcopal clergyman from Cambridge, Massachusetts, and editor of the *Literary World,* and William H. Sale, a former Confederate captain and the proprietor of the Capon Springs Hotel. The two men ultimately (January 12, 1898,) drew up plans for an educational conference. Invitations were extended to approximately sixty persons in different sections of the country who were interested in a discussion of questions of "common interest involved in this problem." The participants of the proposed meetings were to be guests of the Capon Springs Hotel.[1]

The conference met as scheduled on June 29, 1898, and held meetings for four days in a little chapel on the hotel grounds. It was attended by some thirty-six persons, including Bishop T. B. Dudley of Kentucky, J. L. M. Curry of Alabama, A. D. Mayo of Boston, H. B. Frissell of Hampton Institute, and the following North Carolinians: John Wilkes and Jane R. Wilkes of Raleigh, Thomas Lawrence of Asheville, and Charles Meserve.[2] Evidence strongly suggests that problems of Negro education received top priority. Of major concern was the "capacity of the Negro for higher education"; the urgent needs of trained teachers, professionals, and other "leaders for the masses"; and the necessity of training the Negro "to meet the. industrial competition of the South."[3] After deliberation on these problems, the delegates, at the suggestion of Mayo, adopted the name Conference for Education in the South, with Dudley as president, Curry as vice-president, and A. B. Hunter of Raleigh as secretary-treasurer.[4]

It must be emphasized at this point that originally the membership in the Conference for Education in the South was limited to the list of guests invited to share the hospitality of Captain Sales at his Capon Springs hotel. The only qualification for membership was personal presence and a sympathetic record. Thus, what began as a purely voluntary association, with its major emphasis on Negro education and with no clear-cut objectives, was soon to burgeon into a vital force behind a Southern regional educational movement. And North Carolina was to be the proving ground for this worthy experiment.

A second conference was held at Capon Springs for three days beginning on June 21, 1899. The participants at this assembly included Robert C. Ogden, a New York philanthropist, who brought to the Conference in his private coach some twenty-five "ladies and gentlemen" from the North. This was the first of a series of southward trips made by Ogden, which Walter H. Page later dubbed "excursions into ennobling experiences," and commonly known as the Ogden movement.[5] Among the guests were Curry, Mayo, Dr. George S. Dickerman of New Haven, Connecticut, George Foster Peabody of New York, Dr. Albert Shaw of the *Review of Reviews,* St. Clair McKelway of the *Brooklyn Eagle,* Clark B. Firestone of the *New York Evening Mail,* and Stanhope Haus of the *New York Times.* At this conference there was a distinct movement away from consideration of the singular question of Negro education to deliberation

CAPON SPRINGS & BATHS

Hampshire Co., W. Va.

BEST DRAINAGE
TO BE
FOUND.
NO FOGS.
NO MALARIA
NO MOSQUITOES
1800 FEET
ELEVATION

LARGEST
SWIMMING POOL
OF ALKALINE
LITHIA WATER
IN THE UNITED STATES.
90 BY 40 FEET
FINE BAND OF MUSIC
FOR LAWN AND
BALLROOM

W. H. SALE, PROP.

ALKALINE LITHIA AND IRON WATERS.

Resident Physician.
DR. ALFRED H. POWELL.
805 Park Ave., Baltimore, Md.
After June 1st, Capon Springs, W. Va.

Manager,
CHAS. F. NELSON.
Transportation.
S. B. SALE.

Capon Springs, W. Va., May 10th 1899

Dear Sir:--

The Second Capon Springs Conference on Education in the South, will be held here, Wednesday, Thursday and Friday, June 21st, 22nd and 23d.

I take pleasure in extending to you a most cordial invitation to attend this Conference as my guest; and I shall be pleased to have you arrive on Monday, June 19th, if you can conveniently do so.

The closing exercises of the Conference will be held on Friday evening, and you will be expected to remain as my guest until Saturday morning. Round-trip tickets to Capon Springs, W. Va., should be obtained, and on such tickets my Cashier will be instructed to refund the sum of $2.00. You will be doing me a favor if you will let me know at an early date, if you can arrange to be present. Hoping that you will be with us, I am,

Yours very truly,

W. H. SALE.

M. B. S. Dickerman
Hampton Inst.,
Hampton Va.

An invitation to attend the Second Capon Springs Conference, extended by William H. Sale, proprietor of the Capon Springs (W. Va.) Hotel. Courtesy of the Library of Congress on issues involving the entire South. Among the major issues discussed were the dire need for normal schools and the lack of provisions for higher education for women.[6] Although the delegates failed to decide upon any specific plans, a resolution was adopted declaring that "the education . . . in the South is the pressing and imperative need and the noble achievements of the Southern Commonwealths in the creation of a common school system for both races deserve . . . the sympathetic recognition of the country."[7]

By the time the Third Conference for Education rolled around, the faces of McIver and Alderman could be spotted among the delegates, and, as one participant of the assembly observed: "McIver made a pleasant impression at this conference."[8] Meanwhile, Ogden had forged ahead to become its leader and was giving it greater impetus. Robert C. Ogden achieved his "greater renown late in life as a benefactor and promoter of Southern education." Born on June 20, 1836, in Philadelphia, he moved with his family to New York in 1854 and secured a position with Donlin and Company, clothiers. In 1879 he resigned and took charge of John Wanamaker's Oak Hall clothing store in Philadelphia. Six years later, he became the general manager and partner in the Wanamaker firm and in 1896 established a New York branch of Wanamaker's.[9] Besides possessing great business acumen, Ogden was profoundly religious and was deeply involved in the affairs of the Presbyterian church both in Philadelphia and in New York. He served on both boards of trustees and on the building committee of Union Theological Seminary, and was noted for "various philanthropies and disaster relief activities."[10]

Ogden's involvement with Southern education began early in life, following his meeting Samuel Chapman Armstrong, founder of Hampton Institute, in 1869. He maintained a steady correspondence with Armstrong's successor, Dr. H. B. Frissell and with others associated with Hampton. Ogden also served as a trustee and for a time as president of the boards for both Hampton and Tuskegee Institutes. He was elected president of the Conference for Education in the South in 1900 and held the position until his death in 1913. Of his personality, Booker T. Washington wrote in 1910: "The impression the first sight of such a man as Mr. Ogden made upon me, I shall never forget." He was well over six-feet tall and had a "vigorous physique" and later in life he wore a distinguished-looking white beard and pince-nez glasses.[11]

After being elected president of the conference in 1900, Ogden led in organizing the sessions and took the first positive move in deciding the direction in which the organization should go. He believed strongly that progress was most likely to occur when the "best men" of the North and the South became aware of conditions in the South, discussed the situation with each other, and engaged in cooperative efforts to deal with the problems. His views on the course the organization should take were expressed in a speech in which he advocated the application of business methods to all activities of the conference, while maintaining that the conference could "find a wide sphere of salutary influences by bringing the subject of popular education urgently before the business men of the South as a business proposition."[12]

The Conference for Education gained national recognition during its fourth meeting at Winston-Salem, scheduled for three days beginning April 18, 1901. Believing that the problem of education in the Southern states was national in scope and should attract the attention of both North and South, Ogden engaged a special train of Pullman cars to accommodate more than seventy persons as his guests for the Winston-Salem meeting. They included editors, capitalists, publishers, and such notable figures as Dean James E. Russell of Teachers College, Columbia University; George Foster Peabody, Wall Street banker and philanthropist; the Reverend Dr. Walter Buttrick, noted Baptist clergyman of Albany, New York; Walter H. Page; John D. Rockefeller, Jr.; and William H. Baldwin, young president of the Long Island Railroad. They joined the entourage at various points, such as Philadelphia, Pennsylvania; Hampton, Virginia; Atlanta, Georgia; and Greensboro, North Carolina. Ogden's objective for this tour was to enable his guests to visit interesting places in the South, with the meeting at Winston-Salem serving as the chief point of visitation. The *New York Times* ran an editorial and reported the event to be "the most notable gathering of educators in the country."[13] Local editors were even more enthusiastic in their praise. "Even the National Education Association," declared the *Daily Sentinel* of Winston-Salem, "can boast of no more distinguished members in all walks of life than the Conference for Education in the South." Winston-Salem—the "twin city" with its ideal railroad facilities—was viewed as ideal for the meeting. Bishop Edward Ronthaler of the Moravian Church and Dr. J. H. Caldwell, president of Salem College, made available to the conference the buildings of their institutions, while the local citizens made great plans for the entertainment of the members of the conference in their homes.[14] With President Ogden presiding, Governor Aycock extended a welcome to the diversified group and spoke eloquently of a new era in public education.[15] He was followed by Bishop Rondthaler, who addressed the assemblage on the subject of the definition and aims of the conference. Other stirring addresses were delivered on fundamental problems of Southern education. Dr. George S. Dickerman of New Haven, Connecticut, compared the South with the North in

NINTH ANNUAL CONFERENCE FOR EDUCATION IN THE SOUTH,
LEXINGTON, KY., MAY 2, 3 AND 4.
ANNIVERSARY OF HAMPTON INSTITUTE, MAY 7 AND 8.
SPECIAL TRAIN TO BOTH THE ABOVE, WILL LEAVE NEW YORK
ABOUT NOON, TUESDAY, MAY 1 (POSSIBLY MONDAY, APRIL 30) AND
WILL ARRIVE ON RETURN EARLY WEDNESDAY, MAY 9.
COMPLETE DETAILED INFORMATION WILL BE SUPPLIED IN
ADVANCE OF THE DATE FIXED FOR DEPARTURE.

REQUESTING YOUR ATTENTION TO THE ABOVE, I DESIRE TO
ASK THAT

WILL DO ME THE HONOR TO BE MY GUEST   FOR THE PROPOSED
EXCURSION.
THE LEXINGTON PEOPLE ARE VERY DESIROUS FOR A THOR-
OUGHLY REPRESENTATIVE ASSEMBLY FROM ALL SECTIONS OF THE
COUNTRY.
THE PROGRAM FOR THE SESSIONS OF THE CONFERENCE
PROMISES UNUSUAL INTEREST IN HARMONY WITH THE PROGRES-
SIVE EXPERIENCE OF FORMER YEARS. THE HAMPTON ANNIVERSAR-
IES ARE UNIQUE AND IMPRESSIVE.
SIMILAR EXCURSIONS FOR SEVERAL SUCCESSIVE YEARS HAVE
PRODUCED LARGE RESULTS IN THE PROMOTION OF EDUCATIONAL
INTERESTS AND NATIONAL SPIRIT.
YOU WILL PROBABLY RECEIVE THE GENERAL CIRCULAR
CONCERNING THE CONFERENCE. IF YOU ACCEPT THIS INVITATION
PLEASE IGNORE THE REQUEST TO NOTIFY THE COMMITTEE AT
LEXINGTON. MY OFFICE WILL ATTEND TO THAT FOR YOU.
KINDLY USE THE ENCLOSED ENVELOPE FOR REPLY.

YOURS VERY TRULY,

Robert C. Ogden

*An invitation from Robert C. Ogden to attend the Ninth Annual
Conference for Education in the South.* **Courtesy of the Library of
Congress**

educational requirements.[16] McIver delivered a unique speech on
his pet theme, the education of women.[17] However, it was Charles
W. Dabney, a former North Carolinian and the current president
of the University of Tennessee, who electrified the delegates with
a frank and uncompromising address on the deficiencies of Southern
education. Among the major problems he touched upon were the

need for secondary schools, for increased teacher pay, and for expert supervision in the rural areas. He told his audience that education of the Negro was essential. Dabney recognized that if the South was to have an efficient system of public schools, educational legislation and methods of taxation had to be completely "turned around." In conclusion, he strongly emphasized the need for a central propaganda agency "which shall conduct a campaign for free public education," and he urged the conference to "take steps to establish such an agency."[18]

Taking its cue from Dabney's proposal, the conference passed special resolutions designed to initiate a great public school movement aimed at redeeming what Page earlier had dubbed the "Forgotten Man."[19] One resolution authorized the president of the conference to appoint an executive board of seven, "fully authorized and empowered to conduct a campaign of education for free schools for all people."[20] At this juncture the reformers were searching for an organization structure for their educational objectives and destined to endure would be the Southern Education Board. After a series of meetings in New York City, Ogden named the executive board: Dr. Buttrick, Curry, Peabody, Frissell, McIver, Alderman, and Dabney. At the suggestion of Dabney, the newly created executive board shifted its operations to North Carolina. Curry called a meeting of the Southern members to assemble in Greensboro on September 13, 1901. Only Frissell, Dabney, and McIver were able to attend, and they proceeded to draw up plans for an organization that included a supervising director; a general Southern agent to advise on all Southern questions; and a literary bureau" to investigate state public school systems and individual schools and colleges, to recommend improvement on reforms, to conduct campaigns of education by publishing and distributing literature to school officers and newspapers, and to advise on school legislation. District directors were also appointed: McIver for North Carolina, Alderman for Louisiana, and Frissell for Virginia. The two field agents chosen were Dickerman, whose job it was to direct work in public meetings and to conduct campaigns for increased taxation, and Booker T. Washington, who was responsible for the education of Blacks, with "leading whites to be induced to aid in the direction of colored schools." And finally, Edgar Gardner Murphy was made executive secretary.[21]

In time, Curry and Alderman joined Dabney, Frissell, and McIver at Asheville, where the five men proceeded to complete the organization of the board, which became known as the Southern Education Board. They finally completed this task in November of 1901 in New York City, choosing Ogden as president, McIver as secretary, and Peabody as treasurer.[22] Thus, the great Southern Education

Board came into existence. It was comprised of both Northern and Southern progressives. Members from the North included Ogden, Baldwin, Peabody, Page, Buttrick, and Shaw, while the Southern representatives were McIver, Curry, Dabney, Murphy, and Washington. For initial financial support Peabody pledged forty thousand dollars annually for the first two years. At the outset, it was decided that none of the board's funds would be used to assist schools but, instead, would be applied exclusively for the purpose of stimulating favorable public sentiment toward local taxation for the purpose of establishing better schools and longer school terms, instituting a compulsory-school-attendance law, and consolidating rural schools.[23] In brief, the Southern Education Board was strictly a publicity agency, designed to stimulate favorable educational sentiment through propaganda. "Preach a Crusade against Ignorance" was the motto adopted. In keeping with this objective, accordingly, there was created an agency called the Bureau of Investigation and Information, established at Knoxville, Tennessee. Dabney was named director, a position he held for two years. He then became president of the University of Tennessee. The bureau began its work on February 1, 1902, by inaugurating an extensive survey of the educational conditions of schools, particularly rural schools. By fall the bureau was issuing three types of publication: (1) circulars that contained reports and discussions of the conference; (2) bulletins issued under the title of *Southern Education* that contained material on educational conditions in each Southern state and provided brief arguments and statements for use by campaign workers; and (3) *Southern Education Notes.* The last was published biweekly and contained all types of information suitable for republishing in newspapers.[24]

The educational leaders soon sired an allied organization—the mammoth General Education Board. Its originators reasoned: "If the facts known by them were to be made public, and if information was brought forward from trustworthy sources, large sums of money would be given in the course of the next few years."[25] Indeed, they were correct. In a short time the board became the greatest of the educational philanthropies. Its prodigious finances were the result of a single benefactor, the oil tycoon John D. Rockefeller, Sr. Young Rockefeller was the person primarily responsible for the establishment of this philanthropy. He had become interested in the movement following the Winston-Salem tour. After returning home, he had influenced his father to make a donation for the cause of Southern education.[26] On June 30, 1902, young Rockefeller announced his father's initial gift of $1 million. In January 1903, this philanthropy was incorporated as follows: "*Be it Enacted by the Senate and House of Representatives of the United States of America. . . . that*

William H. Baldwin, Jr., Jabez L. M. Curry, Frederick T. Gates, Daniel C. Gilman, Morris K. Jesup, Robert C. Ogden, Walter Hines Page, George Foster Peabody, and Albert Stowe; and their successors . . . constitute a body corporate . . . (and) that the name of such a body shall be GENERAL EDUCATION BOARD."[27]

On October 1, 1905, Rockefeller, Sr., added $10 million to the above sum under the condition that the principal was to be held in perpetuity as a foundation to promote a comprehensive system of higher education in the United States. Again on February 5, 1907, he contributed securities valued at $32 million; "one-third was to be added to the permanent endowment of the Board and two thirds to be applied to objects with the corporate purpose of the Board as either the donor or his son might from time to time direct." Later, on June 29, 1909, he added securities valued at $10 million to the permanent endowment of the board, making a grand total of $53 million.[28]

Being a sagacious businessman, Rockefeller insisted on following two rigid principles in his philanthropies: (1) to give where his gifts would do the most good for the majority of people, and (2) to give where his benefactions would stimulate the spirit of philanthropy in others. Hence, he would not give alone, expecting others to do something toward matching his gifts. Dr. Buttrick became the first executive secretary of the board and, as we shall see, adopted this policy, with North Carolina being the first state to receive financial assistance under these terms. Specifically, what was the function of the organization? The initial goal of the General Education Board was "to hold and disburse funds for the benefit of Southern education."

Thus, there emerged two great educational agencies—the Southern Education Board and the General Education Board. Both were interwoven with all philanthropic organizations in the public school movement. Moreover, all the leading forces in Southern education were members of both boards, and several Southern members were their salaried agents. Professor Woodward viewed the two boards as an interlocking directorate or "holding company for vast philanthropic interests." "The interlocking nature of the several boards of directors," he points out, "indicates that the disposal of large funds was in the hands of relatively few people."[29]

The stage was now set for the launching of the Southern regional educational movement. Fearing that the Southern Education Board might be labeled as a "Yankee notion," or as being interested in the education of the Negro, the board resolved to work behind the scenes. It decided to leave the work in the hands of Southern men. This was viewed as a principle of statesmanship. "The men on the

215

ground," wrote Dr. Dickerman, "are in the foremost place . . . they know the situation . . . [and] we have to wait for these master spirits of the South to bring in the new order."[30] This viewpoint reflected the theory that Southern people must work out their destiny by their own efforts and under the direction of Southern leadership. Accordingly, the Conference for Education in the South instructed its Southern delegates to inaugurate educational movements in their respective states. And the initiation of such a movement in North Carolina fell upon the shoulders of Charles D. McIver.

McIver began his task by carefully compiling a list of educators, clergymen, editors, businessmen, and civic-minded persons who would be in sympathy with an educational movement and who would be of the most service.[31] In collaboration with State Superintendent Toon and Governor Aycock, McIver called for a conference to meet in Raleigh on February 23, 1902. Plans for the proposed conference, to a large degree, were not made public. The reason for this precautionary measure was the fear that the anticipated gathering might be identified with some political party or Northern agency. The press, however, wrote of the proposed meeting but carried few details. The *Biblical Recorder* predicted that the conference would be condemned throughout the state by thoughtful and progressive people. It warned: "About twenty leading educators will meet in Raleigh . . . to advise with the governor about the free schools. Some of them will spend their time advising the governor to get a subsidy for themselves, and advising the free schools to call upon the people to raise funds by special tax." In contrast and in defense of the conference, the *Raleigh News and Observer* replied that the spirit displayed by the *Biblical Recorder* was not shared by anyone in Raleigh.[32]

The Raleigh Conference was held as scheduled and was attended by approximately forty persons who represented all lines of educational work. It was held in the Senate chamber and presided over by the governor.[33] McIver, however, was the pivotal force of the conference, and he opened the meeting with a frank address on the major educational problems, informing the delegates of the necessity of a statewide educational campaign geared to the following objectives:

1. To inaugurate a systematic and popular movement for local taxation.
2. To inaugurate a movement toward a consolidation of school districts and schoolhouses.
3. To inaugurate a movement toward consolidation of school buildings and improvement of grounds.[34]

To carry out these objectives, the Central Campaign Committee for the Promotion of Public Education was established. And finally, a statement was issued to the public under the title "Declaration against Illiteracy." This document, in brief, was a summation of the state's low educational status. It urged all patriotic citizens to aid in alleviating this problem.[35]

During the initial stages of the preparation for the Raleigh Conference, Superintendent Toon became desperately ill with pneumonia, which, to some degree, delayed McIver's plans. A few days after the opening of the Raleigh Educational Conference, Superintendent Toon died suddenly of a heart attack.[36] Governor Aycock appointed James Y. Joyner to the position of state superintendent. Although Joyner was under forty years of age, he had had successful experiences as both a county and a city superintendent. At the time of this appointment, he was a professor of English at the State Normal and Industrial College. In praising Joyner, a local paper wrote: "Everybody in Greensboro regrets the loss of Professor Joyner from active citizenship here but a city loses nothing, all things considered, by contributing such a man to the entire state."[37]

The veteran campaigner McIver, the pivotal figure in the North Carolina educational movement, offered a prediction that turned out to be quite accurate when he said: "The next ten years will witness the development of a group of men who will go upon the hustings and fight . . . the real battles of universal education for every child in the South." "This group of statesmen," he continued, "will preach with all the fervor of a crusader the doctrine which school teachers have believed in for many years, and from time to time have timidly tried to impress upon the public mind and heart."[38] No Southern state can better testify to the accuracy of McIver's prophecy than North Carolina, which took the lead in the regional movement.

On April 3, 1902, North Carolina inaugurated its public school movement, and the bugle call was sounded at Greensboro. Key figures at this assembly were Governor Aycock; McIver; Dr. Buttrick; the executive secretary of the General Education Board; and the new state superintendent of public instruction, Joyner. Every college in the state was also represented by either its president or a member of the faculty. Also present were teachers, school committeemen, and numerous county superintendents, whose railroad fares were paid out of a campaign fund provided by the Southern Education Board. Governor Aycock opened the rally with a stirring speech, followed by Dr. Buttrick who advanced this proposition: "The General Education Board will duplicate all private subscriptions . . . to the amount not exceeding $4,000." In making the proposition, he tactfully told his audience: "I am not doing a favor but accepting one."[39] In a short time, four thousand dollars was raised, and eight thousand dollars was realized for the rural schools of Guilford County.

Several points concerning the urban campaigns must be made

clear. It was not the purpose of these campaigns to promote urban schools, which were believed by some leaders to compare favorably with the public graded schools of the cities and towns of any state in the South. Rather, their major purpose was to give the state superintendent of education an opportunity to confer with the county superintendent; together, they would work out a uniform campaign policy in accordance with the plans adopted at the Raleigh Conference.[40] Another aim was the raising of money to be employed in rural areas to stimulate the voting of special school taxes. Guilford County school district, located about six miles from Greensboro, provides a good illustration of how the urban funds were to be disbursed. The district had already voted a special tax of thirty-three and one-half cents on each bne hundred dollars of property to supplement the state tax of eighteen cents on each one hundred dollars of property. In addition, the district was endeavoring to raise money by private subscription to erect a larger schoolhouse. To encourage this movement, the Executive Committee of Greensboro offered to give one dollar for every two raised by the local community for this purpose.[41]

The Executive Committee of Greensboro took its cue from the Guilford County school district. While not making a hard and fast rule for the distribution of the eight thousand dollars, the committee, in general, adopted a principle of giving one dollar for every two raised by private subscription to build and furnish schoolhouses, provided that a district also voted a local tax. To illustrate, a district that voted a local tax and raised eight hundred dollars was given four hundred dollars, making a total school building fund of twelve hundred dollars. In this case, the General Education Board and the Executive Board of Greensboro would each have contributed two hundred of the four hundred dollars.

Another rally was held for two days at Charlotte beginning on May 1, 1902. The sponsors of this event made an attempt to surpass the work of the Greensboro Conference by raising six thousand dollars. In advertising the event, the *Charlotte Observer* announced: "GRAND RALLY TONIGHT." Among the principal speakers were Superintendent Joyner, McIver, Walter Hines Page and Governor Aycock.

The Charlotte conference and rally were well attended by friends of public education and some twenty-two superintendents, whose railroad fare was paid out of campaign funds supplied by the Southern Education Board. Again Dr. Buttrick agreed to match the amount raised with the understanding that two-thirds would go to the rural schools of Mecklenburg County and one-third to the public schools of Henderson County, situated in the mountainous section of the state.[42]

The success of these two gatherings stimulated Oxford, Henderson, Washington, Goldsboro, and other cities in every section of the state to request the privilege of sponsoring a district conference. Notwithstanding this manifestation of favorable sentiment, the urban campaigns came to an end. By this time, the Executive Committee of the Central Campaign Committee decided to send directly into the rural counties the best speakers available to conduct an active campaign for local school taxation.

Meanwhile, Eugene C. Brooks, one of the outstanding educators in the state, was appointed campaign manager. Brooks opened his headquarters in June of 1902 in Raleigh in the office of the state superintendent. Charles L. Coon succeeded Dabney as editor of the Bureau of Investigation and Information of the Southern Education Board at Knoxville, Tennessee, was requested by Brooks, McIver, and Superintendent Joyner to prepare a special propaganda document.[43] In a short time the document was ready; it contained 176 pages devoted to educational problems in North Carolina. The data were carefully gathered, clearly recorded, and conveniently arranged, and were related to teacher salaries, county supervisors, consolidation of school districts and schoolhouses, illiteracy, school enrollment, and attendance. Every attempt was made to shape all topics along the lines of local taxation.[44] Some ten thousand copies of the document were printed and Superintendent Joyner and McIver distributed over seven thousand of them throughout the state among the press and campaign workers.

The leaders of the North Carolina educational campaigns recognized early that the press was a potent agency for shaping public policies and for promoting movements for public welfare. Naturally, it was mobilized to create favorable sentiment on the subject of improving the public schools during the "Campaign era." At the Raleigh conference, a duty of the Central Campaign Committee was "to distribute news items once each week to every newspaper in the state with a request to publish short consecutive articles bearing upon the great value of better schools."[45] Immediately after they began to spend more money annually, all the leading newspapers, county ones included, began carrying articles of one to two thousand words on education as special features in their. Sunday editions, especially during the campaign months of July, August, and September. Typical editorials were "Education and Its Advantages," "The Ills of Illiteracy," and "Growth of Education in the South."[46]

The press had certain limitations as a campaign agency. Recognizing this fact, Brooks, McIver, Joyner, and other leaders decided to put their case directly before the people by means of attractive speakers employing the power of oratory and persuasion. "In a democracy," contended one noted educational campaigner, "public sentiment is all-powerful and the appeal in every great movement must be in the mass meeting . . . through the ear . . . from the platform and from the stump."[47]

Guided by a determination to saturate every county with strong proeducational propaganda, Brooks planned a systematic educational crusade for the months of July, August, and September. By the means of the telegraph and correspondence and conference with county superintendents and other interested persons, Brooks, McIver, and Coon petitioned for corps of suitable people to campaign for the doctrines of local taxation and universal education. The response to the clarion call was most favorable. To defray the initial cost of the ensuing campaign, the Southern Education Board appropriated a sum of four thousand dollars. By mid-June of 1902, corps of campaigners were ready to take the field. Among them were educators, politicians, editors, clergymen, physicians, businessmen, and lawyers.[48]

On June 19, 1902, the educational campaigners "fired their opening gun—a double-barrelled one," at a rally at Wentworth in Rockingham County. This rally was attended by some fifteen hundred people and included more than one hundred school committeemen and every teacher in the county. Music was furnished by the Third Regiment Band of Reidsville. For two hours, between numbers by the band, North Carolina's most illustrious speakers held the audience spellbound. Ex-Governor Jarvis spoke in the morning, employing an emotional approach that at times was both "pathetic and soul-stirring." In closing, he said "that he was an old man, that his face was turned toward the setting sun; that never again would he solicit suffrage of the state for himself." He prevailed upon his audience "to keep the churches and the schoolhouses open. Do this, and the future will be glorious; neglect it, and we go back to barbarism." McIver's afternoon speech was more practical and followed the main theme as laid down by the Central Campaign Committee. He spoke in a strong and convincing manner on the need for local taxation, school consolidation, and improvement of school buildings.[49]

The Wentworth rally was typical of the scores of rallies conducted during the summer of 1902. To what extent were they successful? According to the record, only fourteen counties adopted local taxation, and elections were pending in twenty-four more districts.[50] This result shows that the public school movement in North Carolina was dilatory in picking up momentum. Moreover, some of the educational campaigners received a cold reception from their agrarian audiences. For example, Central Campaign Director Brooks privately chided Superintendent Joyner: "I hear you had a bum meeting even if you did orate."[51] Public apathy was so great in the western county of Buncombe that McIver concluded that it would be futile to send anyone there "who would be of service to the general cause of education."[52] What about the Black Belt counties of the east? One concerned county superintendent described the situation as follows: "The awakening has just begun. Many are stretching their limbs and rubbing their eyes, and considering the wisdom of taking a second nap, while thousands have never heard the alarm of our noble Governor and Superintendent of Public Instruction. They lie in deepest sleep of ignorance and are snoring in bliss. . . . Let us hope for an awakening, especially in the east."[53]

To surmount the walls of public apathy, Alderman said: "The thing for us to do is to hammer on until the desire for better schools, and all that belongs to better schools, becomes a contagion with the people."[54] Accordingly, Chairman Brooks, as early as March of 1903, began preparations for a more extensive campaign by ferreting out educational orators from every section of the state. The response to this call was most favorable. As one willing campaigner responded: "If you can use an old stick as I am you may have my services anytime between July 15 and August 15. I would prefer to work in the mountain counties." At the same time, Brooks's office was overwhelmed with requests for speakers to appear throughout the state. The tone of some requests, however, suggested that many school committeemen and county superintendents anticipated vigorous opposition to local taxation. Superintendent Way of Ashe County wrote: "I am going into the stronghold of opposition and I want the strongest men for speakers." Likewise, Ira Tarlington said: "Send me one of your men . . . they have a fight on here." From Person County, Nat C. Newbold declared: "This county needs about two Walter Pages, if you have any men of that stock, please send them." F. B. Rankins had observed that a previous attempt for a local tax had failed, but he requested two powerful speakers in the hope that they would effect subsequent passage of a special school tax in his district.[55]

An unparalleled enthusiasm for public education was generated among whites, but, as usual, racism soon raised its ugly head. Racism did not spring up suddenly; it was there from the beginning of the Aycock Administration. There were forces, particularly identified with the Black Belt region, agitating to amend the state constitution to provide for a racial division of the school tax fund. This movement provoked wide discussion both inside and outside the state.[56]

But the real undercurrent of this racism, a legacy of the old Dortch days, was the insistence by whites that all taxes voted be employed solely toward their schools.[57] A case in point was an experience of campaigner R. F. Beasley of Monroe in the Black Belt Roberson County. He reported to Brooks of the town of Moriah (known also as Branchville) : "After the speech a majority stood up and said they'd vote the tax—but they won't divide with the negro." Beasley was instructed to write the young county superintendent to push for the local tax, while advising the town people to "devise some plan for leaving the negro out."[58]

Meanwhile, Governor Aycock was having his own trouble with the problem of racism. Appearing before the General Assembly in 1903, he informed his audience that some members were instructed by the conventions that nominated them "to secure the adoption of an amendment to the constitution by which the taxes paid by the whites shall go to the education of the white children and the taxes paid by the Negroes shall go to education of Negro children." With sincerity, he contended that universal education included the Black population. The Governor's stand on Negro education alarmed some political leaders and newspaper editors. "It would be a blessing to the state," declared one indignant editor, "if our Educational Governor would be stricken with lockjaw."[59] Other racists accused some campaigners of trying to promote equality of the races, of trying to put the bottom rail on top.

With the election safely under his belt, the governor resolutely opposed this movement from the beginning. Appearing before the General Assembly, he said: "I had confidently hoped that this matter would not be before you." He admitted that universal education was a failure and did not use the term *race* when asking the legislature "to make ample provision for the education of the whole people —rich and poor alike." He informed the legislators that he was also "bound by promise and necessity to oppose with utmost effort" any direction or suggestion to enable whites to divide taxes so that Black schools would receive the returns from Negro direct taxes.[60]

Earlier, some members of the Southern Education Board had encountered white racism. "Is there a nigger in the woodpile?" Walter Hines Page was asked from the floor by a newspaper editor. The distinguished Page blushed, but he soon composed himself and answered: "You will find when the woodpile is turned over, not a 'nigger' but an uneducated white boy. We want to train both the white boy and the black boy. But we must train the white boy first, because we cannot do anything for the Negro until his white friend is convinced of his responsibility to him."[61]

Racism caused campaign managers to shift their strategy on the assumption that education of whites must precede that of Blacks and that the former would in turn provide education for the Negro. This strategy was not new and rested on an earlier philosophy of prominent educators and others. At the close of the third conference at Capon Springs, for example, "it was agreed by all members that the best way to provide training for Negroes was first to provide adequate school and training for the neglected whites."[62] Moreover, whites who were familiar with education knew that the South was to play a major role in Negro education. In April of 1901, Governor Aycock ventured to lecture to a Northern group of educators on race relations. "If the negro is ever to be educated," he told them, "it will be by the aid of Southern white men. . . . Education of the white will precede the education of negroes. Philanthropists in the North may think they can educate the negro without the help of Southern whites, but they are mistaken."[63]

It must be recognized that some of these educational philosophies were influenced strongly by the doctrine of white supremacy as nurtured by Curry, now general agent for both the Peabody and Slater philanthropies and rocognized as the white spokesman on Negro education. Jabez Lamar Monroe Curry of Alabama was well known throughout the nation as an influential figure in Southern education.[64] He was born in Lincoln County, Georgia, in 1825, graduated from the University of Georgia in 1843, and attended the School of Law at Harvard. His political positions included membership in the Alabama legislature, the United States House of Representatives, and the Confederate Congress. He also served as a lieutenant colonel in the Confederate Army. As an educator, he was the author of several books, president of Howard College (Alabama), and professor of constitutional and international law at Richmond College (Virginia). From 1885 to 1888, he served as minister to Spain.[65] And yet this distinguished educator and statesman was ultraconservative in his racial views. For example, on numerous occasions he defended before Northern audiences the doctrine of white supremacy as the only means by which "permanent advancement" of Blacks was to be accomplished.[66] Hence, his educational and social philosophy was identified with that of the dominant white racists. For example, the "achievement of a handful of Negroes did not impress him," and, like Southerners in every walk of life, he assumed that the supremacy of the white race was both inevitable and desirable.[67] Curry's sentiments indeed destroyed the myth that education goes hand in hand with the tenets of liberalism and democracy. The irony in this case was that this white racist since 1891 had headed the only Black educational philanthropy—the Slater Fund. He was certainly a far cry from its first general agent, the liberal Atticus G. Haygood.

A word needs to be said about philanthropy and racism. The early movements advocating a racial division of school taxation reflected that Negro education was a thorny problem. Thus, it appeared that the best course was to evade completely the question of education for Blacks. Likewise, the General Education Board and its agents acquiesed to Southern racism. Executive Secretary D. Buttrick had sought to mitigate suspicion of whites by making it clear that the work of the board had no "designs on Southern civilizations," that members of the board did not come into the South as "meddlers but [as] helpers . . . [and] recognized that the education of the negro is in the hands of white people of the South and must ever remain there."[68] Reflecting on the problem, historian Louis R. Harlan wrote: "The General Education Board with its millions, prestige and relative independence might have been expected to balance the caution of the Southern campaigners with its own boldness." But its executive secretary, Buttrick, was "a bit frightened by the emotional timbre of Southern racism." In defense, Buttrick reasoned and wrote confidentially: "But we are confronted 'with a condition and not a theory' . . . and if equal philanthropy for the Negro was advocated . . . we shall err and invite defeat."[69] In facing this dilemma, both boards and campaigners remained silent on the subject of Black education. This could mean only one thing: Negro educational opportunities would dwindle in light of the accelerated expansion of educational opportunities for whites.

On returning to campaigns, we find that, despite the advent of racism, the educational rallies continued to gain momentum. By 1904 a tidal wave of favorable public sentiment was sweeping the state. North Carolina had never before witnessed such a phenomenon. The educational rallies drew larger crowds than the hottest political debates. For instance, Governor Aycock declared that his "audience at fifteen educational speeches was larger than the audience he addressed at any fifteen political gatherings. . . . Times have definitely changed, before the 'Campaign Era' the surest way to insure a small crowd was to announce an educational discussion."[70] Likewise, Philander P. Claxton, a native North Carolinian and the major force behind the Tennessee campaigns, declared that no political gathering within the last ten years had brought together such large crowds of people.[71] He also frequently left his office in Tennessee to deliver campaign addresses in North Carolina and stated: "Educational rallies had become so common that one could hardly get off a train without meeting an educational campaign orator."[72]

To be sure, the great majority of campaigners did not have the advantage of convenient railway travel. Moreover, it was quite common for some of them to address an audience in the afternoon in one town and then journey to an adjacent town to give an evening address. On one occasion, McIver complained to Secretary Brooks that speaking in the afternoon at Nashville and then driving fourteen miles by buggy through the country to speak later at Spring Hope was too strenuous an undertaking for his physical condition.[73] In contrast, John E. Ray, the "Old Stick," stated: "I have received the second list of appointments and shall be glad to fill them to the best of my ability. I have really learned to love the work and feel I have done some good where I have been."[74]

The following is a typical speaking schedule of a campaigner:[75]

White Cross	September 16 (Day)
Buck Horn	" 16 (Night)
Caldwell	" 17 (Night)
Elm Grove	" 18 (Night)

Several media were employed for advertisement of the rallies. The majority of Southerners were God-loving and God-fearing people who filled the churches each Sunday. Cognizant of this important medium of communication, the Campaign Committee submitted a written request to each minister to "preach a crusade against ignorance" and to announce and attend rallies and convince his colleagues to do likewise. In a short time, local ministers of every denomination threw their support behind the educational campaigns. From the pulpit they extolled the values and blessings of education, emphasizing how it would enable one to read and understand the word of God. They also described education as a necessary tool for moral training, and as a way in which to eke out more "bread and butter" from a restricted life. Ministers generally concluded such sermons by prevailing upon the congregation to support the objectives and principles of the school campaigns.[76] At the same time, school superintendents, committeemen, and other sponsors were supplied with posters that urged citizens to attend an "educational rally to be held at [the place] on [the date]." Such posters were readily sought. J. L. Foust wrote Secretary Brooks: "Please send Superintendent Thomas A. Sharpe . . . two or three hundred posters to put up in the community in which we are waging a local tax campaign in the county."[77] The press, especially the *Raleigh News and Observer,* cooperated with the movement by listing speaking engagements.

The educational rallies had the appearance of both political and old-time religious revivals. They varied in duration and size. For an all-day affair, the festive event might include a field day, a band concert, a school fair, or a Confederate parade, and was accompanied by basket dinners, barbecues, and "watermelon cuttings." In addition to the main speeches, diplomacy demanded that county and local prominent citizens, politicians, and orators be given a place on the rally program. Persons who commonly filled the speakers' platform were county superintendents, members of boards of education, judges, magistrates, commissioners, local bankers, businessmen, ministers, lawyers, teachers, and outstanding farmers. Such an array of county and local talent not only served as an added attraction to the rallies but definitely placed such leaders on the side of the educational campaigners.

A typical rally was held at Ellenboro in 1905; its schedule was as follows:[78]

9:45 A.M. ...... Welcome address by G. B. Pruett.

10:00 A.M. ...... Address to the Old Soldiers by L. J. Hoyles and others.

11:00 A.M. ...... Address to Knights of Pythias by A. M. Lyles, A. A. Whiteners and others.

12:00 A.M. ...... One hour for dinner and everybody is invited to bring well-filled baskets so all may have something to eat.

1:00 P.M. ...... Educational address by Walter E. Sikes of Wake Forest College, Harry L. Smith, President of Davidson College, D. F. Morrow and A. L. Rucker.

The outdoor educational rallies, or "open-air meetings," were held in country yards, picnic grounds, schoolyards, and fairgrounds, or "drummed up from the stump." The indoor ones were held in courthouses, schoolhouses, public auditoriums, and churches. The speeches were the main attraction, with the orators "speaking in the morning and again in the afternoon."[79]

"A man," said Claxton, "who had come twenty miles to hear a speaking wants to hear a great deal of it." Southern people by tradition had been attracted to political meetings and revivals. They responded in "mass meetings" to "appeals through the mouth and through the ear." People came from miles around in wagons, buggies, on horseback and on foot, bringing their basket dinners with them.

Some concluding remarks need to be said about the nature of the educational addresses. Many of them by county and local citizens ran the gamut from mere rumbling to oratory. In great contrast, the more experienced campaigners were "pros" and possessed the ability to say effectively and eloquently what needed to be said in behalf of public education. Each speaker carried his own individual and distinctive appeal to his rural audience, but whatever his manner of approach, each sought to accomplish the same end. From the stump and platform some told interesting anecdotes, while appealing to civic pride. "What are we here for?" Superintendent Alexander Graham of Charlotte asked his audience. "I tell you what we are here for. We have conquered the big cities, we have conquered the towns . . . and now we are here to conquer the townships. . . . I want to say to you of the country, you have the advantage of the town." He went on to prevail upon his listeners "to wipe out this old North

Carolina and paint the new North Carolina with her face turned toward the dawn."[80] In a similar vein, President Francis P. Venable of the University of North Carolina emphasized the blighting effects of ignorance and illiteracy when he said: "We have the material all through the state, natural products, but ignorance is the thing which threatens everywhere. . . . I tell you North Carolina is poor—even poorer in some ways than she knows. Where does she stand in the illiteracy column? Next to the last. Thank God for South Carolina."[81]

The veteran campaigner McIver often came straight to the point by asking his agrarian audience to levy higher taxes for schools. Concomitantly, he declared that "ideas are more valuable than acres." He also expounded that aversion to taxation was due to ignorance of the facts and that taxation was simply an exchange of a little money for something better. He blasted the old political theory that the best government was the one that levied the smallest taxes and predicted that the future would modify that doctrine. "Liberal taxation, fairly levied and property applied," McIver declared, "is the chief mark of a civilized people. The savage pays no taxes."[82]

Superintendent Joyner, like McIver, dealt with facts and offered remedies that were easy to grasp. He also played on the sympathy of his rural audiences by telling them that a duty was owed to the rural schools and to children. Referring to the latter, he said: "It is no wonder, that when the God man was on earth He took up little children . . . and blessed them."[83] And some campaigners stressed the cultural and economic rewards of education. But whatever the approach to the problem, all sought to stimulate a more favorable public view of the adoption of local taxation as a permanent means of improving the public schools.

The educational crusades, picking up momentum beginning in 1903, lost impetus some time before the end of the decade. Former Populist Superintendent Mebane, now secretary of the Central Campaign Committee, reported that the biggest campaign was carried on during the spring of 1909, breaking all records; 132 districts voted for local taxation within 90 days. For the first time, an entire county (New Hanover, which was predominantly Black) voted for local taxes for its schools.[84] It was at this point that the unifying forces of education had generated within white society consciousness of a new public school idea, thus ending one historical era and initiating another.

Notes

1. Robert C. Ogden, "The Origin, Purpose and Plans of the Conference for Education in the South," Robert Curtis Ogden Papers, Southern Historical Col-

lection, University of North Carolina, Chapel Hill, N.C.

2. *Proceedings of the Capon Springs Conference for Education in the South,* (1898), p. 37.

3. Helen Ogden Purvis, "Notes on the Annual Conference for Education in the South," 1898, Robert Curtis Ogden Papers, Library of Congress, Washington, D.C.

4. Robert C. Ogden, "The Conference and Its Growth, 1898–1914," Robert Curtis Ogden Papers, Southern Historical Collection, University of North Carolina, Chapel Hill, N.C.

5. Charles W. Dabney, *Universal Education in the South,* 2 vols. (Chapel Hill, N.C., 1936), 2: 29–30, 504–5.

6. Helen Ogden Purvis, "Notes on the Second Capon Springs Conference," 1899 Robert Curtis Ogden Papers, Library of Congress, Washington, D.C.

7. *Proceedings of the Second Capon Springs Conference* (1899), pp. 73–79.

8. H. E. Fries to H. B. Frissell, July 3, 1900, George S. Dickerman Papers, Southern Historical Collection, University of North Carolina, Chapel Hill, N.C.

9. "Biographical Note" Robert C. Ogden Papers, Library of Congress, Washington, D.C.

10. P. W. Wilson, "An Unofficial Statesman: Robert Ogden," Robert Curtis Ogden Papers, Library of Congress, Washington, D.C.

11. Booker T. Washington, "Mr. Robert C. Ogden," written for the *Metropolitan Magazine,* Booker T. Washington Papers, Regular Correspondence, 1910, Library of Congress, Washington, D.C.

12. Robert C. Ogden, "A Few Suggestions upon the Objects of the Capon Springs Educational Conference, as Seen by a Northern Business Man," *Proceedings of the Third Capon Springs Conference* (1900), pp. 24–28.

13. *New York Times,* April 19, 1901.

14. *Special to the New York Times,* April 23, 1901, and Rev. Caldwell to G. S. Dickerman, November 30, 1900, George S. Dickerman Papers, Southern Historical Collection, University of North Carolina, Chapel Hill, N.C.

15. *Proceedings of the Fourth Conference of Education in the South* (1901), pp. 2–4.

16. Helen Ogden Purvis, "Notes on the Winston-Salem Conference," Robert Curtis Ogden Papers, Library of Congress, Washington, D.C.

17. Charles D. McIver, "Two Open Fields for Investment in the South," *Proceedings of the Fourth Conference of Education in the South* (1901), p. 32.

18. Charles W. Dabney, "The Public School Problem in the South," in *Proceedings of the Fourth Conference of Education in the South* (1901), pp. 39–57.

19. See chap. 4.

20. *Southern Education Board: Its Origin and Purpose,* April 1902, Circular no. I, pp. 4–5.

21. Charles W. Dabney Papers, 1901, Southern Historical Collection, University of North Carolina, Chapel Hill, N.C.

22. Executive Board of the Conference for Education in the South, *A Brief Statement concerning the Origin and Organization of the Southern Education Board,* Robert Curtis Ogden Papers, Library of Congress, Washington, D.C.

23. *Southern Education Board: Its Origin and Purpose,* pp. 5–6; "The Conference for Education in the South and the Southern Education Board," in *Report of the United States Commissioner of Education,* 1907, 1: 327.

24. *Proceedings of the Fifth Conference for Education in the South* (1902), pp. 38–40. In February of 1903 Charles L. Coon succeeded Eggleston, Jr.

25. Dabney Papers, 1901, and Rose Wickliffe, "The Educational Movement in

the South," *Report of the United States Commission of Education,* 1903, 1: 377–80.

26. Allen Nevins, *John D. Rockefeller,* 2 vols. (New York, 1940) , 2: 484–89.

27. *The General Education Board: An Account of Its Activities, 1902–1914* (New York, 1915) , app. 1, pp. 212–13.

28. Letters Announcing Gifts to the General Education Board and Replies Thereto, in ibid., pp. 216, 218–19, 222. By 1921 Rockefeller had contributed approximately $128 million to the board. Abraham Flexner, *Funds and Foundations* (New York, 1952) , p. 30.

29. C. Vann Woodward, *Origins of the New South, 1877–1913* (Baton Rouge, La., 1951) , p. 403 n.

30. Rose, "Educational Movement in the South," pp. 379–80.

31. McIver to Peabody, February 10, 1902, Charles D. McIver Papers, University of North Carolina, Greensboro, N.C.

32. *Raleigh News and Observer,* February 13 and 14, 1902.

33. Charles Branlley Aycock Papers, 1902, North Carolina Department of Archives and History, Raleigh, N.C.

34. Charles D. McIver, "Current Problems in North Carolina," *Annual of the American Academy of Political and Social Science* 22 (1903) : 52.

35. McIver Papers, 1902, and Charles L. Coon Papers, Southern Historical Collection, University of North Carolina, Chapel Hill, N.C.

36. *Raleigh News and Observer,* February 20, 1902.

37. *Greensboro Telegram,* April 7, 1902. Clipping in College Scrapbook, McIver Papers, vol. 10.

38. *Journal of Proceedings and Addresses of the Southern Educational Association,* (1901) .

39. *Greensboro Telegram,* April 7, 1902.

40. *Biennial School Report,* 1902–1904, p. lvii.

41. *Proceedings of the Fifth Conference for Education in the South,* (1902) , p. 70; *Raleigh News and Observer,* April 8 and 10, 1902.

42. *Charlotte Observer,* May 2, 1902.

43. Coon Papers, 1903.

44. Southern Education Board, *North Carolina Education* Southern Education Bulletin no. 10 (May 14, 1903) , 121 ff.

45. Aycock Papers, 1901.

46. James Yadkin Joyner Papers, June–September 1910, Southern Historical Collection University of North Carolina, city? N.C.

47. Philander P. Claxton, "Methods of an Educational Campaign," *Proceedings of the Seventh Conference For Education in the South* (1904) , pp. 66–67 and (1908) , p. 74.

48. *Biennial School Report,* 1900–1902, pp. lii–lvii.

49. Ibid., pp. 380–81.

50. Ibid., p. ix.

51. Brooks to Superintendent Joyner, June 16, 1902, James Yadkin Joyner Papers, Southern Historical Collection, University of North Carolina, city? N.C.

52. McIver to Brooks, July 22, 1902, in ibid.

53. Charles A. G. Thomas, "Some Observations of a County Superintendent." Clipping in James Yadkin Joyner Papers, Southern Historical Collection, University of North Carolina, city?, N.C.

54. Edwin Alderman, "Report from the Field," *Proceedings of the Sixth Conference For Education in the South* (1903) , p. 62.

55. F. E. Ray to Brooks, June 19, 1903; Superintendent Way to Joyner, June 1, 1903; F. B. Rankins to Brooks, June 20, 1903; Nat C. Newbold to Brooks, July

11, 1903; H. L. Smith to Brooks, June 15, 1903; M. C. S. Noble to Brooks, June 16, 1903; President Venable of the University of North Carolina to Brooks, June 24, 1903; and President Taylor of Wake Forest to Brooks, June 20, 1903, Joyner Papers, 1903.

56. *Raleigh News and Observer,* January 14, May 31, November 1, 1903.

57. See chap. 2.

58. R. F. Beasley to Brooks, September 9, 1903, Joyner Papers. Quoted in Louis R. Harlan, *Separate and Unequal: Public School Campaigns and Racism in the Southern Seaboard States, 1901–1915* (Chapel Hill, N.C., 1958), pp. 95–96 n.

59. Aycock Papers, 1902.

60. *North Carolina Public Documents,* 1903, no. 1, pp. 7–8. The struggle for a racial division of local tax funds was to die a slow death. Governor Aycock's successor, Robert B. Glenn, also had his problems with the struggle, coming directly from legislation from the east. *Raleigh News and Observer,* January 10, 1905, and January 11, 1907.

61. *Columbia State,* April 24, 1903. Quoted in Dabney, *Universal Education in the South,* 2: 45–46.

62. Henry A. Bullock, *A History of Negro Education in the South* (Cambridge, Mass., 1967), p. 93.

63. *New York Herald,* April 27, 1901. Clipping in Ogden Papers.

64. Merle E. Curti, *Social Ideas of American Educators* (New York, 1935), pp. 264–65.

65. Jabez Lamar Monroe Curry Papers, 1908, vol. 15, Library of Congress, Washington, D.C.

66. J. L. M. Curry, Speech before the Pennsylvania Society of New York, October 31, 1899, in ibid., 1899–1901, vol. 13.'

67. *Curti, Social Ideas of American Educators,* pp. 278–79.

68. *Daily Progress,* April 15, 1902. Clipping in Philander P. Claxton Papers, University of Tennessee, Knoxville, Tenn.

69. Quoted in Harlan, *Separate and Unequal,* p. 94.

70. Aycock Papers, 1903.

71. "Miscellaneous Expense Account of Claxton," Philander P. Claxton Papers, University of Tennessee, Knoxville, Tenn.

72. Charles L. Lewis, Philander Priestly Claxton, Crusader for Public Schools (Knoxville, Tenn., 1905), p. 115.

73. McIver to Brooks, August 3, 1905, Joyner Papers.

74. Ray to Brooks, August 6, 1903, in ibid.

75. C. E. Maddrey to Brooks, August 27, 1903, in ibid.

76. S. E. Mercer to Secretary Brooks, April 6, 1910, Eugene C. Brooks Papers, Duke University, Durham, N.C.

77. Foust to Brooks, August 8, 1903, and I. C. Gibson to Brooks, August 21, 1903, Joyner Papers.

78. Joyner Papers, undated clipping [1905].

79. Claxton to Ogden, October 23, 1908, Claxton Papers.

80. *Raleigh Post,* April 9, 1902, and *Charlotte Observer,* May 2, 1902. Editorials in College Scrapbook, McIver Papers, vol. 10.

81. Ibid., undated clipping.

82. Charles L. Coon, "Charles Duncan McIver and His Educational Services, 1886–1906," *Report of the United States Commission of Education,* 1907, 1: 334–36.

83. McIver Papers, clipping in College Scrapbook, vol. 10.

84. Charles H. Mebane, *More Than a Million Dollars in Local Taxation* (Raleigh, N.C., 1909), p. 3.

8

A Giant Step toward the Massachusetts' School System

A new and remarkable era in education followed in the wake of the public school movement in North Carolina. Between 1902 and 1913, spectacular progress was made on all fronts of the public school system. The purpose of this chapter is to describe this progress, with the view of demonstrating that the public school system by 1913 had changed significantly from that reported in the first two chapters of this work.

Promotion of local taxation was the first objective of the educational campaigns. Overwhelmed by the crusades, the reactionary school forces soon faltered. When the campaigns began in 1902, there were only 46 local tax districts. But by the end of the 1913–14 academic year there were 1,629 such districts scattered from the "seashore to the mountains." Progress in local taxation may be inferred from the following figures:[1]

Year	Number of Local Tax Districts
1902	46
1903	181
1904	227
1905	329
1906	423
1907	583
1908	687
1909	748
1910	995
1911	1325
1912	1439
1913–1914	1629

While the educational progressives were waging localized battles to increase school taxation, the state supreme court inevitably came under attack. It should be recalled that the court in the old Barksdale decision hampered education by restricting all taxes within the constitutional maximum of sixty-six and two-thirds cents per one hundred dollars of property.[2] From the beginning of the educational campaigns, the leaders awaited the auspicious moment to challenge the Barksdale ruling.[3] Under the direction of Superintendent Joyner, the groundwork was laid for litigation. In 1907 he instructed all county superintendents to request their commissioners to levy taxes above the constitutional limitations. For legal expenses, he utilized seven hundred dollars from the General Campaign Fund appropriated by the Southern Education Board. Franklin County was selected as the test case. After some difficulty, he located a taxpayer named J. R. Collie to enjoin the collection of the tax, and attorney W. H. Ruffin was employed by Superintendent Joyner to represent the taxpayer by swearing out an injunction. To round out the lawsuit, A. B. White was named to represent the county board of education, while ex-Governor Aycock was to represent the State Department of Education. In brief, the legal situation was the same as before and the arguments were identical, but supporting sentiment had developed in the interim. Unmistakably, during the campaign era, it became clear that the state supreme court would no longer be an obstruction to school progress, for there now sat on the bench an "enlightened court," headed by the legal progressive Walter Clark. The court reversed the Barksdale decision and maintained that a four-months school term was mandatory as required by article 4, section 3 of the state Constitution.[4] In addition, from funds accrued by increased school taxation, local communities were now raising sizeable amounts of school money from loans and bonds, reflecting a new trend in educational support. Local tax campaigns played a paramount role in influencing this development. Revenue from such sources, for example, increased between 1909–1913 from $220,071 to over $1,500,000. All in all, the total school fund increased from $1,018,143 in 1900 to a total of $6,119,603 by 1913. This increase meant better school buildings, equipment, and teachers' salaries, and a general improvement of the entire school system.

Construction of school buildings was the most discernible manifestation of change in the status of the public school system. Information on the urban schools is limited. Such institutions, it should be recalled, were located in towns with population of 2,500 and above and operated autonomously under a special charter by the General Assembly, while levying a special tax to support their general school fund. Their school officials were not required by law to make annual reports to the state superintendent. Charles L. Coon, however, after patiently researching the local newspapers, did manage to compile some figures and tables on the subject, which are believed to be reliable. His data show that there were approximately ninety-one urban schools constructed between 1901 and 1910.[5] The record also shows that after 1910 school construction in the cities reached a standstill. Considering that North Carolina was 82 percent rural in 1900, the inevitable conclusion is that the majority of towns and cities had, in general, provided what were considered ample school facilities by 1910. Most of them provided secondary instruction along with the lower grades in one building. Only the cities—Charlotte, Asheville, Durham, Greensboro, Raleigh, Wilmington, and Winston-Salem—had separate high school buildings.[6]

School construction was most conspicuous in the rural areas, where white schoolhouses were built at an average of more than one per day. Progress in school construction between 1902 and 1913 may be seen from the following figures:[7]

Year	Number of white rural schools built
1901	63
1902	278
1903	295
1904	307
1905	340
1906	359
1907	303
1908	324
1909	284
1910	280
1911	278
1912	296
1913	315
Total	3,742

Progress in school construction was accompanied by an improvement of the overall quality of public school facilities. For example, the old log structures declined in number from 715 to 61 by 1913, and the old one-teacher common schools were rapidly replaced by graded schools having two or more teachers. Moreover, the new buildings were built according to approved plans of modern school architecture. These plans were prepared by the most competent architects under the supervision of the State Department of Instruction. Some 3,045 of the new schools were equipped with patented desks produced by manufacturing, and most had blackboards, maps, and pictures.[8] While no brick or stone structures existed in the rural counties in 1900, a large number of such buildings had come into existence by 1913. They were symbolic of the general trend to "dignify education by making the schoolhouse one of the most attractive buildings in the community." Likewise, the average value of the rural schoolhouse increased from $160 in 1900 to $852 in 1913, while the total value of rural schools stood at $5,792,629, an approximate increase of $4,250,000 since 1900.[9]

The Permanent Loan Fund for the Building and Improvement of Public Schools, commonly known as the State Literary Fund, provided a great stimulus to school construction and improvement. This fund was created by the General Assembly in March of 1903, and State Superintendent Joyner was the major force responsible for its origin. Under the rules adopted by the state board of education, a loan could not be less than $250. Nor could this amount be made to a school district with fewer than sixty-five children, or exceed more than one-half the cost of a new schoolhouse and grounds or the improvement of an old school. All schoolhouses, furthermore, were required to be constructed in strict accordance with plans approved by the state board of education.[10] Duly negotiated loans were payable in ten annual installments, bearing interest at 4 percent, and were made secure by making the loans a lien upon the total school property of the county "in whatsoever bonds such funds may be entrusted," and, if necessary, the state board of education was authorized to deduct a sufficient amount for payment out of any funds due a county from any special state appropriation for public schools. By 1913, accordingly, loans had been made to ninety-eight counties, ranging from $270 in Yancey County to $11,700 in Buncombe County.[11]

Another significant development that reflected change in the public school system was the establishment and rapid growth of rural libraries. Educators had long recognized the great need for libraries to supplement the child's schoolwork, but no such rural facilities existed in 1900. Earlier, Superintendent Mebane and the Literary and Historical Association of North Carolina had led the agitations for rural libraries.[12] In March of 1901, the Democratic legislature responded and passed an "Act to Encourage the Establishment of Libraries in the Public Schools of the Rural Districts" by appropriating the parsimonious sum of five thousand dollars.[13] Whenever friends or patrons of any school district or incorporated town raised ten dollars by private donation, the county board of education was required to appropriate ten dollars from the general school fund. Afterward, the state superintendent was required to send ten dollars from the state appropriation. Accordingly, these little collections of

DECLARATION AGAINST ILLITERACY.

Address to the People of North Carolina, by Conference of Educators, Held in the Governor's Office in Raleigh, February 13th, 1902—The Names of the Signers.

Profoundly convinced of the prophetic wisdom of the declaration of the Fathers, made at Halifax in 1776, that "Religion, morality, and knowledge being necessary to good government, schools and the means of education shall forever be encouraged"; and cognizant of the full meaning of that recent constitutional enactment which debars from the privilege of the suffrage, after 1908, all persons who cannot read and write, and relying on the patriotism and foresight of North Carolinians to deal with a great question which vitally concerns the material and social welfare of themselves and their posterity, we, in an educational conference assembled in the city of Raleigh this February 13, 1902, are moved to make the following declaration of educational facts and principles:

1. Today, more fully than at any other time in our past history, do North Carolinians recognize the overshadowing necessity of universal education in the solution of those problems which a free government must solve in perpetuating its existence.

2. No free government has ever found any adequate means of universal education except in free public schools, open to all, supported by the taxes of all its citizens, where every child regardless of condition in life or circumstance of fortune, may receive that opportunity for training into social service which the constitutions of this and other great States and the age demand.

3. We realize that our State has reached the constitutional limit of taxation for the rural schools, that she has made extra appropriations to lengthen the term of these schools to 80 days in the year. We realize, too, that the four months' term now provided is inadequate, for the reason that more than 20,000,000 children of school age in the United States outside of North Carolina are now provided an average of 145 days of school out of every 365; that the teachers of these children are paid an average salary of $48 per month, while the teachers of the children of North Carolina are paid hardly $25 per month, thus securing for all the children of our sister

duties of life. And we realize that, according to the latest census report and the report of the U. S. Commissioner of Education, for every man, woman and child of his population, the country at large is spending $2.83 for the education of its children, while North Carolina is spending barely 67 cents; that the country at large is spending on an average of $20.29 for every pupil enrolled in its public schools, while North Carolina is spending only $3 or $4, the smallest amount expended by any State in the Union. And still further do we realize that the average amount spent for the education of every child of school age in the United States is approximately $9.50, while North Carolina is spending $1.78.

These facts should arouse our pride and our patriotism, and lead us to inquire whether the future will not hold this generation responsible for the perpetuation of conditions that have resulted in the multiplicity of small school districts, inferior school houses, poorly paid teachers, and necessarily poor teaching; that have resulted in twenty white illiterates out of every 100 white population over ten years of age; in generally poor and poorly paid supervision of the expenditure of our meagre school funds and of the teaching done in our schools; and, finally, in this educational indifference which is the chief cause of the small average daily attendance of about 50 pupils out of every 100 enrolled in our public schools.

We believe the future will hold us responsible for the perpetuation of these unfavorable conditions, and, therefore, we conceive it to be the patriotic, moral, and religious duty of this generation of North Carolinians to set about in earnest to find the means by which all our children can receive that education which will give them equal opportunities with the children of other sections of our common country.

4. Viewing our educational problems and conditions in the light of educational history and experience, we declare it to be our firm conviction that the next step forward for North Carolina, in education, is to provide more money for our country public schools, making possible the consolidation of small school districts, the professional teacher, and skilled supervision of the expenditure of all school funds and of the teaching done in the schools.

The history of the adoption of the principle of local self help by our S[tate]

graded school towns and cities must surely be an inspiration and an example to every village and rural community in North Carolina. Those towns and cities have adopted the only means at hand for the adequate education of their children. In adopting this principle, local taxation, they secured: first, adequate school funds; second, competent supervision; third, skilled teachers. Lacking any one of this educational trinity no community has ever yet succeeded in establishing the means of complete education for its children.

Those 35 towns and cities within our borders have followed the lead of other sections of the United States in adopting first the means of education, local taxation. The fact that 69 per cent of the total school fund of his Union is now raised by local taxes, while North Carolina raises only 14 per cent of her funds by that means, and lags behind all her sister States in every phase of public education, has both its lesson and its warning.

5. Remembering that in the last year nearly thirty communities in North Carolina, some of them distinctly rural, have adopted the principle of local taxation for schools, we think this time most auspicious to urge a general movement of all our educational forces in that direction, and, therefore, we appeal to all patriotic North Carolinians, men and women, who love their State, and especially that part of their State which is worth more than all its timber, lands, mines, and manufacturing plants, to band themselves together under the leadership of our "Educational Governor" and the State Superintendent of Public Instruction, aided by the Southern Education Board, to carry forward the work of local taxation and better schools, to the end that every child within our borders may have the opportunity to fit himself for the duties of citizenship and social service.

And, finally, heartily believing in the Christlikeness of this work of bringing universal education to all the children of North Carolina, we confidently rely on the hearty co-operation of all the churches of the State, whose work is so near the

hearts of all the people, and, therefore appeal to the pulpit to inculcate the supreme duty of universal education.

Charles B. Aycock, Governor of North Carolina; T. F. Toon, Superintendent of Public Instruction; John Duckett; Charles B. McIver, President State Normal and Industrial College; F. P. Venable, President University of North Carolina; George T. Winston, President College of Agriculture and Mechanic Arts; Charles E. Taylor, President Wake Forest College; Edwin Mims, Trinity College; Henry Louis Smith, President Davidson College; Charles H. Mebane, President Catawba College; O. Atkinson, Elon College; T. D. Bratton, President St. Mary's College; R. T. Vann, President Baptist Female University; L. L. Hobbs, President Guilford College; C. G. Vardell, President Red Springs Seminary; J. D. Carlyle, Wake Forest College; J. L. Kesler, Baptist Female University; J. Y. Joyner, The State Normal and Industrial College; D. H. Hill, College of Agriculture and Mechanic Arts; L. W. Crawford, Jr., Rutherford College; J. I. Foust, The State Normal and Industrial College; M. C. S. Noble, University of North Carolina; Henry Jerome Stockard, Peace Institute; F. P. Hobgood, President of Oxford Seminary; Robert Bingham, Bingham School; I. A. Holt, Oak Ridge Institute; Hugh Morson, Raleigh Male Academy; D. Matt Thompson, Superintendent Statesville Public Schools; C. Coon, Superintendent Salisbury Public Schools; E. P. Moses, Superintendent Raleigh Public Schools; R. J. Tighe, Superintendent Asheville Public Schools; T. R. Foust, Superintendent Goldsboro Public Schools; E. P. Mangum, Superintendent Wilson Public Schools; E. C. Brooks, Superintendent Monroe Public Schools; Alexander Graham, Superintendent Charlotte Public Schools; Frank H. Curtis, Superintendent Burlington Public Schools; Harry Howell, Superintendent Washington Public Schools; W. D. Carmichael, Durham Public Schools; W. S. Long, County Superintendent of Alamance; J. A. Anthony, County Superintendent of Cleveland; J. A. Butler, County Superintendent of Iredell; J. E. Ray, Superintendent of the School for the Deaf, Dumb and Blind; E. McK. Goodwin, Superintendent of the School for the Deaf and Dumb.

Raleigh News and Observer, *February 14, 1902*

books became known as "thirty dollar libraries."[14] They did indeed grow slowly, but, paralleling the erection of new schools, some 906 libraries were established by 1903. In this year an additional twelve hundred dollars was appropriated (later increased to seventy-five hundred dollars) to supplement previously established libraries.[15] Because of the accelerated growth of these institutions, the need for some type of organization became evident. Accordingly, in 1909 the General Assembly created the North Carolina Library Commission. Its purpose was to prepare a school library handbook recommending essential books that all public schools were required to stock in their libraries. By 1913 there were 3,609 original libraries and 1,525 supplemental ones.[16]

The movement for school consolidation, the second objective of the campaign leaders, also gained impetus during this era. Educational leaders recommended combining two or more districts into smaller ones so that three miles would be the greatest distance a child would be from school.[17] By 1912 more than twelve hundred small districts were abolished. Yet the prevailing type of consolidation in the state was the "union school of two teachers."[18] Obviously, there was still a great need for a wider type of consolidation, which made pupil transportation a necessity.

Pupil transportation, a movement that had become quite successful in Ohio and Indiana and that was gaining momentum in both Virginia and Louisiana, was inaugurated in North Carolina in 1908 by the town of Wentworth in Rockingham County. This form of school service was provided by the township, which owned the vehicles that were used. Each cost about $160 and was a "common-type one-horse wagon," providing for "about twelve pupils in each wagon at least." The pay of the driver was $15.00 per month.[19] The horses were generally furnished by the driver, usually a "farmer of the community of character and reliability, who was held responsible for the safety and good conduct of the children." In 1911 the General Assembly amended the public school law, empowering the county boards of education to pay the daily cost of pupil transportation out of the school fund.[20] At this time, two more counties, Wake and Cumberland, were transporting pupils to school.[21] Nevertheless, true effectiveness of this system had to wait for the "good or at least better roads that followed or rather led the automobile."

Improvement and beautification of the environmental setting of the typically unattractive rural school was the third objective of the educational campaigns. McIver was the mainspring of this movement, and he desired to formulate a program that would give it permanency by generating among the general public an awareness of and civic pride in school buildings and grounds. He decided to enlist the aid of the women of the state. As president of the Women's College at Greensboro, he called a meeting of the junior and senior classes on March 20, 1902. After explaining his idea and plan, he urged these young women to act·as missionaries and to go into each community of the state and organize branch associations or small clubs around each public schoolhouse. Thus emerged a society, as article 1 of its constitution reads: "The name of this organization shall be The Woman's Association for the Betterment of Public Schoolhouses of North Carolina." It soon became statewide in scope. Hundreds of branch clubs sprang up in local communities.[22] These clubs were composed of three or more women. Their duties were to plant trees, shrubbery, and flowers, and to hang pictures and perform other essential work to improve the "school environment of the state's future citizens." The Women's Association raised thousands of dollars for the purchase of pictures, library books, and even the construction of schoolhouses. In brief, the association played a significant role in making school buildings and grounds the most attractive public buildings in the community, while increasing the value of school property.[23]

The organization of the Woman's Association was McIver's last great service for the educational cause. "Dr. McIver died suddenly today on a train near Hillsboro," came the shocking news to his old friend, Walter Hines Page.[24] Educational leaders, friends, and others throughout the state and nation were stunned by McIver's death. He died from a stroke, from which he never recovered consciousness. The press, including the *New York Times, World's Work, Outlook,* and *Review of Reviews,* eulogized him as one of the foremost leaders in education, and Page wrote a tribute to him.[25] McIver's aggressive leadership was assumed by Superintendent Joyner.

Another remarkable development reflecting change in the public school system was the founding of rural high schools. The high school movement followed in the wake of an enactment in 1907 by the General Assembly entitled "An Act to Stimulate High School Instruction in the Public Schools of the State."[26] Under the law, one or more schools could be established in localities with twelve hundred or more inhabitants. To promote the movement, forty-five thousand dollars was appropriated to match any amount for a single school up to five hundred dollars raised by local taxation, private donations, or local appropriation. Not more than 4 high schools in any one county were entitled to receive state funds under the provisions of the act. Some 145 rural secondary schools were established during the first year, and by the end of 1913 there were 212 of these institutions in 94 counties. A number of the counties provided dormitories in which rural students could secure room and board at actual cost and pay for it with cash or with farm provisions at market cost. Of these schools, 61 offered four-year courses of study, 74 offered three-year courses of study, and 77 offered two-year courses of study.[27] These institutions added the "second story" to the North Carolina public school system. Hence, the state had taken an essential and a "giant step" toward placing secondary school opportunities within easy reach of the masses of agrarian youths, while concomitantly supplying the necessary link between the rural education system and the colleges.

The General Education Board played a significant role in the

Old school buildings (left-hand column) *as compared to the new structures that replaced them* (right-hand column).

high school movement in North Carolina as well as throughout the South. It took up the problem of Southern education where the Peabody Fund left off, but initially made a systematic study of the educational needs of the South.[28] North Carolina was the first state chosen for the comprehensive study. On the basis of results obtained, Executive Secretary Dr. Butterick reached the tentative conclusion that the region's greatest need was an adequate system of high schools. He wrote Superintendent Joyner: "Secondary education . . . seems to be largely in the hands of private or denominational academies. A large proportion of these academies are short lived. In 1900, 486 private schools and academies were reported; 328 of these are not reported in 1903. Of the 283 reported in the year (1903), 125 were not reported in 1900." Dr. Butterick was blunt and advocated that the state take over the private academies, "creating out of them county high schools here and there."[29]

Dr. Butterick's bold proposal never materialized. He did, however, sell the board of trustees on his scheme to promote secondary education in the South. Soon the General Education Board had inaugurated a policy of providing inspectors of high schools for all the Southern states by paying an annual salary of twenty-five hundred dollars, along with one thousand dollars in traveling expenses. Working behind the scenes in pursuance of his objective, Dr. Butterick approached each state university with the proposal that it install such a person as a regular faculty member. These high school inspectors spent half their time as professors of education and half in the field investigating high schools.[30] The state board of education appointed Nathan W. Walker, a trained specialist, to the position in the fall of 1905. Prominent among his duties were the pointing out defects in the high schools and the making of recommendations for improving instruction, textbooks, and equipment. His ultimate goal was to prepare the schools for accreditation, which in the final analysis would answer a most relevant question: What constitutes a good high school? Concomitantly, he began campaigning for a state law that would make possible the establishment of rural high schools. To marshal public sentiment behind such a law, he appeared before local school authorities, businessmen, and state and county teachers' conferences. And Walker almost individually campaigned before the General Assembly for the state law that made possible the establishment of rural high schools in 1907.[31]

In 1911 a strong standardization movement emerged in the South, and the Southern Association of Colleges and Secondary Schools was the major force behind the movement. The chief functions of this association were: "(1) to organize Southern schools and colleges for mutual assistance; (2) to elevate the standards of scholarship and to effect uniformity in college entrance requirements; and (3) to develop high schools and abolish secondary work in the colleges. While member colleges were required to have written examinations for admission, the Association's By-Laws declared: "certification may be accepted from duly accredited preparatory schools in lieu of entrance examinations at the colleges."[32]

When the General Education Board took up the work of assisting the development of public high schools, the term *high school* conveyed no definite meaning as an educational entity, as it does today. Moreover, the relationship between the high schools and the colleges was unsatisfactory. As secondary schools began to emerge and expand, the higher institutions were already "weighed down and held back by preparatory departments." Of necessity was a criterion to distinguish colleges from high schools. Accordingly, the major objective of the Southern Association was the establishment of minimum academic norms as guidelines for membership in the association for both colleges and high schools. For membership in the Southern Association, the colleges were required to abolish their preparatory departments. At the same time, high schools were encouraged to become accredited institutions, and membership in the association was mandatory. A student with the right credentials from an accredited high school could use them in lieu of entrance examinations at all colleges and universities.[33]

In order to qualify for membership in the Southern Association, the first obligation of high schools was to establish a secondary department with a minimum of three teachers, each possessing a college degree from an approved college, or its equivalent, and giving full time to high school instruction. The high school curriculum had to include a four-year course of study embracing at least fourteen Carnegie units. Another obligation was to maintain a school year of thirty-six weeks, with recitation periods of at least forty hours. And finally, the institution had to possess libraries, laboratories, and other equipment essential for good instruction in the courses offered.[34]

Immediately, Inspector Walker moved toward these goals. The General Education Board had no authority and desired none to force its views upon schools or public officials. Similarly, Inspector Walker—like the other high school inspectors—never attempted to enforce the standards of the Southern Association upon the high schools, but modified them to meet local conditions. In consequence, there ultimately emerged two lists of approved schools whose graduates were not required to take college entrance examinations: (1) the Southern Association list, which was honored throughout the South and in other sections of the country, and (2) the list compiled by the state inspector of high schools, which was honored by the state university and colleges in the state. The second list was tacitly permitted by the Southern Association partly on the grounds that state-supported institutions were sometimes required by law to accept graduates of properly classified high schools. The number of accredited public high schools in the South increased from 5 to 125 between 1911 and 1913 and rose to 340 during the next biennial. Twenty-six of the schools were located in North Carolina.[35] While the secondary schools of North Carolina, as a whole, still had a long way to go toward achieving standardization, one thing was certain: no longer was the completion of nine grades sufficient academic preparation to enter college, as it had been in 1900. It was pointed out earlier that the colleges were in competition for students and looked upon the expansion of high school opportunities with disapprobation. However, by 1913, or before, there was growing recognition that the accelerated expansion of high schools posed no threat to the colleges, as their preparatory departments moved toward their demise.

In some variables, it was evident that the North Carolina schools were approaching national averages. For instance, short school terms, low enrollment, and poor attendance had been cited as the most glaring weaknesses of the public school system in 1900. Between 1902 and 1913 significant advancements were made along these lines. To illustrate, in 1900 sixty-nine of the state's counties maintained school terms of less than the four months required by the Constitution, but by 1908 all the counties provided at least a four-months term. At the end of the 1913–14 academic year, the average length of the school term was 121.9 days, an approximate increase of 51 days. Likewise, the total school enrollment increased from 270,447 to 409,728. Equally important were the notable gains made in secondary school enrollment. Whereas in 1900 few, if any, rural students were in attendance, some 8,316 were enrolled in the secondary schools by 1913.[36]

It was only natural that these improvements would have the effect of lowering the high rate of illiteracy that prevailed in the state in 1900. Nevertheless, the rate was still high as compared with the national average, and the "gap" widened even further when North Carolina was compared with selected Northern states. Furthermore, a high rate of illiteracy still persisted in the Blue Ridge regions and, to some extent, in the Coastal Plain region. Also, a large number of children, as was the case in 1900, were not enrolled in school at all, and the attendance of many of those enrolled was most irregular. For example, only 78.2 percent of the state's white children of school age were enrolled in 1913, and only 70.6 percent of that group were in average daily attendance.[37] Obviously, there was a pressing need for a compulsory-school-attendance law.

Educators, reformers, and humanitarians had long agitated for compulsory-school-attendance and child labor laws. Edgar Gardner Murphy, an agent for the General Education Board; Alexander V. McKelway, editor of the *Presbyterian Standard* (leader of the movement in North Carolina), Coon, Joyner, Daniels, Aycock, and Bailey threw their weight behind the movement. At the same time, labor strongly supported both laws.[38] It was quite evident that child labor was a potent factor in lowering industrial wages. Efforts to put such

241

laws on the statute books failed in 1903 and 1905. Two years later a local "optional law" was enacted, requiring compulsory school attendance for four months annually for all children between the ages of eight and twelve.[39] This failed to satisfy even the most moderate reformer, and agitation continued for a more effective measure. Two years later the law was amended, granting the county board of education the "power to order an election or to grant a petition or to refuse to do either."[40] In 1910, nevertheless, only a few school officials availed themselves of the law or adopted compulsory-attendance laws. Only in 1913 did the General Assembly enact a mandatory-school-attendance statute, and the law was weak; it required compulsory school attendance for a mere four months for children between eight and fourteen years of age.[41]

Child labor legislation emerged simultaneously with the compulsory-attendance law. A law enacted in 1907 forbade the employment of a child in a factory unless he could read or write. This law reflected the views of some political leaders—specifically, Governor Aycock. It also prohibited the employment of children under fourteen years of age in manufacturing establishments betwen 8:00 A.M. and 5:00 P.M.[42] The irony was that the capitalist could still use children at night. This law, as might be expected, failed to satisfy the progressives. They desired a measure that would at least limit the age by day to fourteen for *all* children and to sixteen for night work.[43] In 1913 the reformers got everything they were seeking. The law proscribed the employment of children "between the ages of twelve and fourteen." The compulsory-attendance and the child labor laws complemented each other, and though their standards were low, their impact was soon evident. They went into effect in 1914, and there was at that time an increase of 75,919 children in school attendance. According to Superintendent Joyner, this was the largest increase in enrollment and attendance "during any one year in the history of North Carolina or perhaps in the history of any other State in the South."[44] And this figure was expected to increase still further.

Along with the twin bills of child labor and compulsory school attendance emerged a movement for a longer legal school term. A minimum "six months' term in the elementary schools" was the early goal of Superintendent Joyner.[45] However, it was not until 1913 that the General Assembly saw fit to enact such a law and, with it, to set up the "state equalizing fund." Its purpose was to bring terms in "all districts to a minimum of six months or near thereto." To participate in the above fund, a county was required first to provide from its own sources sufficient revenue to maintain its schools for four months and, if necessary, to levy a special tax of fifteen cents on every hundred-dollar valuation of real and personal property and forty-five cents on every taxable poll. No part of the fund was to be used for any other purpose than for payment of teacher salaries. Such salaries apportioned from the fund were not to exceed forty dollars per month for first grade teachers, thirty dollars per month for second grade teachers, and twenty dollars per month for third grade teachers.[46]

Any marked educational transformation during a specific period will have its impact upon the curriculum, but "the general curriculum shifts of great moments do not sweep away everything." Under the public school law, it was mandatory that spelling, reading, arithmetic, drawing, language lessons, composition, English grammar, geography, history of North Carolina and United States history, and the elements of physiology and hygiene, including the nature and effects of alcoholic drinks and narcotics, be taught in the elementary schools.[47]

Considering the shortness of the school terms and of the legal school day (of six hours), Superintendent Joyner logically concluded that this curriculum was "sheer folly."[48] In 1904, accordingly, to bring "order out of chaos," he requested Professor Coon to prepare a course of study for the elementary schools. It contained a schedule of recitations for one-, two-, and three-teacher schools, respectively, with the essential courses arranged (first through the seventh grade) so as to give emphasis to each subject according to its importance. It also included valuable suggestions to teachers on how to give instruction in the several grades.[49] Joyner had it published in pamphlet form and sent a sufficient number of copies to every county superintendent with the following instructions: "See that every teacher in your county has a copy of this course of study, and . . . will be held responsible for its adoption."[50]

The public school law authorized the state superintendent to prescribe requirements for admission and courses of study for all schools established under the high school law.[51] The course of study was molded around the classical curriculum and "tended in time to become part of the classical or academic course of study."[52] It was established with the objective of preparing the more capable students for college and gave no consideration to the youth destined to lead an agrarian life. Industrial education was strongly favored for whites, as for Blacks, by leading educators and Northern philanthropic bodies. This educational philosophy was expressed in these words: "Let the farm boy learn a little less of foreign exchange and Greek history, if need be, but teach him at the outset that farming is not drudgery, but an intellectual pursuit that, like other callings, pays handsome returns for intelligent, scientific care and management."[53]

Guilford County took the lead in providing a curriculum closely associated with agrarian pursuits. In March of 1911 the General

Assembly decreed that "there shall be maintained in one or more of the public high schools of Guilford County . . . with department of agricultural instruction, and a department of training in domestic science and home economics in order to better prepare the boys and girls of said county for farm and home-making."[54] The educational philosophy behind this type of program saw the role of the curriculum, especially that of the rural schools, as the preparation of students for college as well as for agrarian pursuits.

The law was extended to any other county that complied with the "conditions herein required of Guilford County." Schools offering a curriculum such as the one described above were to be known as "county farm-life schools" and were not to be located in any city or town of more than one thousand inhabitants, or within two miles of the corporate limits of any city or town of more than five thousand inhabitants.[55] An annual sum of twenty-five thousand dollars was appropriated by the state for the establishment of such schools, with twenty-five hundred dollars available to assist each county in the effort provided that the county or township voted permanent taxation of twenty-five hundred dollars for maintenance of the institution. In addition, by "bond · issue or otherwise," it was to provide buildings and equipment necessary for efficient instruction in the prescribed course of study.[56] By law these county farm-life schools were required to conduct agricultural extension and demonstration work and to make available short courses for adults. This was good, for people now saw a close affinity between the schools and the community, while developing a deep loyalty toward them.

Increases in teacher salaries and the establishment of additional normal schools and summer institutes accompanied the expansion of educational opportunities. The maximum salary a teacher could receive in 1900 was controlled by law according to the type of certificate he or she held, a situation that remained unchanged until 1905. In this year the scale was raised from $25 to $35 per month for holders of second grade certificates. Those with first grade certification could bargain for such compensation as agreed upon between teacher and county board of education.[57] With the increase of rural school terms from 70.8 to 115.5 days, the average annual teacher's salary jumped from approximately $70 to $235.[58] It seems reasonable to assume that this development raised the prestige of the teacher, especially in the rural areas. At least it could no longer be said that the average pay of the teacher was less than the state allowed the county jailer for feeding criminals.[59]

During this period the white teaching force increased from 5,382 to 8,344, which meant a larger teacher-pupil ratio. There was also a strong trend toward employment of women teachers in preference to males. For example, the number of female teachers increased from 2,474 to 7,853, while there was a decided decrease in the number of male teachers.[60]

To make training available to more people, in 1903 the Appalachian Training School (currently Appalachian State University) was established in the town of Boone in Watauga County. This institution was created to provide training for teachers in the western part of the state—the mountainous counties in the Highland region. Under the provisions of the law, citizens were required to raise fifteen hundred dollars by private subscription, and the state agreed to appropriate an equivalent sum for the erection of a building, in addition to appropriating two thousand dollars for the maintenance of the school.[61]

The result was that the school began with an "excellent plant" containing two well-equipped brick administration and science buildings and three large wooden buildings, two of which served as dormitories, the third one being comprised of classrooms.[62] The Appalachian Training School opened its doors on October 5, 1903, and 324 students enrolled the first year.[63]

On March 8, 1907, the General Assembly made arrangements for the establishment of a normal school for "young white men and women under the corporate name East Carolina Teachers' Training School" (located at Greenville, and now East Carolina University). This normal school was created under the High School Law of 1907. The reason for this strategy was that the representatives of the eastern section of the state opposed high schools, and the establishment of such an institution was a compromise measure between eastern and western legislators. Consequently, it was forbidden by law to maintain a curriculum that went beyond the stage of preparing a student for unconditional entrance into the freshman class at the University of North Carolina.[64] Under the provision of the law, citizens of the town that established the school were required to raise not less than twenty-five thousand dollars toward the construction of buildings and equipment, while the state agreed to appropriate fifteen thousand dollars toward that end, in addition to appropriating an annual five thousand dollars for maintenance of the school. At length, the county and the town of Greenville voted fifty thousand dollars, and the institution opened its doors on October 5, 1909, with an enrollment of 174, which two years later increased to 359.[65]

In addition to the two normal schools, North Carolina created another medium for the professional improvement of in-service teachers—namely, the county teachers' institutes. These were originated in 1889 and later became a volunteer county responsibility. An amendment to the law in 1905 made it mandatory that a two-weeks teachers'

Four of the new high school buildings reflecting educational progress.

institute be held in every county, and every white teacher was required by law to attend "regularly and continuously."[66] And finally, the County Teachers Associations and County Reading Circles came into existence around 1907. The former was organized for the purpose of continuing the work of teacher-training along the lines laid down by the institutes, which was to be accomplished by the holding of monthly meetings.[67] The purpose of the latter was to provide a home-study course for teachers by making available an annual selected course in reading to fit the professional needs of teachers. These readings were comprised of a number of books recommended by the supervisor of teacher training, subject to the approval of the state superintendent of public instruction. Teachers became members of the reading circles upon payment of a dollar enrollment fee, which entitled them to use books that the county superintendent was required to keep in his office. The teacher who successfully completed a course, as evidenced by a written examination prepared by the supervisor of teacher training, was rewarded with an attractive diploma. It was signed by the state superintendent of public instruction and the supervisor of teacher training, with a space left for the signature of the county superintendent.[68] It may be safely concluded that all the aforementioned institutions played a paramount role in improving the quality of teaching.

As noted previously, North Carolina placed little emphasis upon administration and supervision. But between 1902 and 1913 new trends were shown in these areas. By 1913 the salary of the state superintendent of public instruction had increased from $1,500 to $3,000 annually, and he was permitted a larger budget and office personnel.[69] It should be pointed out once again that the salary of the county superintendent was fixed by law, allowing compensation for no more than the county's school term. The compensation should not be "less than two dollars nor more than three dollars per day." In 1903 the law was changed so that if any county's total school fund exceeded $15,000, the county could employ a superintendent "for all his time at such salary as may be fixed by the said board." During this decade, the record shows a continuous increase in the annual salary of county superintendents from an average of $233 to $1,041, while some of the wealthy counties paid up to $1,800 annually.[70] At one time, the county superintendents were little more than mere clerks to the county boards of education, spending little or no time visiting and inspecting the schools. A law enacted in 1903 mandated that "the county superintendent shall be required to visit the public schools of his county . . . and shall inform himself of the conditions and needs of the various schools under his jurisdiction, and reside in the county where he is employed."[71] There also came into existence the State Association of County Superintendents. Its purpose was the discussion of common problems among members and with the state superintendent at annual conferences, along with the formulation of plans to achieve more uniformity in the various aspects of school management. A state law enacted in 1903 required all county superintendents to attend its meetings continuously during all sessions, with traveling and per diem expenses to be paid for by the county boards of education out of the school fund.[72]

For the further improvement of county supervision, L. C. Brogden was added to the State Department of Education in 1909 as supervisor of rural elementary schools. His annual salary of two thousand dollars and his travel expenses of one thousand dollars were paid by the Peabody philanthropy. Faced with the prospect of the dissolution of the Peabody Fund in 1914, the General Education Board assumed responsibility for its operation.[73] All in all, these developments lead one to the conclusion that North Carolina was beginning to recognize the value of professional supervision as a prerequisite for a successful school system. Between 1902 and 1913, the educational progressives had effected spectacular progress on all fronts of the public school system. Their ultimate goal was the creation of a school system modeled after the Massachusetts pattern. Yet, despite these significant achievements, two negative trends persisted. There was a discernible discrepancy between the educational opportunities offered by rural and urban school systems. The state, conscious of this situation, enacted legislation to assist the rural schools. However, the problem of rural education was national in scope and not to be solved during this era. But what about Negro education? Except for the futile efforts by some whites to secure racial division of the school tax funds, a complete hush settled over the question of education for the Black population. Examination of this problem is our next task.

Notes

1. *Biennial School Report*, 1900–2, p. 105; 1902–4, p. 9; 1904–5, p. 9; 1906–8, p. 247; 1908–10, p. 117; 1910–12, p. 9; 1912–14, p. 9.

2. See chap. 3.

3. *Raleigh News and Observer*, June 8, 1907; Joyner to Alderman, July 17, 1907, James Yadkin Joyner Papers, Southern Historical Collection, University of North Carolina, Chapel Hill, N.C.

4. J. R. Collie, *Appellant* v. *Commissioners of Franklin County*, in *Biennial School Report*, 1906–8, pt. 3, pp. 219–20.

5. Charles L. Coon, *A. Decade of Educational Progress* (Raleigh, N.C., 1910), p. 15.

6. "Annual Report of the State Inspector of High Schools" in *Biennial School Report*, 1912–14, pt. 2, p. 43.

7. Ibid., 1902–4, p. 9; 1904–6, pp. 65–84; 1906–8, pp 209–16; 1908–10, pp. 49–50; 1910–12, p. 9; and 1912–14, p. 9.

8. James Y. Joyner, "Educational Expansion in North Carolina," James Yadkin Joyner Papers, June–August 1910, Southern Historical Collection, University of North Carolina, Raleigh, N.C.

9. *Biennial School Report*, 1912–14, pt. 2, p. 151.

10. *Public Laws of North Carolina*, 1903, chap. 567, secs. 1, 3, and 4.

11. *Biennial School Report*, 1902–4, pp. 17–18, and pt. 2, pp. 190–91.

12. Ibid., 1898–1900, p. 250.

13. *Public Laws of North Carolina*, 1901, chap. 662, secs. 6–11.

14. Francis L. Spain, "High School Libraries in the South," in Carson W. Ryan, ed. *Secondary Education in the South* (Chapel Hill, N.C., 1946), p. 97.

15. *Public Laws of North Carolina*, 1903, chap. 226, sec. 7; Coon, *Decade of Educational Progress*, p. 15.

16. *Public Laws of North Carolina*, 1909, chap. 179; *Biennial School Report*, 1912–14, pt. 1, p. 79.

17. Ibid., 1906–8, pt. 1, p. 40.

18. L. C. Brogden to Superintendent Joyner, January 12, 1912, Joyner Papers.

19. L. C. Brogden et. al., "Consolidation of Rural Schools and Public Transportation of Pupils," *Proceedings of the Fifteenth Conference for Education in the South* (1912), pp. 235–36.

20. *Public Laws of North Carolina*, 1911, chap. 135.

21. *Biennial School Report*, 1912–14, pt. 1, p. 54.

22. *Greensboro Telegram*, April 7, 1902; Southern Education Board, *Woman's Women's Education*, Southern Education Bulletin no. 19 (December 1, 1903).

23. *Proceedings of the Eleventh Conference for Education in the South* (1908), pp. 114–18.

24. C. B. McIver, Jr., to Page, September 17, 1906, telegram, Walter Hines Page Papers, Houghton Library, Harvard University, Cambridge, Mass.

25. Ibid.

26. *Public Laws of North Carolina*, 1907, chap. 802.

27. "Annual Report of the State Inspector of Public High Schools," in *Biennial School Report*, 1913–14, p. 17.

28. Hal Ayres, *Seven Great Foundations* (New York, 1911), p. 43.

29. Dr. Buttrick to Superintendent Joyner, December 18, 1903, Joyner Papers.

30. *The General Education Board: An Account of Its Activities 1902–1914* (New York, 1915), pp. 78–83.

31. Nathan W. Walker, "Recent High School Development in North Carolina," High School Bulletin, vol. 2 (Oct. 11, 1911), pp. 1–5.

32. *Proceedings of the Southern Association of Colleges and Secondary Schools*, (1895), pp. 6–7; *Constitution and By-Laws of the Southern Association of Colleges and Secondary Schools* (1896), p. 27.

33. *Proceedings of the Southern Association* (1912), pp. 30–31.

34. Ibid. (1915), pp. 22–24.

35. Ibid., p. 19.

36. *Biennial School Report*, 1912–14, pt. 2, pp. 131–45. The length of the average school term in the urban areas was 166 days, while in rural regions it ranged from 88 days in Madison County to 160 days in New Hanover County.

37. Ibid., pp. 131–32.

38. Elizabeth H. Davidson, *Child Labor Legislation in the Southern Textile States* (Chapel Hill, N.C., 1939), pp. 114–119, 149, 156–60.

39. *Biennial School Report*, 1906–8, p. 25.

40. Ibid., 1909, chap. 525.

41. Ibid., 1913, chap. 173.

42. Ibid., chap. 894.

43. Davidson, *Child Labor Legislation*, p. 159.

44. *Biennial School Report*, 1912–14, pt. 1, p. 10.

45. Coon, *Decade of Education Progress*, p. 7.

46. *Public Laws of North Carolina*, 1913, chap. 33.

47. Ibid., 1901, chap. 4.

48. *Biennial School Report*, 1902–4, p. 44.

49. Charles L. Coon, *Course of Study for Primary Schools* (Salsbury, N.C., 1901), pp. 5–39; idem, *English and History in the Elementary Schools: A Manual for Leaders* (Raleigh, N.C., 1905), pp. 1–39.

50. "Circular Letter of the State Superintendent," September 1905, in *Biennial School Report*, 1904–6, pp. 329–330.

51. *Public Laws of North Carolina*, 1907, chap. 820, sec. 3.

52. Nathan W. Walker, *Handbook for High School Teachers* (Raleigh, N.C., 1907), pp. 10–23.

53. Southern Education Board, *Southern Education Notes*, ser. 1, June 1902.

54. *Public Laws of North Carolina*, 1911, chap. 84.

55. Ibid., chap 84, secs. 5, 6, and 7. The farm-life schools were already quite common in the New England and South Atlantic states. Around 1900, few, if any, schools existed, but in 1910 there were two thousand such institutions scattered

throughout the nation. D. C. Crosby, "Agriculture in Public High Schools," in *Yearbook of the United States Department of Agriculture* (1912), pp. 471–86.

56. Around 1906 the General Education Board, under the leadership of Dr. Seeman A. Knapp, began to promote farm demonstration work among adult farmers. It was theorized that the Southern people would gladly support better schools if they could be aided in their major economic endeavor—farming. From this activity emerged the Boys Corn Clubs and Girls Canning Clubs. See *General Education Board: An Account of its Activities, 1902–1914*, pp. 22–27, 57–58, 62–68; *Biennial School Report*, 1912–14, pt. 1, p. 13.

57. *Public Laws of North Carolina*, 1905, chap. 820, sec. 4.

58. *Biennial School Report*, 1912–14, pt. 2, pp. 139–45. Annual teachers' salaries in the counties in 1913 ranged from $139.00 to $481.00 in the counties of Bladen and Durham, respectively. The average annual urban salary increased from $275.00 in 1900 to $481.00 in 1913.

59. Southern Education Board, *North Carolina Education*, Southern Education Bulletin no. 10 (May 14, 1903), p. 121.

60. *Biennial School Report*, 1912–14, pt. 2, pp. 139–145, 161.

61. *Public Laws of North Carolina*, 1903, chap. 798.

62. B. B. Dougherty to Superintendent Joyner, May 25, 1903, Joyner Papers.

63. *Biennial School Report*, 1902–4, pp. 515–16.

64. *Public Laws of North Carolina*, 1907, chap. 820.

65. *Biennial School Report*, 1906–8, pt. 1, p. 17, and *North Carolina Public Documents*, 1913, no. 22.

66. "Report of the Supervisor of Teacher Training," in *Biennial School Report*, 1908–10, pt. 1, pp. 10, 108–12.

67. Ibid., 1910–12, pt. 3, p. 64.

68. *Biennial School Report*, 1910–12, pp. 46–47.

69. *Public Laws of North Carolina*, 1903, chap. 435, secs. 8, 13, and 1907, chap. 820, sec. 3; "Circular Letters of the State Superintendent" *Biennial School Report*, 1904–6, pt. 3, pp. 332–33.

70. Chief Clerk to Dr. Abraham Flexner, January 22, 1915. Joyner Papers; *Biennial School Report*, 1900–1912, passim., and 1912–14, pt. 1, p. ii.

71. *Public Laws of North Carolina*, 1903, chap. 435, sec. 8; *Public School Laws of North Carolina*, 1907, chap. 820, secs. 4141, 4139.

72. *Biennial School Report*, 1912–14, pt. 1, pp. 10–12.

73. Wickliffe Rose to Superintendent Joyner, March 10 and 24, 1908, and October 12, 1909; Joyner to Rose, March 24, 1908, Joyner Papers. *General Education Board: An Account of Its Activities, 1902–1914*, pp. 179–87.

9

Negro Education: "Spend Nothing Unless Absolutely Necessary"

This final chapter will consider the negative ways and means by which Negro education was promoted during the decade of the public school movement. Since Negro education was supplemented by Northern philanthropy devoted to the problem exclusively (the Slater, Jeanes, and Rosenwald Funds), efforts will be made to evaluate the effectiveness of such financial assistance and to determine whether such funds were geared to uphold the dominant philosophy of Southern racism.

Negro schools trudged far behind in the march for education. Ironically, in 1896 the United States Supreme Court in the *Plessy* v. *Ferguson* decision in effect ruled that the meager and inadequate Black educational facilities were "separate but equal" to those of whites. That the *Plessy* doctrine involved interstate commerce was purely incidental. For example, in the late 1880s a lower federal court upheld an Ohio law authorizing the school board to organize separate schools for the races, "so long as educational opportunities for Negroes were substantially equal to those for whites." In the *Cummings* v. *Richmond* case in 1900, the Court had ruled that education supported by public taxation was a matter "belonging to the respective states, and interference could not be justified except in a case of 'clear and unmistakable disregard of the rights secured by the supreme law of the land.' "[1] In sanctioning the doctrine of "separate but equal" facilities for Blacks, the nation's highest tribunal ignored the real condition of inequality of Negro educational facilities; it was well known that rarely, if ever, were such facilities equal to those designed for whites. As in the historic 1954 court decision, an appeal to the sociological method of interpretation of the Constitution was unthinkable during this era. Just as there were marked differences between educational facilities for white and Negro children, there was a still greater chasm between the educational opportunities for rural Black and urban Black children.

After the North Carolina public school movement, a large discrepancy prevailed between the educational opportunities offered the white population and those offered Blacks, and this was especially true in the rural counties; consequently, Blacks were bequeathed a cruel legacy. In 1934 the noted Black scholar Horace Mann Bond wrote: "While the per capita expenditures for white children in the rural sections may frequently be from twenty to thirty times as great as for Negroes, the variation in the cities rarely exceeds the proportion of four to one and in most cases less."[2]

More urban schools were constructed for Blacks during the decade beginning in 1902. However, the number is not known because of limited data. In 1913 the total value of white school property in the urban areas was $3,668,795, contrasted to $510,253 for Negro school property.[3] The average value of each white city schoolhouse was $17,159, compared to $3,855 for the Negro urban schoolhouse. Average annual teacher salaries for Blacks were a little more than half those of whites, Black teachers receiving $253 and white teachers earning $416. The Negro fared significantly better in such variables as length of school term and enrollment. For example, the average length of school terms in Black schools, 167 days, was almost equal to that in white institutions, 169.5 days. During the decade beginning in 1900, there was a significant jump in black school enrollment, which increased from 10,159 students to 32,325.[4] Were Negro parents preparing their children for the mandatory suffrage requirements after 1908? It could be argued that racism in the counties and depressed agricultural conditions had caused a Negro exodus from the counties to the cities, which had an impact on school enrollment.

North Carolina's Negro population constituted one-third of the state's total population, and most Blacks were identified with agriculture. The state constitution mandated that the school fund be apportioned equally on a per capita basis of school population. Then, theoretically, the source of funds for Negro schools was the same as that for all children in the public schools.

Racism pervaded the rural areas. In placing the educational appropriation in the hands of local authorities, the Negro schools in the Black Belt were irretrievably doomed to inferiority. The all-white school boards, committees, and superintendents, "elected by the patrons of the schools . . . naturally considered their first duty to the white children."[5] This lack of sensitivity and responsibility for the Negro schools under their supervision led to the practice of channeling most of the per capita school tax to whites. Succinctly stated, white schools in the Black Belt "profited from Negro numbers on their rolls."

True, there was a decided trend to lesser educational expenditures for rural Blacks after 1902; nevertheless, stimulated by the educational crusades, some school construction for them did occur. The extent of construction is indicated by the following figures:[6]

Year	Number of Black Rural Schools Built
1902	51
1903	52
1904	39
1905	49
1906	74
1907	72
1908	80
1909	72
1910	57
1911	75
1912	89
Total	710

But figures tell little. To what extent was this school construction identified with the Piedmont region? What was the pattern of school construction in the Black Belt counties? At the same time, we need to know something about the quality of equipment, such as patented desks, blackboards, and so on. One thing is certain: schools for Blacks were often built as cheaply as possible. Even Superintendent Joyner accepted the premise that schoolhouses for Blacks could be built "for much less money" than white schoolhouses.[7] Adhering to this concept, the total value of all school property for the Negro population in 1912–13 was recorded at $510,253, and the average value of each rural schoolhouse was $231.[8] The value of some of the bizarre structures called schools in the Black Belt counties was far less than is indicated by the average.

An analysis of the eighteen Black Belt counties, in which the educational problem was compounded, will put the matter in better perspective. While there was a marked increase in school funds and expenditures in white schools in response to the educational campaigns, there was a decided trend to decrease the amount of money spent on Negro education. By 1905 Blacks were receiving less than one-fifth of the school fund. But this was a statewide average. In the Black Belt region in the period 1912–13, Negro students represented approximately 60 percent of the school population, but only 36.94 percent of the teachers were Black, and these received only 31.60 percent of the expenditures in teachers' salaries. Yet these statistics are too vague and do not portray the entire story. There were many Black schools with incompetent teachers in rooms with only benches and no blackboards or texts for students. As many educators with keen eyes observed, then and afterward, the ingenuity on the part of some Black teachers and pupils alike was extraordinary. In regard to such items as teacher salaries and the value of school property, the *Plessy* v. *Ferguson* doctrine of "separate but equal" held true in some Black Belt counties in 1900. The average monthly teacher salary for Black teachers exceeded that of white teachers in the counties of Bertie, Edgecombe, and Hertford, while two differed by only a few cents in five of the other counties. Likewise, the average value of Black school property in Halifax and Hertford Counties was greater than that of white school property, and the respective values of each differed by only a few hundred dollars in the other counties.[9] By 1913, however, an enormous chasm had evolved in New Hanover County; Negro school property was valued at $19,255, as compared to $200,371 for white school property, while the average annual salary of the white teachers exceeded that of Black teachers by $157. Halifax County, which had a Negro population of 64.1 percent, paid its white teachers an annual salary of $301.00, as compared to $121.45 for its Negro teachers; school property in the county stood at $72,116 and $15,940 for white and Negro property, respectively. The Halifax situation was mirrored throughout the Coastal Plain region and, in general, throughout the state. For a better look at the problem, see Table 4, in which some of the relevant data are presented.

TABLE 4
SELECTED COMPARATIVE EDUCATIONAL VARIABLES FOR
NORTH CAROLINA'S BLACK COUNTIES, 1912–1913

County	Percentage of Blacks	Number of Schools White	Number of Schools Black	Value of School Property White	Value of School Property Black	Annual Teacher Salary White	Annual Teacher Salary Black
Bertie	57.6	64	52	$ 59,800	$ 9,775	$200.24	$102.26
Caswell	54.6	41	34	15,700	5,200	197.15	85.25

County	Percentage of Blacks	Number of Schools White	Number of Schools Black	Value of School Property White	Value of School Property Black	Annual Teacher Salary White	Annual Teacher Salary Black
Craven	60.2	48	33	110,525	16,725	311.94	136.00
Edgecombe	62.4	42	38	79,332	17,092	385.40	161.12
Granville	51.1	55	43	69,500	5,700	235.10	100.16
Anson	53.4	47	42	69,000	14,000	273.67	92.34
Chowan	57.0	19	15	27,500	5,600	262.30	99.20
Halifax	64.1	43	51	77,116	15,940	305.58	121.45
Hertford	58.7	34	30	24,745	6,765	159.71	94.34
New Hanover	50.8	19	14	200,371	19,225	457.62	300.55
Northampton	57.3	41	42	47,750	7,350	287.27	91.36
Paaquotank	51.4	34	17	72,500	9,000	352.28	186.63
Pender	51.6	42	36	36,300	5,700	241.30	105.63
Pitt	50.2	81	52	110,000	20,200	238.56	96.30
Vance	58.6	30	23	62,500	21,000	293.57	153.05
Wake	68.2	85	64	287,074	62,900.50	370.45	164.33
Warren	68.5	39	40	28,055	10,450	259.73	98.82
Washington	50.6	31	19	41,700	10,000	185.33	132.72

The conclusion is inescapable that the majority of rural whites were opposed to educational equality for Blacks. Thus, a crucial question was, How much education should the Negro population receive? As much as Negro taxes would provide, advocates of the racial division of taxes would have surely answered. Romanticists nurtured a proclivity toward paternalism, while advocating a training different from that of whites, especially "for the making of character."[10] On the other hand, a large group of white Southerners argued a priori that the Negro needed no more than the bare essentials of education to assure that he would always "keep his place" in the biracial political, economic, and social order. One dominant Southern creed was best expressed by Thomas P. Bailey, thusly: "In educational policy let the Negro have the crumbs that fall from the white man's table. . . . Let there be such education of the Negro as will best fit him to serve the white man."[11] Likewise, Aycock's philosophy of Negro education left much to be desired. We saw earlier how he opposed the idea of dividing taxes along racial lines, meaning segregation of local assessments, and limited the amount of public education to the amount of taxes paid by Blacks themselves. His idea of universal education was a four-months school term, which, he said, "includes the negro school districts." Sometimes he used amusing racist statements to get his point across. He once told an audience:

"Yes, I believe in the education of niggers . . . [and] my fellow citizens, you believe in the education of a mule; you train your setter pups and fox hounds . . . I think more of a nigger than I do of a mule or a dog."[12] It is extremely difficult to find in the literature and/or his private papers where he took a strong stand in defense of Black education. At the same time, Blacks could not agitate for more educational opportunities. Survival was their greatest concern. "It was an art that all blacks . . . had to master."[13]

While rural whites had grudingly assented to the principle of a rudimentary education for Blacks, another particular need of the latter remained unmet—teacher training. The rural schools of North Carolina, as in other Southern states, had no immediate institution by which the elementary school student of promise could bridge the gap from his first course and a teacher-training course. Teacher-training facilities increased in number for whites during the decade following 1902, but such facilities for the Black population were actually reduced in number. However, it must be made clear that this was a progressive move. Since their inception, the six Negro normal schools had experienced an uncertain and precarious existence in inadequate quarters. Superintendent Joyner concluded that diffusion was weakness and that concentration over which better supervision could be exercised, was strength. He saw the wisdom of consolidating into three institutions the six Negro normal schools and of establishing each of them at some strategic and permanent location.[14] Charles L. Coon was appointed in July 1904 as superintendent of the Negro normal schools, at an annual salary of $1,500, plus $150 for expenses. After considering all potential sites, he established one at Elizabeth City in Pasquotank County for the Tidewater region; one at Fayetteville in Cumberland County for the upper or Western Coastal Plain, and one at Winston-Salem in Forsyth County for the Piedmont region. For the permanent location of these institutions, the state by 1906 expended a total of $25,300, of which $5,100 was from its annual appropriation. Friends of the normal schools were required to raise monies through "collections and pledges for a building fund," while the state appropriated a meager $500 each for the schools at Fayetteville and Elizabeth City.[15]

The financial resources of the Negro normal schools were limited. The 1912–14 biennial state appropriations were $10,000 to the Winston-Salem Normal and Industrial School; $9,398 to the school at Fayetteville, and $5,448.32 to the school at Elizabeth City. The per capita cost to the state for training students in 1914 at the Fayetteville State Normal School was $2.16 a month, everything included. And at Elizabeth City it was less. The total enrollment of the three combined was 860 students. So restricted were the accommodations

Institute for White Teachers.

The Forsyth County Teachers' Institute for White Teachers will begin at ten o'clock on Monday, July 31st, 1905, and continue two weeks. The Institute will be held in the Salem Academy Chapel, Winston-Salem, and will be conducted by Mr. Charles L. Coon.

The Institute will devote its entire time and attention to the studies taught in the Public Schools--Spelling, Reading, Writing, Arithmetic, Geography, History, English Grammar, Physiology, Drawing, Agriculture, and Civil Government. Teachers should not fail to bring the State Text Books on all these subjects.

The daily work of the Institute will be based on the Elementary Public School Course of Study prescribed by the State Superintendent of Public Instruction, and will attempt to enable Public School Teachers to extend their knowledge of the Public School branches, as well as afford them some instruction in the best methods of teaching those branches to children.

All White Public School Teachers of Forsyth County are required, according to law, to attend this Institute regularly and continuously, unless providentially hindered, which means that all Teachers must be present promptly at ten o'clock on the opening day and attend all the sessions of all the following days. This is a regulation of the Public School Law.

I hope all Teachers will not fail to bring all the Public School Books, which they teach. It will be impossible to have a real school, unless the Teachers bring these books. I also urge that Teachers attend promptly. There should be no time lost on account of tardiness and lack of prompt attendance.

A Public Examination will be held the week following the Institute, the time and place to be announced at the close of the Institute.

W. B. SPEAS,

Co. Supt. Forsyth Co.

July 6th, 1905.

Charles L. Coon's announcement of a County Teacher's Institute. **Courtesy of the Library of Congress.**

at one school that it was necessary to have four and five females in a room, and the problem was more acute among the males.[16] And since most of the appropriations were paid to maintain the teaching force, little was left for capital investment in equipment. The Southern dual system of education imposed a dual pattern of educational standards. It is safe to conclude that the majority of whites did not care about the caliber of Black teachers. At the same time, progressive Negro educators tacitly expected Black teachers to produce results equivalent to those of white teachers with superior facilities.

Even today there prevails the belief that Negro institutions must always adopt programs geared to the academic background of their students, and certainly this was the philosophy of the three normal schools of North Carolina.

Both the curriculum and the textbooks were on a fifth grade level. The four-year course of study was designed for elementary schools of four grades. Some instruction was given in agriculture, gardening, use of simple tools, and domestic science for girls, but, because of the lack of equipment, only the Slater Industrial School at Winston-Salem actually attempted to teach all of these subjects. Eventually, a more advanced course of study was added to the school's normal curriculum, which appeared to have reached in 1908 at least a parity with beginning high school classes.[17] The state's philosophy concerning the education of Black leaders was in accordance with the Southern tradition. These normal schools were really doing a job of training young teachers out of the "agricultural tradition they had known," and returning them to their communities, perhaps, to inspire other young Black persons to become teachers like themselves. One Negro educator put the problem in focus when he wrote: "The finished products of these (institutions) were 'all right for the Negro community,' but generally inadequate for service in the larger American community."[18]

We have seen how Northern philanthropy was inextricably interwoven with the efforts to promote the public school movement in North Carolina. The mammoth General Education Board as well as the Peabody Fund bypassed the Negro. This left only the Slater philanthropy of $1 million to give any consideration to the educational problems of Blacks, but function of the fund was different from that of the other foundations.

From 1891 to 1903, Curry, the ultraconservative on racial issues, proposed no progressive program for the fund. He merely passed out doles to Black college heads, contingent upon their including vocational education in their curriculum. After Curry's death, the equally cautious executive secretary, Dr. Wallace Buttricks of the General Education Board, acted as agent for the fund from 1903 to 1910. He continued Curry's policy of aiding the selected sixteen colleges that taught industrial education.[19] Naturally, he ignored completely those higher institutions constructed on the liberal arts curriculum. So the only real function of the fund was the maintenance of a record of statistical handouts (gratuities). Negro education, certainly, could not be "improved by tinkering at it in spots."[20] Only after Dr. James H. Dillard was appointed field director in 1910 did the Slater Fund finally come forward with a constructive program, designed to create secondary school opportunities. The need for high school facilities for the Negro population remained unfulfilled. Public laws in North Carolina recognized no Negro secondary education before 1918, and until 1921 the growth of Black high schools was slow.[21] One explanation may be found in local hostility toward the idea of Negro high schools, especially in the rural areas. Throughout the South Dr. Dillard promoted the county training school, defined as a large central institution maintaining a curriculum of eight grades or higher and open to children from all parts of the county.[22] County training schools had their inception in Louisiana. County Superintendent A. C. Lewis of Tangipahoa Parish became interested in the establishment of a rural high school for Negro children. He wrote to Dr. Dillard for financial assistance. Dr. Dillard complied by contributing five hundred dollars, earmarked for the salary of an industrial teacher. Superintendent Lewis called his school the Parish Training School for Colored Children. It was located at Kentwood in Tangipahoa Parish.[23] The local school board supplied the teachers and equipment, and a lumber company furnished the material for the house and gave ten acres of land. Meanwhile, Dr. Dillard was badgered with other requests for funds from county superintendents in Arkansas, Mississippi, and Virginia. From this auspicious development, he concluded that the time was ripe to establish these schools throughout the South. He realized that this type of institution would serve two purposes; they would (1) provide secondary opportunities for the Negro in rural areas, and (2) be utilized as a potential medium for the preparation of elementary rural teachers.[24]

In taking up the task of promoting the establishment of county schools, Dr. Dillard set up certain conditions and guidelines. Local school boards were required to appropriate teacher salaries of not less than $730 from public funds raised in state, county, or district territories. The school term was to be at least eight months long. And the school was to be a part of the public school system, and its property was to belong to the state or county.[25] The Slater Fund employed the following diminishing scale in granting financial aid: $500 annually for the first three years; $250 annually for the next two years; and a final $100 for needed equipment after operating for five years. After this time, it was assumed, the institutions would have become well-organized public schools and would be supported completely by their respective counties. Thus, such institutions were assured of "success and permanence."[26]

Through the respective state officials entrusted with public education, Doctor Dillard made known the philosophy of the trustees of the Slater Fund and concomitantly urged the establishment of county training schools.[27] "I approve most heartily your suggestion of a county industrial training school for Negro teachers," responded Superintendent Joyner.[28] Slowly, these schools began to spring up in the South. Counting the Parish Training School in Louisiana, only seven such institutions had been established as late as 1914—one in Newton County, Mississippi, one in Hempstead County, Arkansas, and another in Sabine Parish, Louisiana. The other three were located in North Carolina—one at Smithfield in Johnston County, one at Method in Wake County, and one at Stonewall in Pamlico County.[29] Each of them received a mere five hundred dollars from the Slater Fund, and two years later only five were still operating. From the beginning they had a serious handicap. There was a grave shortage of teachers. Their curriculum was geared to industrial instruction, and there was no equipment. Industrial equipment was expensive and neither the county nor the state saw fit to purchase any.

The county training schools were the origin of public high school opportunities for Southern rural Blacks. Their course of study consisted of the seven elementary grades, in addition to the state's high school course of study in the eighth and ninth grades. Black history was substituted for ancient history, and teacher training and industrial work for the classics. And to give practical training to Blacks, instruction was provided in agriculture (gardening), manual training, cooking, sewing, housekeeping, and laundry work.[30] As Horace Mann Bond keenly observed, it was a striking commentary upon the state of rural schools for Blacks in 1910 that the Slater Board required that instruction should extend through a minimum of eight years, adding at least two at the most propitious time.[31]

Thus, Dr. Dillard and the Slater Board gave the advocates of rural education a new direction, without arousing those in the white community opposed to the idea of high schools supported by taxation. Had they ignored this factor, these institutions could not have been established without incurring the wrath of the white racists. In dealing with this problem, the Slater Fund officials were extremely cunning. When they extended secondary educational opportunities to the Negro to train teachers, they did it through the county training schools, where subjects above the elementary level were quietly taught, without the fanfare of the term high schools. This helps to explain the common practice of naming Negro high schools in the South after their respective county or town, in contrast to the practice of naming white schools after prominent local, state, or national individuals.

An educational philanthropy bearing the name Anna T. Jeanes came into being in 1907. The Jeanes Foundation was to give recognition by accident to a distinct Negro public school problem. Miss Jeanes was a Quakeress of Philadelphia. Her interest in Negro education originated in appeals from Booker T. Washington, Hollis B. Frissell of Hampton Institute, and others. On April 17, 1905, she responded by contributing a sum of two hundred thousand dollars to the General Education Board. This sum was accompanied by a letter that succinctly stated: "I enclose my cheque for two-hundred thousand dollars ($200,000) as a special fund for the assistance of the Negro Rural Schools in the South."[32] Following through with this idea, on September 30, 1907, she created an endowment of $1 million to be devoted solely to the assistance of rural schools for Southern Blacks.[33] Thus came into existence the Negro Rural School Fund, incorporated by an Act of Congress, November 20, 1907.

The tentacles of the "interlocking directorate" represented a virtual monopolistic control of educational philanthropy in the South. There was a lesson in democracy in the establishment of the Jeanes philanthropy to be learned by ultraconservatives like Dr. Buttricks, Baldwin, the late Curry, and others. Among the seventeen-member board of trustees were President William H. Taft, Andrew Carnegie, Peabody, Ogden, Page, Dr. Dillard, Frissell, and Washington. There were four other outstanding Black members. These were Abraham Grant of Columbus, Georgia, Bishop of the African Methodist Church; Robert R. Moton, Secretary of Tuskegee, and later to succeed Washington as principal of Tuskegee Institute; James C. Napier of Nashville, Tennessee, banker and former register of the United States Treasury; and Robert L. Smith of Waco, Texas, a former deputy marshal and, at the time, a successful banker.[34] Dillard was elected president of the fund. In 1909, B. C. Caldwell of Louisiana was appointed field agent and was responsible directly to the president of the board.

Exercising no clear-cut plan during the first two years, the fund disbursed a total of $94,700 in twelve states ($11,300 in North Carolina) to supplement salaries of rural teachers. Just as the Slater trustees came up indirectly with the novel idea that led to the establishment of the county training schools, the trustees of the Jeanes Fund come up with another unique idea in quite a roundabout way. Jackson Davis, superintendent of schools in Henrico, Virginia, met a Negro teacher named Virginia Randolph, whose school was distinctly superior, having its "windows and floors clean, stove polished and yard tidy." Could not this idea be extended over the entire county? In any event, Davis wrote Dr. Dillard and requested some funds, which were granted.[35] Thus, Virginia Randolph became the forerunner of a group of supervisors who became known throughout the South as the Jeanes Teachers, and with the passing of the years they became the equivalent of supervisors of the Black rural school system.

According to the record, some thirteen counties in North Carolina were employing Jeanes Teachers by June 1913.[36] They were recognized as regular employees of the county school system and were responsible to the county superintendent and school board, and performed duties somewhat similar to the Woman's Association for the Betterment of Public Schoolhouses. Two years later there were thirty-one Jeanes Teachers (one teacher in each county) in the state, and toward their salaries the counties paid a total of $3,619, in addition to the total $6,681 contributed by the fund.[37] This amounts to an average annual salary of about $334, a much higher wage than that paid in the Black Belt counties. But there are little available data concerning the payment of personal expenses such as travel and lodging. The salaries of Jeanes Teachers in Louisiana ranged from $470 to $800 annually, with room and board sometimes as high as $45 per month.[38] As public support for the program grew, the state of North Carolina—like other states—gradually accepted the responsibility for assuming support of this philanthrophy and its incorporation in the general system of public education for Blacks.

Five years after the establishment of the Jeanes Fund, the Julius Rosenwald philanthropy came into existence. Negro schoolhouses symbolized the Negro public school problem. Some were boxlike shacks of "old slabs and scrap lumber," or log cabins, while some sessions were held in churches or lodges or old stores. The Rosenwald foundation evolved a new plan for the improvement of schools for Blacks, which involved its assisting in the construction of rural schoolhouses. Rosenwald, president of Sears, Roebuck Company, a trustee of Tuskegee Institute, and a close friend of Washington, was the force behind this benevolence.[39] The idea originated with Washington, however, who sought Rosenwald's financial assistance in the construction of rural schoolhouses in Alabama. He told Rosenwald "that it would hardly be possible to help through the medium of the state, as the states do not recognize the matter of race with reference to dealing with the public schools," and he charged the county boards of education with dividing as they saw fit the funds sent by the state into the various counties, with "the colored school receiving very, very little." The result was that some of the Negro schools in the South "are as bad as stables."[40] Illustrating his point, he described the situation in an Alabama County statistically, as shown in Table 5.[41]

TABLE 5

	White	Colored
Number of children of school age	2,000	10,769
Number of schools	53	49
Average number of children of school age for each school	38	219
Number of teachers	67	53
Average number of children of school age for each teacher	30	209
Enrollment in public schools	1,200	2,318
Percent of school population enrolled	60	20
Average length of school term in months	7.3	3.9
Schools running 5 months or more	46	0
Average yearly salary		
Male	544	73
Female	360	71
Annual expenditures for public schools	$28,998	$3,569
Annual expenditures per child of school age	$14.49	$.20

Rosenwald was moved by Washington's letter and replied: "I expect to celebrate my 50th birthday on the 12th of this month, and would like to announce this gift. . . . My idea would be to make the announcement . . . in this manner: $25,000 for colored schools that have grown out of Tuskegee Institute." He also advised Washington to send a telegram "collect," making it full and complete as if it were a letter and to substitute a name, so the burden of distribution would not be "put upon Tuskegee for distribution."[42] Accordingly, on August 12, 1912, the Chicago newspapers announced Rosenwald's gift of twenty-five thousand dollars on his fiftieth birthday. Washington was empowered to name the schools that could participate, the purpose of each school, and the amount to be allotted to each until the entire sum had been consumed. Rosenwald, like John D. Rockefeller, was a sagacious man. He also believed that his benefactions would stimulate others to do something toward matching his gifts, and, as a condition for distribution of the fund, each school designated was to raise an equal amount. He was convinced that such an "incentive will be great for others to give."[43]

The announcement of the Rosenwald gift immediately released flood of petitions (some full of pathos) from Black principals, who badgered Washington from the beginning. From Allen L. Young of Wake Forest, principal of the Presbyterian Mission School—School to Prepare Colored Boys and Girls to Practical Duties of Life, by Educating the Head, Heart, and Hand, came: "Having learned of the $20,000 placed in your charge for the distribution of same among schools like ours, I beg to say that we are making strenuous efforts to complete our new industrial building . . . we are forced to appeal to our distant friends for financial aid, and believing that you will be one of the many friends who will respond favorably to our appeal, I therefore ask that you prayerfully consider the cause."[44] "Last year a school bond was floated and lost," lamented principal J. H. Michael of the mountain city of Asheville. He assured Washington that he would "appreciate anything that you may do for us . . . if you can see your way clear to give us $500."[45] Such pathetic requests came from all over the South.

It should be understood that the Rosenwald Fund began as an experimental school building program solely for Alabama. In requesting the philanthropy, Washington informed Rosenwald that it would be wise "to begin in one or more states, letting the plan develop gradually and learning by experience." Immediately after the Chicago announcement, Washington launched the program with the help of an assistant, whose salary the donor had agreed earlier to pay. The scheme was successful and by June 24, 1913, only $2,100 of the initial fund remained undesignated. In a special appeal to Rosenwald, Washington requested, and was granted, permission to use the remainder to construct six one-room schools. Washington's plan of financial assistance was quite simple. He offered aid wherever the local Blacks, the county, or the state would contribute funds for the construction of modern schools for the Negro population. For example, the first schoolhouse constructed under the arrangement was at Loachapoka in Lee County, Alabama. The total cost of the building was $842.50; some $410 was raised locally; $142.50 in labor was volunteered; and $300 was donated by Washington.[46]

The success of the Alabama undertaking motivated Rosenwald to offer assistance to the entire state of Alabama and then to the entire South. Effective on August 10, 1914, and over a period of five years, Rosenwald made available a total of $30,000 for the purpose of assisting in the erection of approximately one hundred rural schoolhouses. The maximum amount of aid available for a single school was three hundred dollars (later five hundred dollars), and the Blacks of the community were required to make a substantial contribution in cash, labor, or materials.[47] Washington suggested that "a good strong man" be employed to oversee the expenditure of the fund and to work with the state and county authorities. Any school built with the assistance of the fund was required to be modern and reasonably equipped and would be owned and operated by the respective counties as part of the public school system.[48] Moreover, Washington emphasized that the "counties understood thoroughly that you (Rosenwald) would give a certain amount provided they do likewise to increase over what is being done. . . . The Southern white man likes to be talked to, but does not like to be talked about . . . (so) let the county officials feel as far as possible that they are doing the work—in a word, to place the responsibility upon them." Both men were in accord that, as a beginning, publication of the "general scheme" in the Southern newspapers "would create a good deal of discussion pro and con."[49] Thus, the Rosenwald school program was an extension of the Tuskegee idea as inaugurated by Booker T. Washington. The late Charles W. Dabney neglected to identify Washington with the fund.[50] In consequence, historians, in general, have been remiss in crediting him with the original idea. Indeed, the Rosenwald resources were the major impetus behind the rural-school-building movement identified with the donor's name. It quickly spread beyond the borders of Alabama. Sensing its far-reaching impact, Washington wrote Rosenwald that the fund was effecting a "real revolution in the attitude of Southern people toward Negro Education."[51]

The Julius Rosenwald Fund was identified with the Slater Fund in the construction of the county training schools. And some improvement occurred in Negro public education. During the scholastic year of 1914–15, the Rosenwald Fund began its operation in North Carolina, at which time the state received $1,865 in appropriations. This amount was used to assist in the construction of eight schoolhouses. The next year the state realized $6,000 from the fund, which was employed to help build thirty-five schools in twenty-five counties.[52] Between 1914 and 1928 the fund assisted North Carolina in the construction of 683 Rosenwald Schools, as they came to be known. This number surpassed the number of schools in Mississippi by 206, Tennessee by 279, Alabama by 325, Texas by 329, and Louisiana by 332, and was two or three times greater than the number of schools in the other states.[53] While the individual Rosenwald contributions were relatively small, the fund had the most constructive program of all the philanthropic bodies.

The Rosenwald Fund may have had some influence upon the General Education Board. Much belatedly, after the public school campaigns had run their course, the prestigious board, with financial resources more than thirty times larger than the combined funds of the Peabody, Slater, and Jeanes philanthropies, identified itself with the cause of Negro education. With the advent of the county training schools, the board inaugurated a policy of purchasing industrial equipment for these institutions. It contributed $1,164 for the purchase of such equipment for the first three county training schools established in North Carolina.[54] In the spring of 1914 it made an appropriation of $1,000 to promote the organization of the Homemakers Clubs. These clubs performed work similar to that of the Canning Clubs in white schools.[55] And finally, the board in 1913 made provisions for the appointment of special white agents for the Negro schools in all the Southern states. For the support of these agents, the board appropriated $2,500 each for salary and $1,000 each for necessary expenses.[56] The general function of these agents, to a large degree, was identical to those of the rural supervisors of white schools. Nathan C. Newbold was appointed to this position in North Carolina and began his duties in June of 1913.[57]

As the year 1914 drew near, the Black schools of North Carolina did not reflect the doctrine of separate but equal educational opportunities for the two races. In spite of the efforts of the philanthropic bodies to modify the dismal status of Negro public schools, they remained both the lowest and the poorest rung of the state's educational ladder.

Evidence strongly suggests that the situation was even worse in the Deep South. The wretched condition of Black schools early struck Superintendent Joyners's moral sensitivity. In 1905 he suggested to McIver the possibility of admitting Negro women to the "Woman's Association for the Betterment of Public Schoolhouses." McIver reacted negatively and maintained that there was "absolutely no necessity for mixing of the races in the meetings . . . the Woman's Association for the Improvement of Public Schools that has been organized admits to membership . . . only white women."[58] So the majority of the Negro schools were destined to remain in a deplorable state. From firsthand experience, W. T. B. Williams, field agent for the Slater Fund, could write in 1912 of the North Carolina schools: "In comparatively few cases did I see efforts toward making the grounds and exterior of the buildings attractive . . . the approaches to most of the schools varied from untidy to positively filthy. Ash heaps often adorned the front yards, while at barely respectable distances leaned ugly outhouses in unscreened and shameful imprudence. Their interiors were too often unspeakable. Within the schools themselves there was little that was inviting."[59] Such was to be the legacy of Black schools in the wake of the North Carolina public school movement. And the state of affairs in North Carolina is more or less representative of conditions throughout the South. Yet there were few Southern whites during the Progressive era, or even later, who were prepared to face the thought of equal educational opportunities for the Negro.

Notes

1. With one dissenting vote, the United States Supreme Court in the *Plessy* case upheld a Louisiana "Jim Crow" law as a reasonable exercise of the state's police powers. Earlier, one of the petitioners, an octaroon in whom Negro blood was not discernible, was arrested for sitting in a coach reserved "FOR WHITE." "Our Constitution is blind," said Justice John Marshall Harlan of Kentucky, ironically the only Southern member of the court. His "dissent strikingly presaged the Court's opinion in *Brown* v. *Board of Education of Topeka* [1954]." Rayford W. Logan, *The Betrayal of the Negro* (New York, 1967), pp. 119–21; Edward Conrad Smith, *The Constitution of the United States with Case Summaries* (New York, 1936), p. 145.

2. Horace Mann Bond, *Education of the Negro in the American Social Order,* (New York, 1934), p. 457.

3. *Biennial School Report,* 1912–14, p. 51–52.

4. Ibid., pt. 2, p. 131.

5. Charles W. Dabney, *Universal Education in the South,* 2 vols. (Chapel Hill, N.C., 1936), 2: 448–49.

6. Ibid., 1902–4, p. 9; 1904–6, p. 9; 1906–8, p. 247; 1908–10, p. 119; 1910–12, p. 9; 1912–14, p. 9.

7. Joyner to J. E. Debnam, February 5, 1903, James Yadkin Joyner Papers, Southern Historical Collection, University of North Carolina, Chapel Hill, N.C.

8. *Biennial School Report,* 1912–14, p. 52.

9. Ibid., 1898–1900, pp. 268–85.

10. Merle Curti, *The Social Ideals of American Educators* (New York, 1935), p. 290.

11. Thomas P. Bailey, *Race Orthodoxy in the South* (New York, 1914), p. 93.

12. Rupert B. Vance, "Aycock of North Carolina," *Southwest Review* 18 (Spring 1933) : p. 296.

13. Lawrence Goodwyn, *Democratic Promise: The Populist Movement in America* (New York, 1976), p. 305.

14. Superintendent Joyner to Coon, July 23 and 25, 1904, Charles L. Coon Papers, Southern Historical Collection, University of North Carolina, Chapel Hill, N.C.

15. *Biennial School Report,* 1904–6, p. 346.

16. "Report of the Superintendent of the State Colored Normal Schools and the Croaton Normal Schools," in ibid., 1912–14, pt. 3, p. 103.

17. Ibid., 1904–6, p. 348; 1906–8, pt. 3, pp. 52–53.

18. Henry A. Bullock, *A History of Negro Education in the South* (Cambridge, Mass., 1967), pp. 184–85.

19. H. Leon Prather, Sr., "Origin of the Slater Philanthropy in Negro Education, 1812–1913." *Journal of Social and Behavioral Sciences* 15 (Spring 1970) : 32–40.

20. See chap. 1.

21. Hollis M. Long, *Public Secondary Education for Negroes in North Carolina* (New York, 1932), p. 3.

22. Edward E. Redclay, *County Training Schools and Public Secondary Schools for Negroes in the South* (Washington, D.C., 1935), p. 8.

23. B. C. Caldwell, "Work on the Jeanes and the Slater Funds," *American Academy of Political and Social Science* 32 (September 1913), p. 175.

24. John F. Slater Fund, *Occasional Papers,* no. 14, p. 3.

25. John F. Slater Fund, *Proceedings of the Trustees and Reports,* 1914–15, p. 53.

26. John F. Slater Fund, *Occasional Papers*, no. 23, p. 10–11.

27. "Letter addressed to the State Superintendent," in ibid., no. 14, p. 1.

28. "Extracts of Replies of State and County Superintendents," in ibid., p. 27.

29. "Report of the State Agent of Negro Rural Schools," in *Biennial School Report*, 1912–14, pt. 3, p. 128.

30. Ibid., 1914–16, pt. 3, pp. 117–19.

31. Bond, *Education of the Negro*, p. 134.

32. *The General Education Board: An Account of Its Activities, 1902–1914*, (New York, 1915), app. 2, p. 224; Benjamin Brawley, *Doctor Dillard of the Jeanes Fund* (New York, 1930), p. 1.

33. "Extract of the Will of Anna T. Jeanes," in Arthur D. Wright and Edward D. Redclay, *The Negro Rural Fund, Inc., 1907–1933* (Washington, D.C., 1933), p. iii.

34. Ibid., pp. 175–77.

35. Ibid., pp. 170–71.

36. "Report of the State Agent of Negro Schools," in *Biennial School Report*, 1912–14, pt. 3, p. 126.

37. Ibid., 1914–16, pt. 3, p. 113.

38. James H. Dillard, "Fourteen Years of the Jeanes Fund," *South Atlantic Quarterly* 27 (July 1928): 197.

39. Dabney, *Universal Education in the South*, 2: 465.

40. Washington to Rosenwald, June 21, 1912, Booker T. Washington Papers, Regular Correspondence, 1912, Library of Congress, Washington, D.C.

41. Quoted (some parts deleted) from an undated manuscript, Washington Papers.

42. Julius Rosenwald to Washington, August 5, 1912, Washington Papers.

43. Untitled newspaper clipping dated August 12, 1912, Washington Papers.

44. Allen L. Young to Washington, September 27, 1912, Washington Papers.

45. J. H. Michael to Washington, November 6, 18, 1912, Washington Papers.

46. *The Julius Rosenwald Fund: A Review to June 30, 1928* (Chicago, 1928), p. 24.

47. J. Scott McCormick, "The Julius Rosenwald Fund," *Journal of Negro Education* (October 1934), pp. 607–11.

48. *Julius Rosenwald Fund, A Review to June 30, 1928*, p. 26.

49. Washington to Rosenwald, June 21, 1912, and Rosenwald to Washington, August 5, 1912, Washington Papers.

50. Dabney, *Universal Education in the South*, 2: 465.

51. Quoted in McCommick, "Julius Rosenwald Fund," p. 611.

52. "Report of the State Agent of Negro Rural Schools," p. 118.

53. *The Rosenwald Fund, Review to 1928*, pp. 26–28.

54. John F. Slater Fund, *Occasional Papers*, no. 23, pp. 10–11.

55. "Report of the State Agent of the Negro Rural Schools," pp. 125–26.

56. *General Education Board: An Account of Its Activities, 1902–1914*, pp. 195–96.

57. "Report of the Agent of Negro Rural Schools," pp. 123–24.

58. McIver to Superintendent Joyner, December 5, 1905, Joyner Papers.

59. Thomas J. Jones, *Negro Education: A Study of the Private and Higher Schools for Colored People in the United States*, (Washington, D.C., 1917), 1: 32.

Epilogue

North Carolina is a truly remarkable anomaly in Southern history. The state today reflects a vista of liberalism in politics, race relations, education, and modernity in recreation and tourism. Indeed, the state is impressive with its scenic Blue Ridge mountains in the west, its industrialism and research in the Piedmont region, and the seashore and resort areas in the east. Superhighways connect the three vast and distinct socioeconomic regions of the state, where natural resources abound. Writing in 1949, V. O. Key portrayed North Carolina as the "Progressive Plutocracy."[1]

Certainly, North Carolina has done much to eliminate its once-prevailing "cultural lag." But hereby hangs a historical tale. Throughout its history, North Carolina has given the appearance of being unique and liberal when compared with other Southern states. No slave revolts occurred in the state. It also permitted free Blacks to vote until 1835. While most Southern states practiced Black disfranchisement after Reconstruction, North Carolina continued to allow Negro participation in government. Yet at the turn of the twentieth century, the state became acutely racist, unscrupulously employing political propaganda to deceive a credulous white electorate, while using violence against innocent Blacks. The state surrendered to the racial ideology of the Deep South—more specifically to that of Mississippi—which gives credence to Professor Woodward's model: "The Mississippi Plan as the American Way."[2] And indeed, this raises three significant questions: Does the state's current image represent a distortion of reality within its illustrious history? Are North Carolina's historians allowing their present beliefs to cloud their view of the state's past? And if the Black experience described in chapters 5 and 6 could happen in a liberal state like North Carolina, what was happening to Blacks throughout the South?

The Redeemers of North Carolina, like those throughout the South, successfully undid the work of the Reconstruction radicals and laid the foundation for white supremacy, while demanding white solidarity as its guardian. Representatives of the "New Order," ardent defenders of white supremacy, erected an emotional dike around memories of Reconstruction, supported by the apparition of Negro rule. They sought to prohibit any division of class interests, of issues, and of candidates for the sake of white supremacy. Like Henry Grady, they too were convinced that economic progress was the key to their region's development. And while having little time for engrossment in the romanticism and the nostalgia identified with the "Lost Cause," the Redeemers did, however, drift into "case-hardened Bourbonism of an office-holding caste." They neglected reforms, including those involving public education.

"White supremacy," the "bloody shirt of Southern politics," has always been a fantastic phenomenon, and North Carolina offered a classic example of it. The "New Order" had not solved pressing socioeconomic problems. Latent agrarian radicalism under the banner of populism surfaced to crack the dike. The entrenched groups were able to hold the onrushing flood waters at bay, but not in the rest of the South, and only there did the Populist revolt move into a new dimension—Fusion politics. Populism had begun as a noble democratic ideal, based on the belief that poor whites and Blacks would work in unison in a quest for social justice. Neither populism nor republicanism could do it alone, but Fusion politics was able to join the white Republicans of the Carolina Highlands and the Negro Republicans of the Black Belt, truly creating the model Professor Woodward has named "procrustean bedfellows."[3] And after a political hegemony of some twenty years, the Democrats were toppled from power by the so-called Fusion ticket. Throughout the Black Belt there occurred a clean sweep of public offices, with the Republicans rewarding their Black cohorts with some of the small offices. To the dismay of the Democrats and other whites, Negro leaders again appeared on the political scene.

Most white Southerners of this period considered Negroes inferior and absolutely unfit to hold public office. Moreover, any such office-holding in the Black Belt was propagandized with cries of "Negro Rule," or "Black Domination," with their connotations of ignorance, incompetence, and corruption. Having served as the shibboleths of past controversies, the phrases *Black Domination* and *Negro Rule* acquired a new meaning in the vocabulary of North Carolina politics. They were of much use to the Democratic propaganda machine in creating party loyalty, in deceiving white masses, and in exciting

270

passions that led to racial hatred and so "to human violence." Although in actuality erroneous, these racial expressions were converted into symbols and stereotypes that emerged to describe all Black politicians of the Fusionist era. Historians, I fear, have been influenced by these interpretations. At this point one might raise two crucial questions: What was the caliber of Black political leadership during the Republican-Populist coalition? Who were the leading Blacks, and what can be said about them as a group?

The careers of many of North Carolina's Black political leaders paralleled the career of Booker T. Washington. Based upon the evidence presented in chapter 3, one could argue very cogently that some were better educated and more articulate than Washington and, for that matter, Charles B. Aycock as well. These would include John C. Dancy, James H. Young, George H. White, and James E. Shepard. And evidence strongly suggests that Young was more of a progressive than was Aycock. To be sure, these men were intellectuals and indeed, representatives of W. E. B. Dubois' model—the "talented tenth." The late Wilber Cash in his *Mind of the South* spoke of America as the land of pushing men who pushed past those who stood still. North Carolina's Negro political forerunners had surpassed the masses of downtrodden whites to make a mockery of this thing called white supremacy. They had achieved, more or less, the summum bonum of Southern civilization, and such an accomplishment was made without the loss of racial consciousness.

Moreover, North Carolina's Black political leaders represented a continuing Black Republican bloc, which was not to suffer disfranchisement until 1900. Led by Jim Young, their coalition meant Fusion success in 1896. In effect, the Republicans had to pay their Populist debt. Convinced of the need for reforms, the Populists, as demonstrated in chapter 4, attempted to work through both the political and the educational systems. Trying to deal constructively with the education problem, they put at the helm the competent Charles H. Mebane as superintendent of public instruction. Progressive school tax laws were enacted, only to be invalidated by the state supreme court. Undaunted, the friends of the public schools launched an educational movement in 1897. Walter Hines Page, the expatriate North Carolinian, arrived on the scene to lend his rare forensic skills to "the cause" with his "Forgotten Man" address. After a day or two this successful editor, writer, and lecturer departed, while his friends formulated plans for the redemption of illiterate children of the forgotten men. The campaigns that followed were centered on galvanizing communities to vote school taxes beyond the state's constitutional limitation, but the vanguard of the reactionary forces frustrated the movement on all sides. Yet North Carolina progressives, early in the next decade, were to successfully borrow and retain much from populism.

If Populism had succeeded, perhaps the coalition of poor whites and Blacks could have enacted progressive reforms to alleviate some of the economic ills. But in the final analysis, racism proved to be more powerful than self-interest. Fear of Black equality was stronger than revulsion at one's own wretchedness. Thus, the glue that held Fusion politics together came undone. During the vicious white supremacy campaigns of 1898 and 1900, the poor whites and economic oligarchies had a brief honeymoon, only to part later along traditional lines. Leaders of the Democratic party, with their middle-class values and attitudes, left the lower-class whites where they found them, destined to a way of life that failed the Southern farmers. The New South and its economy did not take into account the masses of whites.

The Fusionist triumph of 1896 resulted in a resurgence of the Democrats' aim of returning their party to power. A small clique of elitists inaugurated emotional white supremacy campaigns, employing all means, politically and legally, to obtain their objectives. To avoid a division that would split white men, class lines were blurred, and competency or weakness of candidates, along with local issues (to say nothing of national ones), all had to be ignored for the sake of white solidarity. Furnifold M. Simmons, "Czar of Tar Heel Politics," and his cohorts clouded the real issues during the infamous white supremacy campaign of 1898. They used lower-class whites as instruments to accomplish their own selfish ends by inciting their passions, and the racial issues were their stimuli.

Now it was time for the Democrats to pay their dues to their constituents. The white supremacy campaign was also fought on a pledge to bar the Negro from politics, and promises had been made that no white man would be disfranchised. Mississippi, followed by South Carolina and Louisiana, had shown the way to void the United States Constitution. The 1899 General Assembly adroitly fashioned a suffrage amendment with a temporary "grandfather clause" to legally and permanently checkmate Black voters. To insure its success in the gubernatorial election of 1900, the Democrats employed their stratagems of the previous campaign to a greater extent and brought the political wrath of the entire state upon the Negro. Racism appears to have been more virulent in the cities than in the small towns and in the rural counties; the great margin of victory of the suffrage amendment was partly a result of the tremendous support it received in urban areas.[4] In a representative government, it is a crime to perpetrate extralegal means—intimidation and vio-

272

lence—to achieve political goals. Historians, much too often, have written such activities off as a "temper of the times." For the physical and social terror used against Populists, Republicans, and Blacks to secure the adoption of the amendment itself, besides bringing dishonor upon the state.

The suffrage amendment was contrived under the banner of white supremacy. Even if the absurd claim of inherent superiority of the Anglo-Saxon race were admitted, this, in itself, would not justify the disfranchisement of the inferior race. The Democrats were willing to hold Blacks responsible for the Southern crime of keeping Negroes in compulsory ignorance for more than two centuries.

Once disfranchisement became a fait accompli, the historical implications strongly suggest that in order to participate in future politics, the Negro had to obtain the summum bonum of Southern civilization. I have no objection to an educational qualification for the suffrage, if it were applied equally to both Negroes and whites. It is easy to find fault and to suggest what might have been done. There is wisdom in the conclusion of the ex-slave who said "we are not prepared for this suffrage. But we can learn. Give a man the tools and let him commence to use them, and in time he will learn a trade. So it is with voting."[5] If we believe in the lofty ideals of democracy, there can be no justification for giving one illiterate segment of the population the right to vote, while denying it to the other.

The suffrage amendment with its "grandfather clause" had steamrolled through the legislature, to invalidate the formidable Black Republican bloc. Accordingly, it would be impossible for the Black Second Congressional District, which had elected more Negro congressmen than any other, to have another such representative.

The somewhat militant Congressman George H. White of North Carolina was particularly disturbed about Black disfranchisement and representation and was well aware that such practices were glaring violations of the Constitution. He stood alone, the sole representative of seven million Blacks. In this unique role he would occasionally lecture to Congress on the racial problem. "No matter what the topic under discussion might be," wrote one scholar, "White, like Cato of Rome, could always bring it around to a discussion of Negro rights."[6] A typical example of this strategy occurred on February 26, 1899. The topic being debated was the Cuban question, including territorial acquisitions resulting from the recent war with Spain. After completing his speech, Congressman Marsh said: "Mr. Chairman, I now yield twenty minutes to the gentleman from North Carolina." White arose and immediately thanked Marsh for the floor. As his colleagues listened attentively, he spoke these words: "Mr.

Chairman, I supported very cheerfully all measures tending to bring about the recent war for liberating a very much oppressed and outraged people . . . Being a member of this great Republic and one of the Representatives on this floor, I give my support in voice and in every way that I could to all measures tending to the liberation of these poor people in Cuba. I now favor the acquisition of all the territory that is within our grasp as a result of that war. [Applause]."
Ultimately, he adroitly digressed with the following transition: "Mr. Chairman, it is another problem, possibly more vexing than the one we have now under consideration. I know that you will pardon me if I do not address myself to the question before us when you recollect that I am the only representative on this floor of 10,000,000 people from a racial standpoint. They have no one else to speak for them from a race point of view, except myself."[7]

George H. White touched on many themes as they related to Blacks. He reminded the Southern members of the House that their states were overrepresented to the extent to which Blacks were deprived of the franchise. "Our representation is poor," he said, and in keeping with the principles of the Fourteenth Amendment, he believed that representation in Congress should be reduced in proportion to the number of Negro votes suppressed.

On several occasions White had heard some of his Southern colleagues sprinkle their House speeches with plantation dialect stories about their favorite "darkies." But he was not amused by such antics. "I have sat in my place," he told his listeners, "and heard discussions pro and con; I have heard my race referred to in terms of anything else than dignified and complimentary. I have heard them referred to as savages, as aliens, as brutes, as vile and vicious and worthless, and I have heard but little or nothing said with references to their better qualities, their better manhood, their developed American citizenship."[8] In reminding his fellow congressmen that Blacks were making a social transition, he said: "We are passing, as we trust, from ignorance to intelligence. The process may be slow; we may be impatient; you may be discouraged; public sentiment may be against us because we have not done better, but we are making progress." He then raised a provocative question: "Do you recollect in history any race of people placed in like circumstances who have done any better that we have?" He noted that Black achievements were made despite job discrimination, Jim Crowism, and lynching. He requested of his fellow congressmen: "Give us a chance, and we will do more. We plead to all of those who are there legislating for the nation that while your sympathy goes out to Cuba—and we are legislating for Cuba." Alluding to centuries of American slavery, he told his audience to "remember those who have worked for you;

remember those who have loved you, who have held up your hands, who have felled our forests, have digged your ditches, who have filled up your valleys and have lowered the mountains, and have helped to make the great Southland what it is today. We are entitled to your recognition."

White emphasized that there had never been, nor would there ever be, "Negro Domination" in North Carolina, and no one knew it better than the Democratic party. He pointed out that Blacks "do not ask for domination," but ask and expect a chance to legislate and would be content with nothing else. White continued by illustrating the importance of man through the words of a poet:

> "Were I so tall to reach the pole,
>   Or mete the ocean with my span,
> I must be measured by my soul
>   The mind's the standard of the man."

Choosing his words carefully, and with the right emphasis on gesture and eloquence, White brought his address to a dramatic conclusion by asking the congressmen to recognize its Negro citizens "at home . . . [and] at [their] door, give them the encouragement, give them the rights that they are justly entitled to." He then asked that stable and fixed governments "be established for Cuba, Puerto Rico, the Philippine Islands, and the Hawaiian Islands, and then "make happy" . . . the black man, the white man . . ." and all the people of the earth that are "coming to our shores will rejoice with you in that we have done God's service and done that which will elevate us in the eyes of the world." A prolonged applause was accorded him when he sat down.

On January 29, 1901, White appeared on the floor of the House for the last time. "I bid adieu," he said, "to these historic walls on the 4th day of next March." He was apologetic, for he told his colleagues that he did not want to digress from the question at issue and detain the House, but strongly felt the necessity "to enter a plea for the colored man, the colored woman, the colored boy, and the colored girl of this country." He asked the House to act on his antilynching bill, which still languished in committee, though petitions supporting it had poured in from all over the country. He employed his usual, relaxed speaking style, while both colleagues and gallery accorded him rapt attention. As for the rights of the Black man, he said: "Treat him as a man; go into his home and learn of his social conditions, learn of his cares, his troubles, and his hopes for the future; gain his confidence; open the doors of industry to him." And in conclusion, he said: "This, Mr. Chairman, is perhaps the Negroes' temporary farewell to the American Congress; but let me say, phoenix-like he will rise up some day and come again."[9] According to Rayford W. Logan, one of America's most distinguished historians, "White's retirement from Congress, in 1901, was hailed as public thanksgiving in his own state."[10]

The prediction of George H. White has yet to become a reality in the South, where the Negro masses still dwell; indeed, the region was without an elected Negro representative to Congress for more than three generations. The record will show that between 1882 and 1898 North Carolina elected four Blacks to Congress (James E. O'Hara and George H. White served two terms each).[11] Yet during the entire twentieth century the state has not elected another one. As late as 1978, there were only three Black Congressmen from the eleven Southern states. Only in larger cities of the South has the Black political picture changed significantly. In 1975 there were 125 Black elected officials on the municipal levels in North Carolina.[12] But in the Coastal Plain, where the Negro population is still heavily concentrated, public officeholding by Blacks is still very much tokenism. For example, in the same year, there were only seventeen elected county officials, and five of these were in law enforcement. Moreover, black registration remains below the rest of the state.[13] And in great contrast to the period of the Populist-Republican coalition, the Black Belt suffers from a lack of Black political leadership. At the same time, Blacks of North Carolina represent 19.4 percent of the voting age populations,[14] while constituting only 3.5 percent of the state's 5,504 elected officials, which is lower than that of South Carolina, Alabama, and Mississippi.[15] In North Carolina, despite the fact that currently the quality of Blacks (politically and otherwise) is high in terms of ability and leadership potential, there were only six Blacks in both houses of the General Assembly in 1975. It should be recalled that during the Fusion era there were ten Blacks elected to the General Assembly—three in the state Senate and seven in the state House of Representatives.[16] Also in 1975 the state's six Black legislators represented less than any of the states of the Deep South, except Mississippi.

It is ironic that during the period of black disfranchisement white representatives continued to be elected to Congress by white minorities from the Black Belt and contiguous counties, where masses of Blacks were voteless. It is also ironic that a provision of the Constitution reads: "Representatives shall be apportioned among the several states according to their respective numbers, counting the whole number of persons in each state. . . . But when the right to vote at any election . . . is denied to any of the male inhabitants of such State, being twenty-one years of age, and citizens of the United

States, or in any way abridged . . . representation therein shall be reduced in the proportion. . . ." Scholars and others have given tacit approval to this abridgement of the voting rights of Black minorities under the nomenclature the "Unwritten Consitution." Nevertheless, words of the Constitution held little meaning for Blacks. Abandoned now by their white political allies, Blacks in the South ceased to struggle for reforms in the face of the "harsh imperatives of resurgent white supremacy;" they were forced to wait for a new age. And as Professor Lawrence Goodwyn reminds us, "When the banner of reform was again raised in the South in the 1960s the hands holding it aloft were Black."[17]

Most tragic is the fact that Black disfranchisement in North Carolina rode to power on the Democratic "enameled lie." The "White man's government," wrote historian Bassett, "is full blast in this state, [North Carolina] and they are arranging a suffrage amendment which will disfranchise the Negro and not disfranchise the ignorant white. At best it is an enameled lie . . . It is one more step in the educating of our people that it is right to lie, steal, and to defy all honesty in order to keep one party in power."[18] The Democratic "enameled lie" was based on the twin myths of Black domination and Fusion corruption, with "white supremacy" being the theme song. The Democrats wanted offices, and to get them they exhausted their vituperative vocabulary in their effort to array weak and gullible whites against the Blacks. Often overlooked in analyses of the struggle is the underlying force of economics, which fed the passions of white racism. Once the Democrats got control of the offices, the "boiling political sea" suddenly cooled down. Thus, the adage "The wild ass brayeth not when he hath grass, nor does the ox low when he hath fodder" held true.

Some Progressives insisted that this corrupting influence in government be eliminated. But did Negro political participation mean corruption? "Yes!" some Southern leaders would have answered categorically. Charles B. Aycock "promised in 1899 that disfranchisement would bring 'a larger political freedom and a greater toleration of opinion . . . The Republican party will be freed from the stigma of influence in making a shaping of wholesome public opinion. Discussion of politics and principles will take the place of heated declamation and partisan abuse."[19]

Some historians have alluded to the absurd notion that Black disfranchisement was a major facet of Southern progressivism. But such a conclusion is strictly false. I am inclined to believe that, in several ways, Southern progressivism was a myth. While Southern progressivism was antimonopoly with some business, an examination of the evidence might reveal that reform measures benefited the middle classes most. Moreover, we need to know the extent to which these measures were beneficial to the majority of Southerners. Abolishment of political bossism was a chief reform of the Progressives. Nevertheless, a tyrannical state-party machine persisted in North Carolina, dominated by the Democratic organizations with Furnifold Simmons at the helm, until his defeat in 1930 after serving five terms in the Senate. What was the value of the direct election of senators, the direct primary, the initiative and referendum and recall, and the like, when countless Southerners were still trapped within the clutches of the crop-lien system, still paying exorbitant interest rates, and still ridden with debts? At the same time, labor was unorganized, and low wages had reduced much of the white population to the living standard of Blacks. Hence, the forces that created populism persisted after the Progressive era. Professor Woodward put it well when he wrote: "Progressivism had its day in the South as elsewhere, but it no more fulfilled the political aspirations and deeper needs of the mass of people than did the first New Deal Administration."[20]

If labels matter, and I think that they do, concensus historians are not likely to agree with the interpretations here. American textbooks glorify progressivism. Yet some historians believe, as I do, that the Progressive era needs a new label. The problem seems to begin with terminology. Historians have used the term *Progressive era* as an umbrella term to describe the political and social reforms (municipal, state and national) that occurred during the Roosevelt, Taft, and Wilson administrations. The locution sounds more positive than the evidence turns out to be, and scholars do not have to study the evidence closely to reach the conclusion that the era became less and less progressive. Remaining untouched by progressivism were the inarticulate urban masses of the North, trapped in their teeming sweatshops and tenements. In the South were the masses of "unredeemed farmers," both Negro and white.[21] The downtrodden remained after progressivism had run its course. Too many questions remain unanswered or unresolved, both in the North and in the South. Was the Progressive era one of conservatism? Should historians follow the bold new lead of Gabriel Kolko, who saw the era as a triumph of big capitalists who obtained their objectives with the aid of government?[22] Was Southern progressivism purely a middle-class urban phenomenon? Was Southern progressivism a collaboration—on specific issues—between the urban middle classes and capitalism?

Extended economic interests within the Democratic party did hamper Southern progressivism. Governor Aycock, reflecting the viewpoint of the political bosses and of party machinery, was more a friend to the "tax-dodging corporations" than to public education. In order to obtain campaign funds, the Democrats had promised the railroads that there would be no increase in taxes. Leading educators, along with the Populists, had censured the railroads for not paying taxes, which would have done wonders toward providing needed monies for public education. Yet Governor Aycock reached an understanding with them. As governor, however, he did use his influence to present laws allowing for a racial division of the educational funds. Since Blacks constituted 33 percent of the population and held less than 5 percent of the property, they would have received little or no education if the racial division laws had passed. Hence, the labeling of Aycock as a progressive is an enigma.

Black disfranchisement and Jim Crow laws were the work of groups whose leaders are identified by some scholars as progressives. Among the latter are demogogues of diabolic proportions, who are yet classified as reformers. Notably Ben Tillman of South Carolina, James K. Vardeman of Mississippi, and Hoke Smith of Georgia.

Virulent racism was the Democrats' theme song, and Charles B. Aycock carried the main speaking load in the white supremacy campaign of 1898. In the words of one scholar: "Two years later he race-baited his way to the governorship."[23] While he did not wear a Red Shirt, he quickly became identified with Ben Tillman and became the idol of thousands of Red Shirts.

Many North Carolinians, know "of all the naked ruthlessness of the 1900 Red Shirt Campaign that elevated Aycock to the governorship on a platform of white supremacy." Rupert B. Vance wrote: "There was nothing in the background of Charles B. Aycock to mark him as different from the ordinary political agitator on the race question. His stock was that of the common man of the South; any Yankee journalist would have described it as 'Southern poor-white' without batting an·eyelash."[24] Plagued by ambivalence, Vance was not able to follow his hypothesis to its logical conclusion. The same was true of many North Carolinians who knew of Aycock's racism and vilifying of Blacks in the 1898 and 1900 white supremacy campaigns. Yet history has exonerated him. The passage of time has added to the reputation of the name that now stands emblazoned in public places. Why this disparity? Aycock has emerged not as a champion of white supremacy like Tillman, Vardaman, Hoke Smith, Jeff Davis of Arkansas, and Cole Blease of South Carolina, but as an educational governor, a claim it would be well to forget, for evidence strongly suggests the existence of an Aycock myth.

Professor Arthur S. Link has written: "Progressives are usually persons who strive for reforms that alleviate the ills of society."[25] In every social movement, there are certain men and women, oftentimes unknown to the general public, who, "like the Hoosier schoolmaster and the teacher in *The Virginian,* stood out against the background at the clearing and the range," and, with insight and conscience, looked about their world and saw certain social ills to be corrected by education. North Carolina's young Wataugians— Walter Hines Page, Edwin A. Alderman, and Charles D. McIver— had long remembered the "Forgotten Man." As young progressives, they were cognizant that equality had long been a potent American ideal and that education was commonly accepted as a powerful tool for opening the doors of opportunity for the underprivileged. Unlike their political counterparts, they made no promises they could not keep. Employing rhetoric, to no avail, they tried to persuade the farmers that support for public educational reform would be advantageous to them. To be sure, education needed a stimulus—provided by political development related to racism.

The suffrage amendment proved of great educational significance, for section 4 of the amendment mandated that after 1908 only literate persons would be franchised. The amendment encountered staunch opposition in the western Republican counties, where there was a high rate of white illiteracy. The Democrats were compelled to promise universal education to obtain support in these areas; they failed miserably to fulfill their promise. But an educational vacuum had been created, and an elitist group of educators and reformers came forward and filled it. The men who made the greatest contribution to the movement were: Charles D. McIver, James Y. Joyner, Eugene C. Brooks, and Charles L. Coon. They inaugurated the great educational crusades by sending forth orators, on the stump and in the schoolhouses and churches, to expound the gospel of universal education. The campaigners sought to impress upon the people the concept that a tax-supported free public school system was a community responsibility. And numerous fundamental changes were realized on the educational front by 1913.

Northern philanthropy was inextricably interwoven with the efforts to promote public education in the South and was closely identified with the North Carolina public school movement. In fact, both the Peabody Educational Fund and the mammoth General Education Board made their debut in the state. The charters of the philanthropic bodies were phrased in broad terms to enable them to move from one educational problem to another. Their significant behind-the-scenes activities were less discernible, but the influences on school legislation were impossible to determine. Without Northern philanthropy, the public school movement would have been less dramatic and probably less effective.

The overly cautious trustees of the General Education Board, with its prodigious millions and prestige, avoided the issue of Black education during the educational campaigns. They were in complete agreement with the philosophy that the education of whites must precede that of Blacks. Only after the educational campaigns had run their course, and naturally had lost their momentum, did philanthropy identify itself with Negro education. Whereas its belated financial policy for Blacks was parsimonious and gratuitous, financial assistance for whites was rendered not as charity, but as a means of motivating philanthropy in others. For the Blacks it came in the form of charity, rather than full-fledged philanthropy, and the bequests were indeed small. Hence, philanthropy brought no permanent relief, and improvement of the quality of Negro education was impossible. This raises a provocative question: Would the cause of Negro education during the Progressive era have been better off without philanthropy? There were three philanthropic bodies set solely to aid Negro education—the John F. Slater Fund, the Anna T. Jeannes Fund and the Julius Rosenwald Fund. Their total resources of less than $2.5 million (the Slater philanthropy of $1 million had been in existence since 1882) were placed under the administration of white men. All educational boards were interwoven with the philanthropic organizations active in the public school movement. Curry of Alabama, reflecting the dominant racist attitude of his state, sat on all of them, and his views pervaded each board. Booker T. Washington was the only Black of acceptable stature for service on the various boards. At the same time, the boards ignored him, while he solicited funds to operate his institution constructed upon a curriculum of industrial education. Only the Quakeress Anna T. Jeannes insisted that other Blacks besides Washington be placed on the board of trustees of her philanthropy.

An inevitable question is: To what extent did philanthropy assist Black education? Quantitatively, the answer cannot be determined. Moreover, attempts at any other type of answer must be considered against the backdrop of the era. It could be argued that the philanthropic bodies stimulated and supported key educational functions yet unrecognized by public authorities. While this is true, it is also true that they promoted and kept alive substandard Negro education. Their policies demonstrated to both state and local school officials how cheaply Negro education could be maintained, and public officials have continued these policies to the present day. It could also be argued very cogently that some education is better than no education. In light of the accelerated educational opportunities offered the whites, the chasm widened to such an extent that the Black child had difficulty in bridging the gap.. Thus emerged the legacy of Negro educational inequality. Negro public school principals and heads of the various state colleges were tacitly obligated to public officials and state legislatures to uphold the social order, while soliciting meager funds to build and equip substandard schools. This vicious wheel now turns on itself. White children are presently being bused into the Black communities and now find substandard schools at the end of the line.

The greatest praise can be given the altruism of the donors John Fox Slater, Anna T. Jeannes, and Julius Rosenwald. Nevertheless, those who administered the funds compromised with the Southern social order. They accepted industrial education as a tool for keeping the Negro in his "proper place." This type of training was identified with physical labor—not mental labor—and carried with it the connotation that the Negro "was incapable of anything but industrial education." Worst of all, there was nothing in industrial education for the exceptional Blacks with outstanding aptitudes for the professions and politics. North Carolina's John C. Dancy, James H. Young, George H. White, Thomas Fuller, and James E. Shepard head a list of such men scattered throughout the South, including W. E. B. DuBois, James Weldon Johnson, Thomas E. Miller of South Carolina, and John Mercer Langston of Virginia. The list is almost endless. The Supreme Court decision of *Plessy* v. *Ferguson* did not deceive the philanthropic agents or the boards of trustees. But they were faced with the dilemma of Southern racism, and they solved the problem by acquiesing and surrendering to it.

The term *progressivism* suggests progress, and expansion of public school opportunities for the white population between 1902 and 1913 was the most remarkable achievement of the New South. The suffrage amendment with its "grandfather clause" nullified the Black man's political power and deprived him of any political spokesman for his schools. Yet no racial minority is likely to achieve progress without the ballot and political participation. "Keep quiet," was the advice given Blacks during the educational crusades. That advice was followed. The new educational currents that changed the school system of North Carolina and the South swept past the Negro, leaving him isolated in his ordained role of tenant farmer, common laborer, and domestic servant, "the drawer of water and hewer of wood." And what education was recommended and extended to him was designed to insure perpetuation of white supremacy. Meager training provided him with skills essential for reading the printed page and for counting money but not with motivation toward thrift and farm ownership. The Black Belt landlords were not interested in making it possible for Blacks to become property holders; they only wanted tenants and a cheap supply of labor. Worse still, the availability of just an elementary education was already outmoded by the nation's dynamic twentieth century industrialism. Consequently, the children of one-third of North Carolina's population were denied the opportunity to develop to their fullest potential and were also denied an equal and rightful chance to train for leadership. Surely, this was an irretrievable loss to themselves, the state, and the nation.

The salient public school movement, "a crusade against ignorance," had exploded throughout the South. Its impetus came from North Carolina, and the remarkable progress effected between 1902 and 1913 reflected a salutary trend toward reassessing and ameliorating the existent system of education. Put in the perspective of time, the movement can be labeled under Professor Woodward's model: "Progressivism For White Only."[26] Accepting the "white only" model, the expanded educational opportunities, to be sure, reflected no class lines.

True, the rights of the Negro to equal education were largely ignored during the "campaign era"; these blatant inequalities created an ineffable blot upon the American democratic way of life. Nevertheless, this does not disqualify the South from a viable role during the Progressive era. The Southern Progressives, particularly middle-class professional people—educators, clergymen, and editors—by their dedicated and exhaustive efforts in the cause of public education laid a sound foundation upon which to build an ever-improving and even more democratic school system. For the region's masses, truly, this was clearly the most discernible and outstanding achievement of Southern progressivism. Far too many historians have neglected to interpret the notable public school movement as a significant progressive measure, and to put it in its proper perspective, a reassessment of this phase of the history of the region is essential.

A fundamental tenet of Jeffersonian political and progressive educational thought advocates a periodic reexamination and revision of laws to ensure their keeping abreast of changing times. A contemporary application of this philosophical doctrine occurred in 1954 when the Supreme Court overruled the *Plessy* v. *Ferguson* decision of 1896 by declaring: "Separate educational facilities are inherently unequal . . . in the field of education the doctrine of separate but equal has no place." In light of the complex and ever-changing nature of modern society, a reexamination of educational theories and practices in each state, and in the nation as a whole, is vital to the welfare of all citizens.

Americans today are still confronted with some of the basic issues of race relations that persisted during the Populist and Progressive eras. Can the attitudes of white Americans be changed to accept the democratic tradition for all racial minorities? The answer is not easy, considering the residual presence of entrenched interests. Economic opportunities were never wide open, and have continued to narrow with the nation's increased industrial technology. As in the Populist and Progressive eras, attitudes are still molded by influences from society, schools, churches, government, the press, and libraries. Some of these forces are undemocratic and designed to preclude social changes. In this age of upheaval, undemocratic forces are an anachronism. Educators, by the very nature of their position, possess important social responsibilities. Much too often the educator's intellectual and social thought reflects his social environment and class, the region he lives in, and his personal temperament. Succinctly stated, educators must transcend the conservative pattern of social thought that causes conflict and impedes progressivism.

More today than in the past, the "modern South"—better stated, "the maturing South"—is a microcosm within the nation. In marked contrast to the first decade of the 1900s, the ideals of universal education have been achieved for all Americans. But crucial educational problems have persisted, while new issues and conflicts have emerged in North Carolina and in the Southern region, and are pervading other parts of the nation. What are the problems of learning in isolation? On the other hand, what are the problems of learning in forced integration? Do both of these contribute profoundly to the social pathology of race relations today? The social scientists and educators included in this category are well acquainted with the power of ideas for which history provides cogent evidence. Some of the propaganda techniques employed during the public school movement in North Carolina, 1902–1913, may prove valuable in resolving our contemporary educational difficulties in the South and elsewhere. In any event, it remains the responsibility of social scientists, educators, and others to include programs in universal education to help Americans understand the salient issues in contemporary education and to employ adequate means to resolve them. This could, indeed, be the fundamental key that opens the door for a still greater American society.

Notes

1. V. O. Key Jr., *Southern Politics in State and the Nation* (New York, 1949), p. 211. For a greatly contrasting interpretation, see Jack Bass and Walter DeVries, *The Transformation of Southern Politics* (New York, 1976), pp. 218 ff. "The progressive image," they write, "the state projected in the late 1940's has evolved into a progressive myth that remains accepted as fact by much of the state's native leadership, despite ample evidence to the contrary. Although North Carolina has changed with the times, it is perhaps the least changed of the old Confederate states." But this conclusion is only partially true. Scholars, I believe, should always qualify the section of the state they were considering. As pointed out in the Prologue, the state actually divides into three natural and clear-cut

physiographic areas that mirror three distinct socioeconomic divisions. The Coastal Plain (Black Belt) is the current problem. It is larger than the other two regions, with a total land area of about half the state, and "embraces wholly or largely forty-five counties." It has an identification with the Deep South, rather than with the upper or border Southern states. "Not only was the region," wrote journalist Bass and Professor DeVries, "bypassed by the Civil Rights movement, but it was also the hotbed of the Ku Klux Klan activity in the 1960's. And the Klan in North Carolina was larger and more virulent than in any state outside of Alabama and Mississippi during that period." On the contrary, in the 1950s, the "bulldozer revolution" had moved into the Carolina Highlands, the beautiful Blue Ridge—giving it an identity with progressivism. It is in the Piedmont area where astounding progress has occurred. Here, indeed, is progressive North Carolina, and when people interpret the state as such, they will be speaking about the Piedmont region.

2. C. Vann Woodward, *Origins of the New South, 1877–1913* (Baton Rouge, La., 1951), pp. 324–49.

3. Ibid., pp. 75–106.

4. Jerry Wayne Cotton, "Negro Disfranchisement in North Carolina: The Politics of Race in a Southern State" (Master's thesis, University of North Carolina at Greensboro, 1973).

5. Quoted in David Lindsey, *Americans in Conflict: The Civil War and Reconstruction* (Boston, 1974), pp. 202–3.

6. Samuel D. Smith, *The Negro in Congress, 1870–1901* (Chapel Hill, N.C., 1940), p. 126.

7. *Congressional Record*, 55th Cong., 3d sess. (1899), p. 1124.

8. Ibid., p. 1126.

9. Ibid., 56th Cong., 2d sess. (1901), pp. 1636–38.

10. Rayford W. Logan, *The Betrayal of the Negro: From Rutherford B. Hayes to Woodrow Wilson* (New York, 1967), p. 195.

11. Smith, *Negro in Congress*, p. 6.

12. Bass and DeVries, *Transformation of Southern Politics*, p. 51. In the background of the increased political activities in the cities was the Voting Rights Act of 1965. It abolished all literacy tests and other devices in states that used them, (twenty six counties in North Carolina were affected). The "right to vote law" authorized federal registrars to oversee voter registration whenever deemed necessary. See Numan V. Bartley and Hugh D. Graham, *Southern Politics and the Second Reconstruction* (Baltimore, Md., 1975), pp. 111–13; John Hope Franklin, *From Freedom to Slavery* (New York, 1969), pp. 639–40.

13. Bass and DeVries, *Transformation of Southern Politics*, p. 242.

14. Ibid., p. 51.

15. Ibid., p. 242.

16. Helen Edmonds, *The Negro and Fusion Politics in North Carolina, 1894–1901* (Chapel Hill, N.C., 1951), pp. 97–112, 116 n.

17. Lawrence C. Goodwyn, *Democratic Promise: The Populist Movement in America* (New York, 1976), pp. 305–6.

18. John Spencer Bassett to Herbert Baxter Adams, November 15, 1898 in *Historical Scholarship in the United States, 1876–1901*, ed. W. Stull Holt (Baltimore, Md., 1938), p. 238.

19. Quoted in J. Morgan Kousser, *The Shaping of Southern Politics: Suffrage Restriction and the Establishment of the One-Party South, 1880–1910* (New Haven, Conn., 1974), p. 72.

20. Woodward, *Origins of the New South*, p. 395.

21. Ibid., p. 175.

22. Gabriel Kolko, *The Triumph of Conservatism: A Reinterpretation of American History, 1900–1916* (New York, 1967), p. 2.

23. Kousser, *Shaping of Southern Politics*, p. 260.

24. Quoted in Rupert B. Vance, "Aycock of North Carolina," *Southwest Review* 18 (Spring 1937): 293.

25. Arthur S. Link, "The Progressive Movement and the South, 1870–1914," *North Carolina Historical Review* 23 (April 1946): 172.

26. Woodward, *Origins of the New South*, pp. 369–95.

Bibliographical Essay

The volume of literature relevant to the subject of this book—manuscripts, documentary publications, memoirs, and monographs—is of enormous proportions. The following essay is selective and makes no attempt to list all sources consulted or utilized in the writing of this book; only the significant works will be cited. Interested readers who are seeking a more comprehensive bibliography can scan the footnotes of each chapter.

Manuscripts

Manuscript collections for this study are voluminous and scattered. The larger collections are located in the Southern Historical Collection (S.H.C.) in the Wilson Library of the University of North Carolina, Chapel Hill, N.C. Considerable manuscript holdings are also available in the following: Duke University Library, Durham, N.C.; North Carolina Department of Archives and History (N.C.D.A.H.) Raleigh, N.C., and the Manuscript Division of the Library of Congress, Washington, D.C. Wading through these immense sources for some sort of synthesis, I sampled only the manuscripts of major political and educational leaders. Falling into the former category are the Charles Brantley Aycock Papers (N.C.D.A.H.) and the Furnifold M. Simmons Papers at Duke University. Less exhaustive manuscripts essential to this study include: Henry G. Connor Papers (S.H.C.); Marion Butler Papers (S.H.C.); Matthew W. Ransom Papers (S.H.C.); and the Daniel L. Russell Papers (S.H.C.—Executive Papers, 1897–1901, at the N.C.D.H.D.). The John Spencer Bassett letters to Herbert Baxter Adams, at Johns Hopkins University, (available in photostatic copies at Duke University), are nonpartisan and full of interesting details of the North Carolina 1898 election. On the same subject, see W. Stull Holt, ed., *Historical Scholarship in the United States, 1876–1901* in Johns Hopkins University Studies in

Historical and Political Science, vol. 56 (Baltimore, Md., 1938). While the Negro in North Carolina was the subject of serious study during this era, depositories of manuscripts relating to this topic are practically nonexistent. The one exception, and a valuable source of materials by a prominent political figure who lived in the state, is the John C. Dancy Collection, Private Papers and Correspondence, in the Andrew Carnegie Library at Livingstone College, Salisbury, North Carolina.

In the use of manuscripts of key educational figures, preference is assigned to the bulky Charles D. McIver Papers preserved at the University of North Carolina Library at Greensboro. The Robert Curtis Ogden Papers throw much light on different aspects of the Southern educational movement. They are divided between the Southern Historical Collection and the Library of Congress. Equally important are the Charles W. Dabney Papers (S.H.C.).

The most notable collections of manuscripts on the educational movement in North Carolina, excluding the McIver Papers, are the James Yadkin Joyner Papers; the Charles L. Coon Papers, the George Sherwood Dickerman Papers, all in the S.H.C., and the Eugene C. Brooks Papers in Duke University Library. There are two MS notebooks containing shrewd educational observations in the Edwin Alderman Papers at the Alderman Library, University of Virginia, Charlottesville, Va. Some of the more important scattered papers include: Walter Hines Page Papers, Houghton Library, Harvard University, Cambridge, Mass.; the Philander Priestly Claxton Papers, main Library of the University of Tennessee, Knoxville, Tenn.; and the Jabez Lamar Monroe Curry Papers and the Booker Taliaferro Washington Papers, both in the Library of Congress, Washington, D.C.

Government Publications: Federal and State

A variety of federal documents were found useful for this study. Publications of the Bureau of Census, especially the *Tenth Census, Eleventh Census,* and *Twelfth Census,* 1880–1900, and *Negro Population,* 1790–1915, contain significant statistical data.

One may turn to the *Report of the United States Industrial Commission,* vol. 10 (1900), for testimony reflecting attitudes on economic conditions, particularly labor practices related to agriculture. The *Congressional Records* reveal Southern attitudes toward the North Carolina Suffrage Amendment. They also provide a close look at the careers and provocative speeches of North Carolina's Black congressmen. On this latter subject, also of some value is the *Biographical Directory of the American Congress, 1774–1927* (Washington, D.C., 1927). Replete with vital statistical data on Southern education are the *Report of the United States Commission of Education,* 1899–1900, 1900–1901, 1902–1903, Washington, D.C.

State publications include bills introduced, debates on them, the complete text of statutes, annual reports of the Department of Labor and Education, significant speeches of legislative members, messages of the governors, and some biographical information. Among the wealth of such materials, the following cannot be ignored: *Public Laws of North Carolina,* 1876–1916; *Public School Laws of North Carolina,* 1890–1914; legislative debates and speeches in the *Journal of the Senate of North Carolina*; and *Public Documents of North Carolina.* A rich source of statistical data on industrial wages and samples of public school attendance laws are available in the *Report of the North Carolina Bureau of Labor and Printing* (Raleigh, N.C., 1900). State party publications may logically be included here. Democratic propaganda documents, being both aggressive and unreliable, pose a problem for research and documentation. Particularly was this true of the *Democratic Party Handbook,* 1898 and 1900, and the *Amendment Cathechism* (Raleigh, N.C., 1900). The *Republican Party Handbook,* 1900, and the *People's Party Handbook of Facts* (Raleigh, N.C., 1898) are valid rebuttals of the Democrats' propaganda.

Official publications of the State Department of Education were indispensable to this study. The *Biennial Reports of the State Superintendent of Public Instruction,* 1877–1916, are the best source of educational history and statistics. The *Annual Reports of the State Inspector of Public High Schools,* 1907–1916 (Raleigh, N.C.) also contain important information. The following monographs offer significant data, as indicated by their titles:

County Farm-Life Law and Explanations by J. Y. Joyner. A Special Circular (Raleigh, N.C., 1913).
Consolidation of Schools and Public Transportation by L. C. Brogden. Educational Bulletin no. 17 (Raleigh, N.C., 1911).
Local Taxation in North Carolina From 1875 to the Present Time. A Special Circular (Raleigh, N.C., 1910).
Local Tax Conditions before and since Local Tax, As Shown by the Testimony of County Superintendent. A Special Circular (Raleigh, N.C., 1910).
Official Instructions as to Forming Special Tax Districts, Holding Elections, Registrations and Qualification of Voters by J. Y. Joyner. A Special Circular (Raleigh, N.C., 1910).

The role and the relation of Northern philanthropy to Southern education are essential facets of this study. The *Proceedings of the Capon Spring Conference for Education in the South,* 1898–1900 and the *Journal of the Proceedings and Addresses of the Southern Educational Association,* 1900–1914, are the most helpful publications on the origin of the Southern educational movement, and the *Proceedings of the Conference for Education in the South,* 1900–1914, also yield excellent data. *The General Education Board: An Account of Its Activities, 1902–1914* (New York, 1915) is the most comprehensive account of the board's numerous activities. The *Proceedings of the*

Trustees of the George Peabody Educational Fund, 6 vols. (Boston, 1875–1916), provide the most information on this philanthropy. Equally important are the *Proceedings of the Trustees of the John F. Slater Fund,* 1883–1915. They should, however, be supplemented by the following:

> *County Teacher Training School for Negroes in the South.* Occasional Papers no. 14 (1913).
> *Documents Relating to the Origin and Work of the Slater Trustees.* Occasional Papers no. 1 (1894).
> *A Study of County Training Schools for Negroes in the South.* Occasional Papers no. 23 (1923).

For a good source of information on the two other philanthropies established solely to promote Negro education, see Anna T. Jeanes Foundation, *Negro Rural School Fund: A Review to June 30, 1928* (Chicago, 1928). The state superintendent's *Biennial Reports,* 1904–1916, surprisingly present important data on all the philanthropic bodies. It is logical to include here Ullin W. Leavell, *Philanthropy in Negro Education* (Nashville, Tenn., 1930).

Among the monographic works issued by the Southern Education Board, the following promotional literature proved to be very fruitful:

> *North Carolina Education.* Southern Education Bulletin no. 10. May 14, 1903.
> *Women's Education.* Southern Education Bulletin no. 19. December 1, 1903.
> *Education of the Negro.* Southern Education Bulletin no. 20. December 21, 1903.

In addition, there are serials containing valuable information prepared for releases to newspapers under the title *Southern Education Notes.* All of these publications were issued by the bureau at Knoxville.

Newspapers

During this era, partisan newspapers covered politics and state legislatures more thoroughly than they do today. Again the researcher is faced with the problem of presentation; the reader should be aware that certain details and facts may not be entirely accurate. The general picture provided by newspapers of the day, however, is quite revealing.

Of the newspapers sampled, top priority was given to the *Raleigh News and Observer* (Democratic), which was published in the state capitol and which exerted wide influence throughout North Carolina as well as outside the state. While it is true that its editor, Daniels, carried on a propaganda crusade against Republicans, Populists, and Blacks in particular, it was a most colorful press and gave wide coverage to politics and educational developments. Other papers found useful (all Democratic) were the *Charlotte Daily Observer, Greensboro Patriot, Wilmington Morning Star, Fayetteville Observer* and the *Asheville Morning Gazette.* Among the better smaller newspapers were the *New Bern Daily Journal,* the *Goldsboro Argus,* the *Pittsboro Chatham Record,* and the *Chatham Citizen.* Of the non-Democratic papers, the *Progressive Farmer,* the *Caucasian* (Populist), and the *Union Republican* were most useful. The *Progressive Farmer* was more of a regional paper in its attempts to analyze and offer solutions to agrarian problems and to keep up a running account of political affairs. All the above newspapers are available on microfilm at the University of North Carolina Library, Chapel Hill, N.C.; the Department of Archives and History, Raleigh, N.C.; and the Library of Congress, Washington, D.C.

Periodicals

Two national weeklies, the *Outlook,* edited by Lyman Abbott, and the *Independent* (New York) were useful. The *Star of Zion,* a quarterly and the official organ of the *African Methodist Zion Church,* was the most ambitious Black publication and contained significant economic, political, and social data.

Autobiographies, Biographies, and Memoirs

Several works of prominent personalities deserve attention because of the significant light they shed on particular aspects of this study. However, the reader should be forewarned that many are full of historical omissions. Indeed, this is true of Alfred M. Waddell, *Some Memories of My Life* (Raleigh, N.C., 1908). Waddell played the pivotal role in the Wilmington race riots and the abolishment of that city's government, yet he relegates less than two pages of his book to these events. Historians have often used R. D. W. Connor and Clarence Poe, *The Life and Speeches of Charles Brantley Aycock* (New York, 1912) as a source of materials as well as of factual data. However, details in this work are not always correct. Oliver H. Orr, Jr., *Charles B. Aycock* (Chapel Hill, N.C., 1961) certainly is work and adds new material and observations. But the book is somewhat disappointing. A logical conclusion, based on the evidence presented in this study, is that there is still a need for an adequate biography of Governor Aycock. While the author finds fault with Fred M. Rippy, ed., *Furnifold M. Simmons, Statesman of the New South; Memoirs and Addresses* (Durham, N.C., 1936), this work should be consulted as an important source of political data.

Robert W. Winston, *It's a Far Cry* (New York, 1937), which offers a penetrating analysis of the political era of the Redeemers. The editor of the *Raleigh News and Observer,* Josephus Daniels, was a skilled writer and a dedicated supporter of the Democratic party. His memoirs, *Tar Heel Editor* (Chapel Hill, N.C., 1939) and *Editor in Politics* (Chapel Hill, 1941), were essential to this study. Both works are exceedingly interesting, informative, and written in a very colorful style. Other important biographies include: Burton J. Hendrick, *The Life and Letters of Walter Hines Page*, vol. 1 (New York, 1923); Rose Holder, *McIver of North Carolina* (Chapel Hill, N.C., 1957); and William B. Gatewood, Jr., *Eugene Clyde Brooks: Educator and Public Servant* (Durham, N.C., 1959). Works by two important prominent Negro politicians are John C. Dancy, Jr., *Sands against the Wind: Memoirs of John C. Dancy* (Detroit, Mich., 1966), and Thomas O. Fuller, *Twenty Years in Public Life, 1890–1910* (Nashville, Tenn., 1910).

Books

Literature dealing with the interrelationship among politics, racism, and public education during this era has been particularly neglected by historians and others. Works by the Black scholar Horace Mann Bond—*The Education of the Negro in the American Social Order* (New York, 1934), *Negro Education in Alabama: A Study in Cotton and Steel* (Washington, D.C., 1939)—provide a classic beginning for studies going beyond the mere institutional approach in historiography. These two books are especially valuable for insights into white attitudes on taxation and expenditures to support separate school systems. Louis R. Harlan, *Separate and Unequal: Public School Campaigns and Racism in the Southern Seaboard States, 1901–1915* (Chapel Hill, N.C., 1958) is a more recent regional and penetrating study. This volume was most useful, and I recommend it highly to those interested in pursuing the subject of this work. Also useful for its insights is Rayford W. Logan, *The Betrayal of the Negro* (New York, 1967); it originally appeared as *The Negro in American Life and Thought: The Nadir, 1897–1901* (New York, 1949). However, before starting to read the specialized monographs, interested scholars should consult C. Vann Woodward's revisionist classic, *Origins of the New South, 1877–1913* (Baton Rouge, La., 1951), a brilliant study of the active socioeconomic forces of this era. V. O. Key, Jr. ed., *Southern Politics in State and Nation* provides the necessary background of regional politics. George B. Tindall, *The Emergence of the New South, 1913–1945* (Baton Rouge, La., 1967) is a vast and fascinating volume. While falling outside the period selected for this study, Tindall's work is valuable in calling attention to the problems of a changing South.

For a description of North Carolina's three socioeconomic regions, no book is superior to S. Huntington Hobbs, Jr., *North Carolina: Economic and Social* (Chapel Hill, N.C., 1930); and idem, *North Carolina: An Economic and Social Profile* (Chapel Hill, N.C., 1958). Albert Bushnell Hart, a competent historian, supplies reliable social and economic data in his small volume, *The Southern South* (New York, 1910). For a multitude of interesting sidelights with some interpretations of the state's social and economic life, see Jonathan Daniels, *Tar Heels: A Portrait of North Carolina* (New York, 1941). An old work, but one that contains some valuable material, is J. G. de Roulhac Hamilton, *History of North Carolina,* vol. 3, *North Carolina since 1860* (Chicago, 1919). However, it is marred by the author's strong sympathy for the Democratic party and his intermittent use of incorrect data from the *Raleigh News and Observer.* Recommended are the more recent and scholarly works of Hugh T. Lefler, *History of North Carolina* (New York, 1956), and of Lefler and Patricia Stanford, *North Carolina* (New York, 1972). The classic of John D. Hicks, *The Populist Revolt: A History of the Farmers' Alliance and the People's Party* (Minneapolis, Minn., 1931) is still the standard work for background information on the agrarian movement. A number of works on Populism have been published recently. One is by Lawrence C. Goodwyn, *The Democratic Promise: The Populist Movement in America* (New York, 1976). Goodwyn's study provides a variety of new insights on the theme, including an excellent chapter on the role of Blacks in the Populist movement. Selective monographs on populism and Fusion politics include Simeon Delap, *The Populist Party in North Carolina,* Trinity College Historical Papers, ser. 24 (Durham, N.C., 1922), and William A. Mabry, *The Negro in North Carolina Politics since Reconstruction,* Trinity College Historical Papers, ser. 23 (Durham, N.C., 1940). Both these studies have been outmoded by Helen Edmonds, *The Negro and Fusion Politics in North Carolina, 1894–1901* (Chapel Hill, N.C., 1951). Professor Edmonds writes within a safe style. Her objectivity suggests an avoidance of antagonizing conservative readers; she fails to take any stand against racism or to come to the defense of any of the outstanding Black political leaders. Nevertheless, Dr. Edmonds's study is indispensable and full of interesting details that shed new light on hitherto unknown or neglected aspects of fusionism. An older work that surveys the careers of all Blacks who served in Congress, including some of the few unsuccessful candidates, is Samuel D. Smith, *The Negro in Congress, 1870–1901* (Chapel Hill, N.C., 1940). Far more informative, and written in a popular style, is Maurice Christopher's *America's Black Congressmen* (New York, 1971).

There is dire need for an educational history of North Carolina. Currently there exist two older works: Edgar W. Knight, *Public Education in North Carolina* (New York, 1916), and Marcus C. S. Noble, *A History of Public Education in North Carolina* (Chapel Hill, N.C., 1930). The latter's treatment of education does not extend beyond 1893, but the volume is an excellent source of background data. Professor Knight takes time out to play the role of a political reformer. He devotes one chapter of fifteen pages to the period

1900–1910, extolling Aycock as a governor pledged to improving education—a portrait that is greatly over-exaggerated. However, the work does have some merit. Among Charles L. Coon's numerous works are two pamphlets of factual data: *A Statistical Record of the Progress of Public Education in North Carolina, 1870–1906* (Raleigh, N.C., 1907), and *Significant Educational Progress in North Carolina, 1900–1906* (Raleigh, N.C., 1907). Of some value is Fred W. Morrison, *Equalization of the Financial Burden of Education among the Counties in North Carolina* (New York, 1925).

Because no work has appeared to replace it, Charles W. Dabney, *Universal Education in the South,* 2 vols. (Chapel Hill, N.C., 1936) remains the most extensive and standard history of public education during this era. Those desiring to gain a regional perspective should consult it. The one major weakness of this work is that the author does not concern himself with the interaction of politics and racism and the resulting impact of this interaction upon education. A unique struggle with historical taproots was waged by advocates of denominational colleges against the state university and colleges, to the extent of crippling the former in the name of a tax-supported system of public education. On this theme there is nothing comparable to Luther T. Gobbel, *Church-State Relationships in North Carolina since 1776* (Durham, N.C., 1938). If not the best, surely Walter Hines Page's "The Forgotten Man" of 1897, was the most famous educational address. Its complete text is in Page, *The Rebuilding of Old Commonwealths* (New York, 1902). Merle E. Curti, *Social Ideas of American Educators* (New York, 1935), is infused with a variety of racial attitudes of the nation's prominent figures.

Several recent works were found extremely useful. J. Morgan Kousser, *The Shaping of Southern Politics: Suffrage Restriction and the Establishment of the One-Party South, 1880–1910* (New Haven, Conn., 1974), utilizes one of the newer research techniques—cleometrics. The study is an excellent treatment of the disfranchisement movement in the ex-Confederate states, during a period closely paralleling that covered by C. Vann Woodward. Kousser appears somewhat critical of the practice of some historians of identifying certain Southern demagogues as progressives. Norman V. Bartley and Hugh Graham, *Southern Politics and the Second Reconstruction* (Baltimore, Md., 1975) is worth examining for its insights on voting behavior in the South during the last three decades. Jack Bass and Walter DeVries, *The Transformation of Southern Politics* (New York, 1976) presents the most current look at politics in the eleven Southern states since V. O. Key's *Southern Politics* in 1949.

Journals

Numerous articles were located; however, only the major ones will be included here. For compactness the following abbreviations will be employed: *A.A.A.P.S.S.* (*Annuals of the American Academy of Political and Social Science*) ; *N.C.H.R.* (*North Carolina Historical Review*) ; and *S.A.Q.* (*South Atlantic Quarterly*). *North* Carolina's peculiar and defective tax structure has been neglected by historians. It is adequately discussed in two articles by Charles A. Raper, "Our Taxation Problem," S.A.Q. 12 (October 1913), and "North Carolina's Taxation Problem and Its Solution," ibid 14 (January 1915). Charles L. Coon, "School Support and Our North Carolina Courts," N.C.H.R. 3 (July 1926) is the best article on the negative attitude of the state supreme court in regard to increasing educational taxes. Recommended for its treatment of racism and educational taxation is Frenise Logan, "The Legal Status of Public Education for Negroes in North Carolina, 1877–1894," N.C.H.R. 32 (July 1955). Clement Eaton, "Edwin A. Alderman—Liberal of the New South," N.C.H.R. 23 (April 1946), utilizes basically the primary sources of the two MS notebooks in the Alderman Papers. The result is a penetrating analysis of varied negative educational attitudes. There is a need for a biography of James Y. Joyner, and steps have been taken in this direction by Elmer D. Johnson, "James Y. Joyner, Educational Statesman," N.C.H.R. 32 (July 1956).

A number of articles treat important aspects of the political developments of the era. John D. Hicks, "The Farmers' Alliance in North Carolina," N.C.H.R. 2 (April 1925) is an indispensable article that concentrates on the origin of agrarian organization. Shedding light on the same theme is Stuart L. Noblin, "Leonidas Lafayette Polk," N.C.H.R. 20 (April and July 1943). The following two excerpts are from larger works: William A. Mabry, "Negro Suffrage and Fusion Rule in North Carolina," N.C.H.R. 12 (April 1935), and "White Supremacy and the North Carolina Suffrage Amendment," ibid 13 (January 1936). Both works, like the main source, suffer from the writer's utilization of data from unreliable Democratic papers; however, good remnants of information remain. The best report of the Wilmington race riot is offered by H. L. West, "The Race War in North Carolina," *Forum* 26 (January 1899).

One may turn, finally, to a number of illuminating articles on particular phases of education. Both interesting and informative is David L. Smiley, "Educational Attitudes of the North Carolina Baptist," N.C.H.R. 25 (July 1958). Edgar W. Knight, "The Peabody Fund and Its Early Operation in North Carolina," S.A.Q. 13 (1914) is a good source of information on the subject indicated by the title. General information may be secured from B. C. Caldwell, "Work of the Jeanes and Slater Funds," A.A.A.P.S.S. 59 (1915). Charles D. McIver, "Current Problems in North Carolina," A.A.A.P.S.S. 20 (1903) provides a brief summary of the state's low educational status, while clarifying the objectives of the ensuing campaigns. Josiah W. Bailey, "Popular Education and the Race Problem in North Carolina," *Outlook*, May 11, 1901, offers keen observations of racial attitudes manifested during the futile educational campaign of the Populists in 1897.

Unpublished Works

An extensive search of doctoral dissertations revealed several significant works. Working through the massive study of John Flake Steelman, "The Progressive Era in North Carolina, 1884–1917," Ph.D. dissertation, University of North Carolina, 1955, one will be rewarded with some interesting sidelights touching on some of the prominent political figures. A study of special value in tracing the origin of laws that sought to create a tax-supported system is Samuel H. Thompson, "The Legislative Development of Public School Support in North Carolina," Ph.D. dissertation, University of North Carolina, 1936. Frederick A. Bode, "Southern White Protestantism and the Crisis of the New South, 1894–1903," Ph.D. dissertation, Yale University, 1969, is a brilliant analysis of the attitude of white ministers, including their propensity for the doctrine of white supremacy (this study has been recently published).

Several master's theses were also found useful. They are: Philip J. Weaver, "The Gubernatorial Election of 1896 in North Carolina," University of North Carolina, 1937; Theron Paul Jones, "The Gubernatorial Election of 1892 in North Carolina," University of North Carolina, 1949; John Elliot Elmore, "North Carolina Negro Congress, 1875–1901," University of North Carolina, 1964; and Jerry Wayne Cotton, "Negro Disfranchisement in North Carolina: The Politics of Race in a Southern State," University of North Carolina at Greensboro, 1973.

Index

Abbot, Dr. Edward, 207
Adams, Spencer R., 185, 195
Agriculture, 66-67. *See also* ruralism
Alabama, Wilcox County, 262–63
Ashby, ("Stump") Harrison S.P., 89
Ayer, Hal, 94

Alderman, Edwin A., 41; conductor of county teachers' institutes 47–51; Institute Statistics, 61; comments on church-state rivalry, 70; on racism and education, 73; farmers, 73; educational crusaders before farmers, 121–23; supports Populist Educational movement, 126, 175, 191–92; at Capon Springs Conference, 210; on Black Belt Educational apathy, 221; mentioned, 280

Appalachian mountain system, in North Carolina, 14, 21
Appalachian Training School (Appalachian State University): establishment of, 245. *See also* teacher training
Arena, 86
Armstrong, Samuel, C., 210
Ashpole affair, 157, 171
Atlanta Constitution, 146
Aycock, Benjamin F., 198–99
Aycock, Charles B., 135, 140; character sketch, 147–48; white supremacy in 1898 campaign, 149–50, 162; supports "Grandfather Clause," 180; nominated gubernatorial candidate in 1900, 184; racist campaign speeches, 189–90; shifts to universal education in Highland region, 191; return to Black Belt and racist theme, 192–94; elected governor, 195;

reminds 1901 General Assembly of educational promises, 197–98; futile one-man educational crusades 200; universal education unfulfilled by 1902, 201; welcomes educational reformers at Winston-Salem, 211; and Raleigh Conference, 216; at Greensboro and Charlotte rallies, 217–18; opposes racial division of school tones, 222; on advocated education of whites first, 223; compares educational and political rallies, 224; represents State Department of Education in Barksdale Case, 222; racist philosophy, 255–56; as an educational progressive, 277, 279

Bailey, Josiah, W., 129–30, 139
Bailey, Thomas P., 255
Baldwin, William H., Jr., 211, 215
Baptists, in church-state rivalry, 70–72
Barksdale V. Commissioners 68
Barksdale decision: impedes educational progress, 69–70, 125; revered, 232
Bassett, John Spencer, 276; on North Carolina Disfranchisement, 277
Beasley, R. F., 221
Benton, A. M., 63
Biblical Recorder, 70, 124, 134
Bingham, Prep School, 63
Bingham, Robert, 65
Blacks, 9, 12, 24–27, 36; population, 93; middle-class, myth of the era, 82n; in Farmers' Alliance, 88–89; disenchantment with Republican Party, 93, 95; distrust Populists, 98; number in 1895 legislature, 100–101; role in 1896 elec-

ism, 223; on McIver's death, 237; mentioned, 261, 271, 280

Peabody, George Foster, 208, 210, 261

Peabody Education Fund: originates in North Carolina, 35–36; ignored negro education, 258, 280

Philanthropy: defined, 35. *See also* individual foundations

Piedmont Region 22, 24; location of the most graded schools, 36, 141

Plessy V. Ferguson, 282–83

Poe, Clarence H.: advocates aparthied for N.C. farm lands, 176

Poor Whites, 26–27, 62, 270, 272

Polk, Leonidas L., 89–91 moves toward Populism 92; death of, 94

Poll Tax, insolvency among negroes and whites, 66

Population, slow development, 22

Populists 10–11, 65, 93–99, 104–7; platform supports education, 117, 123; futile educational campaign, 129–30; in 1898 campaign, 133-68 Passim, number in 1899 legislature, 174; against suffrage law, 181

Private schools, number of, in 1890s, 40; Negro, number of, in 1889, 42

Privot, R. H., 74

Pritchard, Jeter C., 92; advocates Fusionism 99; 158; on suffrage amendment in Congress, 181–83

Progressivism 11, 13; myth of, Southern, 277–79; educational expansion most remarkable achievement of, Southern, 282

Public education, 1900: administration and supervision, State superintendent, part of party ticket, 53; function, 54; superintendents, of city schools, 54, 55; of rural school, patronage of county politicians, 55–56; progress in, by 1913, 247–48

Public education, 1900: automocis city schools, 34; Peabody Fund cooperates with, 35-36; graded school opportunities, 37. Curriculum and course of study, 38; progress by 1913, 233

Public education county, 1900: ungraded common school, number of, 38; school districts, need of consolidation of, 39; school houses, described, 39–40, 41; curriculum and course of study, 42; variables of, school term, enrollment attendance, 41–42; illiteracy compared with selected states, 42–43; progress by 1913, 233–46 *Passim*

Public education, 1900: Negro, city, and rural school opportunities, statistics of, 44–45; average school term, attendance and enrollment, 45. *See also* Public School Movement effect of

Public education, 1900: teachers, certification, pay, and academic preparation, 46; average age and sex 47; pedagogic techniques 47–48; Public education, Teachers training, summer normal schools, Teachers' Institutes, 49; origin of the Normal and Industrial school for young white girls at Greensboro (1891) and the Cullowhee Hight School (1893) in Jackson County, 50–51; progress by 1913, 244–46

Public education: Teacher Training, Negro, normal schools, Parsimon 100s support of, 51–53; trends by 1913, 256–61

Public School movement: salient neglect of Negro education, 252–55

Pruitt V. Commissioners Of Gaston County, 76

Pupil Transportation Movement, 236

Raleigh News and Observer: leading Democratic organ, 84, 92, 99–101, 106, 108, 114–15, 120, 128–29, 133–34, 141–45; cooperates with educational progressives, 225

Raleigh Conference, 217–18

Raleigh News and Observer, 133–39, 141–45

Ramsey, J. L., 94

Randolph, Virginia, 261

Ransom, Senator Matt W., 109–10

Raper, Arthur, 64

Raper, Charles L., 67

Ray, John E., 225

Rayner, John, 84

Redeemers, 24–25, 28n; 54, 68, 99; mentioned, 174, 270

Red Shirts, 13, 133–34; origin of N.C., 156–57; larger numbers in 1900, 173–74, 192–94; decline, 197; mentioned, 203n, 279

Republican Party, 10, 25–26, 85; factionalism between white and negro allies, 92, 95; fusion with Populist 99–100; split within Black ranks, 102–5; elects first Republican governor since Reconstruction, 107; in 1898 campaign